ALTERED LANDSCAPES

Christianity in America, 1935-1985

Edited by
David W. Lotz
with
Donald W. Shriver, Jr.
and
John F. Wilson

GRAND RAPIDS, MICHIGAN
WILLIAM B. EERDMANS PUBLISHING COMPANY

Copyright © 1989 by Wm. B. Eerdmans Publishing Co.
255 Jefferson Ave. S.E., Grand Rapids, Mich. 49503

Library of Congress Cataloging-in-Publication Data

Altered landscapes: Christianity in America, 1935–1985 /
    edited by David W. Lotz with Donald W. Shriver, Jr., and John F. Wilson.
        p.   cm.
    "Essays in honor of Robert T. Handy"—P.   i.
    Includes index.
    1. United States—Church History—20th century.   2. Handy, Robert T.
I. Lotz, David W., 1937-   . II. Shriver, Donald W.   III. Wilson, John Frederick.
IV. Handy, Robert T.
BR526.A37   1989
277.3'082—dc19   88-31785
                                                                        CIP

Cloth ISBN 0-8028-3654-2
Paper ISBN 0-8028-0455-1

Contents

79673

CONTENTS

PART II: THE CHANGING THEOLOGICAL DISCIPLINES

PART III: REFLECTIONS ON RELIGION IN A CHANGING AMERICA

The Contributors

H. GEORGE ANDERSON is President of Luther College, Decorah, Iowa.

JAY P. DOLAN is Professor of History and Director of the Cushwa Center for the Study of American Catholicism at the University of Notre Dame.

GABRIEL FACKRE is the Abbot Professor of Christian Theology at Andover Newton Theological School.

GERALD P. FOGARTY, S.J., is Professor of Religious Studies at the University of Virginia.

EDWIN S. GAUSTAD is Professor of History at the University of California, Riverside.

WILLIAM R. HUTCHISON is the Charles Warren Professor of the History of Religion in America at Harvard University.

WILLIAM BEAN KENNEDY is the Skinner and McAlpin Professor of Practical Theology at Union Theological Seminary, New York.

KOSUKE KOYAMA is the John D. Rockefeller, Jr., Professor of Ecumenics and World Christianity at Union Theological Seminary, New York.

EDWARD LeROY LONG, JR., is the James W. Pearsall Professor Emeritus of Christian Ethics and Theology of Culture at Drew University.

DAVID W. LOTZ is the Washburn Professor of Church History at Union Theological Seminary, New York.

THE CONTRIBUTORS

GEORGE M. MARSDEN is Professor of Church History at the Divinity School, Duke University.

MARTIN E. MARTY is the Fairfax M. Cone Distinguished Service Professor of the History of Modern Christianity at the University of Chicago.

GLENN T. MILLER is Professor of Church History at Southeastern Baptist Theological Seminary, Wake Forest, North Carolina.

WAYNE PROUDFOOT is Professor of Religion at Columbia University.

ALBERT J. RABOTEAU is the Henry W. Putnam Professor of Religion at Princeton University.

DONALD W. SHRIVER, JR., is President of the Faculty and the William E. Dodge Professor of Applied Christianity at Union Theological Seminary, New York.

LEONARD I. SWEET is President of United Theological Seminary, Dayton, Ohio.

GORDON TUCKER is Dean of the Rabbinical School and Director of the Louis Finkelstein Institute for Religious and Social Studies, The Jewish Theological Seminary of America, New York.

JAMES F. WHITE is Professor of Liturgy at the University of Notre Dame.

JOHN F. WILSON is the Agate Brown and George L. Collord Professor of Religion at Princeton University.

BARBARA BROWN ZIKMUND is Dean of the Pacific School of Religion, Berkeley, California.

Preface

The model for this book was one published in 1936, *The Church through Half a Century: Essays in Honor of William Adams Brown* (New York: Charles Scribner's Sons). The eighteen contributors to that volume were all former students of Professor Brown, who for more than forty years was a teacher of church history, systematic theology, and applied theology on the faculty of Union Theological Seminary in New York. Upon his retirement in 1936, the essayists paid tribute to him by surveying the major components of Protestant church history and theological scholarship during the fifty years of Brown's active life as an academic and ecumenical leader. Edited by Samuel McCrea Cavert and Henry Pitney Van Dusen, the book was a festschrift whose breadth of view matched the breadth of Brown's own lifelong labor in the Presbyterian church and the ecumenical movement. In the best tradition of the liberal theology of his era, Brown was intellectually hospitable to all the events that affected the integrity of the Christian movement.

The present volume pays tribute to another scholar of the Union faculty whose teaching career in that school (1950-86) spanned a length of time and embodied an intellectual inclusiveness resembling that of William Adams Brown: Robert T. Handy, the Henry Sloane Coffin Professor of Church History. Because the authors of this book are not all former students of Professor Handy, it is not a conventional festschrift. Further, the authors are not all professional historians. Like the authors of the Brown volume, they come from many disciplines, some outside the formal fields of theological education. Every one of them, however, knows his or her indebtedness to the lifelong scholarly career of Robert Handy. His strict adherence to the technical canons of historical inquiry, his sensitivity to the practical needs of Christian people, his signal labors on behalf of a sophisticated understanding of American church history, and his appreciation for the conceptual ties of history with many other disciplines all mark him, too, as an ecumenical intellectual in the great tradition of a William Adams Brown.

Our tributes to Robert Handy's diverse influences on our lives— as teacher, author, colleague, friend, spiritual helper—attest the fact that we have acquired our debts to him from so many different aspects of his distinguished career. If this volume does not, like the usual fest-schrift, contain formal biography and bibliography from the life of the man it honors, this is partly because Robert Handy has astutely and faithfully guided us toward sharing his own intellectual enthusiasm for the objects of his own academic fidelity: the unfolding history of the Christian movement in America. We write here about that movement, not primarily about *his* writing about it.

As will be evident from many of these pages, however, and from not a few footnotes, this is a book deeply indebted to the intellectual substance of Handy's scholarly publications. Moreover, our knowledge of him through virtually any aspect of his career—pages of a book, papers delivered at conferences, sermons from a pulpit, advice in a committee, or invariably compassionate counsel in private conversation— has benefited us in ways that exceed our acknowledgment.

Also appropriate here are three qualifying comments about three important words used throughout these essays: "Christianity," "America," and "religion." The majority of the religious bodies referred to in the text are the Protestant churches of the United States. "America" implies chiefly the United States, but by the word we mean also a culture and a set of institutional assumptions associated chiefly with the history of this country. As for our primary focus on "Christianity" rather than "religion" in the United States, we are aware that the two are not the same and that (as the introductory essay makes plain) the nation is religiously far more pluralistic today than it was in 1936 or at any other time in its history. In deference to this important fact we had originally commissioned an essay on religious movements outside of Christianity and Judaism during the 1935 to 1985 period; unfortunately, the scholar so commissioned had to decline her assignment late in the publication process. The inclusion of separate essays on Roman Catholicism and Judaism, however, marks an important break from some Protestant assumptions that dominated the 1936 volume, and we gladly confess that it is inconceivable now, on theological no less than on historiographical grounds, for any of us to write about American Protestantism in the

1980s without careful attention to its relations with these other ecclesial communities.

By way of a final acknowledgment, it should be duly recorded here that the chief responsibility for the editing of these essays was assumed by Professor Lotz, to whom the remaining two editors express their thanks. The book likewise owes much to the help of Jon Pott, editor of the William B. Eerdmans Publishing Company, who vigorously encouraged the project from the start. It also owes much to a great array of persons in the sixteen schools at which the twenty-one authors of these essays work. As in history itself, the multitude of real actors in any scholarly project outnumbers by far the number of the named. Secretaries who first typed these pages, colleagues who were consulted about their content, and institutions that paid salaries to sustain us in these activities all deserve gratitude—the more so because history as Robert T. Handy has written it always embraces institutions as well as ideas, the actions of the anonymous as well as the actions of the famous. We know that as a historian he loves the truth of history; he loves as well the people who make history. Indeed, among those scholars whom we know, we know of none who better joins the love of truth to the truth of love. So to him, again, we affectionately dedicate these pages.

Donald W. Shriver, Jr.
John F. Wilson
David W. Lotz

Introduction:
Religion in America 1935-1985

Martin E. Marty

Two environmental images, one of hurricanes and the other of glaciers, can inform the observation of American religious change during the past fifty years. Both hurricane and glacial forces leave altered landscapes.

The hurricane represents sudden and drastic change. It uproots, destroys, and occasions new human building. The Second Vatican Council (1962-65) was one of the fairly rare, specifiable, documentable forces for such abrupt and radical change in American Catholicism. Catholics were invited or compelled to leave behind, in a five-year period, practices and concepts that had seemed permanent for five centuries and more. While historians and social scientists can observe such change "from within the eye of the hurricane, . . . where all is calm and intelligible," people in the path of the hurricane experience it without much chance for serenity or intelligibility.[1] Such events and public reaction to them make for the kind of subject historians like to chronicle.

The glacier represents gradual and subtle change. It moves by the pull of gravity and the tempering of weather. In its path there is an altered landscape, a new carving of the terrain and a deposit of moraine.[2] Most American religious change during this most recent one-fourth of the republic's life, these fifty years, has been of the glacial sort. One has an eye on the glacier and does not notice what it carries along.

1. John Murray Cuddihy, *The Ordeal of Civility: Freud, Marx, Levi-Strauss, and the Jewish Struggle with Modernity* (New York: Basic, 1974), p. 9.
2. The image is from Ernest Gellner, *Thought and Change* (Chicago: University of Chicago, 1964), p. 123.

Thus *Brown v. Board of Education*, the United States Supreme Court ruling that helped give momentum to the civil rights movement in 1954, or the invention of television, did not seem to be religious events. Historians of law and technology focus on them. Yet these events evoked religious response and changed the spiritual outlook of America.

Much of the glacial change is easy to overlook because what altered the life of people was not always headline-making "hard" news at all. To grasp it, one must acquire Jacob Burckhardt's eye for the common and the taken for granted. "Everywhere in the past we encounter things which remain unexplained only because they were completely self-understood in their time and, like all daily matters, were not thought necessary to write down."[3] José Ortega y Gasset also alerted observers to pay attention to the soft news that came with change of attitudes in the heart. "Decisive historical changes do not come from great wars, terrible cataclysms, or ingenious inventions; it is enough that the heart of man incline its sensitive crown to one side or the other of the horizon. . . ."[4]

I. Change in the Religious Landscape

Whoever would compare maps suggesting religious predominances across America in 1935 and 1985 would find the basic topography to be apparently constant.[5] Utah and the basin around it were and remain Mormon. A Lutheran presence is strong in the upper Midwest, and was in the 1930s. The mid-South from Maryland to Kansas had a strong representation of Methodism then and has one of United Methodism now. The South was, and is, Baptistdom. Jews were and are urbanites, chiefly in the Northeast. In most metropolises Catholicism was and is prime, though in northern cities it must share power increasingly with formerly southern black Baptists, Methodists, and Pentecostalists.

The appearance of the map can also deceive. One of the best ways to discern the glacial changes on the religious landscape is to picture a professor from Boston or New Haven, New York or Chicago, taking the mythical "foreign observer" on a tour of American regions

3. Quoted from Burckhardt's *Griechische Kulturgeschichte* in Karl J. Weintraub, *Visions of Culture* (Chicago: University of Chicago, 1966), p. 270.

4. Quoted by Weintraub, ibid., p. 269.

5. The best source for correlating demographic data on American religion with the map remains Edwin Scott Gaustad, *Historical Atlas of Religion in America* (New York: Harper and Row, 1976).

2

in 1935 and again in 1985. Then the results of the more subtle, less event-centered shifts would be apparent.

The most vivid change would be in the South, both that of old Dixie and of the new Sunbelt. A Nashville or Atlanta professor could say that much of the change was in the eye of the northern beholder, who formerly could and did overlook the South.[6] In the Depression years the Southeast, for instance, carried a legacy of habitual and devoted church membership. In 1926 61.4 percent of the adults in the Southeast were members when only 54.3 percent were members nationally.[7] Three-fourths of the members were Baptist or Methodist. So what was new now?

Fifty years ago the South appeared to outsiders and many of its own scholars to be chiefly a depressed "Bible belt," made up of poor whites and poorer blacks, "hillbillies" in culture and "holy rollers" in religion. "Born again" was the local vernacular, not something that would show up in the Gallup polls and public media. Yet after World War II, as millions of blacks moved northward and northerners re-moved their factories to the South or retired in its warm and air-conditioned climate, a religious, or at least a Protestant, balance of power began to be subtly visible—but with dramatic effects. The alert and ag-gressive Southern Baptist Convention grew as did no other large body. Methodism, eventually United Methodism, more nearly held its own there than it did in the North. Pentecostalism "moved uptown" and from low-wattage radio stations to the point where it all but dominated re-ligious television, from the empire of Oral Roberts to whole evangelical networks. The Churches of Christ in the Southwest prospered while their nineteenth-century kin, the Disciples of Christ, oxidized somewhat in the Rustbelt.

One might picture this glacial movement, which left its moraine in the North, as only a North to South movement. Yet just as important as the changes in that direction were the South to North influences. The old southern racial attitudes and practices came to characterize most northern church life.[8] What we might call a "country-and-western-ization" of white religion occurred, just as once-southern black gospel

6. Evidence of historians' increased attention to the South appears in Charles W. Lippy, *Bibliography of Religion in the South* (Macon, GA: Mercer University Press, 1985).

7. Cited in George Brown Tindall, *The Emergence of The New South 1913-1945* (Baton Rouge: Louisiana State University Press, 1967), p. 197.

8. David M. Reimers, *White Protestantism and the Negro* (New York: Oxford, 1965), plots the adoption of southern attitudes on race in the North, in Chapter 3, "The North Compromises." This compromise became an intensified pattern in the post–World War II years.

and soul music came to be familiar, at least through the media of television, radio, and records, throughout the whole nation.

The glacial changes shaped a new figurative landscape in the West and Southwest as well. Catholicism and, to a lesser extent, evangelistic Protestantism faced bewildering and promising change as the Hispanic population came to dominate rural and metropolitan life in much of the Southwest and, again in a trickle-up pattern, in the urban North. The Far West presented a bemusing blend of awesomely secular and intensely religious life. Seven of the eight least "churched" states were in the American West, including Hawaii and Alaska, while San Francisco and Seattle bade fair to match European cities for their patent secularity. Yet such cities, to say nothing of the Los Angeles complex, also became proverbial zones of intense spiritual experiment—the public often all but equated California with "cultic" and "occult"[9]—while the population of Asians far outstripped the growth of Occidental America toward the end of this period. Post-war Dallas and Houston, among other expansive cities, were hosts to prosperous Protestant fundamentalisms while Los Angeles saw the rise of "super-churches," evangelical in outlook and high-gloss in tone. They replaced the old bastions of more liberal Protestantism of the Northeast in the public eye.

Younger people in the mid-80s would take all the current landscape for granted. To them what used to be "the old-time religion" is now "the new-time religion." They do not know the Depression and World War II eras, the times when tent revivals gave color to the South or West and Park Avenue churches lent tone to the Northeast. They would be hard-pressed to find histories that explain the "moraine" they confront, the map they inherit. No hurricane-force occasions, symbols of abrupt and decisive events, tell the story. Who bothered to explain the unexplained that was self-understood in its time, the daily matters in religion that changed with population shifts, technology, and nuanced symbolic alterations? Who would think of looking for a history of religious change that featured agents like air-conditioning and television and union practices instead of Bishop This or Council That?

Without reference to a single religious proper name or ecclesiastical event, we have casually smuggled into those topographic and demographic paragraphs at least some signals of many of the major religious events of the half-century. It may seem tiresome to some or dazzling to others to run through a catalog of these, but it helps make the point. Therefore, we recall, in order: Mormon prosperity, church mergers in an

9. See Jacob Needleman, *The New Religions* (Garden City: Doubleday, 1970), pp. 3-4 and 36-37, "What is California?" and "The Place of California."

ecumenical time, Catholic strengthening despite change, black church power, the Born Again movement, Southern Baptist prosperity, mainline and liberal stasis, Pentecostal growth and transformation, burgeoning independency and localism, "ritual" change, the Hispanicization of Catholicism, The Secular City, the visibility of cults and the occult, new-style fundamentalist and evangelical prosperity, and more.

II. Change in the Religious Peoplescape

The dictionary allows the attachment of "-scape," indicating what meets the eye, to other features of what is seen beyond the mere land of landscape. So the mythical foreign visitor who knew America fifty years ago, now, in age, greets the naive if intelligent youthful observer and the two, guided by the professor, try to make sense of changes in the ways American religionists have of dealing with peoplehood.

a. The instance of race

Race would code-name one of the prime realities. It always has, in America, since October 12, 1492, with respect to Native Americans and Iberians, or since 1619 with reference to Virginia blacks and whites. Yet as taken for granted or self-understood as this reality was in 1935, most of the synoptic accounts of American religion from that period pay little attention to it. The Anglo-Saxon racial outlook of imperial Protestantism earlier in the century blinded even liberal Social Gospel advocates to the interracial agenda, and Christian realists like the brothers Reinhold and Richard Niebuhr gave it far less attention than they did most social issues in the churchly zone in the 1930s. In 1955 Will Herberg could write the all but normative broad-brush review of American religion in his time, but *Protestant, Catholic, Jew* hardly alludes to black, red, or yellow peoples and the religious dimension of their peoplehood.[10]

Today such an approach would misguide traversers of the American religious landscape. The major ecclesiastical issues of justice in the second half of this period centered in or were shadowed by the civil rights struggle, which did feature some names like Martin Luther King along with a sequence of memorable events. There was a Native American consciousness-raising and "Red Power" movement. Black churches are often the only significant rivals or partners to Catholic dioceses in major cities. Blacks in the Nation of Islam or in orthodox Islam have not

---

10. Will Herberg, *Protestant, Catholic, Jew* (Garden City: Doubleday, 1955).

been numerically significant, but they came in this half-century to represent spectre or promise to millions beyond the "Judeo-Christian" scope, while distinct Afro-movements in religion carried nonbiblical symbolization even further among blacks. The Asian story has not centered around celebrities or recognized leaders, but it disrupts the conventional pictures from 1935 of Christian America and forces some glossing over by advocates of the return of Christian America after 1985. Race is a reality in serious religious reckoning as it would not have been on any guided tour for the foreign visitor of 1935. The young American, college bred and probably from a metropolis, cannot picture a world in which race was able to be overlooked.

b. The example of ethnicity

Ethnicity would be the second code word for a changed consciousness and reality in respect to peoplehood in this half-century. One is, again, almost embarrassed to cite it, so self-understood would ethnicity be to the majority of the young. Television, mass higher education, mobility, the urban experience, personal experience—all these have made Americans aware of the power of ethnic distinctions, also in religion. Yet one must overcome embarrassment over the obvious in order to bring up the contrast with 1935: ethnicity hardly then entered the reckoning among serious chroniclers.

From the 1930s through the 1950s anti-Catholicism was a more vivid Protestant force than a public can picture in the ecumenical times after Pope John XXIII or the political times after President John F. Kennedy.[11] The only feature relevant here is the small role Catholic ethnicity played in Protestant fears or fearmongering, hopes or hope-spreading. There may well have been, there often was, a documentable anti-Irish bias, but for the most part Catholicism was treated as a monolith. The ethnic factors that all but tore it apart in some decades seemed invisible to polemicists and conscientious historians alike. One now peels back the layers of historical writing that obscured it and finds underneath and through it all great Catholic consciousness of the differences in being, say, Italian, Polish, German, Irish, Czech, black, or whatever inside the "monolith."

What person, what event, what "hurricane force" brought about this change? There were, of course, demographic jostlings, what with Jewish and other exilings and refugee movements from the 1930s to the

---

11. A sample summary from the Catholic viewpoint of conflicts in the middle of this period is John J. Kane, *Catholic-Protestant Conflicts in America* (Chicago: Regnery, 1955).

1960s. The G.I. Bill that brought Catholic peoples into universities and colleges, and the suburbanization that breached and then made irrelevant most Catholic ghetto walls, played their part. They led to ethnic self-consciousness at the time of ethnic diffusion. Yet the change, if drastic, was gradual, camouflaged under non-religious symbols. Today the church extension expert, the suburban planner, the antidefamation groups, and the councils of bishops and ecumenical visionaries all pay attention to this shift that came as the "sensitive crown" of the heart was inclined by thousands of small particular changes in the half-century.

One must single out on this front a particular ethnic awareness, that of Judaism. For a century Reform Judaism and much of Conservatism sought ways to blend traditions of religion with an emerging American identity. The classic Protestants who moved in interfaith circles tended to know best these half-assimilated (and more) Jews, while Orthodoxy was a kind of remote ghetto reality. Even the Holocaust in Hitler's Germany and the birth of Israel in 1948 did not lead to a radical stress on Jewish peoplehood. Will Herberg gave scant mention to these two cosmic events as late as 1955. Many Jewish social scientists suggest that the Six Day War in 1967 was a "hard news" turning point—shall we say the hurricane instead of the glacial movement?—that led to concern over Jewish survival. Yet the growth of survival consciousness and the positive stress on religiously symbolized peoplehood did also have a glacial character. Would our young Jew or foreign visitor think to account for this change by reading histories of the G.I. Bill and its effects, or by suburbanization, or by television comedy? Yet they probably had more to do with the new peoplescape than did named heroes like Abraham Joshua Heschel or any conferences of rabbis.

One can only suggest change on the ethnic front. The visitor of 1935 might know that America's oldest continuously-in-use mosque had been built the year before, in Cedar Rapids, Iowa, but that is not likely. Nor would an accounting of a Muslim presence be important. Fifty years later, according to some accounts, there were as many Islamic people in America as there were practicing Anglicans.[12] Thanks to international news and reports on black Muslims at home, it is possible that people far from both peoples might know (or interestingly missknow) more about Islam than Anglicanism. Through it all, Anglo-Saxons, who somewhere in these fifty years acquired the invidious and then accepted acronym WASP, learned that they also were an ethnic cluster. They were another part of the story of peoplehood. They pro-

---

12. For a succinct review see Martin E. Marty, "Muslims Next Door," in *1985 Britannica Book of the Year* (Chicago: Encyclopedia Britannica, 1985), pp. 366-67.

gressively learned how much of their historical self-consciousness was bonded with religious symbols and claims.

c. The new understandings of and by women

It may seem strange to link the rise in women's consciousness, associated with religious symbols or institutions, with race and ethnicity as issues of "peoplehood." Yet women increasingly engaged in acts of self-definition that changed what we are calling the peoplescape, that which can be observed. They made up more than half the membership in religious groups in 1935 as well as in 1985, be these religious groups largely white or black, Anglo or Hispanic or whatever. The change came when calls for the experience of sisterhood came to create new definitions and new group boundaries in the course of these fifty years.

In 1935 there were almost no ordained women beyond some Holiness and Pentecostal churches; the lonely few in the mainstream Protestant churches could not yet look for much company. Calls for ordination of Catholic women, not yet effective in 1985, were all but unheard of and unthinkable in 1935. While popular evangelicalism has seen an increasing articulation of female "submission" theology, this occurs against the background of an enlargement of women's roles that suggests this theology may be used to try to rein in already unleashed forces. Whatever term they use or legitimation they employ, conservative Protestants are "hearing the Word" from women who minister through the printed page, over television screens, as missionaries and teachers, or anything that disguises their all but overt ministerial roles.

The historian who looks for the specific heroine who made this possible across the denominational and interreligious spectrum would be hard-pressed to find a counterpart to a Pope John or a Martin Luther King in their movements. Instead, a thousand particular movements and inclinations of the "sensitive crown" of the human heart occasioned the changes. Women entered the work force and sought new rationales for changed relations to spouses and children. They entered the professions, and the clerical is among these, almost the only one still denied Catholics and some Protestants. New stresses on marriage led to separation and divorce, also in conservative Protestantisms and Catholicism, occasioning the need for fresh theological interpretation. Technology altered the approaches to conception and child-bearing, and this forced or permitted new ethical understandings of stewardship, parenting, and relations to men. Of course there were influential treatises by the Rosemary Ruethers and Beverly Wildung Harrisons and Virginia Mollenkotts and Naomi Goldenbergs, and there were specific acts like the decision by Episcopalians to ordain women or by Pope Paul VI not to; these all "made history." Yet the changes were glacial. They left a moraine that will be on the landscape indefinitely.[13]

Denominations continued to survive, to attract loyalties. They were faithfully observed by Old Foreign Visitor and Youthful American Native alike along ecclesiastical *Yearbook* lines. Yet in both practical living and social scientific accounting, race and ethnicity, religiously conceived and justified, were more prominent than sectarian boundaries. The color line now often defined more than the denominational line.

III. Change in the Religious Soulscape

While extending the license to connect -scape with nonce words, we invent the concept of the soulscape to observe change in the spiritual configurations apparent in America. Here one has nothing as tangible as the demographic map or the color line to discern, and the choice of what to feature may seem more arbitrary; yet patient chronicling can produce logically coherent sequences for vision.

a. A different religious-secular mix

We can suggest a juxtaposition of observations between the senior and returning foreign visitor on one hand and the alert but ahistorical younger citizen. This is not the place to flesh out documentation behind the suggestion; I present it as hypothesis, hunch, half-ready conclusion, but one that is supportable and can stand up to scrutiny. The suggestion is somewhat controversial for two reasons. The American academy, according to most accounts, is captive to "the secularization thesis."[14] This leads the monitors of social change to work instinctively with the notion that modernity, industrialization, urbanization—and most other "-ation" words that describe the spiritual hurricanes and glaciers of our

13. The historical literature on this subject is growing; see, for beginnings, Rosemary Radford Ruether and Rosemary Skinner Keller, eds., *Women and Religion in America*, Vol. I, *The Nineteenth Century: A Documentary History* (San Francisco: Harper and Row, 1981), and Janet Wilson James, ed., *Women in American Religion* (Philadelphia: University of Pennsylvania, 1980).

14. For a typical sign of the awareness of the secularization thesis, see Rodney Stark and William Sims Bainbridge, *The Future of Religion: Secularization, Revival and Cult Formation* (Berkeley: University of California, 1985), pp. 1-3, 436-37.

time—lead, will lead, and must lead to pervasive "desacralization"[15] and, despite minor and illusory countertrends, to decline of religion, also in America. On the other hand, people in our time are regularly alerted by the defensive aggressors in religion to a "secular humanist conspiracy" and an expansive secularism around them. With this goes a mythical construct of religious "good old days" when the little red schoolhouse and the little white church promoted "Judeo-Christian" values for the whole culture.

The defensible counterhypothesis, based on wide reading in the literature of the 1930s and 1940s, suggests a different picture. While there may be as much secularity and worldliness around now as then, or as ever—who knows how to measure it?—there has been a decline in the ability of assertive secularists to provide a rationale for their ideology. They have also had difficulty accounting for what a black scholar called the "religiocification" of social movements around them,[16] from Iran through Israel and Ireland to North America. Religion may be serenely ignored in much of the academy and the media, but, as Langdon Gilkey has pointed out, it is the progressive-rationalist Enlightenment synthesis that is in disarray.[17] Religious forces are in array. The America of 1935 was the world of "nonreligious" articulation *a la* John Dewey, Joseph Wood Krutch, Walter Lippmann; agnostic conservatisms like that of George Santayana; and atheistic socialisms of Marxist and other sorts. Almost no one spoke of a religious revival in the 1930s and 1940s. Henry C. Link's *Return to Religion* in 1936 was fifteen years ahead of its time. Even it was less a documentation of revival than a prescription for self-help through busyness, based on his own personal outlook and observation.[18]

Since the early 1950s—pick 1952 and the Eisenhower era as a symbolic date—there has been constant talk of ever-changing revival patterns. In the 1950s there was an institutional revival, when church and synagogue prospered as never before. Indicators of preference, membership, attendance, building, educating of children rose as never before. In the 1960s the talk was of an ethical renewal, while institutional religion took to the streets and the forum in support of social change. In the 1970s reporters discovered a new stress on the "spiritual journey," on private

15. See, for example, S. S. Acquaviva, *The Decline of the Sacred in Industrial Society* (New York: Harper and Row, 1979).

16. See Clifton F. Brown, "Black Religion—1968," in Hart M. Nelsen, Raytha L. Yokley, and Anne K. Nelsen, eds., *The Black Church in America* (New York: Basic, 1971), pp. 17-18.

17. Langdon Gilkey, *Society and the Sacred* (New York: Crossroad, 1981), p. 24.

18. Henry C. Link, *The Return to Religion* (New York: Macmillan, 1936).

and individualized spiritual searches. In the 1980s religion has "gone public" again. Sometimes the talk of revival has been rooted in evanescent evidences and ephemeral trends by historically uninformed commentators. Yet it can be shown that the talk itself is significant, not wholly unrelated to the renewal fires beyond the revival-talk smoke.

Concurrent with this change has come a broadening of the definition of religion that makes it hard to find purely desacralized worlds or trends. In 1935 observers were quite content to link religion with religious institution, with church and synagogue. Today, thanks to the spread of religious studies in higher education and the interdisciplinary inquiries that draw on anthropology, sociology, and history of religions, religion is seen to be connected with all sorts of symbol systems. It gets to be hard to find nonreligion in the era after theologian Paul Tillich and of anthropologist Clifford Geertz or sociologist Thomas Luckmann.[19] Yet even without their diffuse and expansive definitions, we have been trained to find religion beyond the conventional institutions, and the public has found it there.

These trends would lead the aging foreign observer to rub her eyes in wonder and to cause the young American to wonder why she is doing it. The rubbing comes in confusion—"Whatever happened to the old lines?" There used to be a "love not the world" dimension to at least conservative religion, a hint of asceticism and world-denial. Yet someone who would have looked at conservative Catholicism preparing its own for the reversals of status after deprivation now and the rewards of heaven then, would be puzzled to see how the backdrop of purgatory and hell has slipped from the Catholic scene. That veteran observer who associated conservative Protestantism with denial of the world, with criticism of social mores and "fleshly" accents on entertainment, sports, cosmetics and fashion, and success, would see a complete transvaluation of values. If liberal Protestantism was once frankly worldly, it turned progressively critical of the "American Way of Life," and may have lost some popular support in doing so. Meanwhile, much of Evangelicalism, Fundamentalism, and Pentecostalism connects Jesus' promise of "more abundant life" not with meaning but with substance. Witness the popular religious self-help books and movements or evangelical television: the Gospel is connected less with denial, suffering, and cross and more with athletic heroes, Christian charm schools and beauty queens, gaining political office and military victory, and personal

19. See the section on "The Diffusion of Religion" in Martin E. Marty, "Religion in America Since Mid-Century," *Daedalus* 3/1 (Winter 1982) 154-57, which includes comment on the Geertzian definition.

financial success. The world is allowed to be loved, so long as some Jesus-symbols are carried over into the transaction.[20]

We hyphenate the religious-secular mix to suggest that in the course of these fifty years a fresh anthropological observation might be productive: the connecting hyphen replaces the dialectical slash bar or the symbol of necessary mutual antagonism. Toward what end this will move theologically it is difficult to hazard. Moderate and liberal Christianity employed the visions of Dietrich Bonhoeffer's "religionless Christianity" or Teilhard de Chardin's Christianized evolutionism to make some of its transit and tempered these with many levels of criticism of national policy and personal striving. Conservative Christianity, despite impressive holding out by some critics within, seemed to be changed more than it changed the culture, to be enworlding the evangel as much as it would evangelize the world.

b. Privatization of religion

While much religion abroad and at home could be characterized as newly or renewally "tribalized," where it was connected with introverted movements of peoplehood, America also saw a countertrend during these fifty years. The canonical name for this, after definitions of Thomas Luckmann, Peter Berger, and others, was "privatization" of religion.[21] It would be hard to sustain the claim that this was not widely dispersed already in 1935. It is not difficult to find justifications for spirituality outside institutions and communities, away from "organized" religion. Critics of church and temple often brought creative insight to the claim that hypocrisy, idolatry, and self-centeredness could find a home in the House of the Lord. They could then move outside or alongside the House in order to judge and, perhaps, purify it or themselves. And the more relaxed were then, as now, claiming that they could be spiritual in a symphony hall or under the cathedral of the heavens as well as or better than when they were in the sanctuary.

Something happened, however, between 1935 and 1985, without "great wars, terrible cataclysms," as Ortega would have it, but perhaps with the "ingenious inventions" to which he referred. Radio and television, religious best-sellers, do-it-yourself spiritual journeying, a la carte and pick-and-choose religion, were all part of what Peter Berger eventually came to call *The Heretical Imperative*.[22] He meant that people must

20. A report on the worldly trends in evangelicalism is Carol Flake, *Redemptorama: Culture, Politics and the New Evangelicalism* (Garden City: Doubleday, 1984).
21. Thomas Luckmann, *The Invisible Religion* (New York: Macmillan, 1967).
22. Peter Berger, *The Heretical Imperative* (Garden City: Doubleday, 1979).

seek meaning. They must "choose," he said, reminding readers that "heresy" came from the Greek noun *haeresis,* choice. Yet the traditional and communal options were not sufficiently coherent or sustaining, so each person would, in a sense, be impelled to put a personal package together to support the search for meaning.

John Murray Cuddihy has spoken of the way "differentiation" was at the cutting edge of the modernization process, "sundering cruelly what tradition had joined," and slicing "through ancient primordial ties and identities, leaving crisis and wholeness-hunger in its wake."[23] That wholeness-hunger led some back to old ties and identities and pushed others to form new ones. Yet there was an increasing premium on religion as a commodity, a personalized consumer item, adaptable to and adapted by each private person. In this noninstitutional and unstable form, then, it did not go away but became, in Luckmann's sense, *The Invisible Religion.*[24] In 1935 it may have been hard to picture a minister citing "privatization" as a greater problem for the church than "secularization." No spiritual hurricane, no sudden trauma produced the change. But thanks to glacial-like processes, by the mid-1980s, in the world of the high-rise apartment and the long weekend, the new styles of living led millions to be religious without community. How does one write the history of the movement or describe the spiritual moraine if there have been no specifiable and decisive events or persons effecting the change? How explain this "self-understood" and thus easily overlooked shift?

c. Ecumenism and interreligiousness

In 1935 a worldwide Christian ecumenical movement with roots in northwest Europe and Anglo-America was shaping up. There had been a sequence of conferences called Faith and Order and Life and Work, and only World War II postponed until 1948 the founding of the World Council of Churches. There had been since 1908 a Federal Council of Churches, which was to become the National Council of Churches in 1951. Church mergers were constant, especially within denominational families. Yet the veteran foreign observer would marvel at how taken for granted ecumenism of all sorts is today. And the young American could not picture the world of 1935, when barriers were high.

This time there are some designatable dates and events and persons like the founding of World and National Councils or the holding

23. Cuddihy, op. cit., p. 10.
24. Thomas Luckmann, op. cit.

of a Vatican Council, like John R. Mott and John XXIII and John Courtney Murray. But the subtle, long-term, glacial-style shifts predominated. The councils often propelled and profited from ad hoc and local ecumenism. Again, higher education, mobility, suburbanization, and now mixed marriage and the personal choice that transcended "privatization" all played their parts. Mass media and rapid travel made the globe smaller. People wearied of controversy and were spiritually moved to make subtle friendly adjustments. Historians can write of highs and lows, advances and retreats in the formal, soon to be bureaucratized, ecumenical movement. Success came so rapidly at some stages that its results seemed boring during the periods of relative stasis or of less coherent motion in others.

The ecumenical point had been made, however, in free societies, not least in America. The formerly antiecumenical evangelical and fundamentalist forces band together or make their sectarian lines apparently irrelevant in their common purposes. And interreligious contact moves far beyond Christian ecumenism. The Vatican document *Nostra Aetate* officially spoke well of non-Christian faiths in specified circumstances and lights. Jews and Christians, including fundamentalists who had earlier been cast, sometimes half miscast, as anti-Semite, united in support of Israel and came to be distant and wary friends, but still friends, in America.

d. Public and civil religion

In 1935 not even many academics would have spoken as did Benjamin Franklin of a "public religion," or as Jean-Jacques Rousseau or Emile Durkheim or, in America, Robert N. Bellah would, of a "civil religion." W. Lloyd Warner had begun isolating and elevating civil rites to see their role beyond the churches.[25] John Dewey was promoting a kind of religious-secular *A Common Faith* in 1934, and some were beginning to hear in Franklin D. Roosevelt a mildly religious rhetoric that helped lift them out of Depression and carry them through War. Yet it was after mid-century, when it became clear that not all religion was private or housed in ecclesiastical institutions, that the naming of civil religion gained some acceptability and observation of it became widespread.

The shift was glacial, not occasioned by a spiritual hurricane even of the scope of World War II. It came subtly with the diffuse piety of Dwight Eisenhower and America's Cold War against Atheistic Com-

---

25. W. Lloyd Warner, *The Living and the Dead* (New Haven: Yale, 1959) and *The Family of God* (New Haven: Yale, 1961) present some of his pioneering explorations.

munism. It came vigorously with the rhetoric of John F. Kennedy and the language heard early in the presidency of Lyndon B. Johnson. Ronald Reagan knew how to promote response to a revanchist and nostalgic version of this public or civil faith, and his approach was popular among the American majority that may not have used the term "civil religion" to explain what they took to be self-understood. Yet any reckoning of these years must call the invention, which the dictionary says means both the finding and the making up, of a public religion to be a major event of the half-century.[26]

e. The premium on experience, authority, identity

It would be hard to picture a religion or a religious complex that survived and prospered if it did not minister to basic human needs. Among these as constants, we may presume, are the valid search for personal and communal experience of God or the Holy; the quest for a sense of authority to give gravity to sacred calls and security to human responses; the seeking for some group where one may find a sense of belonging and a base for human trust and social location.

On those terms, it is not news to find these three among the more frequently sought and claimed elements in American religion in 1985. Yet it might surprise the returning visitor to see the contrasts with 1935. At least in moderate and liberal, certainly in academic religion, there was a regular stress on the way in which the religion of the future must stress rationality and appeal chiefly to the intellect and the will. In 1985 the movements that stress the ordeal of passage to *communitas*, "enlightenment," "being born again," ecstasy, enthusiasm, what some charismatics call *The* Experience, a spiritual "high," centering prayer, meditation, and sacramental piety—the catalog is extensive and appeals to diverse tastes—prosper, while those on the progressive-rationalist trajectory wane.

Similarly, the academic observer of 1935 could well assume that the religion of the future would not be fundamentalist or authoritarian. "The right of private judgment" and "the priesthood of all believers" were the two features that, it was believed, could be torn from Reformation thought and projected into the future. The "invention" or definition of papal infallibility and biblical inerrancy by nineteenth-century Catholicism and conservative Protestantism was seen as a regressive ac-

---

26. Bellah's original essay on this theme appears in Russell E. Richey and Donald G. Jones, eds., *American Civil Religion* (New York: Harper and Row, 1974), pp. 21-44, and is discussed by many other essays in the collection.

tion. Fifty years later it was again clear that, while millions of Catholics chafed over specific assertions of papal and hierarchical authority, there was an appeal to many kinds of authority. Meanwhile, Protestantism that saw all sorts of authority erode declined or disintegrated. Authoritarian groups appealed to huge cohorts while mainstream groups also seriously confronted the issue of authority appropriate to their views of freedom.

Identity, meanwhile, was behind many of the issues of peoplehood—racial, ethnic, denominational, gender-based, movement-directed—that in extreme form spelled tribalism and in moderate form meant more benign "tribal" life. Who am I? To whom do I belong? Whom shall I trust? How will others know to locate me? These were questions that late-modernity posed with surprising urgency.

Was there a specifiable war, cataclysm, or invention? Were there designatable heroes and heroines? Were there decisive turns? Was any of this present with hurricane intensity on a culture-wide basis? It would seem that the world the young person finds unexplained and self-understood, and which the older visitor must have explained and cannot easily comprehend, belongs to the glacial sort of movement. It demands careful observation, a full range of the tools of historians and social analysts, and a regard for the people who made up the sphere of American religion fifty years ago as they do now.

My first response to the festschrift invitation was to review the fifty years in the light of the periodization and stresses set forth by the honoree, Professor Robert T. Handy. I learned from the editors that the purpose of this festschrift was of a different design and that I should reconceive my essay as an approach to main themes in American religious history in this half-century, without necessarily referring to Handy's work. While I have followed the second prescription here, let me at least enter into the record a sense of gratitude for his work and a recognition that rereading his works in the summer of 1985 in preparation for that draft was a rewarding experience that reinforces my sense of debt to him.

PART ONE

The Changing American Churches

1. The Modernization of Protestant Religion in America

Leonard I. Sweet

G. K. Chesterton defined paradox as truth standing on its head with both legs dangling to get attention. A paradox stands at the heart of American religious life today. Seldom has American addiction to religion been higher or American religion more "alive and well";[1] seldom have segments of Protestant religion been in worse shape. The leg of the paradox representing the crumbling of conventional Protestantism may not dangle as noticeably as the more shapely leg of burgeoning religious beliefs, the latter being a "very remarkable psychological problem" that mystified Sigmund Freud in *The Future of an Illusion* (1928).[2] But the plight of institutional Protestantism from 1935 to 1985 is, in its own right, a very remarkable cultural, political, sociological, and theological problem of extraordinary importance.

Nineteen thirty-five spelled the end of the Protestant era in American history, Robert T. Handy has argued. Some would push back twenty years, others ahead twenty years, the watershed dates for this passing of Protestant hegemony in American culture.[3] Nevertheless, there is general agreement that, from 1935 onward, Protestantism has been set upon

---

1. See *Religion in America: Fifty Years, 1935-1985*, Gallup Report No. 236 (Princeton, NJ: Gallup Organization, 1985).

2. Sigmund Freud, *The Future of an Illusion*, trans. W. D. Robson-Scott (New York: Liveright, 1928), p. 47.

3. Robert T. Handy, *A Christian America: Protestant Hopes and Historical Realities*, 2nd ed., rev. and enl. (New York: Oxford, 1984), pp. 185-210; Sydney E. Ahlstrom, *A Religious History of the American People* (New Haven: Yale, 1972), pp. 1093-94; Winthrop S. Hudson, *Religion in America*, 4th ed. (New York: Macmillan, 1987), pp. 388-89; Catherine L. Albanese, *America, Religions and Religion* (Belmont, CA: Wadsworth, 1981), pp. 247-81; and Peter L. Berger, "Religion in Post-Protestant America," *Commentary* 81 (May 1986) 41-46.

by troublesome forces tart enough to sour honey. "Years of Drift and Indecision" and "A Time of Disarray and Disaffection" are the headings one prominent historian used to interpret the last fifty years.[4] A crumbling moral code and shift in values, especially regarding family structure, size, and composition, proved more potent in altering religious beliefs and behavior than did even economics. Traditional standards of marital and fertility behavior became almost as quaint as the words to a popular song: "Love and marriage . . . go together like a horse and carriage." The decline in generativity among certain Protestants brought about dramatic demographic changes—a severe drop in youthful members of some churches and a swelling of blue-haired people on Sunday mornings.[5] The general cultural demand for equality, where an equal sign achieved totemic status and a hierarchical plus or minus sign became anathema, pulled at Protestantism from every angle and democratized leadership styles. The great migrations of the 1970s, bringing 5-7 million people to the United States from Latin America, the Caribbean, Southern and Southeast Asia, nimbussed issues relating to the church's ministry and leadership in new and threatening ways.

Two technological developments had massive consequences for Protestantism. First, America's love affair with the automobile, after lying nearly dormant during the grim 1930s, picked up pace in the 1940s and, by 1950, the highway was dotted by one car for every three households.[6] Beginning in 1957, the interstate highway system's geologic transformation of American topography into a densely packed grid of interminable, anonymous freeways radically altered the character of church life. "Autopia" also cordoned off America's inner cities, allowing Protestantism to pass by on the other side. Second, after tripping over the threshold of the communications revolution, the church rose to stare bewilderingly at electronic media and mass television that had already recast the Christian consciousness in profound and permanent ways.

Protestants found themselves inhabiting a religious landscape populated largely by unbelief and overbelief. On the one hand, there was the secularizing tendency to debunk religion and replace it with holy grails like science, the arts, or a spinning prism of isms. Even

4. Winthrop S. Hudson, *Religion in America,* 3rd ed. (New York: Scribner's, 1981), p. xiii.

5. Robert T. Handy, "The American Religious Depression, 1925-1935," *Church History* 29 (March 1960) 3-16; Benton Johnson, "Winning Lost Sheep: A Recovery Course for Liberal Protestantism," in Robert S. Michaelsen and Wade Clark Roof, eds., *Liberal Protestantism: Realities and Possibilities* (New York: Pilgrim, 1986), pp. 220-34.

6. "The Automobile Age," *Wilson Quarterly* 10 (Winter 1986) 64-81.

church members began identifying more with an ideology or a caucus than with the church. On the other hand, there was the sacralizing tendency to follow a host of usurpant gods and household deities down well-traveled but booby-trapped terrain. Protestants lived through two great religious depressions, one hitting in the 1920s and ending in the 1930s, the other hitting in 1967 with staggering losses suffered in the 1970s and 80s.

In short, from 1935 to 1985 Protestantism came to grips with the forces of modernization—that process by which a culture becomes adapted to rapidly changing attitudes, realities, and values that place a premium on rationality, objectivity, relativity, novelty, science and technology, social action, organization, differentiation, and distributive justice. Modernization takes characteristic form in the different spheres of society. In the religious sphere, it found its fullest expression in, and took the unique form of, what historians used to call "mainline" Protestantism, what they are increasingly prone to call "oldline" Protestantism or "the Protestant establishment," but what this paper refers to as "modernist" Protestantism. In varying degrees the modernization of American religious life has affected all religious traditions. Yet modernization patterns among America's denominations have been asynchronic, with different starting places and pulses. Those Protestant groups that have been most receptive to modernist culture and its embrace of the present, rather than of the past, as a source of creativity, stand as concrete enough historical entities (although of differing forms and intensities) to legitimate a sustained analysis of modernist Protestantism during the last fifty years.

I. From Realism to Modernism

Each of the modernist Protestant denominations swung to the political left during this period.[7] From 1935 to 1940 a pacifist crusade swept through Protestant churches, making it virtually impossible to distinguish the historic "peace churches" from what has been called the modernist tradition of "war churches." Modernist Protestantism marched through World War II more as as duty to be performed than as the customary holy crusade. Socialist sentiment, which was on the side of all the political angels of the day, was never stronger among the clergy, though it failed to make significant headway among the laity. Ameri-

---

7. Robert Moats Miller, *American Protestantism and Social Issues, 1919-1939* (Chapel Hill: University of North Carolina, 1958), pp. 101-12.

can clergy flirted with communism more seriously than at any other period in American history. Reinhold Niebuhr, who contended that there was more left-wing political opinion in the American churches than anywhere else in the entire world of religion, called himself a "Christian Marxist." Even that pragmatic liberal, Harry Emerson Fosdick, did not become overly upset at being included among the "pink intellectual and sobbing socialists."[8] Denominational political and social pronouncements, which one old parson termed the most harmless form of amusement ever designed by the human mind, became a pervasive and perduring feature of mainline religion during this period. Many of the pronouncements were among the most progressive and radical in American history—severe attacks on the profit system, with Soviet Russia openly celebrated (even held up as a model) and socialism encouraged. Methodist youth were given decision cards bearing a pledge to surrender themselves to Christ and to smash the capitalist order.[9]

Troubled by a sense that the pillars of the world were crumbling and confronted by disasters on a global scale, Protestant church leadership moved to the right theologically at the same time that it lurched to the left politically. Christian realism was now the order of the day, as the title of a book by layman Francis P. Miller and theologians H. Richard Niebuhr and Wilhelm Pauck made clear: *The Church Against the World* (1935). Just how much of a change the Depression decade wrought was manifested in the *Christian Century's* 1939 series, "How My Mind Has Changed in This Decade." Of thirty-four contributors, twenty-six (76 percent) registered "considerable change" (seven), "positive change" (eight), or "radical change" (eleven). Only eight claimed "no change."[10] The direction of this "sea-change"[11] was toward social and evangelical liberalism. Over and over again one reads in these articles of "the shattering of liberalism's illusions";[12] "the smashing of ideals" and "the progress of disillusionment";[13] a rediscovery of "the profound depth of sin";[14] a "church-centric gospel"[15] and "the importance of the Christian tradition" ("Ten years ago I had little interest in the church,"

8. Ibid., pp. 64, 104.

9. Ibid., p. 68.

10. Charles Clayton Morrison, "How Their Minds Have Changed," *The Christian Century*, October 4-November 1, 1939, pp. 1194-98, 1237-40, 1271-75, 1300-03, 1332-35.

11. George Craig Stewart, "A Bend of the River," ibid., May 10, 1939, p. 605.

12. Georgia Harkness, "A Spiritual Pilgrimage," ibid., March 15, 1939, p. 350.

13. Frederick D. Kershner, "Realities and Visions," ibid., February 1, 1939, p. 149.

14. Henry Nelson Wieman, "Some Blind Spots Removed," ibid., January 25, 1939, p. 118.

15. E. Stanley Jones, "The Christ of the Kingdom," ibid., May 3, 1939, p. 572.

confessed John C. Bennett);[16] the "flimsiness of our foundations";[17] a new concern for "the conduct of worship";[18] and "a sober and chastened view of the human problem."[19] Neo-orthodox terminology and Karl Barth walked the pages of virtually every one of these articles. Halford E. Luccock spoke for modern Protestants who found themselves going through the "bend in the river" when he said his theme song had gone from "At Length There Dawns A Glorious Day" to "O God, Our Help in Ages Past."[20]

Certain things must be remembered about Protestantism's attempts at theological renewal in the 1930s and 1940s. First, they took place almost exclusively within the seminaries. They had little substantial or sustained achievements outside of academic circles. The process of acculturation continued apace in the pulpits and pews. Second, it is now apparent that neo-orthodoxy marched uncomfortably to the tune of theological conservatism. The international galaxy of neo-orthodox thinkers—including Buber (Jewish), Unamuno (Spanish), Maritain (French), Nygren (Swedish), Berdyaev (Russian), and Brunner (German)—made this movement highly diverse and difficult to put into a single framework.[21] More than anything, however, neo-orthodoxy sought to help liberalism ferry into the future by walking today where Jesus walked. In other words, neo-orthodox theologians were liberal critics of liberalism and, fundamentally, neo-orthodoxy was a movement toward a new and revitalized liberalism. Third, although neo-orthodoxy —as stubbornly as the most hardened atheism—denied to history or to the world any capacity for divine revelation, both history and the world took on enormous significance once the kerygmatic "moment of faith" had occurred. The degree to which renewal, neo-orthodox style, exhibited the essence of modernism—taking the spirit of the age seriously —was symbolized in an image that achieved widespread currency: Karl Barth's definition of the preacher as one who stands in the pulpit with the Bible in one hand and the daily paper in the other. The often observed but mystifying connection between neo-orthodox theology and the most radical of modernist theologies—the "death of God" movement—is both logical (theologically) and linear (historically).

16. John Coleman Bennett, "A Changed Liberal—But Still a Liberal," ibid., February 8, 1939, p. 179.

17. Paul B. Kern, "Hope Sees a Star," ibid., March 29, 1939, p. 412.

18. Albert W. Palmer, "A Decade's Spiritual Pilgrimage," ibid., June 7, 1939, p. 732.

19. Bennett, "A Changed Liberal," ibid., p. 181.

20. Halford E. Luccock, "With No Apologies to Barth," ibid., August 9, 1939, p. 971.

21. Winthrop S. Hudson, *Religion in America,* 4th ed., pp. 350-51.

It was a short haul from the breadlines of the 1930s to the postwar boom in babies, business, and both urban and suburban growth. The fifties were a decade that even now resists interpretation and imposes its own religious terms of reference. Outwardly, there was a thunderous religious revival for modernist Protestantism, with church youth groups surprised by throngs of Brylcreemed boys and beehive-hairdoed girls. Inwardly, there was tumult, anxiety, and fear, or as one book title put it, a *Crack in the Picture Window* (1956). By every external set of measurements, Protestant churches had seldom been in better shape. The quickening religious interest was manifested in mounting membership (the level at which the decade ended—69 percent of the American population claiming church affiliation—has not been attained again) and in peaks of church attendance (in 1955 and 1958, 50 percent of the population claimed to be in church or synagogue each week). There were also unprecedented sales of religious books, a phenomenal pace of congregational development (during this period the Methodists started one new congregation every three days, the American Baptists one every five days), and the biggest boom in church construction in American church history (surpassing a billion dollars a year by 1960). The 1955 *Life* layout celebrating the vitality of American Protestantism testified to a public perception of plushness ("the fortunate fifties") for establishment religion.[22]

Behind the picture window, however, it was a different scene— the furniture of faith formless and in confusion, the table of devotional observance on its last legs. Menacing yellow and black "civil defense" triangles on church walls across America showed just how carefree this happy decade really was. Behind closed doors it was "the haunted fifties," as I. F. Stone put it. Religious and biblical literacy had seldom been lower. Denominational identities were eroded by the forces of public religion, bureaucratization, and modernism's devaluation of tradition. Allegiances were becoming less to denominations than to movements and causes within denominations. The fifties were the triumphant decade for the definition of church membership as going to church rather than being the church, with the individualistic notion of the church as one's private chapel so rampant that gambits had to be devised to thaw the cold wars going on inside the sanctuaries themselves—guest registration pads passed down the pews, "rituals of friendship" during worship, and their more stylish updating in the 1960s as "the kiss of peace."

The evaporation of the old bourgeois culture, based on self-discipline and deferred gratification, was virtually complete, replaced by new bourgeois values of self-gratification, immediate gratification, and

22. "Christianity in the U.S.," *Life*, December 26, 1955, pp. 46-144.

material gratification. Captivated by a consumerist economy, church members were being turned into shoppers and addicts—shopping for churches the same way they would shop for cars, with product style ranked above pedigree and the market's addiction to newness needing the constant and artificial stimulation of newness to keep it going. Clergy were fast going from missionizing to merchandizing, which helps account in part for the remarkable 1960s phenomenon of clergy picking fights with their congregations as the badge of being prophetic. By the 1960s some modernist clergy treated their parishioners as if they were the enemy rather than racism, sexism, and a host of other injustices.[23] To some extent, in all consumerist cultures the consumer becomes the adversary; indeed, in the 1960s fresh ways of assaulting congregations with newness were constantly devised in order to stave off the Gidean paradox—the boredom of novelty, the tedium of ever-newness. Where clergy miscalculated was in believing the marketing axiom that it is impossible to insult the consumer.

During the 1950s modernist Protestantism did prove on issues of race, anticommunism, and ecumenism that it could be in touch with culture without being in tune with it. Within every denomination there were leaders who raised dissenting voices against the way Protestants were holding up a torch of truth that was more nationalistic and materialistic than spiritual, more self-serving than just. In the early 1960s this voice could be heard above the others, but what did not change was the basic acculturation of modernist Protestantism itself and the prevalence of its peculiar sin: "trendier than thou" having replaced the old sin of "holier than thou." In the sixties the distinction between the church accommodating culture and being accommodated to culture was lost in the rush to find more relevant ways of realizing the kingdom of God in America. Modernist Protestantism remained hopelessly estranged from the voices of its past, its members having almost entirely forgotten how to live historically in conversation with their classic traditions.

The case has been made elsewhere for the concept of two very different sixties: the "first sixties" beginning in 1960 and lasting until 1967; the "second sixties" beginning after the long, hot summer of 1967 and lasting well into 1975.[24] In other words, the seventies were the sixties (or more accurately the second sixties) at least until the fall of

---

23. This is an observation that Winthrop S. Hudson has made in private conversations with the author.

24. Leonard I. Sweet, "The 1960s: The Crisis of Liberal Christianity and the Public Emergence of Evangelicalism," in George Marsden, ed., *Evangelicalism and Modern America* (Grand Rapids: Eerdmans, 1984), pp. 29-45. See also Ronald B. Flowers, *Religion in Strange Times: The 1960s and 1970s* (Macon, GA: Mercer University Press, 1984).

Saigon in 1975. The seventies really began in 1975-76. The difference in mood between the first and second sixties in modernist Protestantism can be illustrated by the black power movement in the churches. By the time of the death on April 4, 1968, of Protestantism's greatest leader during this fifty-year period—the tragic assassination of Martin Luther King, Jr., in Memphis—the movement for black power had gone from focusing on integration, reconciliation, and nonviolence to liberation, reparation, and militancy. The first sixties can be further elucidated by means of a hypothesis: what abstract expressionism was to the world of art in the 1950s and early 1960s, modernist Protestantism was to the world of religion in the first sixties. Indeed, it can be argued that what has been called "abstract art" and what might be called "abstract religion" have proved to be the dominant form of artistic and religious expression during the last fifty years. Just as romanticism dominated nineteenth-century American evangelicalism, so modernism has dominated twentieth-century American liberalism. Especially from 1945 to 1975—in sculpture, in painting, in architecture, and in religion—the mainstream was mostly modernist.

The world of church architecture, called by John Dillenberger "the art form of Protestantism," celebrated "the end of the cathedral,"[25] while the shopping mall, with its architectural similarities to the great gothic cathedrals, became the pilgrimage center of American life. Church buildings that were constructed during the second sixties differed from traditional ones in that a new "language of space" spoke a message of minimalism and impermanence. Flat-roofed, common design, low-profile exteriors constructed not of solid stone but of standardized building materials like those used for supermarkets and shopping centers spoke of a church whose position in the community was less dominant, more domestic and derivative than ever before. God's house was now built on sand, not stone. Nondirectional interior space with movable enclosures, movable furnishings, and even changing walls (through the use of banners and posters) spoke of a faith that was people centered and participatory, but with nothing set aside as holy or "high and lifted up." A healthy new orientation toward fostering intimate relationships between one individual and another was featured, but without the restoration of the sacred and the fostering of holy intimacies between this world and the next. Even the three furnishings deemed necessary in church interiors—altar-table, pulpit, and font—

---

25. John Dillenberger, *A Theology of Artistic Sensibilities: The Visual Arts and the Church* (New York: Crossroad, 1986), p. 213; E. A. Sovik, *Architecture for Worship* (Minneapolis: Augsburg, 1973), pp. 63-64.

were put on rollers or otherwise made mobile to fit the ruling ethos of "simplicity, flexibility, intimacy, utility" (with beauty conspicuous by its absence). James F. White did not exaggerate when he called this a "revolution" in church architecture. For the first time in church history, churches were built on the premise that change is the only permanence.[26]

II. Modernism and Popular Piety:
A Loss of Mastery and Mandate

The problem with the modernist affirmation of minimalism and impermanence is that when one casts off the burden of tradition, one also diminishes the capacity to convey certain kinds of content and meaning. Meaning is religion's food and drink, and modernism failed to address the essentially religious question of meaning in full and fulfilling ways. The inability of modernist Protestantism to answer God's two questions of Hagar in the wilderness, which are the two basic questions of existence—where have you come from and where are you going?—helps explain the onset of the second great religious depression in modernist Protestant churches.

Modernist denominations, however, did not so much disregard the problem of meaning as seek to answer it in ways that were either inaccessible or unsatisfying to their constituencies. The basic issue, then, was not the widely touted "problem of meaning."[27] In fact, modern religion (like modern art) has been preoccupied with the question of meaning. Rather, the basic issue was the decline of modernist Protestantism as a popular religion and its deserved reputation for obscurity: its attempt to express spiritual realities in ways beyond the reach of, or at flagrant odds with, popular piety.

At the very time television was becoming the most popular of the public arts and the most powerful mass medium, indeed the primary window to the world that was open to Americans, modernist Protestantism was turning its back on the blinking box and denouncing the family room

---

26. James F. White examined the differences between church architecture in the mid-60s and the mid-70s in "The Church Architecture of Change," Chapter 7 of *Christian Worship in Transition* (Nashville: Abingdon, 1976), pp. 143-55. See also his *New Forms of Worship* (Nashville: Abingdon, 1971).

27. See Dean M. Kelley, *Why Conservative Churches Are Growing: A Study in Sociology of Religion* (New York: Harper & Row, 1972), p. 38. For an attack on Kelley which defends the modernists, see James H. Smylie, "Church Growth and Decline in Historical Perspective," in Dean R. Hogue and David A. Roogen, eds., *Understanding Church Growth and Decline: 1950-78* (New York: Pilgrim: 1979), pp. 69-93.

as little more than a brainwashing chamber. Whether modernist Protestantism would have developed a user-friendly instead of a user-hostile or user-vaguely-acquainted relationship with the electronic media if it had continued to receive free public air time—something that was taken away from the modernists in the 1950s, but something that evangelicals and fundamentalists always had to live without—is a moot question.[28] Suffice it to say that while a few modernist preachers like Harry Emerson Fosdick, Norman Vincent Peale, Ralph Sockman, and Robert Schuller pioneered in the use of mass communications media (radio, television, publishing ventures, computer mailings, etc.), by and large modernist clergy were content to remain inky-fingered, acting as if the communications revolution had never taken place.

Failure to use the mass media of the age led to a failure of rhetoric—the inability to use the symbolic language that can effectively mobilize church members in an electronic culture. In spite of renewed interest in evangelism ever since "Key '73" and Dean Kelley's book of a year earlier *(Why Conservative Churches Are Growing)*, the degree to which emerging forms of modern evangelism (such as vacation evangelism, entertainment evangelism, and electronic evangelism) were not taken seriously and, indeed, were snubbed as "slick" and "acculturated" by modernist Protestantism was but one indication of its decline as a popular religious movement. In spite of their rhetorical status as "the voice of the voiceless," their vaunted identification with the "forgotten man and woman," and their concern for the "conditions of the poor and oppressed," modernist churches made a cult of the cultivated and distanced themselves as never before from their social environment and the religiosity of middle-class Americans. The reasons for this loss of mastery and mandate—mastery of the common touch and mandate of the common faith—are varied and complex and can only be hinted at here.

First, part of this loss was due to modernist Protestantism's failure in the face of privatization to encourage a "shared symbolic order"[29] that could bring together minister and congregation, member and neighbor into a fruitful communal embrace. Tom Wolfe called the seventies "the greatest age of individualism in American history,"[30] and this fragmentation of community life was reflected in the social struc-

28. Dennis Voskuil, "The Protestant Establishment and the Media, 1920-1960" (unpublished manuscript).

29. The words are those of Peter Fuller in *Images of God: The Consolations of Lost Illusions* (London: Hogarth, 1985), pp. 3-16.

30. Tom Wolfe, *Mauve Gloves & Madmen, Clutter & Vine, and Other Stories, Sketches and Essays* (New York: Farrar, Straus, and Giroux, 1976).

tures of the church. Many churches found themselves reduced to commuter communities, with parking lots the scenes of some of the most intense encounters. Many Protestants took their leave of religion because its inaccessibility and its riot of individualism mocked a faith that is communal.

Second, part of this loss was due to a crisis in the devotional life that occurred during the middle years of this century, as evidenced in the transit from Robert E. Speer's popular devotional guidebook, *Five Minutes A Day With God* (1943), to Malcolm Boyd's *Are You Running With Me Jesus?* (1965), where God catches time with us as catch can. By the 1960s a rich devotional tradition of personal piety, involving regular Bible reading, family worship, and disciplined habits of prayer and piety had vanished along with the mid-week prayer meeting, leaving a void both in the arena of public worship, where the sense of the holy became increasingly dim, and in the arena of personal devotion and discipline, for which professional religious leaders were now claiming responsibility. Higher criticism, as James Smylie has astutely argued, "made it more and more difficult for the ordinary Christian to deal with the Bible in devotional terms."[31] By the 1960s modernist hymnbooks no longer reflected popular religious tastes or reinforced daily devotional life but had become bureaucratic rituals and denominational rites of passage. Even Sunday schools, during the 1940s and 1950s, ceased being a training ground for the laity's "taking time to be holy" and became agencies for the professionalization of religious observances carried out by the newly professionalized Christian Education Directors.

Third, part of this loss was also due to the high, at times bordering on gnostic, conception of the role of the minister and theologian in modernism. Clearly, professionals were supposed to know best, and professionals did not aim to please. Further, as with any model of professionalism, there was a foot on the hose in the flow of information from clergy to laity, from seminary to sanctuary, from denominational staff to congregations. Much of modern theology required a heavy cerebral investment in learning new ways of putting words and ideas together before one could even begin to draw strength, say, from Paul Tillich's sermons, not to mention his three-volume *Systematic Theology* (1951-63). In other words, the flashpoint at which the divine erupts was distanced from the constituency, not because the climactic moment and the conviction were not there but because modernism by design left the constituency to itself, unmanacled by rigorous interpretive standards. In

31. James H. Smylie, "Of Secret Family Worship: Historical Meditation, 1875-1975," *Journal of Presbyterian History* 58 (Summer 1980) 95-115.

this way meaning came to be attached to, and reduced to, the appropriating question, "What does it mean *to you?*" By refusing to make meaning antidemocratic, modernism willy-nilly made it too demanding, too difficult, and inevitably and ironically, too undemocratic.

The size of the much talked about "gap" that separated the pulpit from the pew is evident from the liturgical renewal movement of the 1960s and from theological education in the 1960s and 70s. In the name of bringing the laity more into the experience of worship, and in an attempt to communicate the message that faces are more important than furniture, church leaders took away the communion rails where people knelt, the lecterns where people read, and the fixed pews where people sat. Theologians specialized in hermeneutical and methodological crossword puzzles, whose answers were absorbing to the players but useless to the wider public. By focusing on the academic community rather than the worshiping community, theologians allowed those whom Schleiermacher called Christianity's "cultured despisers" to set the theological agenda, until soon some theologians themselves *became* the "cultured despisers." After having created a theological rain forest impenetrable to the unguided mind, both theologians and the clergy they trained only reluctantly served as guides to laypersons brave enough to wish to enter.

Perhaps the most serious consequence of this lack of rapport with the grass roots and this systematic attack on middle-class biases was the way in which denominational staffs consistently made uninformed and, at times, downright maddening decisions about church programs and policies—including the abandonment of new church development in the late 1950s, the dismantling of successful denominational strategies for the campus ministry in favor of ecumenical ones, new ventures in worship, and a new understanding of missions that led to a decline in the deployment of missionaries both at home and abroad.[32] Most controversial of all was the fashionable leftward bias and the disdain for patriotic feeling that manifested itself in "empowerment money" for Angela Davis's defense fund ($10,000 from the United Presbyterian Church in the U.S.A. in 1970), for the "Alianza of New Mexico" and James Forman's "Black Manifesto Movement" ($40,000 and $200,000, respectively, from the Episcopal church in 1969), and for the Patriotic Front in Zimbabwe ($85,000 from the World Council of

---

32. Between 1956 and 1976, the United Presbyterians reduced their overseas staff by more than half. The Episcopalians cut even more dramatically, reducing their foreign missions by two-thirds from the late fifties to the early seventies, and by 1976 reporting a further decline of 14 percent. See "The Employment Situation for Ordained Protestant Clergy," *Yearbook of American and Canadian Churches* (Nashville: Abingdon, 1978), pp. 248-51.

Churches in 1978).[33] Laity were no doubt as bewildered by all this as was Vietcong General Giap, whom a *National Review* cartoon portrayed as reading, with a look of utter puzzlement, a telegram that said: "The Episcopal Diocese of New York stands shoulder to shoulder with you in your resistance to American aggression."

The inability of modernist churches to create a popular consensus for their policies meant that they had to rely increasingly on undemocratic means to achieve democratic ends.[34] Little wonder that church bureaucracies became distrusted for being out of touch with the people, that an antiestablishment spirit emerged in all the modernist churches, and that religious alternatives to denominations proved more and more attractive. The proliferation of parachurch groups from the 1960s to the present, in which 12 percent of all Protestant giving goes to some 5,000 to 10,000 parachurch agencies, reflects the need of even those members remaining in modernist denominations to find more satisfying outlets for their piety. It also testifies to the modernist denominations' signal failure to understand lay piety and to find useful full- or part-time roles for lay men and women in church life.

III. Modernist Sources of Meaning: Ecumenism, Actionism, Pluralism

One source of meaning that proved effective for modern Protestants was ecumenism and interfaith cooperation. A new ecumenical ethos, which no longer revolved around anti-Catholicism, characterized modernist church life after 1960. Early expressions of this ethos were primarily bureaucratic. The National Council of Churches of Christ in America was organized in 1950, with twenty-five Protestant member churches (and four Orthodox). In 1962, the formation of the Consultation on Church Union (currently known as the Church of Christ Uniting) aimed at a church "truly catholic, truly evangelical, truly reformed." By 1968 nine denominations were participating in COCU and in 1970 a "Plan of Union" was distributed. In the 1970s ecumenical initiatives and energies passed from bureaucratic structures to renewal movements, such as the charismatic and liturgical movements, but these pioneering bureaucratic maneuvers achieved lasting influence in three ways. First, they introduced in the 1970s a common church year, a com-

33. The attack was most focused in Clarence W. Hall's "Must Our Churches Finance Revolution?," *The Reader's Digest*, October 1971, pp. 95-100.
34. For Christopher Lasch's similar critique of the left, see "What's Wrong with the Right?," *Tikkun* 1 (1986) 23.

mon lectionary, and fuller liturgical and ordinal uniformity. Second, they gave rise to interfaith centers on college campuses, interfaith chapels in hospitals and at military bases, and an exploding number of community churches (also called "federated" churches, "united" churches, "interdenominational" churches, "covenant" churches). Third, they brought about dialogues among Christians and Jews, Protestants and Catholics, Lutherans and Catholics, Lutherans and Reformed, United Methodists and Lutherans, Protestants and Orthodox, Protestants and Marxists—virtually every modernist body in dialogue with everyone except fundamentalists. While the bureaucratic vision of organic union no longer sparkles today, the grassroots vision of ecumenical encounters and excitements shines as never before.

Another source of meaning for Protestantism was "actionism." Organizer Saul Alinsky lectured modernist churches on the necessity of their acting "as if" they were 100 percent sure, even if they were only 51 percent sure. For a modern religion that was experimenting with living theater, multimedia works, aleatoric music, and action painting, the worst sin of all was not to act. The civil rights movement was the baptizing moment for the equation of spirituality with actionism and for the placing of justice issues at the center of religious consciousness. Modernist Protestantism's three finest hours during this fifty-year period were its "new awakening" to peace issues in the early 1980s;[35] its heroic mobilization against hunger at home and abroad during the mid-1970s, replete with youth "Rock-a-Thons" and "Starv-a-Thons"; and its magnificent showing in the first sixties on desegregation and racial justice, symbolized by the March on Washington on August 28, 1963, in which hundreds of thousands of people participated in what amounted to a modern camp-meeting.

By 1963 most denominations had established racial commissions to respond to the "black revolt"; to study the persistent problems of employment, housing, and schooling; to confront the church with its own discriminatory practices; and, through quota systems and other means, to insert blacks into positions of high responsibility.[36] Whereas in the past the clergy's concern for social issues was likely to stop short of direct political involvement, in the first sixties activist clergy aimed to play a part in changing society through their participation in marches,

35. See Alan Geyer, "From Haunted Sleep to a New Awakening: The Churches and Disarmament in America," in Paul Peachey, ed., *Peace, Politics and the People of God* (Philadelphia: Fortress, 1986), pp. 7-24; and Leonard I. Sweet, *The Lion's Pride: America and the Peaceable Community* (Nashville: Abingdon, forthcoming).

36. John L. Kater, Jr., "Dwelling Together in Unity: Church, Theology, and Race, 1950-1965," *Anglican Theological Review* 58 (October 1978) 444-57.

boycotts, demonstrations, and political parties. For these activists God was to be discovered less in community, or in worship and devotions, than in the streets and struggles of the modern metropolis.[37]

Yet, once again, elitism showed itself in such actionism. To be sure, there were many efforts at civil rights involvement at the local church level (efforts that have largely gone unrecognized and still need to be documented). But the most innovative and meaningful responses of modernist church bodies to the racial crisis came from the top down, and these were ultimately undercut by local church opposition. In this sense, one must be cautious in talking about a civil rights "movement" in modernist Protestantism. Mobilizations that were effected in the streets did not last long. Enthusiasm was aroused only among relatively few church people and it soon evaporated. In moving from the "Book of Numbers" to the "Book of Acts," as the popular saying of the day went, church leaders were perpetuating the same uneven growth pattern of the fifties that they had sought to correct, namely, external growth occurring faster than internal growth. One still entered the kingdom of God through works, not faith.

The most striking feature of the running debate over who "sets the agenda" for the church—the world or the church itself?—was the fundamental agreement that the worst thing of all would be the church's lack of an agenda, of some kind of plan. Churches thus became little more than the sum and channel of human action. James F. Findlay's study of the Delta Ministry from 1964 to 1971 reveals the ultimately fatal absence of theological underpinnings and spiritual formation to this NCC-sponsored attempt to promote racial progress in the Delta region of Mississippi.[38] A good church was not a believing church but a working church, a church of constant "to-ing and fro-ing," with lots of "task forces" and especially lots of committees (those monsters that devoured so many modernist lives during this period). Denominational thrusts in the first sixties were aimed more at activating neighborhood organizations and building civic communities than at activating the church and building Kingdom communities, more at transforming society through political coalitions than at transmitting the Gospel through communities of faith. Among novelist Peter De Vries's most memorable characters was the Reverend Andrew Mackerel of the People's Liberal Church—"the first split-level church in America" with

37. Harvey Cox, *The Secular City: Secularization and Urbanization in Theological Perspective,* rev. ed. (New York: Macmillan, 1966). For a critique of Cox, see Leonard I. Sweet, "Theology a la Mode," *Reformed Journal* 34 (October 1984) 17-22.

38. James F. Findlay, Jr., "'The Justice Place': An Evaluation of the Delta Ministry, 1964-1971" (unpublished manuscript).

a dining area, kitchen, three committee rooms, "one huge all-purpose interior" divisible into an auditorium, gymnasium, and ballroom, and "a small worship area at one end."[39]

Church, in sum, became a place to get things done. A modern church was judged by the activities it kept. Modernist Protestant leaders tried to show the world how much their churches could work, not how well they could believe. In fact, the reigning ideology of pluralism and the moral appeal of relativism made what one believes one's own affair. But act one must. At first, love of God took back seat to love of neighbor. However, as spirituality became more and more oriented to social and political structures rather than to God and persons, love dropped almost entirely from view, except insofar as it was identified with human rights and justice or seen as a by-product of social betterment and liberation. It was assumed that just as modern unbelief had been caused by injustice, so modern faith would be created by justice. The circle was now unbroken: faith had become a kind of reward for good works. The loss of pure (nonmoralistic) faith occasioned by such actionism was well rendered by Karl Barth in his comparison of modern theological discourse to a newspaper photograph taken during a fever-pitch moment at a soccer match. The freeze-frame shot catches opposing players in mid-leaps, shoves, and stretches—bodies and faces strained to their limits. Yet, as Barth pointed out, the object of all this frenzy, the ball itself, is nowhere to be seen.[40]

Exploding interest in religion during the fifties and first sixties led to the construction and expansion of complex denominational bureaucracies. The crisis of membership beginning in the second sixties was not due, as some have insisted, to the growth of these huge bureaucracies. Rather, modernist Protestantism shrank because it did not have what evangelicalism and fundamentalism had: the organizational and theological characteristics required by the modern urban environment.[41] How much the face of modernist Protestantism has changed organizationally over the past twenty years is evident from the architectural message conveyed by the Interchurch Center (1959) or "God Box" at 475 Riverside Drive in New York City, the *locus classicus* for bureaucratic, ecumenical, establishment Protestantism. This aloof, austere structure—eighteen floors of orderly rows of rectangular peepholes that begin at two floors' distance from street level—gives off the

---

39. Peter De Vries, *The Mackerel Plaza* (Boston: Little, Brown, 1958), p. 7.
40. As cited in Gordon E. Michalson, Jr., *Lessing's "Ugly Ditch": A Study of Theology and History* (University Park: Pennsylvania State University Press, 1985), p. vii.
41. See Kevin William Welch, "Church Membership in American Metropolitan Areas: 1952-1971" (Ph.D. dissertation, University of Washington, 1985).

aura of an elevated, even depersonalized Protestantism. Whereas modernist denominations were once proud and vital organizations in the voluntary sector, over the past two decades they have been progressively weakened by widespread distrust for seemingly unloyal leaders, disdain for agencies riddled with "dirty politics" and power games, and by the resultant cutbacks in funding as parishioners increased their giving to local congregations in record-breaking amounts (even during the 1975 recession). Power is ultimately conferred upon any organization by its loyal constituency, and precisely such a constituency came to be lacking in the modernist denomination during the past twenty years.

Notwithstanding its recent enfeeblement, bureaucratic Protestantism has left a lasting and significant legacy. Bureaucratic structures came to replace strong individual leaders, thereby keeping "giants in the land" from emerging and being celebrated. They also flattened theological differences to the point that denominational identity no longer resided in theology but in polity. And since polity matters were increasingly based on general principles of organizational development, not on theological premises, it was almost impossible for denominations to maintain a theological distinctiveness. The triumph of the managerial revolution and the erosion of faith bases in church organizations became most apparent at the 1980 General Conference of the United Methodist Church, when its *Discipline* equated "efficiency" with "effectiveness" and provision was made for pastors to be brought to trial for the chargeable offense of "inefficiency."

Denominations were now being run by an "ecclesiocracy without an ecclesiology," one American Baptist historian charged, and, as churches became preoccupied with their own internal processes, modern religion showed as great a facility for self-regard as did modern art.[42] Church mergers, denominational restructuring, and the relocation of national headquarters all illustrate modernist Protestantism's preoccupation with institutional concerns and procedural matters. Of the scores of proposals for church union between 1910 and 1960, fifteen resulted in actual mergers, but only after expending enormous energies in family feuding and civil lawsuits. Since 1960 significant mergers have been consummated among Lutherans (ALC in 1961, LCA in 1962, and the Evangelical Lutheran Church in America in 1986 [finalized, 1988]), the United Methodists (1968), and the Presbyterians (1983). The structural and administrative changes made during the seventies in all the

---

42. C. C. Goen, "Ecclesiocracy Without Ecclesiology: Denominational Life in America," *Religion in Life* 48 (Spring 1979) 17-31.

modernist denominations, with 1972 a banner year for restructuring among United Methodists, Presbyterians, and American Baptists, gave considerable support to John Fry's controversial thesis about the "trivialization" of modernist religion in America: lots of time lost doing a lot of something while achieving nothing of lasting consequence.[43] In fact, by the 1970s the word "mission" had come to mean everything a church does, from paying the pastor's salary to purchasing robes for the cherub choir.

The most important source of meaning, however, was pluralism. Pluralism became the fairy godmother of modernist Protestantism, non-inclusiveness its wicked stepfather. The power of pluralism as both a theology and a social platform can be seen in what it accomplished in modernist Protestantism: the death of the "WASP" establishment and the birth of the women's movement. Of all the social justice issues confronted by modernist Protestantism during this time—including fights over black rights and reparations, abortion, homosexuality, and bioethics—the entrance through the front door of women into all levels of church life, particularly the ordained ministry, brought about some of the most revolutionary and lasting changes, smashing forever the stereotype of home-bound mothers and work-bound fathers.[44] Edwina Sandys's female Christ on the cross called *Christa* (1975), but even more George Rodart's *Adam and Eve* (1981)—a diptych with Adam's face on one panel, Eve's naked body on another, and a snake slithering between them—speak volumes about the emerging genre of gender, which manifested itself in discussions about feminism, the hemispheres of the brain, the relationship of mind and body and their sex-linking, and the fragmentation of the individual. Every modernist church took valiant strides (though not without much kicking and screaming) toward the inclusion of blacks and women in its power structures, culminating in the 1980 election of Marjorie Matthews as a bishop in the United Methodist Church, the first woman consecrated bishop by any major denomination. The 1983/84 revision of Bible readings for worship, sponsored by the National Council of Churches and published as *An*

43. John R. Fry, *The Trivialization of the United Presbyterian Church* (New York: Harper & Row, 1975).

44. For the ordination of women as one of the major issues in ecumenical and denominational circles, see Barbara Brown Zikmund, "Winning Ordination for Women in Mainstream Protestant Churches," in Rosemary Radford Ruether and Rosemary Skinner Keller, eds., *Women and Religion in America*, 3 vols. (San Francisco: Harper & Row, 1981-86), 3:339-83; "Securing Ordination Rights: No Legal Barriers, 1930-1958," in Lois A. Boyd and R. Douglas Brackenridge, *Presbyterian Women in America: Two Centuries of a Quest for Status* (Westport, CT: Greenwood, 1983), pp. 139-56.

Inclusive Language Lectionary, signaled the abolition of masculine nouns and pronouns in modernist Protestantism's official liturgical life. "Inclusivity" was executed primarily through the joined forces of bureaucratic agencies and advocacy groups (motley clusters of caucuses) intent upon promoting ethnic minority consciousness and interests within the church, and through the institution of quota systems or their equivalent for membership on general boards and agencies.

To the extent that pluralistic theologies led to pluralism as a theology, pluralism exacted a high price. Modernist denominations became a veritable fleamarket of faiths. Pastors could be found playing musical-chairs theology with their parishioners, while the promiscuous pluralisms of theologians afforded the churches little more than the sum of different views. Spurred on by pluralism, and by the Spockean focus on the individual child's powers of self-realization, modernist church members sent their children on individual quests for meaning—and their children often kept going, not into conservative churches but into "secularized" life-styles. Young adults became the "lost generation" in modernist Protestant churches. The modernist inability to hold onto, or attract, younger members testified to the weakness of its theological pluralism, as did the loss of clear theological identity in most modernist churches.[45]

The attempt, as it were, to climb aboard a theological helicopter that could fly over all competing traditions and beliefs, enabling one to look down upon them all with equal dispassion, meant that modernist Protestants became highly skilled in knowing how to respond to changes in the weather. But they were left stranded in the air, able to hover endlessly, but unable to land anywhere. Like the inhabitants of the checkerboard land of "Through the Looking Glass," modernists had to work hard and move quickly merely to stay in the same place. Finally, despite its celebration of pluralism, modernist Protestantism became an isolated, introspective, xenophobic church when treating its own past, in that it regarded ecclesiastical tradition not as a matter of truth but as one of taste and cultural preference. While ostensibly adopting a "Christ against culture" perspective, modernist Protestantism so identified Christian faith with what it considered best in American culture that it actually adopted what it said was the worst of H. R. Niebuhr's five typologies—the "Christ of culture" pattern of faith and life.

---

45. Wade Clark Roof and William McKinney, "Denominational America and the New Religious Pluralism," *The Annals of the American Academy of Political and Social Science* 480 (July 1985) 24-38.

IV. Modernism in Retreat: Antimodernism

In 1984 a Golden Earring song asked the question: "Where am I to go now that I've gone too far?" This song could easily have been the ballad for a disoriented "oldline" Protestantism during the past ten years. As the actionist dream ran out, the only hope for humanity was seen in spiritual solutions. Americans embarked on a massive "search for the sacred."[46] Yet modernists were unequipped to satisfy this yearning. By 1976, which the media christened "The Year of the Evangelical," modernist Protestantism could only ironically or nostalgically be considered the "mainline" religion in America.[47] Major religious initiatives and innovations were now coming from evangelicals, fundamentalists, Pentecostals, even from "laic piety."[48] The ultimate indignity came when modernist Protestantism's last stronghold, political involvement, was seized by evangelicals like Jimmy Carter (Democratic party), fundamentalists like Jerry Falwell (Moral Majority), and traditionally antipolitical Pentecostals like Pat Robertson (the religious Right).

Just how serious things had become for modernist Protestantism can only partially be seen in the staggering losses reflected in church membership statistics from 1967 to 1984: Christian Church (Disciples of Christ)—40 percent decrease; Presbyterian Church (USA)—27 percent decrease; Episcopal Church—19 percent decrease; United Church of Christ—17 percent decrease; United Methodist Church—16 percent decrease; Lutheran Church in America—8 percent decrease. The story was told even better in the 1978 *Christian Century* series on "The Churches: Where From Here?" It makes for somber reading: a square-one "quest for identity" and a blunt prognosis of "hazy future" and "condition guarded."[49] Another indicator of the extent to which the modernist was caught in the grip of angina was the slew of "whatever happened to" books that became tracts for the times in the 1970s, in-

---

46. See the special report entitled "Religion's New Turn: A Search for the Sacred," *U.S. News and World Report,* April 4, 1983, pp. 35-44. Also "Gallup's View of Religion in America: Hopeful," *Signs of the Times,* February 1986, pp. 1-6, which concludes: "There are clearcut signs of renewed religious interest in America, providing enormous opportunity for churches, if they can recognize and understand that interest, tap into it, and form it into solid religious commitment."

47. Kenneth L. Woodward and others, "From 'Mainline' to 'Sideline,'" *Newsweek,* December 22, 1986, pp. 54-56.

48. See Martin E. Marty's "After Ten Years: The Shape of the Decade in Religion," *Context,* October 15, 1979, pp. 1-8.

49. Richard E. Koenig, "Lutheranism: A Quest for Identity," *The Christian Century,* October 25, 1978, p. 1009; Earl H. Brill, "The Episcopal Church: Conflict and Cohesion," ibid., February 15, 1978, p. 164.

cluding *Whatever Happened to . . . "Confession?"* (1970), *"Morality?"* (1971), *"The Gospel?"* (1973), *"The Church?"* (1974), *"Hell?"* (1979), *"Salvation?"* (1979). Most famous of all was Karl Menninger's *Whatever Became of Sin?* (1973),[50] which focused on ministers like poet Phyllis McGinley's Reverend Doctor Harcourt, of whom she wrote in "Community Church":

> And in the pulpit eloquently speaks
> On divers matters with both wit and clarity:
> Art, Education, God, the Early Greeks,
> Psychiatry, Saint Paul, true Christian charity,
> Vestry repairs that must shortly begin—
> All things but Sin. He seldom mentions Sin.[51]

In 1975 *Christianity and Crisis*'s theme issue on "Whatever Happened to Theology?" was precipitated by an editorial meeting where, in the frank admission of the editor, "the conversation was brisk and animated so long as we discussed social, economic and political questions, but when someone suggested that we begin talking about theology, there was dead silence!"[52]

With everything gone, there was little reason for people to stay. The 1980s was a time when one had to go no further than the nearest bridge to see how many people had fallen between the cracks. Nor did one have to go further than the nearest modernist church to see how many people had simply fallen away. A 1978 Gallup study of "The Unchurched American" confirmed the existence of vast numbers of "believers on the outside" because it was colder on the inside, the church having become preoccupied with organizational matters and "management science" techniques rather than with theological and spiritual concerns.[53] In the year 1984, the twentieth straight year of net membership loss for United Methodism—the largest and in many ways the most representative of the modernist churches—42 percent of United Methodist churches had no constituency rolls, 60 percent had no confirmation or membership training classes, and 38 percent did not

---

50. Menninger's social commentary was as much a summoning of clergy to moral leadership and a rediscovery of preaching as it was a lament for a word that had dropped out of the church's vocabulary because of the dominance of therapeutic (sin as "sickness") and legal (sin as "crime") over theological categories.

51. Phyllis McGinley, *Times Three* (New York: Viking, 1961), pp. 134-35.

52. "Whatever Happened to Theology?," *Christianity and Crisis* 35 (May 12, 1975) 106.

53. William McKinney, "The Unchurched—Believers On the Outside," *A.D.*, February 1979, pp. 26-30; and James Solheim, "Unchurched Americans Say Church Is Not Spiritual Enough," ibid., September 1978, pp. 38-39.

receive a single new member by profession of faith. The spectacle of a United Methodist church in trouble and on the defensive became nightly news in 1983. When under attack by *Reader's Digest* and "60 Minutes" for supporting left-wing, even revolutionary causes, United Methodist leaders responded by crying foul. It apparently never occurred to these leaders to counter aggressively and self-confidently with the claim that they had articulated a vision of the faith that was both authentically Christian and American.

Modernism's attempt to remythologize America and Protestantism had not worked. Hence the old myth came back—with Ronald Reagan in politics, with Jerry Falwell in religion. The restoration of severely traditional religion is one of the primary features of American religious life in the 1980s. In every modernist denomination there have emerged powerful conservative movements that harken back to the forms and formats of what is affectionately called "old-time religion." Clearly, antimodernism could become an elegiac lament for the passing of lost values, a mulish opposition to any dialogue with modern forms of thought. But another form of antimodernism also characterized American denominational thought from 1976 to 1985: postmodernism.

In American religion some of the first stirrings of postmodernism can be seen in the flurry of mid-seventies declarations. The "Chicago Declaration" (1973) issued from young evangelicals who criticized their transcendence-minded peers for a lack of interest in social action. The "Hartford Appeal for Theological Affirmation" (1975) issued from liberals who criticized their social-minded peers for a lack of interest in transcendence and for succumbing to thirteen modernist heresies. And the "Boston Affirmations" (1976) did not criticize anyone directly, but instead celebrated the uneasy marriage of politics and spirituality. Despite the media's attempt to bring these declarations into conflict, all three manifestos said basically the same thing from different starting points: first, theology must have something to declare; second, modernists have lost their theological roots and must rediscover spiritual taproots to the truth; and, third, the spiritual and the social belong together.

Postmodernist sentiments can also be seen in Protestantism's renewed attention to the Bible in worship (it was the lectionary that returned the Bible to modernist sanctuaries) and in its new focus on biblical themes in educational programming; in the recovery of roots through study of the church's teaching and tradition; in an increased concern for spiritual formation, liturgical renewal, and community building, with the postmodernist metaphor of "body" dominating all these discussions; in an attempt to restore to religion all the faith that modernism had removed;[54] and in a painful recognition of the perils of lacking a theological identity, well-advertised by the landscape of corpses left by unchecked viruses that had rapidly worked their way to the heart of oldline Protestantism.

To be sure, some who claimed to be postmodernists were really unrepentant modernists. Some postmodernist expressions, such as liturgical renewal, could actually mask subtle forms of Christian agnosticism, the redemption of ritual coming close to what one British theologian called *Taking Leave of God* (1980) but not of the "bells and smells" of God.[55] And in spiritual renewal's role-definition of "spiritual directors," a professionalism as hardened as anything modernism had produced raised its head under a new guise.

In the 1980s, modernism was in retreat. It had been called into question by a generation in search of spiritual meaning—a generation unconvinced that modernist religion could be truly spiritual.

54. Leonard I. Sweet, "Theology a la Mode."
55. Don Cupitt, *Taking Leave of God* (New York: Crossroad, 1980). For the way in which liturgical renewal can be a form of "'as if' faith" or a religion of make-believe, see A. N. Wilson, *How Can We Know?* (New York: Atheneum, 1985).

2. Religion and Social Change in the American Catholic Community

Jay P. Dolan

Reading through American newspapers published in 1935 is a good way to realize how remote those days really are. Automobiles were selling for six or seven hundred dollars and new homes could be purchased for seven or eight thousand dollars. People could not imagine earning more than $5,000 a year. In 1935 Congress passed legislation that established the social security system. Jane Addams died in 1935 and Huey Long was assassinated in September of that year. Adolf Hitler was a name that appeared in the press with some degree of frequency and the emperor worship of the Japanese intrigued American people. The daily news had a very international flavor to it in 1935 and, judging from all reports, trouble seemed to be brewing throughout Europe. In the world of religion Catholics, Protestants, and Jews were united in their opposition to immorality in the movies and were praising the success of the newly established Legion of Decency. In fact, the Catholic journal *America* claimed that movies were now 99.5% pure.[1] Fifty years later, in 1985, the Legion of Decency no longer existed; the social security system was taken for granted; Hitler was dead; and $700 was not enough to buy even a good used car. The passage of time does indeed change things and the passage of fifty years changes things a great deal. The challenge for the historian is to discern the changes and make sense of them so that, in understanding the past, the present might be better served.

In this essay I want to focus on some major changes that have

1. Gerard B. Donnelly, S.J., "The Outstanding Catholic Achievement," *America* 52/13 (January 5, 1935) 298.

taken place in the American Catholic community in the area that Martin E. Marty labeled "peoplescape" in his introductory essay. In focusing on the people, I hope to demonstrate how decisive social movements are in shaping the religious landscape, in this case the American Catholic dimension of that landscape.

In 1932 Arthur M. Schlesinger, Sr., wrote an essay entitled "A Critical Period in American Religion 1875-1900."[2] It was a somewhat celebrated essay since Schlesinger, one of the preeminent American historians of his time, had ventured into an arena of history ordinarily thought to be reserved to church historians. What Schlesinger wanted to show was how "the pronouncements of science and scholarship" (intellectual change) and "rapid urban and industrial development" (social change) had challenged organized religion. In the last fifty years American historians have come a long way, and there is now much more crossover and cross-fertilization between "church history" and "secular history." This is most visible in the area of social history, where a distinct and well-delineated area of religious social history has emerged. One of the fundamental assumptions of this new school of history is that social change influences religion. At first glance this seems obvious, but taken seriously it means that historians of religion must be acutely aware of the influence of social change on the historical development of religion.

Without question the major social movement of the past fifty years was the civil rights movement, which swept through the nation much like the Second Great Awakening did in the early nineteenth century and transformed everything in its path. To appreciate the dramatic changes inaugurated by this movement one has only to ponder the reality that from 1933 to 1935 "lynch mobs murdered sixty-three Negroes while southern sheriffs and deputies often looked the other way."[3] The lynching of black Americans in 1985 would have been unimaginable. Although black Americans were the first social group to benefit from the civil rights movement, the demand for an end to discrimination and for equal rights for all eventually affected numerous minority groups. In this essay I will concentrate on both black and Hispanic Americans and examine how the civil rights movement, especially the awakening that took place in the critical decade of the 1960s, altered the historical development of Roman Catholicism in the United States.

---

2. Arthur M. Schlesinger, Sr., "A Critical Period in American Religion 1875-1900," *Massachusetts Historical Society Proceedings* 64 (June 1932) 523-47.
3. Richard Polenberg, *One Nation Divisible* (New York: Penguin Books, 1980), p. 32.

I. The Black Catholic Community

The civil rights movement influenced the American Catholic community in a substantial manner. Prior to the mid-twentieth century black Catholics were a rare breed. By 1928 an estimated 203,986 blacks belonged to the Catholic church; this was less than 2 percent of the total black population. About half of the black Catholic population lived in Louisiana. The next largest concentration was in New York City, where about 25,000 lived; then came Baltimore and Washington, D.C., with a combined total of about 22,000. The remainder were scattered across the country. There are various reasons why so few blacks were attracted to Roman Catholicism, but institutional indifference and racial discrimination were the primary ones. Another key reason was the simple fact that most blacks lived in the South and most Catholics lived in the North. This changed in the post–World War I era when millions of blacks migrated north, with the result that by 1960 about half of black America lived in the North. When they moved north, they gravitated toward the city and the old immigrant neighborhoods, which formed the heartland of the Catholic immigrant church. When blacks moved into these white ethnic neighborhoods both church and people were ill-equipped to deal with the newcomers.

One American trait that Catholic immigrants and their children adopted was racial prejudice. In city after city, neighborhood after neighborhood, Catholic priests and people let it be known that "Negroes" were not wanted. Pastors would stand on the church steps on Sunday mornings and direct any black Catholic newcomers to go to their own church, i.e., the Catholic church in the city that had been designated, for all practical purposes, as the exclusively black church. What transpired in St. Louis in the 1930s and 40s was not much different from what happened in other northern cities.

In St. Louis the color line ran right through the heart of the Catholic community, segregating churches, grade schools, high schools, and colleges. A small black Catholic high school, St. Joseph's, "could not even engage in competitive sports within the city's Catholic High School League." The archbishop of St. Louis, John J. Glennon, had no desire to remove the color line in the Catholic community and remained adamant in this position throughout the 1930s and early 40s. Like most Americans he believed in the separate but equal doctrine as regards the civil rights of black Americans.[4]

---

4. Jay P. Dolan, *The American Catholic Experience: A History from Colonial Times to the Present* (New York: Doubleday, 1986), p. 368.

Times were changing, however, and the 1930s proved to be a decisive decade in the development of a concern for social and racial justice. A new breed of clergy and laity was surfacing in the Catholic community and it pushed both church and people toward integration and racial justice. At the parish level this concern for racial justice took the form of evangelization among the black newcomers, or, as it was called in those days, convert-making. One of the first priests to become involved in this apostolate was William McCann, pastor of St. Charles's Parish in Harlem, New York City's black metropolis. In cities like New York, Philadelphia, and Chicago, convert-making became the principal work of parish priests interested in the welfare of the black newcomers. An important element in this convert crusade was the parochial school. The idea of private school education at a nominal fee appealed to many black newcomers, and it was not long before parents and children were taking instruction in Catholic doctrine; in fact, in some parishes Protestant children could attend the school only if their parents took such religious instruction. In this manner the school became a port of entry for the clergy into the adult black community.

In St. Louis a number of both priests and laity, in this instance black Catholic laity, wanted more than convert-making; they wanted "equal rights" in the church. What this meant was the abolition of Archbishop Glennon's separate but equal policy and the implementation of integration in the church's institutions. It came at the stroke of a pen when Glennon's successor, Joseph E. Ritter, issued an edict in 1947 that required the integration of parochial schools. Anyone who opposed Ritter's policy was threatened with excommunication. Ritter exemplified a new type of bishop in the church, one concerned with racial justice. Francis J. Spellman in New York, Vincent S. Waters in North Carolina, Patrick A. O'Boyle in Washington, D.C., and Robert E. Lucey in San Antonio were other advocates of racial justice who demanded integration in their dioceses.[5]

The 1930s witnessed the beginnings of two extraordinary movements, the Catholic Worker and the Friendship House, which were founded by Catholic laywomen. Dorothy Day's name has become synonymous with the Catholic Worker movement, and Catherine de Hueck will best be remembered as the foundress of Friendship House, which was founded specifically to promote interracial justice in the Catholic community. Though the Catholic Worker movement had a broader vision, one of its primary objectives in the 1930s and 40s was to promote racial justice in both church and society. Another important organiza-

5. Ibid., pp. 366-68.

tion in the 1930s was the Catholic Interracial Council. Made up of both white and black laymen it promoted a biracial approach to racial justice. The key person in the organization was a Jesuit priest, John La-Farge, who became nationally known and respected for his promotion of racial justice.[6]

The work of people like LaFarge and de Hueck at the national level, along with that of numerous parish priests like McCann in Harlem, helped to awaken the Catholic community to the need for racial justice in the church as well as in society at large. The strong pro-integration stance of bishops like Ritter of St. Louis and Spellman of New York, together with the prophetic witness of numerous black Catholic laity, reinforced this awakening. Because of this awakening in the 1930s and 40s, American Catholics were fairly well prepared to participate in the major phase of the civil rights crusade that began in the 1950s under the leadership of Martin Luther King, Jr.

The militancy of the civil rights movement influenced the Catholic community in such a manner that clergy and laity began to move beyond convert-making and interracial education programs like those of Friendship House and the Catholic Interracial Council. The concern now was for community organization programs and direct action on behalf of social justice issues. The migration of millions of blacks to northern cities and government-sponsored urban renewal programs in the 1950s and 60s had highlighted the special needs of the urban church. The civil rights movement provided both a rationale (equal rights) for these needs and a tactic (civil disobedience) to deal with them. Because of its prominent presence in the inner city, the Catholic church could not ignore the needs and the demands of the urban newcomers. Before long urban ministry became very popular as scores of clergy and laypeople flocked to the inner city.

The church's increased commitment to racial justice and its rather intense involvement in urban affairs eventually persuaded more and more black Americans to cast a friendly eye toward the Catholic church, and a sizable number even joined the church. By 1959 the number of black Catholics had increased to 595,155—almost three times the number in 1928. This represented slightly more than 3 percent of the total black population, a proportion about twice as large as in 1928. Even more significantly, the number of black priests had increased; by 1961 they numbered 120, whereas in 1935 there had only been six black Catholic priests in the United States. Despite such substantial gains and

---

6. Ibid., pp. 369, 409-14.

the increased commitment of Catholics to racial justice, racism still remained a serious problem in the church throughout the 1950s and 60s.[7]

In the 1960s the world was turned upside down. Mass movements for equal rights for minority groups took hold throughout the world; the student movement mobilized young people in places as diverse as Berkeley, California, and Munich, Germany; and the women's movement forever changed the way men and women thought about one another. All of these movements and more swept across the American landscape and transformed both religion and society. Of course, one of the most significant developments was the civil rights movement and the awakening of black consciousness that accompanied it. The Civil Rights Act of 1965 indicated how far the nation had progressed since 1935, when people were still lynching blacks with impunity. Stokely Carmichael's dramatic introduction of the slogan "black power" in 1966 symbolized the militancy and ethnic awakening that was transforming the black community. The assassination of Martin Luther King, Jr., and the subsequent long hot summer of 1968, when burning and rioting took place in 168 cities and towns, intensified the rage and militancy of civil rights activists.

The civil rights revolution of the 1960s influenced the Catholic community in a variety of ways. At the institutional level the hierarchy issued strong statements against racial discrimination and for equal rights for all people. Catholic parishes in the South as well as in the North began to be racially integrated. A new organization, the National Catholic Conference for Interracial Justice, was established and it mobilized Catholic support for the famous march from Selma to Montgomery, Alabama. It also was instrumental in organizing a national interfaith conference on religion and race in Chicago in 1963.[8] In the black Catholic community more significant and long lasting changes were taking place. Clergy and laity began to talk about black theology and black culture. A Cincinnati priest, Clarence Rivers, introduced black-flavored music into Catholic worship and the popularity of folk music in the liturgy enhanced this development. The concern for racial and social justice superseded the concern for convert-making, and the number of black converts dramatically decreased. Catholic schools in the black community were no longer linked to the idea of convert-making.

---

7. Ibid., pp. 370-71.

8. Richard A. Lamanna and Jay J. Coakley, "The Catholic Church and the Negro," in *Contemporary Catholicism in the United States,* ed. Philip Gleason (Notre Dame: University of Notre Dame Press, 1969), pp. 147-94; William A. Osborne, *The Segregated Covenant* (New York: Herder, 1967); and Michael J. McNally, "A Peculiar Institution: Catholic Parish Life in the Pastoral Mission to the Blacks in the Southeast, 1850-1980," *U.S. Catholic Historian* 5/1 (1986) 67-80.

"More and more the church began to look at its schools in black communities as a service to those in need, since the public schools in the areas were often so inadequate. This service of education came to be seen more as a witness to the Gospel ethic of charity and neighborly concern than a way of bringing people into the Catholic church. Convert classes became smaller or nonexistent, and it seemed to be understood that neither black students in the parochial schools nor their parents were likely to become Catholics."[9] Many black Catholics resisted and resented these developments, but the times were changing and the demand for black theology and black Catholic liturgies increased rather than diminished.

The militancy and rage of the 1960s fired the imagination of the black Catholic clergy. In April 1968 the first meeting of the National Black Catholic Clergy Caucus took place in Detroit. From that meeting came a three-page statement in which the Catholic church in the United States was described as a "white racist institution, a part of America's racist society." The clergy continued to meet and soon demanded what they called a "share in the power of the church,"[10] which they sought to gain through the establishment of a National Office for Black Catholics. Their demand was met in 1970 when such an office was set up in Washington, D.C. Black Catholics, like the immigrants before them, also wanted their own black bishops and eventually got them. The first black Catholic bishop in the twentieth century, Harold R. Perry, was appointed in 1965 as an auxiliary bishop in New Orleans. By 1985 nine more black Catholic bishops had been appointed, but only one, Joseph L. Howze, bishop of Biloxi, Mississippi, was the head of a Catholic diocese; the rest were assistant bishops in dioceses with a large black Catholic population.

During the 1960s and 70s the number of black priests increased so that by 1985 they numbered 350; there would have been more, but some left the active ministry during those years. The same phenomenon was noticeable among black women religious; nonetheless, their number increased to 850 by 1985. Since 1960 the number of black Catholics has also increased so that by 1985 there was a total of 1.2 million; in other words, about 5 percent of the black American community is Catholic; in 1960 the corresponding figure was about 3 percent.[11]

9. Edward K. Braxton, "Authentically Black, Truly Catholic," *Commonweal* 112/3 (February 8, 1985) 76.

10. Lawrence Lucas, *Black Priests/White Church* (New York: Random House, 1970), pp. 186, 190.

11. Braxton, "Authentically Black, Truly Catholic," p. 74; Dolan, *The American Catholic Experience,* p. 370; John Harfmann, S.S.J., *1984 Statistical Profile of Black Catholics* (Washington, D.C.: Josephite Pastoral Center, 1985).

These numbers represent a sizable gain and compare favorably with the 1930-1960 period when convert-making was so much in vogue. Still, black Catholics make up a very small part of the Catholic community and when people speak of the black church, they invariably mean the black Protestant church. As Edward Braxton wrote,

> When we hear that the church is the source of values, culture, community, solidarity, and political influence in the black community, the *Catholic* church is not meant. . . . When there is talk of the Catholic church as an important religious, educational, cultural, and political force in our land, we do not mean *black* Catholics. The estimated 1.2 million black Catholics in this country seem invisible in comparison to the over 50 million white Catholics. Black Catholics are seen as a negligible minority in the larger white Catholic community.[12]

To accept the validity of Braxton's claim that black Catholics are a negligible minority in the larger white Catholic community does not preclude acknowledging that substantial change has taken place in the black Catholic community in the period 1935-1985. To grasp the magnitude of this change one has only to read the 1984 pastoral letter of the black bishops on evangelization, *What We Have Seen and Heard,* wherein they celebrate black culture and values, proclaiming that "there is a richness in our black experience that we must share with the entire people of God."[13] They go on to ask for leadership and authority positions for black Catholics; they emphasize the importance of an authentically black liturgy, of parochial schools, and of social justice; and they quote their fellow white bishops in calling for an end to racism in the Catholic church in the United States.

What it means to be black and Catholic has changed substantially from the 1930s. The 1984 pastoral letter, the first of its kind, is a clear sign that the black Catholic community has come of age. In the 1980s there is a heightened sense of black cultural awareness or pride in being black and in the richness of that unique heritage; blacks have claimed the Gospel and the church for themselves not in a separatist, divisive manner but in a way that recognizes racial and cultural particularity in a religion that espouses religious universalism. They want to be both authentically black and truly Catholic.

It is clear that black Catholics will no longer wait for white priests and bishops to tell them what to do. As one priest put it, "black Catholics [must] become missionaries to themselves."[14] Equally important for

---

12. Braxton, "Authentically Black, Truly Catholic," p. 75.
13. "What We Have Seen and Heard," *Origins: N.C. Documentary Service* 14/18 (October 18, 1984) 275.
14. Braxton, "Authentically Black, Truly Catholic," p. 77.

the future are two questions that have been pondered since the urban awakening of the 1950s and 60s. What is the role of the church in the inner city and what should be its relationship to the large number of blacks, both Protestant and Catholic, residing there? Will the white Catholic community and the white power structure in the institutional church "welcome sincerely the Black person and utilize the existing facilities and services to assist him or her to adjust in the urban environment and to develop educationally, socially, economically, and religiously?"[15] The survival of the black Catholic community depends a great deal on how these questions will be answered in years to come.

II. The Hispanic Catholic Community

The civil rights movement of the 1950s and 60s was not limited to the black community. It transformed the entire American society as people became more conscious of the "flagrant discrepancy between American ideals and American racial practice."[16] The democratic ideal of equality and justice for all now became both a popular slogan and a cherished goal. By the 1960s the shift in thinking was very noticeable as the campaign for equality and justice for all moved beyond the concept of race and beyond the black community and sought to include other minority groups. In 1965, the same year that the Civil Rights Act was passed, Congress also passed a new immigration law that abolished discriminatory quotas based on national origins. A major influence on the passage of this bill was the new climate of racial and ethnic toleration. As one member of Congress put it, "just as we sought to eliminate discrimination in our land through the Civil Rights Act, today we seek by phasing out the national origins quota system to eliminate discrimination in immigration to this nation. . . ."[17]

Coupled with this rising commitment to universalist principles was an increasing commitment to ethnic group loyalty and solidarity. Symbolized by the slogan "black power," this emphasis on group solidarity and group interest transformed the thinking of many minor-

15. Lamanna and Coakley, "The Catholic Church and the Negro," p. 191, and George Shuster, S.S.J. and Robert Kearns, S.S.J., *Statistical Profile of Black Catholics* (Washington, D.C.: Josephite Pastoral Center, 1976), p. 41.

16. Philip Gleason, "American Identity and Americanization," in *Harvard Encyclopedia of American Ethnic Groups*, ed. Stephan Thernstrom (Cambridge: Harvard University Press, 1980), p. 52.

17. David M. Reimers, *Still the Golden Door* (New York: Columbia University Press, 1985), p. 83.

ity groups. From this emerged the women's movement, the rise of ethnic consciousness among descendants of various European immigrant groups, the revitalization of the American Indian community, and the Hispanic *movimiento* or what Chicanos called "the struggle for liberation."[18] The tension between an intensification of the particularistic emphasis on group consciousness and the universalist ideal of equality and justice for all regardless of race, religion, sex, or national origin was indeed real. In fact, the interaction of these two forces constituted much of the social history of the late 1960s and early 1970s. This shift in thinking clearly affected the Catholic church in the United States, as it did Protestant churches. Within the Catholic church one of the most significant developments was the emergence of the Hispanic *movimiento* and the subsequent transformation of the Hispanic Catholic community.

By 1800 an estimated 20,000 Mexicans lived in the New Mexico area. After the 1848 Mexican-American war, when the United States annexed about half the territory belonging to the Republic of Mexico, 80,000 Mexicans became part of the United States. By 1900 the Mexican American population numbered close to half a million. Immigration increased substantially in the decades prior to the Depression so that by 1930 an estimated 1.4 million people of Mexican descent lived in the United States, and that was an admittedly low estimate.[19] The vast majority of these people lived in five states of the Southwest: Arizona, California, Colorado, New Mexico, and Texas. Initially the Mexicans were attracted to rural settlements and jobs in the agricultural industry, but as the nation became increasingly more urbanized so too did Mexican Americans. As a group Mexican Americans were economically very poor. The Catholic bishop of Amarillo, Robert E. Lucey, described Mexican Americans in Texas as "a people apart, ostracized and held in social and economic subjection." He went on to note that "if a Mexican is murdered, the officials do little or nothing about it. The Mexicans in Texas, even if born here, are classed with the Negroes."[20]

Even though Protestant missionaries had been evangelizing the Mexican American population since the mid-nineteenth century, the overwhelming majority of the community in the 1930s was Roman Catholic. As was true with various immigrant communities, the national

18. Moises Sandoval, "The Church and El Movimiento," in *Fronteras: A History of the Latin American Church in the U.S.A. Since 1513*, ed. Moises Sandoval (San Antonio: Mexican American Cultural Center, 1983), p. 377.

19. Carlos E. Cortes, "Mexicans," in *Harvard Encyclopedia of American Ethnic Groups*, pp. 697, 699.

20. Saul E. Bronder, *Social Justice and Church Authority* (Philadelphia: Temple University Press, 1982), pp. 63-64.

parish became the norm in the Mexican community. In cities with a sizable Mexican community certain parishes were designated as the Mexican parishes. The clergy working in these parishes most often belonged to a religious order of priests that the local bishop had designated as solely responsible for the Spanish-speaking apostolate. In Los Angeles and Chicago, for example, the Claretians were responsible for Mexican Catholics. The tendency, then, was for other clergy to waive any responsibility for the Mexicans. This served to isolate and segregate the Mexicans from the rest of the Catholic community.

After World War I a large number of Mexicans emigrated to the United States and both Protestant and Catholic churches made a strong effort to evangelize the newcomers. The response of the Catholic church in cities like Chicago and Los Angeles was impressive; one reason for this was the threat of Protestant competition. In Los Angeles in 1920 there was only one church serving the Mexican community, but by 1930 thirteen churches were engaged in some type of ministry in the Mexican community. Chicago had two Spanish-speaking parishes in the 1930s, whereas in 1920 it had none. The settlement house was another very important institution in the church's evangelization efforts. Lay men and women staffed these neighborhood institutions and became actively involved in home visitation and catechetical (religious education) programs. The catechetical movement had become very popular by the 1930s and in the Southwest United States where there was a severe shortage of priests, lay catechists proved to be especially advantageous. In cities like Chicago and Los Angeles the organization of a catechetical center was often the first step in the establishment of a Spanish-speaking parish.[21]

Living in the United States posed a mighty challenge for Mexican newcomers. Discrimination and prejudice confronted them at every turn and society reminded them at every opportunity that they had to become American. What this meant was that every trace of foreignness—such as language, customs, clothes, and patterns of behavior—had to be cast aside and replaced by corresponding American characteristics. The churches were as adamant in this regard as was the rest of American society. Priests, both Spanish-born and American-born, told the newcomers "to learn the language and adopt the customs of the United States."[22] They were asked to conform to the American "Mass and sacraments" style of Catholicism in which the quality of religion was measured by regular attendance at Sunday Mass and the

---

21. Dolan, *The American Catholic Experience*, pp. 371-79.
22. Quoted by Dolan, *The American Catholic Experience*, p. 374.

frequent reception of the sacraments. The religion of Mexican Americans, however, was family centered, not church centered; for this reason domestic family rituals and the public celebration of a saint's feast day were much more important than regular attendance at Sunday Mass. Anglo-American priests never understood this and sincerely believed that the Mexican Americans were "almost entirely ignorant of their duties to God and church."[23] Such prejudice was slow to disappear.

Discrimination in the church took a variety of forms. In some churches they had to sit in special pews in the back of the church; other churches had signs, "Mexicans Prohibited." Another common practice was to have one Mass on Sunday for Mexicans; if they attended any other Mass, they were asked to leave. The use of the Spanish language by the clergy was discouraged and Mexican-American-born priests were often not even assigned to Mexican-American parishes. Archbishop Patricio Flores, the first Mexican-American bishop, recalled that for his first pastoral assignment as a priest, "I was sent to a parish where I was asked not to use Spanish to communicate with people who did not understand English."[24] Such prejudice and discrimination alienated many Mexicans.

In the 1940s and 50s a major development occurred in the Mexican Catholic community. Both priests and people began to become concerned about issues of social justice, which had been of central concern in the Mexican-American labor movement in the 1930s. By the 1940s the public conscience had been sufficiently awakened and this concern spread to the institutional church. A main agency in the development of a social justice apostolate in the Mexican Catholic community was the Bishops' Committee for the Spanish Speaking. Organized in 1945, the committee focused its activities on the Southwest. The key person in the organization was Robert E. Lucey, archbishop of San Antonio, who led a crusade against social injustices in Texas. In the Mexican community the principal weapon in his fight for justice was the Bishops' Committee. It sponsored catechism and child-care programs, established health clinics and community centers, and also became involved in public housing and unionization efforts. In the 1950s Lucey turned the committee into a "virtual farm workers' organization, using it to expose the migrants' plight and broaden the church's involvement in confronting this injustice."[25]

23. Ibid., p. 371.
24. Quoted by Moises Sandoval, "Effects of World War II on the Hispanic People," in *Fronteras*, p. 371.
25. Bronder, *Social Justice*, p. 76.

As a result of the committee's success in raising public awareness of the problems of migrant farm workers, dioceses in California and Florida inaugurated a traveling mission to work with the migrants during the 1940s and 50s. In California, priests involved in this ministry eventually became concerned with social justice issues and encouraged farm workers to organize unions. In this manner Cesar Chavez was introduced to the labor movement and to the cause of social justice. Then, in 1962, he organized the National Farm Workers Association and launched the farm workers' movement, popularly known as *la causa*.

In the 1960s Congress began to fashion a new immigration law. Enacted in 1965, it sought to put a cap on immigration from nations in Central and South America as well as in the Caribbean. But owing to loopholes in the legislation, immigrants from these countries increased rather than decreased in the post-1965 period. During the 1960s 1,283,434 immigrants arrived in the United States from these countries; during the 1970s the number climbed to 1,811,801. In addition, immigrants from Spain and Puerto Rico added to the number of Spanish-speaking newcomers.[26] As a result of this large influx of immigrants the Hispanic population in the United States has skyrocketed in the past quarter-century. In 1985 the Bureau of the Census reported that there were 16.9 million people of Spanish origin in the United States; in 1960 the number of persons with Spanish surnames was 3.5 million. Not to be forgotten are the large number of Hispanic immigrants who have entered the country without the proper documentation (i.e., illegally); depending on which study is cited, their number varies from 3 to 10 million.[27]

Within the Hispanic community there is great diversity. The people have come from nineteen different Latin American republics plus Puerto Rico and Spain. The largest group, about 60 percent of the total, are Mexican Americans. In the last quarter-century Hispanics have settled in every state in the nation and "over 85% are found in large urban centers like New York, Chicago, Miami, Los Angeles, San Antonio, and San Francisco." Though there has been some improvement over the generations, Hispanics as a group are at the bottom of the

---

26. *1984 Statistical Yearbook of the Immigration and Naturalization Service*, U.S. Department of Justice (Washington, D.C.: U.S. Government Printing Office, 1984), p. 5.

27. Frank Ponce, "Spanish-Speaking Catholics in the United States," in *Pro Mundi Vita: Dossiers* (January 1981), p. 5; Leo Grebler, Joan W. Moore, and Ralph C. Guzman, *The Mexican American People* (New York: Free Press, 1970), p. 16; *Persons of Spanish Origin in the United States: March 1985* (Advance Report), U.S. Department of Commerce, Bureau of the Census, Series P-20, No. 403 (December 1985), p. 1.

economic ladder, with the proportion of Hispanic families living below the poverty level "more than double that of non-Hispanic families (25 percent versus 11 percent)."[28]

As a social movement that has substantially altered the ethnic character of American society during the past quarter-century, immigration has also had an obvious impact on the churches. When this is coupled with the civil rights movement of the 1960s and the subsequent awakening that took place in the Hispanic community, it is clear that the past twenty-five years have been a most unique period in American social and religious history.

One decisive effect of the Chicano movement was that Hispanics began to display a new self-consciousness and to achieve a new self-identity. They publicly celebrated their own cultural heritage and advocated integration into American society rather than assimilation. They wanted to retain their native language and culture rather than become transformed into white, Anglo-Saxon Americans. This awakening of group consciousness powerfully aided Hispanics in their "struggle for liberation."

As in the black community, Hispanics became filled with anger and rage at the discrimination and prejudice they encountered in the United States. Many became militant advocates of social justice and committed themselves "to struggle ceaselessly," as one manifesto put it, "until the promise of this county is realized for us and our fellow-Americans: *one* nation, under God, *indivisible*, with liberty and justice for *all*."[29] Sit-ins, demonstrations, and protest marches—the proven tactics of the black civil rights movement—became the chosen tactics in the Chicano movement. In 1965 in Delano, California, Cesar Chavez and the United Farm Workers launched a nationwide boycott of grapes; they dramatized the action with a march of protest, or pilgrimage as they called it, of hundreds of farmworkers and their supporters to the state capital. In Texas militant Hispanics organized *la raza unida*, a new political party, and were successful in winning some local elections. By 1974 the Chicano political awakening had become so powerful that two Chicanos were elected to governorships in New Mexico and Arizona. In East Los Angeles the Hispanic community boycotted the local schools in 1968 to protest inferior education. In other cities Chicanos protested segregated schools and advocated bilingual education. In these areas of education, politics, and economics, the Chicano

---

28. *Persons of Spanish Origin*, p. 3; *The Hispanic Presence—Challenge and Commitment: A Pastoral Letter On Hispanic Ministry* (Washington, D.C.: National Conference of Catholic Bishops, 1984), p. 6.

29. Armando B. Rendon, *Chicano Manifesto* (New York: Macmillan, 1971), p. 336.

movement effected decisive changes and permanently altered American society.[30]

The Chicano movement also confronted the Catholic church and was equally successful in effecting change. In Los Angeles a group of young Hispanic activists organized *Catolicos por la Raza* (Catholics for the People) to protest the Catholic church's wealth and its lack of support for Hispanics in their struggle to achieve political and social justice. At a 1969 Christmas Eve Mass celebrated by the cardinal archbishop of Los Angeles in a new multimillion dollar church, *Catolicos por la Raza* organized a demonstration to denounce the church's wealth. When this crowd of 400-500 sought entrance to the church, a violent confrontation with the Los Angeles riot police took place. Arrests were made, charges filed, and anger spread throughout the Los Angeles Catholic community. What happened in Los Angeles was extreme, but it was scarcely an isolated event in the turbulent 1960s. The *movimiento* also captured the imagination of Catholic clergy. In 1969 a group of Mexican-American priests organized PADRES (an acronym for Priests Associated for Religious, Educational and Social Rights). They wanted to become "the voice of the voiceless" and transmit "the cry of our people" to the "decision makers of the Catholic Church of America." Two years later a group of militant Hispanic women religious met in Houston for the first meeting of Las Hermanas (the Sisters), an organization designed to be a source of power to Hispanic Catholics.

Without a doubt one of the most symbolically significant events in the Hispanic Catholic community was the appointment in 1970 of Patricio Flores, a member of PADRES and a former migrant worker, as the auxiliary bishop of San Antonio. Flores was the first Mexican-American bishop in the history of the American Catholic church. It was obvious that Hispanic Catholics were making their voices heard and church authorities were beginning to respond in a positive manner.[31]

Another significant development in the Catholic church in the late 1960s and early 1970s was the establishment of regional offices designed to meet the special pastoral needs of Hispanic Catholics. A Midwest office opened in Lansing, Michigan, in 1967 and later moved to South Bend, Indiana; an office on the West Coast opened in California in 1968 and five years later a Southwest regional office was set up in Texas. At the national level an office for Spanish-speaking Catholics was

30. Cortes, "Mexicans," in *Harvard Encyclopedia of American Ethnic Groups*, pp. 712-19. David F. Gomez, *Somos Chicanos, Strangers in Our Own Land* (Boston: Beacon Press, 1973), pp. 100ff.

31. Gomez, *Somos Chicanos*, pp. 156ff.; Sandoval, "The Church and El Movimiento," in *Fronteras*, pp. 397-410.

established in Washington, D.C., at the national headquarters of the American Catholic church. Managed by Hispanic clergy and laity, these offices focused attention on the special needs of Hispanic Catholics and sought to promote many of the ideas articulated in the Chicano movement of the 1960s and 70s. In 1971 another very important development took place with the founding of the Mexican American Cultural Center (commonly known as MACC). Located in San Antonio and guided since its founding by the Rev. Virgil Elizondo, MACC has become "the national center for the development of liturgy for the Spanish-speaking, for research on Hispanic vocations, for the creation of materials of religious education in Spanish, for training missioners going to Latin America, and for acculturating Anglos and Hispanics alike to minister more effectively to the Spanish-speaking in the United States." As one writer put it, "no institution created to serve the Spanish-speaking approaches the impact, significance, and promise of the Mexican American Cultural Center."[32]

No doubt the most significant and substantial development in the Hispanic Catholic community in the last fifty years was the national *encuentro*, which can be described as a national pastoral congress for Hispanic Catholics. The idea came from a Colombian priest, Edgard Beltran, and was presented to a group of Hispanic leaders in 1971. A year later the first national *encuentro* took place in Washington, D.C. Two hundred and fifty people took part in the meeting, whose aim was to plan pastoral care for Hispanics in the United States. Though many topics were discussed, the two chief resolutions were a demand for greater participation by Spanish-speaking persons in the leadership and decision-making roles, at all levels, in the church, and the establishment of regional centers for research, reflection, and Christian leadership programs. It is fair to say that to a large degree these goals have been achieved. By 1985 there were eighteen Hispanic bishops in the United States; in 1972 there was only one. In addition to the national secretariat for Hispanic Affairs in Washington, D.C., by 1985 there were six regional offices across the country. Funded by the church, these offices seek to bring into active church participation as many as possible of the millions of Hispanic Catholics living in the United States. Also, since 1972, the church has established institutes where men and women are trained for ministerial work in the Hispanic community.[33]

While church leaders were working to achieve the goals set forth

---

32. Sandoval, "Church Structures for the Hispanics," in *Fronteras*, p. 431.
33. Ponce, "Spanish-Speaking Catholics in the United States," p. 28. The text of the First National Encuentro may be found in *Origins: N.C. Documentary Service*, 3/1 (May 31, 1973) 1-14.

by the first *encuentro,* the second national *encuentro* took place in 1977 and was clearly "a watershed in the life of Hispanic Catholics."[34] A grass roots movement, it involved more than 100,000 people meeting in over 12,000 small groups scattered across the country. These groups elected 600 delegates to the national meeting. Over 1,000 lay people attended along with clergy and more than fifty members of the hierarchy. The document produced by the second *encuentro* is one of the most impressive documents to come out of the post–Vatican II American Catholic church. It represents an understanding and vision of the church that is truly prophetic and evangelical; it also reflects much of the thinking of the Chicano movement of the 1960s and 70s. The *encuentro* focused on six themes: evangelization, ministry (both lay and clerical), human rights (especially for undocumented immigrants and farm workers), integral education (i.e., bilingual and multicultural education), political responsibility, and unity in pluralism. The conclusions of this *encuentro* became the Hispanic Catholic agenda for the 1980s.

A very important achievement of the *encuentros* is that they have channeled the enthusiasm and spirit of the Chicano movement in a positive direction. As one writer said, "they provide a mechanism whereby Hispanos can come face to face with the top levels of authority in the Church to express their frustrations and demands for equality and opportunity in the community of believers. The *encuentros* have legitimized protest and demonstrated the Church's willingness to listen to the oppressed."[35]

A third national *encuentro* took place in 1985 and followed a format similar to the second *encuentro.*[36] Based in local parish communities, the process of discussion, formulation of priorities, and election of delegates to the national meeting took place over the course of two years. The themes discussed were similar to those examined in 1977; one noticeable difference was the new concern for Hispanic youth. The Hispanic population is one of the youngest in the country, with a median age in 1985 of 25.0 years. Given this social reality, many Hispanics are calling for more attention to the pastoral needs of younger people, most of whom have little contact with the church.

The success of the *encuentro* process at both the local and national level suggests that the Hispanic Catholic community is alive with a new

34. Ponce, "Spanish-Speaking Catholics in the United States," p. 28. The text of the Second National Encuentro may be found in *Origins: N.C. Documentary Service,* 7/23 (Nov. 24, 1977) 353-68.

35. Sandoval, "Church Structures for the Hispanics," in *Fronteras,* p. 431.

36. See *Prophetic Voices: The Document on the Process of the III Encuentro Nacional Hispano de Pastoral* (Washington, D.C.: United States Catholic Conference, 1986).

enthusiasm. Hispanics have always placed a high priority on religion, but they have not directed this commitment to the church in the same degree that other ethnic groups have. The *encuentro* suggests that this situation may be changing. Hispanics are, in a sense, reclaiming the church as their own; they are articulating a sense of ownership of the church and the Gospel unheard of in the history of American Catholicism. As the Hispanic bishops put it in a 1983 pastoral letter, a "new era" is unfolding and they want to "harness" the resources of the church to support "the call to Hispanic ministry."[37] What is even more striking is that Hispanic Catholics are moving ahead on their own and are not asking church authorities how they should proceed. In commenting on the resolutions of the second *encuentro,* one observer put it this way: "What is notable about these conclusions is that they refer much more to what the Hispanic commits himself to doing than to what he asks of structures. He simply expects the structures to help him in his commitment."[38]

It is clear that Hispanic Catholicism has come a long way in the last fifty years. As in the case of the black Catholic community, Hispanic Catholics have moved up from the rear of the church. They have their own Hispanic bishops; they have exhibited a new cultural self-awareness; and they have acquired a political sophistication unheard of in the pre-1960 era. They are proud to be Hispanic and to celebrate the distinctiveness of their own value system, which sets them apart from the more individualistic and consumer-oriented Anglo society. Hispanic Catholics have identified their pastoral needs, have set their priorities, and are now moving forward in the task of evangelizing the millions of other Hispanics who spiritually live hundreds of miles from the church.

III. Toward the Future

In this essay I have not mentioned the Second Vatican Council. That was intentional since I believe that too much has been made of the council's influence on the development of contemporary Roman Catholicism. I certainly acknowledge the great influence that the council has had on the church. Nevertheless, as a historian I want to insist on a more nuanced and comprehensive view of contemporary developments. To make this point I have focused exclusively on the influence of social change on religion and have tried to demonstrate how the civil rights

37. *The Hispanic Presence—Challenge and Commitment,* pp. 29, 31.
38. Ponce, "Spanish-Speaking Catholics in the United States," p. 29.

movement of the last fifty years has influenced the black and Hispanic Catholic communities. I believe that the changes that have taken place in both communities would have come about without the council. The council had an influence, to be sure, but not a decisive one; it was more peripheral than central.

What the future holds for black and Hispanic Catholics in the United States is not certain. In both communities great emphasis is being put on the importance of lay ministry. Both communities, especially the Hispanic, have acquired a new sense of maturity as Catholics in the United States, and with this has come a spirit of independence unknown in earlier decades. In the era of Pope John Paul II, however, such independence is not encouraged and the model of a clerical church is being resurrected. In addition, unity rather than pluralism, be it cultural or theological, is the rallying cry of church authorities in Rome and elsewhere. Such developments suggest that the future will witness tension and even conflict, but, one hopes, reconciliation and compromise as well. In the case of black and Hispanic Catholics the stakes are very high indeed. Church authorities are not dealing with a dissenting theologian or a liberal bishop; they are dealing with millions of people who, after decades of feeling alienated from the church, have at last claimed it as their own and found a welcome where before both signs and gestures told them they were not wanted. How long that welcome lasts remains to be seen.

3. Unity and Diversity in the Evangelical Resurgence

George M. Marsden

Carl F. H. Henry, looking back in 1980 as part of *The Christian Century*'s "How My Mind Has Changed" series, observed, "During the 1960s I somewhat romanced the possibility that a vast evangelical alliance might arise in the United States to coordinate effectively a national impact in evangelism, education, publication and sociopolitical action." Billy Graham, Henry thought, might have provided the leadership necessary to unify evangelicalism. Graham had decisively broken with the separatist fundamentalists, had made inroads into the major denominations, was immensely popular, and stood almost alone as a recognized evangelical leader. Henry and some of his intellectual cohorts, often known at the time as "new evangelicals" or "neo-evangelicals," had provided the movement with some ideological leadership. *Christianity Today*, under Henry's editorship, modeled itself after *The Christian Century* but had a larger circulation. The neo-evangelicals and Graham even talked seriously about founding an evangelical university in the New York City area. The movement was advancing on a number of fronts and Henry could plausibly imagine that the core group of new evangelical reformers of fundamentalism could successfully mobilize a cohesive united evangelical front, reminiscent of the heyday of American evangelicalism in the nineteenth century.

"By the early 1970s," Henry recollected, "the prospect of a massive evangelical alliance seemed annually more remote, and by mid-decade it was gone."[1] Evangelicalism was thriving more than ever and

---

1. Carl F. H. Henry, "American Evangelicals in a Turning Time," *The Christian Century* ("How My Mind Has Changed" series), November 5, 1980, p. 1060.

awareness of it was reentering the national consciousness. Yet by 1976, when *Newsweek* proclaimed "The Year of the Evangelical," the hopes of the neo-evangelicals for unity under their leadership had dissipated. Having a Southern Baptist and a Democrat elected to the White House did not advance their party's cause. In addition, for them 1976 brought increasingly open internal strife, centered on "the battle for the Bible." As evangelicals gained some of the national prestige they had once only dreamed of, the neo-evangelical leaders could no longer agree among themselves as to what an evangelical is.

Certainly one of the most remarkable developments in American religion from 1935 to 1985 has been the reemergence of evangelicalism as a force in American culture. Probably it is the one least likely to have been predicted in 1935. Fundamentalism appeared to have been defeated in those major northern denominations in which it had raised serious challenges during the 1920s, and progressives were in control. All that remained to be carried out, according to prevailing sociological theories, were mopping-up operations. Conservative religion would die out as modernity advanced. The backward South would become more like the industrialized North. Fundamentalists had their own version of this theory, expecting secularization to advance steadily in churches and culture until Christ returned. Few thought the South would rise again to set the religious-cultural tone for much of the nation.[2] Few would have thought that fifty years later the progressive denominations would be in a state of steady decline, while evangelical and conservative groups would be flourishing.

The "neo-evangelical" reformers of fundamentalism were among the first to anticipate the possibility of an evangelical resurgence. Already in the 1940s they were talking grandiloquently not only about such a comeback, but even about "the restating of the fundamental thesis and principles of a Western culture"[3] and, as Carl Henry put it, "remaking the modern mind."[4] They were convinced that if the voice of fundamentalism could be tempered slightly, evangelical Christianity could "win America."[5] They saw themselves as standing in the tradition of Dwight L. Moody, Charles Finney, Jonathan Edwards, and George

---

2. This important feature of recent evangelical developments is discussed by Grant Wacker, "Uneasy in Zion: Evangelicals in Postmodern Society," in *Evangelicalism and Modern America*, ed. George Marsden (Grand Rapids: Eerdmans, 1984), pp. 17-28.

3. Harold J. Ockenga, "The Challenge to the Christian Culture of the West," First Opening Convocation address, Fuller Theological Seminary, Pasadena, California, October 1, 1947, pamphlet.

4. Carl F. H. Henry, *Remaking the Modern Mind* (Grand Rapids: Eerdmans, 1946).

5. Harold J. Ockenga, "Can Christians Win America?," *Christian Life and Times*, June 1947, pp. 13-15.

Whitefield, representing the long-standing transdenominational center of the American evangelical tradition. An American evangelicalism once again more-or-less organized, they thought, could still be a formidable force in American culture and a challenge to the dominant trends toward secularism in the West.

The success that the movement had attained by the 1970s was only partly what its leaders had envisioned. The movement got far beyond their control and grew as the result of forces never anticipated in their plans. The extent to which their plans actually shaped the movement is difficult to estimate. It is important not to mistake a few prominent spokespersons for a movement. Nonetheless, by focusing first on these visionaries and organizers, we can find a window through which to see the larger movement, both as it fit their vision and as it did not.

Given the bewildering diversity of American evangelicalism, it might seem remarkable that any one party would have supposed it could provide unifying leadership. Timothy L. Smith has argued, with some persuasiveness, that evangelicalism is like a kaleidoscope. It is made up of fragments as diverse as black Pentecostals, Mennonite peace churches, Episcopal charismatics, Nazarenes, and Southern Baptists. It is a grouping for which no one party could presume to speak.[6] From this perspective, one could regard evangelicalism as a unity only in a very broad sense. Evangelicals might agree in a general way on the two essentials of evangelicalism: "that the sole authority in religion is the Bible and the sole means of salvation is a life-transforming experience wrought by the Holy Spirit through Faith in Jesus Christ."[7] Other than that, they represent largely independent, even if related, traditions.[8]

Despite the general validity of these observations, which must qualify any talk about a single "evangelicalism," twentieth-century American evangelicalism has had more unity than its denominational diversity might suggest. This degree of unity grows not only out of a common basic profession but also out of a considerable common heritage and experience. Even most black Protestants, who have been almost entirely separated from whites since the Civil War, have enough common heritage to be readily indentifiable as "evangelical," though they seldom use the word. As for white evangelicals, with whom this

6. Timothy L. Smith, "The Evangelical Kaleidoscope and the Call to Christian Unity," *Christian Scholar's Review* 15/2 (1986) 125-40.

7. Grant Wacker, *Augustus H. Strong and the Dilemma of Historical Consciousness* (Macon, GA: Mercer University Press, 1985), p. 17. This is not an exhaustive definition, but it is economical and carefully framed.

8. The conceptual questions involved in relating the whole to the parts of evangelicalism are discussed by George Marsden, "The Evangelical Denomination," in *Evangelicalism and Modern America*, ed. Marsden, pp. vii-xix.

essay is primarily concerned, the bondings of their common heritage were reinforced during the first half of the twentieth century by the shared experiences of most of them in fundamentalist reactions against "modernist" theological innovations and certain cultural changes.

In the 1930s "evangelicalism" was not a term much used in American religious life. The white Protestant world was still dominated by the mainline denominations, and these were divided by wars between "fundamentalists" and their sympathizers and "modernists" and their sympathizers. Both sides had earlier claimed the appelation "evangelical," so that it was no longer of much use to either. Strictly speaking, most American Protestants, clergy as well as laypeople, were neither fundamentalists nor modernists, but were located somewhere in between. The fundamentalist/modernist wars, however, had forced many such moderates to choose sides. In the North, most clerics favored tolerance of modernism and most laypeople did not want a fight. In the South, most of both groups were willing to hold the line with the fundamentalists.

By the 1930s the northern white churches were undergoing realignment,[9] as fundamentalists relocated and built their own networks of separate institutions. Uncounted numbers of fundamentalists left the major denominations to join or to found independent local Bible churches, or they forsook a more liberal denomination for a smaller, more conservative one. Most fundamentalists, nonetheless, remained quietly within the major denominations, hoping to work within existing structures, especially through conservative local churches. At the same time they increasingly gave their support to a growing network of trans-denominational fundamentalist evangelistic agencies.[10]

Fundamentalism embodied two paradoxical impulses that its advocates always had difficulty reconciling. What chiefly distinguished fundamentalism from earlier evangelicalism was its militancy toward modernist theology and cultural change. Metaphors of warfare dominated its thinking, and the rhetoric of "no compromise" often precipitated denominational showdowns. Once it became apparent after 1925, however, that fundamentalists could not control the major northern denominations,[11] the logic of their no-compromise position pointed

9. The classic exposition of the condition of the mainline churches during this era is Robert T. Handy, "The American Religious Depression, 1925-1935," *Church History* 29 (1960) 2-16.

10. Joel A. Carpenter, "Fundamentalist Institutions and the Rise of Evangelical Protestantism, 1929-1942," *Church History* 49/1 (March 1980) 62-75.

11. The fundamentalist developments during the earlier era are discussed in George Marsden, *Fundamentalism and American Culture: The Shaping of Twentieth-Century Evangelicalism, 1870-1925* (New York: Oxford University Press, 1980).

toward separatism. Dispensational premillennial interpretations of history, which had spread widely among fundamentalists, supported this separatist tendency. Dispensationalism taught the apostasy of the major churches of "Christendom" as part of a steady cultural degeneration during the present "church age." By the 1930s the strictest fundamentalists increasingly were proclaiming the duty of ecclesiastical separatism.

Fundamentalism, however, also incorporated a positive impulse that often worked at cross-purposes with this negativism. Antedating fundamentalist antimodernism was the evangelical revivalist tradition out of which fundamentalism had grown. The overriding preoccupation of this tradition was the saving of souls. Any responsible means to promote this end was approved. As American revivalism developed, it did so with basically sympathetic ambivalence toward the major denominations. To be sure, part of the appeal of the revival impulse was based on dissatisfaction with what the denominations were doing. A few revivalists, such as Alexander Campbell, founded their own denominations, but the most successful, such as Charles Finney and Dwight Moody, worked alongside the respected denominations, often building their own evangelistic organizations to supplement denominational efforts. The evangelical denominations, for their part, encouraged revivalism and promoted it through both denominational and extradenominational agencies.

The negative fundamentalist impulse in the 1930s to abandon the major denominations was countered by its prior, ongoing agenda to win America and the world for Christ. This agenda seemed to require believers in "the fundamentals" to hold on to their entrenched positions in the respected denominations. If they gave up all connections with these denominations, how could they get a hearing to win the nation? Though most fundamentalists by the 1930s had put aside the discouraging business of political programs in favor of emphasizing soul winning, they still (contrary to the cultural pessimism of dispensational teaching) entertained at least lingering aspirations to a wider social, spiritual, and moral influence such as evangelicals had enjoyed only a generation earlier. Retaining some connections with the major denominations suited this positive strategy.

This positive strategy involved only a half-way separation of most fundamentalists from the denominational mainstream. While some fundamentalists built new institutions that were strictly separatist, more were building institutions that were in practice separate, but had not in theory repudiated the mainstream. During the 1930s the lines between these two kinds of separatism were not always clear. Some leading fundamentalists insisted on repudiating oldline denominations. Others, equally prominent, stayed in. The situation was fluid, so that for most groups in the transdenominational coalition separatism was not yet a test of faith.

In this ecclesiastically unsettled atmosphere, fundamentalists moved ahead by building their network of largely evangelistic agencies. The radio offered a particularly effective way to build up ministries that, consistent with long-standing revivalist practice, ignored denominational considerations. By the early 1940s, Charles E. Fuller of "The Old-Fashioned Revival Hour" had gained the largest radio audience in the country. In the 1920s Fuller had been a typical fundamentalist militant and had split a local Presbyterian congregation to form his own group; but by the time he became a national figure, he had adopted the positive fundamentalist stance of refusing to engage in controversy or to make separatism a test of orthodoxy.[12]

By the early 1940s fundamentalists, typically working through recently formed organizations, were seeing signs of revival on a number of fronts. Most notably successful of the new organizations was Youth for Christ. During World War II youth evangelists such as Jack Wyrtzen and Percy Crawford had sponsored remarkably successful mass rallies in American cities, notably New York and Chicago. In 1945 Youth for Christ International was organized to consolidate a considerable revival. During its first year, Youth for Christ sponsored nearly 900 rallies nationwide, with about 1 million constituents.[13] The new organization chose a young graduate of Wheaton College, Billy Graham, as its first full-time evangelist. By the end of the decade, Graham carried the revival movement to massive national success.

Graham's base was a network of positive fundamentalists who had been organizing for such a revival throughout the 1940s. The most visible institutional manifestation of this network was the National Association of Evangelicals, founded in 1942 as a loose affiliation of diverse evangelical denominations and individuals, primarily to promote evangelism. The NAE was the national outgrowth of the earlier New England Fellowship, headed by J. Elwin Wright. Harold John Ockenga, a former student of the scholarly J. Gresham Machen and pastor of the Park Street Congregational Church in Boston, became the chief organizer of the NAE and also headed a number of other important agencies founded during the next two decades. At the center of these organizations was a

12. Daniel P. Fuller, *Give the Winds a Mighty Voice: The Story of Charles E. Fuller* (Waco, TX: Word Books, 1972).
13. Joel A. Carpenter, "From Fundamentalism to the New Evangelical Coalition," in *Evangelicalism and Modern America*, ed. Marsden, p. 15.

group of people, predominantly Baptist and Presbyterian, most of whom had connections with institutions such as Wheaton College, Moody Bible Institute, Dallas Theological Seminary, Gordon College and Seminary in Boston, and those followers of Machen who were not strict separatists.

This group built up a broad constituency, as is evident from the NAE, which by 1947 included thirty small denominations, representing 1,300,000 members. The NAE leadership reflected the more or less mainstream heritage of fundamentalism. Many of its leaders still belonged to major denominations. Working from this broad fundamentalist base, they also brought in some evangelical groups that had been on the periphery of the earlier fundamentalist movement. Groups with ethnic origins, such as the Swedish Baptists and the Evangelical Free Church, found the national movement a congenial form of Americanization. Holiness groups, such as the Nazarenes and the Wesleyan Methodists, found their distinctive emphases being reshaped by the fundamentalist-led movement. And even some Pentecostal denominations, which had been pariahs among the earlier negative fundamentalists, were invited into the fellowship of the positive movement. The Southern Baptist Convention, which would have swelled the numbers of the NAE immensely, had representatives at some early meetings but had too distinct an identity to join the movement. The smaller Christian Reformed Church joined and then left the NAE, but some of its leaders were always important contributors to the movement. William B. Eerdmans, for instance, became its most respected publisher. Missouri Synod Lutherans, by contrast, usually remained more aloof from such versions of Americanization.[14]

The constituency of this emerging movement was, however, considerably larger than the numbers of people who could be counted in its organizations. The vast audiences who listened to Charles E. Fuller, or later to Billy Graham, were at least part-time supporters of the network and were being shaped by its message. Local radio stations, such as WMBI at the Moody Bible Institute in Chicago, similarly kept people from many denominations in the positive fundamentalist orbit. Most of these people, no doubt, belonged to the major denominations. On the West Coast, for instance, the movement long had substantial support from the large and pivotal conservative Presbyterian congregations.

Although all fundamentalists had sought national revival, the stricter militants were becoming increasingly uneasy about the alliances

---

14. Ibid., pp. 13-14. Also see Joel Carpenter, "The Fundamentalist Leaven and the Rise of an Evangelical United Front," in *The Evangelical Tradition in America,* ed. Leonard Sweet (Macon, GA: Mercer University Press, 1984), pp. 257-88, for an important discussion of these interrelationships.

being forged during the positive fundamentalist resurgence of the 1940s. The most vocal spokesman for this more separatist view was Carl McIntire, another former Machen student and an indefatigable organizer of opposition movements. In 1941, apparently anticipating the formation of the NAE, McIntire founded the American Council of Christian Churches on a strict fundamentalist basis—no Pentecostals and, especially, no denominations (or their members) affiliated with the Federal Council of Churches. McIntire's strictness kept his organizations small, but his vigorous promotions through publications and radio and his sensational attacks on liberals and their agencies, often emphasizing Communist connections, gave him disproportional influence. During the 1940s, however, it was not clear to the heirs of fundamentalism that a split was shaping up over the relative importance of the negative and the positive components of their heritage. Both sides had some of each. Efforts were made, for instance, to merge the American Council and the NAE, and a few people belonged to both.[15]

The issues that were emerging, however, were not just negative versus positive or separatist versus inclusivist. Some ideological questions were important as well, above all the role of dispensational premillennialism in the movement. During the 1930s this doctrine was taught in the overwhelming majority of fundamentalist (and Pentecostal) churches. Dispensationalism's pessimistic view of the prevailing culture encouraged a deemphasis on social causes in the movement. Dispensationalism's negative estimate of major churches encouraged separatism.[16]

As part of the effort for an American and world revival after World War II, a group of positive fundamentalist intellectuals began organizing a move away from dispensationalist emphases. With America's emergence into world leadership after the war, they saw a unique opportunity for reconstituting Christian civilization, if America's evangelical tradition could be revived. To attain this ambitious goal, they recognized that it would be necessary to build on fundamentalism's claim to stand in the broad tradition of Augustinian orthodoxy, rather than to promote the more narrow dispensationalist teachings of recent invention. They also deplored fundamentalism's emphasis on personal ethical prohibitions at the expense of a positive social program, a theme enunciated in Carl Henry's *Uneasy Conscience of Modern Fundamentalism* in 1947. They were embarrassed, furthermore, by the anti-intellectual-

15. The author has discussed these developments in his *Reforming Fundamentalism: Fuller Seminary and the New Evangelicalism* (Grand Rapids: Eerdmans, 1987).

16. The cultural implications of dispensational teaching are discussed in Marsden, *Fundamentalism and American Culture*.

ism that had come to be associated with dispensational fundamentalism, which had been promoted primarily through Bible institutes and pragmatic popularizers.

Their most notable effort to counter such trends was the founding of Fuller Theological Seminary in Pasadena, California, in 1947. Charles E. Fuller provided the early funding but left most of the management of the institution to the intellectuals, headed by Harold Ockenga as president and including among its early faculty an impressive lineup: Carl Henry, Edward J. Carnell, Wilbur M. Smith, Everett Harrison, Gleason Archer, Harold Lindsell, George E. Ladd, Daniel Fuller, and Paul K. Jewett. Though the Fuller faculty deemphasized dispensationalism, they did not immediately repudiate their fundamentalist heritage. They were sincerely dedicated to Charles Fuller's ideal of positive evangelism and were close associates of Billy Graham (who eventually became a trustee). The school paid its sincere respects to fundamentalist doctrinal militancy, as well, by requiring creedal assent to the inerrancy of Scripture.[17]

During the 1950s, Billy Graham's success was rapidly changing the status of this predominantly positive evangelicalism that had been growing out of fundamentalism. Graham's vast popular appeal gave him virtual independence. The election of Eisenhower and Nixon in 1952 gave him entry to the White House. Support from politically conservative business leaders, most notably J. Howard Pew of Sun Oil, added to his resources, though Graham played down the political implications of his connections.[18]

Most importantly, Graham's move toward the respectable centers of American life precipitated a definitive split with the hardline fundamentalists in 1957. For his New York City crusade, Graham accepted the sponsorship of the local Protestant Council of Churches. Strict fundamentalists were deeply offended by this cooperation with liberals and they anathematized Graham.[19] In the aftermath of the resulting schism within the coalition, "fundamentalism" came to be a term used almost solely by those who demanded ecclesiastical separatism. They called their former allies "neo-evangelicals," picking up on the term "new evangelicalism" coined earlier by Ockenga. Others in the reforming group called themselves simply "evangelical," the term that eventually became common usage both for them and for the wider movement.

---

17. See note 15.

18. Richard V. Pierard, "Billy Graham and the U.S. Presidency," *Journal of Church and State* 22 (Winter 1980) 107-27.

19. This split is ably discussed by Butler Farley Porter, Jr., "Billy Graham and the End of Evangelical Unity" (Ph.D. dissertation, University of Florida, 1976).

Recognizing that the emerging movement needed some intellectual guidance, Graham sponsored the establishment of *Christianity Today* under the editorship of Carl Henry. Ockenga was the chairman of the board and Pew the chief financial supporter. Most of the pieces were now in place for promoting their vision of a movement that would not only evangelize the nation but would also lay the foundations for a unified evangelical social and intellectual program. Perhaps the high-water mark in their efforts to organize a culturally significant and coherent evangelistic coalition came in 1967 with their sponsorship of the World Congress on Evangelism, a notable display of unity among most of the main evangelical leaders from America and around the world. The congress witnessed to a feature of the American evangelical coalition that had been important since the nineteenth century: it was part of a wider transatlantic movement with major missionary ties.

By 1967, however, it was becoming impossible to regard American evangelicalism as a single coalition with a more or less unified and recognized leadership. In part the reason for this was negative, the result of an internal crisis. The core ex-fundamentalist movement that the neo-evangelicals hoped to speak for was splitting apart. The political issues of the 1960s were becoming sources of sharp dissensions. During the 1940s and 1950s, when neo-evangelical spokespersons had called for an evangelical social program, they had assumed it would be a Christianized version of Republicanism. By the 1960s their movement and a growing number of colleges associated with it were producing a second generation that was calling for more progressive political stances. Vietnam polarized everyone over these issues, and arch-conservatives like J. Howard Pew demanded that evangelicals take unreservedly pro-nationalist and procapitalist positions. Carl Henry, though solidly Republican, nonetheless lost his job at *Christianity Today*, partly owing to his unwillingness to be sufficiently militant. He was replaced in 1968 by Harold Lindsell, who readily provided Christianized versions of the rhetoric of Spiro Agnew during the Nixon era. This militantly conservative political stance of the evangelical "establishment" sparked a reciprocal action on the left. In 1971 dissident students at Trinity Evangelical Divinity School (a leading center for "establishment evangelicalism") organized The People's Christian Coalition and founded an underground newspaper, *The Post-American,* later becoming *Sojourners,* published by the radical evangelical Sojourner's Community in Washington, D.C. Senator Mark Hatfield became the best-known supporter of this movement. During the 1970s a spectrum of well-represented evangelical political stances emerged. By now there were articulate evangelical groups championing women's equality, pacifism, and progressive versions of social justice.[20] A conservative old guard advocated opposing views. Evangelical social-political involvement, which neo-evangelical leaders had called for in the 1940s and 1950s, now indeed emerged, but as a prime source of division.

At the same time there emerged the closely parallel issue of biblical inerrancy. Although the new evangelicals had attempted to reform fundamentalism, an important group in this "establishment" party had never wanted to break with fundamentalist militancy. "Inerrancy," a real concern in its own right, also symbolized other concerns. Progressive evangelicals usually were relatively sensitive to the importance of historical context for understanding the absolute claims of the Gospel. This stance opened the door to more progressive interpretations of the Gospel's social implications, and also engendered an openness to nondestructive aspects of higher criticism. Hence, for progressive evangelicals, the "inerrancy" of Scripture usually implied a wooden hermeneutic that tended to interpret the Bible simply as a set of true propositions, without adequately taking into account the original biblical standards of meaning. Conservatives reasoned that inaccuracies in the original Scriptures would be unworthy of God and would undermine biblical authority. Conservatives on this issue were unlikely to have made even modest concessions to the relativizing tendencies of progressive modern thought.[21]

By the early 1970s, two major evangelical denominations, the Southern Baptist Convention and the Lutheran Church—Missouri Synod, were embroiled in controversies over inerrancy. In 1976 *Christianity Today* editor Harold Lindsell successfully revived inerrancy as a primary issue in transdenominational evangelicalism, suggesting in his much-discussed *The Battle for the Bible* that whoever denied inerrancy was not an evangelical at all.[22]

The transdenominational movement to reform fundamentalism was thus irreparably split over a combination of political and doctrinal issues. "Neo-evangelicals" were so divided among themselves that the term lost its meaning. By the late 1970s, no one, not even Billy Graham, could claim to stand at the center of so divided a coalition.

---

20. These developments are discussed by Richard Quebedeaux, *The Young Evangelicals: Revolution in Orthodoxy* (New York: Harper & Row, 1974) and *The Worldly Evangelicals* (San Francisco: Harper & Row, 1980), and by Robert Booth Fowler, *A New Engagement: Evangelical Political Thought, 1966-1976* (Grand Rapids: Eerdmans, 1983).

21. A partial bibliography of the works debating this issue is provided by Mark A. Noll, "Evangelicals and the Study of the Bible," in *Evangelicalism and Modern America*, ed. Marsden, pp. 198-99.

22. Harold Lindsell, *The Battle for the Bible* (Grand Rapids: Zondervan, 1976).

In addition to these negative forces dividing the movement there were positive ones related to evangelical success. As evangelicalism in the late 1970s reemerged into prominence in American public life, the movement produced spinoffs that shone more brightly than the fragmenting ex-fundamentalism that once provided a sort of center. One of these was the Moral Majority, arising from the unexpected quarter of separatist fundamentalism. Jerry Falwell was in fact a reformer of fundamentalism, whose role in some ways paralleled that of Graham and his new evangelical cohorts of the 1950s. "Neo-fundamentalist" is an appropriate term for Falwell's movement. While holding to the fundamentalist heritage of ecclesiastical separatism (and hence remaining distant from Graham), Falwell tried to bring fundamentalists back toward the centers of American life, especially through political action. Politics meant making alliances. Stricter fundamentalists, like Bob Jones III, condemned Falwell as a pseudofundamentalist. Falwell, nonetheless, proved that the fundamentalist militant "either-or" style suited the political mood of the era. While the evangelical "establishment" was immobilized by internal divisions, Falwell took over the program of its right wing and mobilized many Americans with fundamentalist decisiveness.[23]

The Moral Majority rode the Reagan wave to success, a strategy apparent from their almost uncritical endorsement of the new president's domestic and foreign policies. The Reagan administration, in turn, adopted some of the rhetoric of the religious Right, but it did little substantively (except through court appointments) to promote such leading concerns of the right-wing as antiabortion and prayer in public schools.

Although impossible to measure, perhaps evangelicalism's greatest political impact on American policy during the past fifty years has been its role in broadening the popular base for an almost unreserved support for the state of Israel. The Moral Majority only articulated a much more widely held evangelical view on this issue. Dispensationalist teaching, so widespread in the movement since the 1930s, centers on predictions that the state of Israel will play a crucial role in God's plan for the end time. Even most of those neo-evangelicals who abandoned the details of dispensationalism still retained a firm belief in

---

23. A fine discussion of the extensive literature on the fundamentalist Christian right is Richard V. Pierard, "The New Right in American Politics," in *Evangelicalism and Modern America*, ed. Marsden, pp. 161-74. Falwell's differences with stricter fundamentalists are well described in Jerry Falwell, with Ed Dobson and Ed Hindson, *The Fundamentalist Phenomenon: The Resurgence of Conservative Christianity* (Garden City, NY: Doubleday, 1980).

Israel's God-ordained role. This belief is immensely popular in America, though rarely mentioned in proportion to its influence. For instance, during the 1970s the best-selling book in America (though never on the *New York Times* "best seller" list) was Hal Lindsey's *The Late Great Planet Earth*.[24]

The largest group to hold such prophetic views and, more broadly considered, the largest evangelical force to overwhelm the old fundamentalist reform movement was the charismatic movement. By 1979, 19 percent of all Americans identified themselves as charismatic or Pentecostal.[25] This phenomenal development on the American religious scene would have seemed bizarre to predict in 1935. One of the manifestations of religious resurgence in the 1950s had been the growth of healing revivalism among Pentecostal evangelists. An offshoot was the formation, in 1951, of the Full Gospel Business Men's Fellowship International under the leadership of David du Plessis, an Assemblies of God minister and a friend of the leading faith healer, Oral Roberts. Du Plessis worked assiduously and successfully during the next decade to carry the Pentecostal message beyond the traditional Pentecostal denominations and beyond the poorer economic groups with which it had been largely associated. By the early 1960s charismatic renewal movements had begun in Episcopal, Presbyterian, Lutheran, and other mainline denominations. Soon it reached the Catholic church, where it also found fertile soil. By 1979, 18 percent of all American Catholics were charismatic.[26]

This development fostered a major shift in evangelicalism, substantially bringing to an end hostilities that had still been intense as late as 1960. (The Moral Majority's adoption of the traditionally Roman Catholic "family issues" further promoted this shift.) The spread of the charismatic movement throughout Christendom was due not so much to central leadership, or to prominent personalities, as to effective decentralization. Through the agency of small groups and intense communities, the movement grew at seemingly geometrical rates, thus bringing renewal and spreading the Gospel at home and abroad.[27] The burgeoning charismatic movement also changed the character of much of evangelicalism in important ways. The emphasis shifted both toward

---

24. Grand Rapids: Zondervan, 1970. Lindsey's work and related views of the Middle East are discussed in Timothy P. Weber, *Living in the Shadow of the Second Coming: American Premillennialism 1875-1982*, enlarged edition (Grand Rapids: Zondervan, 1983).

25. Richard Quebedeaux, *The New Charismatics, II* (San Francisco: Harper & Row, 1983), p. 84.

26. Ibid.

27. Ibid., *passim.*

the experiential aspects of Christianity, a sense of closeness to Jesus through the Spirit dwelling within, and toward its therapeutic aspects. The reputed benefits of Christianity for health, success, and personal fulfillment became one of the movement's most common themes.[28] Messages incorporating such emphases were proclaimed by the prominent television evangelists who flourished in the 1970s and 1980s. Among those with the largest ministries, Oral Roberts, Jimmy Swaggart, Jim Bakker of the "PTL Club," and Pat Robertson of the "700 Club" were all charismatic. By 1985 Oral Roberts, for instance, was operating with a budget of close to $2 million dollars per week.[29] In such circumstances the demands of the market were bound to have some impact on the messages preached. By the mid-1980s Pat Robertson was showing himself particularly adept at combining the popular therapeutic emphases of healing Pentecostalism with the equally popular political patriotism and conservatism that had won such wide support for (the noncharismatic) Jerry Falwell and the Moral Majority.

Such developments had to be viewed with mixed feelings by the former reformers of fundamentalism who had attempted to build an evangelical coalition around Billy Graham in the 1960s. Evangelicalism was succeeding in remarkable ways. Its most prominent representatives, however, seemed to be moving away from the group that had a plausible claim to embody the core of the transdenominational evangelical tradition that could be traced back through fundamentalism to the days of Moody, Finney, Edwards, and Whitefield. Political fundamentalism picked up one strand that had always been present in that tradition, but ran to what seemed an extreme of self-serving nationalism. The charismatic revival picked up another important strand, namely, concern for individual spirituality, which could be traced back to the Great Awakening. This revival, however, also marked something of a departure from the tradition, especially since the message of health and prosperity seemed to intimate that one need not expect to give up the world to follow Christ, but that one would gain the whole world.[30] It can be plausibly argued that evangelicalism's rounding off of the sharp edges of the Gospel message between 1960 and 1985 paralleled the gentle modifications of the Gospel by Protestant liberalism in the later

28. James Davison Hunter documents these themes in his *American Evangelicalism: Conservative Religion and the Quandary of Modernity* (New Brunswick, NJ: Rutgers University Press, 1983).

29. David Edwin Harrell, Jr., *Oral Roberts: An American Life* (Bloomington: Indiana University Press, 1985), p. 485.

30. A number of the authors in the *Christianity Today* supplement, "Into the Next Century: Trends Facing the Church," 30/1 (January 17, 1986), pp. 1-I to 32-I, express concern over such trends.

nineteenth century. Still, many found it difficult to argue with success, which was always at a premium in evangelicalism. People were being converted and brought into churches where most of the essentials of the evangelical message remained unchanged.

In any case, no individual, group, or institution was in a position to control such trends, since one of the key peculiar features of American evangelicalism is its general disregard for the institutional church. Except at the congregational level, the organized church plays a relatively minor role in the movement. Even the local congregation, while extremely important for fellowship purposes, is often regarded as a convenience to the individual. Ultimately, individuals are sovereign and can join or leave churches as they please. Often they seem as likely to choose a church because it is "friendly" as to do so because of its particular teachings. Denominational loyalties, although still significant for substantial numbers of evangelicals, are incidental for many others, especially those with a transdenominational consciousness who have attempted to bring unity to the movement.

Given this situation, it is remarkable that American evangelicalism has the degree of coherence it does. Little seems to hold it together other than common traditions, a central one of which is the denial of the authority of traditions. Nonetheless, one can attend apparently unconnected evangelical churches at opposite ends of the country and, as likely as not, find nearly identical teachings on most subjects. Probably the principles of the mass market, which emphasize standardization and national campaigns, are primary forces that help maintain this considerable evangelical uniformity.

Whether such centripetal forces for coherence or some countervailing centrifugal forces will prevail is difficult to tell. Perhaps what has been happening over the past two decades is that the traditional transdenominational core has become subordinate to several parties (the charismatic, the conservative-nationalistic political, the progressive evangelical), and that these parties will soon be as distinct as were the mid-twentieth-century fundamentalist and modernist heirs to nineteenth-century evangelicalism. One cannot predict with assurance. Yet, given evangelicalism's typically informal sense of the church, it is difficult to see how any single party could come to dominate and hold the larger movement together. Perhaps it will continue to develop in the form of sympathetic parallel manifestations of related traditions.

One other chief consequence of the lack of an institutional churchbase, and of the declining role of the traditional denominations, is that evangelicalism's vaunted challenge to the secular culture becomes increasingly difficult to sustain. The movement depends on free enterprise and popular appeal. To some extent conservative churches grow because they promise certainty in times of uncertainty, in the name of the old-time Gospel. Yet, with few institutional restraints on what message may legitimately be proclaimed, the laws of the market invite mixes of the Gospel with various popular appeals.[31] So the evangelical challenges to the secular "modern mind" are likely to be compromised by innovative oversimplifications and concessions to the popular spirit of the age. Hence, as is so often the case in church history, the advance of the Gospel is bound up with the advance of secularization within the church. Perhaps this conjunction is inevitable in a fallen world. The tares will grow with the wheat.

31. Nathan O. Hatch, "Evangelicalism as a Democratic Movement," in *Evangelicalism and Modern America,* ed. Marsden, pp. 71-82, discusses these dynamics of the movement.

4. The Black Church: Continuity within Change

Albert J. Raboteau

During the past fifty years, sweeping economic, political, social, and cultural changes have profoundly affected the religious institutions of black Americans. Migration, urbanization, and the civil rights movement, to mention only the most obvious examples of large-scale social change, have fundamentally altered the conditions of life for Afro-Americans. In this context, the church has served both as a source of stability and as a vehicle of change. By conserving traditional religious culture, black churches gave black communities and individuals a significant sense of continuity with the past. By evoking familiar religious symbols to interpret novel circumstances, black pastors helped their people to accommodate disruptions caused by rapid change. As the mention of civil rights suggests, the churches not only reacted to social and political change; they also participated in bringing it about. In addition to external factors, internal theological, liturgical, and institutional developments have been major sources of change in black religious life over the past five decades.

For most of that period, the "great migration" of Afro-Americans, which began around World War I, continued to shift the black population from rural areas to urban centers, and from South to North. While the Depression slowed migration during the 1930s, between 1940 and 1970 4.4 million black southerners left the South, with the vast majority settling in northern and, to a lesser extent, western cities. Even those blacks who remained in the South (never less than 52 percent of the total black population) moved in ever increasing numbers to cities.[1] This

1. Although historical study of the effects of migration and urbanization upon the

massive movement of people disrupted congregations, transplanted religious customs, taxed the resources of urban churches, and formed, in
the burgeoning ghettos, favorable conditions for religious innovation.

Facing an unfamiliar urban environment, rural migrants looked
to the church to reaffirm the traditional values and communal ties that
had always given them a sense of social location back home. In some
instances they joined already established churches, in others they
founded new ones of their own. The sheer number of migrants enlarged
the membership of existing churches and tested their capacities to ab-
sorb the new arrivals. In the early years of the migration, some churches
were so overcrowded that they had to hold double services. As the migrants continued to flood in by the thousands, pastors and church
boards embarked on extensive and expensive building programs to increase the seating capacity of their buildings. Some churches established
social auxiliaries to assist the migrants. Abyssinian Baptist in New York,
Olivet Baptist in Chicago, and First Congregational in Atlanta, for example, conducted employment bureaus, day-care centers, kindergar-
tens, adult education classes, drama groups, orchestras, social clubs, athletic events, and various youth programs, even in the depths of the
Depression.[2]

While some of the newcomers took pride in the size and prestige of the large city churches, others missed the intimacy and status
they had enjoyed in smaller churches "downhome." Differences in educational and economic levels and in styles of worship distinguished
migrants from some long-time residents and from each other. These dis-
parities, as well as the usual divisiveness of church politics, splintered
congregations and multiplied the number of churches in urban black
neighborhoods. The proliferation of congregations, many of them so
poor and so small that they had to gather in storefronts or homes for
worship, prompted the popular remark that ghettos had at least one

---

black church has tended to focus exclusively on the movement of rural black southerners
to the North, significant urbanization of blacks occurred in the South and the West. In
the last decade, moreover, a sizable black migration has gone from North to South. See
Harry A. Ploski and Ernest Kaiser, *The Negro Almanac* (New York: Bellwether, 1971), pp.
343-67; William C. Matney and Dwight L. Johnson, *America's Black Population 1970 to 1982:
A Statistical View* (Washington, D.C.: U.S. Bureau of the Census, 1983).

2. Louise Venable Kennedy, *The Negro Peasant Turns Cityward: Effects of Recent Migrations to Northern Centers* (New York: Columbia University Press, 1930), pp. 202-06; Carter G. Woodson, *History of the Negro Church* (Washington, D.C.: Associated Publishers,
1921; reprint ed., 1972), pp. 252-60; Henry Hugh Proctor, *Between Black and White: Auto-
biographical Sketches* (Boston: Pilgrim, 1925), pp. 106-08; William M. Welty, "Black
Shepherds: A Study of the Leading Negro Clergymen in New York City, 1900-1940"
(Ph.D. dissertation, New York University, 1969), pp. 283-85.

church on every block and led some sociologists to wonder whether the black community was "overchurched."[3]

Besides increasing the size and number of urban black churches, migration also increased the variety of black religious life by exposing people to new religious options. Accustomed to deciding between Baptist, Methodist, and maybe Holiness-Pentecostal churches back home, migrants to the cities encountered black Jews, black Muslims, black Spiritualists, and the disciples of a host of charismatic religious figures like Father Divine and Daddy Grace, to name two of the most famous. In the cities black Protestants came into contact with Roman Catholicism, usually for the first time, since Catholics had been scarce in the rural South except for lower Louisiana and Maryland, the traditional centers of black Catholic population. The parochial school, which offered urban blacks an appealing alternative to public education, became an important mechanism for the conversion of black Protestants to Roman Catholicism. Catechism classes and mandatory attendance at Mass exposed black school children, and through them their parents, to the doctrines and rituals of Catholicism. Some social scientists have speculated that the desire for education and upward social mobility influenced the decision of black Protestants to convert to Catholicism. However this may be, the number of black Catholics increased dramatically between 1940 and 1975, due mainly to conversion. During that period, the black Catholic population grew from 296,988 to 915,854, an increase of 208 percent. From 2.3 percent, black Catholics increased to 4 percent of the black population.[4]

Another intensive movement of people, this time from beyond our national borders, made a new and surprising contribution to the religious variety of urban America. Immigrants from Puerto Rico, Cuba, and, more recently, Haiti, have introduced the traditional gods of Africa to the United States. Over the last two decades the religions of santeria and voodoo, which originated during slavery in Cuba and Haiti respectively, have spread to black and Hispanic communities across the country. Here, as in Cuba and Haiti, initiates celebrated the feasts of the gods in rituals of drumming, singing, and dancing that derived ultimately from West and Central Africa. Underlying these rituals was the

---

3. St. Clair Drake and Horace R. Cayton, *Black Metropolis: A Study of Negro Life in a Northern City* (New York: Harcourt-Brace, 1945), pp. 632-36; Benjamin E. Mays and Joseph W. Nicholson, *The Negro's Church* (1933; reprint ed., New York: Russell & Russell, 1969), pp. 198-229.

4. Drake and Cayton, pp. 641-46; Arthur Huff Fauset, *Black Gods of the Metropolis: Negro Religious Cults in the Urban North* (1944; reprint ed., Philadelphia: University of Pennsylvania Press, 1971); George Shuster and Robert M. Kearns, *Statistical Profile of Black Catholics* (Washington, D.C.: Josephite Pastoral Center, 1976), p. 34.

belief that the gods rule over all aspects of life. By offering them praise and sacrifice, people attracted their favor and activated their powerful intercession in times of illness or misfortune. In ceremonies of spirit possession, entranced mediums made personal contact between gods and humans possible by embodying the god for the community. Whenever something inexplicably went wrong, priest-diviners determined the cause and prescribed the means for setting things right. In these ways, santeria and voodoo preserved a view of life as personal and relational in the midst of a society that seemed increasingly impersonal and atomistic. Although the number of North American blacks that converted to these religions was small, the number of their adherents, according to news reports, was growing. In the 1960s reawakened interest in the African heritage prompted some Afro-Americans to adopt African names, styles of dress, and religious traditions. In 1970 one group of black Americans went so far as to establish an "African" village in South Carolina patterned on the culture of the Yoruba people of Nigeria. Yoruba and Yoruba-derived religious communities in Nigeria, Cuba, Brazil, and the United States recently established formal links with one another by instituting annual "Orisa Tradition" conferences (*orisa* being the Yoruba word for the gods). The third conference was held in 1986 in New York City.[5]

Historical studies of twentieth-century black religion have emphasized the dichotomy between "mainline" established churches and storefront congregations in urban black communities. The former were supposedly middle-class bastions of traditional Protestantism, while the latter housed the esoteric sects and cults preferred by the lower classes. It is important to remember, however, that numerous storefront churches were Baptist and Methodist missions, newly formed congregations too poor to afford a regular church building. The stereotypical contrast between the ecstatic worship of the storefront and the sedate liturgy of the mainline church has been overdrawn. Mainline churches provided a greater variety of musical and liturgical styles than has been recognized. Significant theological and liturgical differences did divide black churches during this period, but they did not conform neatly to the storefront-mainline model or to the church-sect typology.[6]

One of the most significant theological and liturgical develop-

---

5. Robert Farris Thompson, *Flash of the Spirit: African and Afro-American Art and Philosophy* (New York: Random House, 1983), pp. 3-97; Carl M. Hunt, *Oyotunji Village: The Yoruba Movement in America* (Washington, D.C.: University Press of America, 1979).

6. Drake and Cayton organized their discussion of urban black religion around class distinctions, but their own evidence suggests that the situation was more complex. See Drake and Cayton, pp. 673-79.

ments over the past fifty years was the growth of the Holiness-Pentecostal family of churches into one of the largest denominational groups, alongside Baptists and Methodists, in black America. Contrary to Baptist and Methodist doctrine, Holiness and Pentecostal evangelists preached an experience subsequent to conversion, called baptism of the Holy Spirit, which was attested, they claimed, by reception of the Spirit's gifts of healing, teaching, prophesying, discernment of spirits, and especially speaking in tongues. Since the Spirit's gifts empowered women no less than men, Holiness and Pentecostal churches proved much more willing to accept women as pastors than did the Methodists or the Baptists, though the majority of their pastors and elders remained male. Their emphasis upon the literal experience of the Spirit's power encouraged Holiness-Pentecostal worshipers to manifest their religious emotions in ecstatic displays of shouting, singing, and dancing that elicited the pejorative nickname "holy rollers" from those who favored a more sedate liturgy. By introducing the use of guitars, pianos, and drums in church music, the Holiness-Pentecostal congregations significantly affected the development of black gospel music and gradually influenced the musical tastes of churches that once banned such instruments as tools of the devil. The sanctified churches, as they were also called, required their members to observe a strict moral ethic that prohibited tobacco, alcohol, narcotics, gambling, and "worldly" entertainment. In effect, the sanctified churches themselves constituted little social worlds in which the music and ecstasy of religious worship afforded tired and downtrodden people a recreative catharsis that helped them face an oppressive and frequently hostile larger world. The values inculcated in the lives of the sanctified church members—honesty, thrift, hard work, and discipline, combined with the moral asceticism mentioned above—structured their daily lives around a coherent system of beliefs and, within the limits of racial discrimination, tended to promote upward mobility.[7]

Social critics have complained that the proliferation of black churches fragmented the black community into competing sects. If only they had overcome their differences, the argument goes, black churches might have pooled their resources and become an effective force for the economic and social development of the black community. Perhaps so,

---

7. Melvin D. Williams, *Community in a Black Pentecostal Church: An Anthropological Study* (Pittsburgh: University of Pittsburgh Press, 1974); Benton Johnson, "Do Holiness Sects Socialize in Dominant Values?," *Social Forces* 39 (May 1961) 309-16; Joseph R. Washington, Jr., *Black Sects and Cults: The Power Axis in an Ethnic Ethic* (New York: Doubleday, 1972); Paul Oliver, *Songsters and Saints: Vocal Traditions on Race Records* (New York: Cambridge University Press, 1984), pp. 169-98.

but the fact remains that individual ministers and churches did cooperate to better the condition of the race. During the 1930s, for example, ministers in Harlem organized "Don't buy where you can't work" boycotts against stores and agencies that refused to hire black employees (anticipating Operation Breadbasket and PUSH by thirty years). It should be noted that their efforts, though rarely successful, depended upon a well-established network of cooperation between black ministers and congregations of various denominations. In 1933, a group of black clergymen organized the National Fraternal Council of Negro Churches, an ecumenical structure designed (like the Federal Council of Churches) to promote cooperative action among member denominations in social as well as religious causes. During the 1940s and 1950s the Fraternal Council vigorously protested racial discrimination and, by means of its Washington bureau, lobbied Congress for the passage of civil rights legislation.[8]

Interdenominational cooperation did not disguise the serious doctrinal divisions that separated black Baptists from black Methodists and black Pentecostals. But, despite their doctrinal differences, black Christians shared more with each other than they did with white Christians of the same denominations. The racial segregation of American churches stood as a continual reminder that Christianity had failed to build biracial religious community in this country. None were more zealous in exposing this failure than were various groups of black Muslims and black Jews. Since the days of slavery, Afro-Americans had identified themselves metaphorically with biblical Israel in prayer, sermon, and song. The first organization to take this identification literally was the Church of God and Saints of Christ, founded in 1896 by William S. Crowdy in Lawrence, Kansas. Crowdy preached a heterodox version of Judaism based upon his assertion that black people were descended from the ten lost tribes of Israel. Similar beliefs inspired the development of other black Jewish congregations. In the 1920s Wentworth A. Matthew formed around a nucleus of West Indian immigrants the Commandment Keepers Congregation of the Living God, for years Harlem's largest congregation of black Jews. The Commandment Keepers believed that Afro-Americans were "Ethiopian Hebrews" or Falashas, who had been stripped of their true religion by slavery. Judaism was the ancestral heritage of the Ethiopians, whereas Christianity was the religion of the "gentiles," i.e., whites. The Commandment Keepers rejected Christianity as the religion of a corrupt white society

---

8. Mays and Nicholson, pp. 224-27; Welty, pp. 243-44, 300-11. See also Spurgeon E. Crayton, "The History of the National Fraternal Council of Negro Churches" (M.A. thesis, Union Theological Seminary, New York, 1979).

that would destroy itself in atomic warfare. They condemned emotionally expressive worship, so characteristic of black shouting-churches, as "niggerition." Moral restraint and dignity presumably distinguished the behavior of the Ethiopian Hebrew from the immorality and self-indulgence of the typical "Negro." While they rejected racist stereotypes as applicable to themselves, black Jews accepted them as accurate descriptions of black behavior and black culture.[9]

Black Muslim groups closely resembled black Jews in the rejection of Negro identity as pejoratively defined by whites, and in the invention of a new religious-racial identity for Afro-Americans. The original religion of black people, they claimed, was Islam. The first organized movement of black Americans to identify itself as Muslim was the Moorish Science Temple founded in Newark, New Jersey, in 1913 by Timothy Drew. The Noble Drew Ali, as his followers called him, taught that Afro-Americans were not Negroes but Asiatics. Their original home was Morocco; their true nationality was Moorish-American. To symbolize recovery of their true identity, members of the Moorish Science Temple received new names and identity cards issued by Noble Drew Ali. Knowledge of their true selves, Ali taught, would empower them to overcome racial oppression.[10] The Moorish Science Temple survived Ali's death in 1929, only to be eclipsed by another esoteric Muslim group that gained much more notoriety among blacks as well as whites.

In 1930 a peddler, W. D. Fard, began teaching poor blacks in Detroit that they were members of a Muslim "lost-found tribe of Shabbazz" and that salvation for black people lay in knowledge of self. Before disappearing in 1934, Fard provided an institutional base for his movement by establishing a Temple of Islam, a University (actually an elementary and secondary school) of Islam, a Muslim Girls Training Class, and a paramilitary corps, the Fruit of Islam. Under Fard's successor, Elijah Muhammad, who guided the movement for the next forty years, the Nation of Islam grew from two small congregations in Detroit and Chicago to dozens of mosques embracing thousands of members in every section of the country. By claiming that Fard had actually been the incarnation of Allah and that he was Fard-Allah's messenger, Elijah Muhammad asserted his authority to proclaim an elaborate gospel that owed much more to the racial situation in America than it did to the

9. Howard M. Brotz, *The Black Jews of Harlem: Negro Nationalism and the Dilemmas of Negro Leadership* (New York: Schocken, 1964); Deanne Shapiro, "Double Damnation, Double Salvation: The Sources and Varieties of Black Judaism in the United States" (M.A. thesis, Columbia University, 1970).

10. Fauset, pp. 41-51.

tenets of Islam. His revelation that white people were a race of devils, the product of a black scientist's malicious genetic experiment, was heresy in the eyes of orthodox Muslims, but to Messenger Elijah's disciples it seemed a plausible explanation for endemic white racism and an effective antidote to the pervasive myth of white supremacy and black inferiority.

The black Muslims, most notably Malcolm X, castigated black Christians for accepting the "white man's religion" and denounced the black church for keeping black Americans ignorant of their true selves. They pointed to their successful record in rehabilitating criminals, drug addicts, and alcoholics, to prove that Islam was better fitted than Christianity to save the outcasts of America's society. Black Muslims, like black Jews, rejected behavior associated with popular black culture and disciplined their membership to observe strict dietary and social regulations. Moreover, black Muslims insisted on a new national as well as religious identity. Elijah Muhammad taught his followers to reject the rituals of American civic piety, such as saluting the flag, voting, and registering for the draft. Claiming that they constituted a black nation, the black Muslims demanded that the federal government set aside a separate section of the country for black people in compensation for the unpaid labor of their slave ancestors.[11]

Black Jewish and black Muslim attacks on Christianity highlighted a problem that had long troubled black churches: the racist attitudes and behavior of white Christians. From slavery days on, black Christians had resisted the temptation to identify Christianity as a religion "for whites only" by distinguishing "true" Christianity, which preached the equality of all races, from "false" Christianity, which countenanced slavery and discrimination against blacks. There were always those, however, who failed to see the distinction and who scorned Christianity as the religion of the oppressors. Given the history of white brutality against blacks, how could blacks accept the same religion as whites? The national identity of black Americans was threatened by the same dilemma. A history of slavery, disfranchisement, and discrimination in America made Afro-Americans feel like aliens in their own land. Black Jews and black Muslims solved the dilemma by embracing their alienation from Christianity and from America. By identifying with Judaism and Islam, respected religions embraced by millions of "nonwhite" people around the world, Afro-Americans figuratively escaped

---

11. C. Eric Lincoln, *The Black Muslims in America* (Boston: Beacon, 1961); E. U. Essien-Udom, *Black Nationalism: A Search for Identity in America* (Chicago: University of Chicago Press, 1962).

to a religious homeland outside the racial boundaries that imprisoned them in America. For some the migration became literal. The Original Hebrew Israelites, for example, a black Jewish group from Chicago, emigrated in 1967 to Liberia and in 1969 to Israel, where their claims to original ownership of the land created ongoing problems for Israeli authorities.[12]

Afro-Americans also converted to orthodox forms of Islam and Judaism in twentieth-century America. As more black Americans were exposed to the interracial character of worldwide Judaism and Islam, the racialist doctrines of Crowdy, Ali, and Fard seemed false or at least outmoded. After the death of Elijah Muhammad in 1975, his son Warrithuddin (Wallace Deen) Muhammad began teaching that his father's doctrines were to be understood allegorically, not literally. He encouraged civic and political participation among black Muslims and even opened membership to whites. As the Nation of Islam moved rapidly toward orthodox Islam, it signified the shift by changing its name in 1976 to the World Community of Islam in the West, and, in 1980, to the American Muslim Mission. These changes were rejected by some black Muslims, however, who remained loyal to the original teachings of Elijah Muhammad. Under the leadership of Minister Louis Farrakhan they resumed the separatist ideals of the Nation of Islam.[13]

Faced with the discrepancy between the creed that American Christians preached and the deeds they performed, black Muslims rejected both America and Christianity, although doing so required them to deny significant aspects of their own history as Afro-Americans. For most black Americans this was too high a price to pay, even to be free of the American dilemma. Instead, like generations before them, they refused to believe that America was a white man's country or that Christianity was a white man's religion. With increasing militancy, they continued to call upon the nation to "rise up and live out the true meaning of its creed," as Martin Luther King, Jr., put it in his keynote address at the 1963 March on Washington. And they used the symbols and the rhetoric of the black religious tradition to do so.

Though some critics, including some black clergy, have claimed that the black church became apolitical and that black protest was secu-

---

12. Merril Charles Singer, "Saints of the Kingdom: Group Emergence, Individual Affiliation, and Social Change Among the Black Hebrews of Israel" (Ph.D. dissertation, University of Utah, 1979); Ben Ammi, *God the Black Man and Truth* (Chicago: Communicators Press, 1982).

13. Yvonne Yazbeck Haddad, "Muslims in the United States," in *Islam: The Religious and Political Life of a World Community*, ed. Marjorie Kelly (New York: Praeger, 1984), pp. 265-71.

larized during the twentieth century, the black church remained more political and black protest more religious than some have thought.[14] Clergy were extensively involved, for example, in the organization and activity of the National Association for the Advancement of Colored People, the Urban League, and Marcus Garvy's Universal Negro Improvement Association. Reflecting their experiences in national and international ecumenical bodies like the YMCA, northern and southern black ministers played active roles in several movements for interracial cooperation antedating the civil rights movement. The black Congregationalist churchman, George Edmund Haynes, a founder and the first executive director of the Urban League, used his position as executive secretary of the Federal Council of Churches' Commission on Race Relations, from 1922 to 1947, to establish local interracial clinics designed to bring whites and blacks together to study, discuss, and act upon racial issues. Gordon Blaine Hancock, a black Baptist minister and college professor from Richmond, Virginia, organized the Conference on Race Relations, an important meeting of southern black leaders held in Durham, North Carolina, in 1942. Out of this all-black meeting came the Durham Manifesto, a challenge to white southern leaders to cooperate with blacks in improving race relations. As a result of the Durham meeting, the Southern Regional Council, one of the few interracial organizations in the pre-civil rights South, was organized in 1943 at Atlanta University. Neither the Durham Manifesto nor the Southern Regional Conference seemed militant by later standards, but they were bold and significant achievements given the state of race relations at the time.[15]

Occasionally acts of discrimination did stir black churches to take more militant action even in the South. In 1935, for example, Martin Luther King, Sr., led several thousand black demonstrators on a march from Ebenezer Baptist Church to the Atlanta city hall to protest the denial of voting rights to blacks. A decade earlier, Adam Daniel Williams, Martin Luther King, Jr.'s, maternal grandfather, organized rallies at Ebenezer to protest a municipal bond issue that contained no plans for high-school education for black youth. The history of economic boycotts and political demonstrations by southern and northern blacks before the civil rights movement remains to be written. When it is, it

14. See Gayraud S. Wilmore, *Black Religion and Black Radicalism: An Interpretation of the Religious History of Afro-American People*, 2nd ed. rev. (Maryknoll, NY: Orbis, 1983), pp. 167-91.

15. Samuel K. Roberts, "George Edmund Haynes: Advocate for Interracial Cooperation," in *Black Apostles: Afro-American Clergy Confront the Twentieth Century*, ed. Randall K. Burkett and Richard Newman (Boston: G.K. Hall, 1978), pp. 97-127; Raymond Gavins, *The Perils and Prospects of Southern Black Leadership: Gordon Blaine Hancock, 1884-1970* (Durham: Duke University Press, 1977).

will very likely confirm the conclusion of one recent study that the activism of black ministers and black congregations, as well as the legal struggles of the NAACP and the Urban League, laid the groundwork for the civil rights movement that erupted in the 1950s.[16]

In city after city, from Montgomery to Memphis, the involvement of black clergy and black churches was crucial to the day to day conduct of the civil rights struggle. The black church influenced the philosophy and spirit behind the movement as well. In large part, the movement was a revival, an attempt to reawaken the nation to the ideals upon which it was founded—and the most eloquent expression of these ideals was formulated in the cadences of the black church. As the son, grandson, and great grandson of Baptist ministers, Martin Luther King, Jr., was deeply rooted in the Afro-American religious tradition. He drew instinctively upon that tradition to inspire the movement's nonviolent wing to "save the soul of the nation," as the motto of the Southern Christian Leadership Council expressed it. Studded with frequent references to biblical images like Exodus and Promised Land, King's speeches marshalled the evocative power of the black sermon to convince Americans of both races that desegregation was a religious, not just a political cause. Time after time, he motivated his followers by teaching them that they, like the prophets and martyrs of the Bible, had to be willing to suffer and die for justice in the knowledge that unmerited suffering is redemptive.[17]

The demonstrations themselves took on the feel of church services. Local campaigns, like the Montgomery Bus Boycott of 1955-56, were structured around frequent rallies in black churches, which quickly became primary targets for white terrorist bombings. These rallies consisted of song, prayer, scripture reading, discussion of goals and tactics, and an exhortation to action that frequently resembled a sermon. The importance of these quasiprayer meetings for keeping up morale and maintaining momentum was incalculable. In this sense the black church was truly the soul of the movement.[18]

Although King attracted widespread support from local black churches, it was never unanimous. Some clergymen disagreed with his

16. Martin Luther King, Sr., with Clayton Riley, *Daddy King: An Autobiography* (New York: Morrow, 1980), pp. 84-87; Aldon D. Morris, *The Origins of the Civil Rights Movement: Black Communities Organizing for Change* (New York: Free Press, 1984).

17. A broad selection of King's speeches is available in *A Testament of Hope: The Essential Writings of Martin Luther King, Jr.,* ed. James M. Washington (San Francisco: Harper & Row, 1986).

18. Martin Luther King, Jr., *Stride Toward Freedom: The Montgomery Story* (New York: Harper & Row, 1958).

philosophy of social activism because they believed that Christian ethics was fundamentally about personal morality, not social reform. Society would only be changed by obedience to God, not by political agitation. Others, including Joseph H. Jackson, then president of King's own denomination, the National Baptist Convention, U.S.A. Inc., believed that civil disobedience led only to lawlessness and was totally inappropriate in America, where legal means of redress were available to every citizen. King's most cogent critic came from outside the Christian churches. Malcolm X, as spokesman for the Nation of Islam, derided both integration and nonviolence as forms of black self-hatred. Before and after his conversion to orthodox Islam, Malcolm X preached that blacks, like any other people, were justified in taking their freedom "by any means necessary." In 1964 he founded the Organization of Afro-American Unity for the purpose of uniting all people of African descent in a common struggle for human rights. His assassination in 1965 cut short the development of the OAAU, but the posthumous publication of his autobiography spread his ideas to a wide audience and gained Malcolm greater respect than he had known during his life.[19]

In 1966 the cry, "black power," could be heard, signifying that some black activists were disappointed with the slow pace of racial change and disillusioned with the tactics of nonviolence. Black power quickly became a rallying cry for those who adopted a more radical position than King's. While King rejected the demand for black power as a slogan without a program, in 1966 the National Committee of Negro Churchmen (later renamed the National Conference of Black Churchmen) distanced itself from King by issuing an extended theological defense in the July 31 issue of the *New York Times*. The assassination of King in 1968 led to massive rioting in urban areas around the country and seemed to confirm that the period of nonviolent protest had passed. Self-determination, community control, and liberation replaced desegregation and integration as the catchwords of the movement. Radical militants joined the black Muslims in attacking the black church for being otherworldy, compensatory, and reactionary. Assertions of black pride and celebrations of black cultural identity marked a new mood of independence among black Americans. Separatism seemed to be on the rise while integration seemed discredited even in ecumenical circles.

In 1967, for example, black delegates to a National Council of Churches conference on urban problems insisted on splitting the meet-

---

19. For a careful treatment of the differences between King, Jackson, and Malcolm X, see Peter J. Paris, *Black Leaders in Conflict* (New York: Pilgrim, 1978); George Breitman, ed., *By Any Means Necessary: Speeches, Interviews and a Letter by Malcolm X* (New York: Pathfinder, 1970), pp. 33-67.

ing into two caucuses, one black and one white. Black Christians in white churches established ongoing caucuses to deal with issues of black identity and black autonomy. Between 1968 and 1970, black Catholics organized the Black Catholic Clergy Caucus, the National Office of Black Sisters Conference, the Black Catholic Lay Caucus, and finally the National Office of Black Catholics, which proceeded to characterize the Catholic church in America as primarily a white racist institution. In 1969 tensions between black clergy and white churches were exacerbated further when the civil rights activist, James Forman, presented a "Black Manifesto" demanding that white Christian churches and Jewish synagogues pay out $500 million for black economic development in reparation for slavery and racial oppression. Support for the Manifesto by the National Conference of Black Churchmen led to bitter controversy between black clergy and white denominational boards over how much money should be given and to whom.[20]

In this context of militancy, separatism, and heated rhetoric, black churchmen began developing a black theology to articulate systematically the distinctive character of Afro-American religious experience. The most prolific and prominent of the black theologians was James H. Cone, professor at Union Theological Seminary in New York, whose first book, *Black Theology and Black Power,* appeared in 1969. As the title suggests, Cone's book was in part a response to the challenge presented to black Christians by the black power movement. What did Christianity have to do with the liberation and empowerment of black people? Cone's answer, further elaborated in successive books, was that God identifies himself in human history with the struggle of black people and has evidenced their ultimate victory in the resurrection of Jesus, who came to liberate the oppressed. Cone's black theology also leveled a strong attack against white theologians for failing even to consider the experience of the oppressed, which, he claimed, is the primary locus of God's saving presence in the world. Whereas Cone made liberation the major theme of his theology, other black theologians, like J. Deotis Roberts, emphasized reconciliation, or, like Charles Long, stressed the non-Christian components of black folk religion. During the last fifteen years, black American theologians have entered into discussion with African, Asian, feminist, and liberation theologians and have begun to add the issue of class to their theological reflections.[21]

Even before King's assassination, for reasons too numerous to

---

20. Gayraud S. Wilmore and James H. Cone, eds., *Black Theology: A Documentary History, 1966-1979* (Maryknoll, NY: Orbis, 1979), pp. 15-111.

21. Wilmore and Cone, pp. 609-23.

summarize here, the civil rights movement had lost momentum, but his death, more clearly than anything else, marked the end of an identifiable movement for racial equality on the national level. No black leader of national stature arose to take his place, although the Rev. Jesse Jackson attempted to revive the spirit of the movement in his 1984 and 1988 political campaigns for the Democratic party's presidential nomination. Significantly, black churches played a strategic role in the local organization of his campaign nationwide. The absence of a national black political movement has distracted observers from considering the activity of black churches on the local level, where issues of community organization, housing, education, economic development, and employment have continued to trouble black Americans for the past fifty years and more. A highly successful and widely imitated model of church-sponsored black economic development on the local level was the Opportunities Industrialization Center (OIC) founded in 1964 by Leon H. Sullivan, author of the "Sullivan Principles" and pastor of Zion Baptist Church in Philadelphia. The OIC trained unemployed and underemployed black and white workers for skilled positions in industry and assisted them in finding jobs to match their newly acquired skills. By the end of the decade similar OIC programs were established across the country. OIC was preceded by a "selective patronage campaign" in which, on a given Sunday, 400 black ministers urged their congregations not to patronize a particular company because it discriminated against blacks in employment. An estimated twenty-nine selective patronage campaigns between 1959 and 1963 opened up many jobs formerly closed to blacks in Philadelphia and inspired the Southern Christian Leadership Conference to establish a similar program, called Operation Breadbasket, in 1962. In numerous black communities, black churches have sponsored housing improvement and neighborhood development programs, health care clinics, day-care centers, and senior citizen facilities.[22]

For most of the past fifty years, scholars have asserted that secular alternatives were diminishing the extent of the black church's power in the black community—a difficult assertion to verify. Evidence is conflicting, and what type of evidence to use is unclear. Recently, for example, social analysts have listed the waning influence of religious values upon inner-city blacks as a contributing factor to the current crises of mounting teenage pregnancies, illegitimate births, absent-father households, drug abuse, and "black on black" crime. Yet the same social planners looked to the black church as the primary community

22. Leon H. Sullivan, *Build Brother Build* (Philadelphia: Macrae, 1969).

agency to deal with these intractable problems of America's black underclass. Certainly black Americans, like whites, were exposed to modern secular culture. But, statistically at least, the black church remained strong. In 1936 the United States Census for Religious Bodies estimated that there were 5.7 million church members in a black population of 12.8 million. According to the 1986 edition of the *Yearbook of American and Canadian Churches,* black Baptists numbered over 9 million, black Methodists roughly 4 million, and the black Holiness-Pentecostal family probably exceeded 4 million members. While these figures, based on church reports, were surely inflated, there is no reason to doubt that a large percentage of the approximately 28 million black Americans are church members. Yet the efficacy of social programs and the size of membership rolls were not the only, nor necessarily the most revealing, measures of the black church's significance over the last five decades. The centrality of the church in the black American's quest for identity and meaning demonstrated its ongoing resilience and creativity during a period of tumultuous change.

5. Ecumenical Movements

H. George Anderson

In his book *The Unfinished Reformation,* published in 1953, Charles Clayton Morrison looked back over the previous seventy-five years and described an "awakening" that had been "gradually evolving." That awakening was the ecumenical movement, which had, he thought, made more progress toward its goal among Protestants in the United States than in any other major country. Even though church bodies might not realize it, they "should be made aware that, without their conscious effort, the Spirit of Christ has been drawing them together over a period of many years, and under many influences, until they are nearer the goal of a united church than they realize. . . ."[1]

This vision and understanding of the ecumenical movement dominated American Protestant thought at mid-century. The metaphor of evolution suggested a virtually inevitable process of growth. When this view of the past was combined with the conviction that the Spirit of Christ was drawing denominations toward the goal of a united church, then past and future formed a coherent pattern leading from separateness to ever greater unity. Like a vast glacier, the ecumenical movement flowed from disparate sources toward a single destiny decreed by nature and nature's God.

Morrison summarized the evidence for his evolutionary view. The movement had begun "in simple, natural fraternization of church leaders across denominational lines." That fraternal spirit prompted "informal projects of cooperation," and the informality gradually "gave rise

---

1. Charles Clayton Morrison, *The Unfinished Reformation* (New York: Harper & Brothers, 1953), pp. 12, 222.

to a formalized cooperation on a national scale under the name of the Federal Council of Churches," which, in turn, produced "the new National Council of Churches" in which several functions, formerly reserved to the churches themselves, were being shared within an interdenominational structure.[2]

Any description of ecumenical activity in the United States needs to reckon with that image and its supporting assumptions because ecumenical history after 1950 often has been judged from its perspective. The ecumenical movement is conceived as a gradually widening series of organizational links encompassing increasingly diverse traditions in a single structure, until at last all Christian denominations will be united in one visible church. Any break in that chain or delay in its linkage becomes a cause for dismay. When the goal of church union is not reached as quickly as some visionaries have hoped, the ecumenical process is declared moribund or scapegoats are found. What about questioning the metaphor? Do ecumenical movements in this country really move toward a single end like a glacier moving toward the sea? Or is there another way to read the record since 1908?

During the first decade of this century the cooperative spirit that prevailed among American Protestants spawned a variety of new interdenominational organizations. Some of them enabled denominational boards to work together in home missions, foreign missions, and other areas of common interest. Other organizations continued the voluntary association principle of the nineteenth century by gathering individual Christians from various church bodies to support causes like temperance, Sunday schools, and Bible distribution. These national structures were supplemented by at least eleven statewide federations and "denominational commissions," chiefly in New England and the upper Midwest.[3]

In 1908 the cooperative process moved beyond boards and individuals to involve entire denominations. Thirty-three church bodies formed the Federal Council of Churches as an instrument of common service, consultation, and witness, and as a means "to secure a larger combined influence for the churches of Christ in all matters affecting the moral and social condition of the people, so as to promote the application of the law of Christ in every relation of human life."[4]

---

2. Ibid., pp. 12-13.

3. Useful reviews of this early period, by an eyewitness, are Samuel McCrea Cavert, *The American Churches in the Ecumenical Movement 1900-1968* (New York: Association, 1968) and *Church Cooperation and Unity in America: A Historical Review 1900-1970* (New York: Association, 1970). The latter volume includes an extensive bibliography by Erminie H. Lanterno, pp. 354-96.

4. "Plan of Federation," quoted in Cavert, *The American Churches in the Ecumenical Movement*, p. 49.

In retrospect, the formation of the Federal Council is often seen as the source of later efforts for wider church union, but at the time of its organization it had no such grandiose aims. In 1908 the denominations were not ready to consider union, so the proposal for the Federal Council explicitly stated that "its province shall be limited to the expression of its counsel and the recommending of a course of action." Its constitution stated that it had "no authority to draw up a common creed or form of government or of worship." The model was much more that of a conference for mutual consultation than of an agency carrying on an independent program—to say nothing of being the first stage of a movement toward a single church. In fact, a conservative Disciples of Christ newspaper opposed the council precisely because joining it would be "to surrender the grand plea for Christian unity on the New Testament platform."[5]

Although the council originally was to provide a forum for consultation on matters ranging from evangelism to Sunday observance and family life, the area of social service gradually became most prominent, not because the council so intended but because societal problems were not being addressed by any other cooperative association or agency. An early leader of the council recalled that, in its first two decades, the council grew "not by the promulgation of clear-cut plans and schemes but by attempts to meet needs and opportunities as they arose and to gather the forces which the hour demanded."[6] World War I required the churches to coordinate their ministries to military personnel. After the war came the call for cooperative efforts to meet the needs of European countries for food and clothing. The League of Nations and peace concerns, Christian-Jewish relations, university evangelism, and the growth of pastoral care all opened new frontiers of service that the churches preferred to address cooperatively rather than separately. The result was that the Federal Council set up committees, then commissions, and finally departments to coordinate these new programs.

Although its membership, measured in terms of denominations, remained relatively constant, the council steadily expanded its influence and its staff. It also assisted in the formation of state and local councils of churches. By 1949 there were forty state councils and nearly 850 local councils, of which over 180 had paid leadership.

During the same period other, more specialized cooperative agencies also proliferated. In addition to the Home Missions Council, the Foreign Missions Conference, and the International Council of Re-

5. Cavert, *The American Churches in the Ecumenical Movement*, pp. 48-53 (quoting *The Christian Standard*, February 3, 1906, p. 8).
6. Ibid., p. 69.

ligious Education, there were the United Stewardship Council, the Missionary Education Movement, the Council of Church Boards of Education, the Protestant Radio Commission, the Protestant Film Commission, the Inter-Seminary Movement, and the United Council of Church Women. Samuel McCrea Cavert, who was the general secretary of the Federal Council during this period, has remarked that ordinary church members "did not even know the names of all of the agencies among which the program of cooperation was parceled out."[7] Beyond these agencies, other very strong organizations—the Young Men's Christian Association and the American Bible Society, to name just two—commanded the loyalty of individuals from many Protestant denominations.

The existing network of relationships was becoming severely overtaxed. It had come to the point where agencies established by the denominations for common work in specific fields were themselves creating a second layer of ad hoc committees to address areas of cooperative work between commissions. By the late 1940s the number of those ad hoc commissions reached twenty-four in one year.

It would have been difficult for an observer in the 1930s to detect a simple pattern in ecumenical affairs. Like the universe, ecumenism seemed to be expanding in all directions at once. The Federal Council had not replaced other cooperative bodies; it had taken its place among them and worked with them for thirty years. Although no new organizational steps had been taken, it was clear that progress was being made. What was the next phase to be? Bishop Holt of the Methodist Episcopal Church South expressed the feelings of many when he observed, "We have far more unity than we have any agency to express."[8]

These dual pressures toward a visible expression of existing unity and a more rational structure for cooperation led to the formation of a new ecumenical instrument, the National Council of Churches of Christ in the United States of America (NCC). During the 1930s various committees and denominations, and the Federal Council itself, had called for a new organization, but it was not until the 1940s that a suitable plan emerged. As the United States was entering World War II in 1941, a study conference was recommending a single corporate structure to integrate the work of eight interdenominational agencies, including the Federal Council. The next year the eight agencies all met at the same time in Cleveland, and the slow process toward unification began. A plan was ready by 1944, but after four more years

7. Ibid., p. 203.
8. Ibid., p. 158.

of negotiation only five of the eight agencies and less than half of the member denominations had approved. Then, in a flurry of activity, helped substantially by the momentum generated by the formation of the World Council of Churches (1948), a total of twelve agencies and twenty-nine denominations agreed to constitute a new body at a convention in Cleveland in December, 1950. The start-up date for the council was set for just a few weeks later, January 1, 1951, the exact midpoint of the twentieth century.[9]

The NCC was described by a friendly observer as "the most complex and intricate piece of ecclesiastical machinery this planet has ever witnessed."[10] Not only did it represent nearly thirty denominations ranging from Quakers to Eastern Orthodox, but it also provided services to an equal number of denominations that did not choose to become full members. Its representative system was complex, reflecting its origin in both denominations and their respective boards. Its working structure was far from sleek; it reminded one of a snake that had swallowed a grand piano. Although there were only four major divisions, each division had from twelve to twenty departments, committees, and commissions; in addition there were General, Central, and Joint Departments that related to entities other than single divisions. No wonder the structure was simplified in 1965 and again in 1986. In general, the council's functions involved sponsoring conferences, research and study, publication, joint administration of major projects such as overseas relief, and development of new cooperative ventures, as well as serving as a contact point with Roman Catholics, Jews, and secular organizations, and speaking on matters of public policy. Although the last of these functions has been the most visible and controversial of the NCC's activities, the importance of the other six has been the reason for continued denominational loyalty to the NCC. Since its founding the NCC has also gained membership through the participation of additional denominations, particularly from the Orthodox tradition. In 1985, the thirty-one denominations belonging to the council included about 40 million members.

Of course there were denominations that remained aloof from the council for doctrinal reasons. Two of these bodies, the Southern Baptist Convention and the Lutheran Church—Missouri Synod, are not active in other interdenominational groups.[11] A sizable number of holi-

9. Ibid., pp. 158-60, 187, 204-06.
10. Ibid., p. 210; the quote is from Henry P. Van Dusen.
11. Glenn A. Igleheart, "Ecumenical Concerns Among Southern Baptists," *Journal of Ecumenical Studies* 17/2 (Spring 1980) 49-61, is a helpful review of Southern Baptist attitudes since World War I.

ness, pentecostal, and conservative bodies, however, formed the National Association of Evangelicals (NAE) in 1942. Although the NAE may originally have served as a rallying point for denominations opposed to the "ecumenical movement"—usually conceived as a church union movement based on lowest common denominator theology—the NAE itself has provided cooperative structures for its member denominations. In 1985 it consisted of forty-three denominations, as well as local associations, schools, and some individual congregations, with a total membership of about 4 million.[12] In some respects it may be regarded as practicing a level of cooperation similar to that practiced by the "mainline" churches in the 1920s.

In hindsight, the formation of the National Council seems to have been inevitable, particularly if one subscribes to the "glacial" theory of ecumenical advance. At the time, however, there were other options advanced by those people who felt that the next logical step was a union of churches rather than another council. The church union vision had earlier glimmered on the horizon and it reappeared during the 1940s, when talk of reorganizing ecumenical cooperation filled the air.[13]

Looking back to the beginning of the century, one is tempted to identify the Federal Council of Churches as the ancestor of modern ecumenical efforts. To do so, however, is to miss the variety and breadth of the early ecumenical movement. The Federal Council was only one strand in a complex tapestry of interchurch agencies and voluntary associations; in fact, observers of the scene in those early decades might well have picked the Young Men's Christian Association as the most vital and promising cooperative movement among the churches. John R. Mott, who dominated the ecumenical scene in those years, was really based within the YMCA and exerted his tremendous influence through that organization.

After World War I, in the heady days of international cooperation that produced the League of Nations, several denominations considered a federation of churches that would have gradually transformed itself into an organic union. Although representatives from a wide variety of church bodies attended the first meeting in 1918, interest soon waned and the plan finally withered in the disillusionment and theological tensions of the 1920s. At the end of that decade there was a brief

---

12. For the beginnings of the NAE, see H. Shelton Smith, "Conflicting Interchurch Movements in American Protestantism," *Christendom* 12/2 (Spring 1947) 165-76. For membership, see Constant H. Jacquet, Jr., ed., *Yearbook of American and Canadian Churches, 1986* (Nashville: Abingdon, 1986), p. 14.

13. A review of these movements, and of others described below, is provided in Cavert, *Church Cooperation and Unity in America*, pp. 324-35.

effort to amend the constitution of the Federal Council itself so that denominations could transfer their functions to it and thus move toward union, but the amendment was never passed.

After World War II the quest for new ecumenical forms produced two movements that may have confused the picture rather than simplifying it. E. Stanley Jones, a Methodist missionary to India who conducted preaching missions in the United States, called for "the next great step" in American church life—the immediate formation of "The United Church of America" as a central body of which each denomination would be a branch. However, denominations were never clear about just what sacrifice of sovereignty would be required of them, and several of them were uninterested in commitments to a union until theological and structural questions had been resolved. During the same years a second project, "The American Conference on Church Union," became the focus of efforts from within the Disciples of Christ and the Congregationalists. These denominations attracted several bodies from the Methodist and Presbyterian families to join in discussing a series of steps designed to produce organic union by working upward from the local and regional level.[14] Although the participating denominations recognized one another's ministries and sacraments, their polities varied from episcopal to congregational, and the idea of dissolving existing structures was too radical to succeed. After a decade of discussion the "Greenwich Plan," as it was popularly called, faded away in 1959.

Denominational survival tendencies did not, however, prevent the merging of church bodies on an individual basis. Advocates of broader church union could point to a steady series of denominational mergers, usually within a single faith tradition but occasionally bridging confessional barriers. A survey of the period from 1910 to 1952 identified twelve successful organic unions, three of which crossed confessional lines. Eight more negotiations were in progress, and four of those eventually resulted in mergers; one of the four involved differing confessional backgrounds. Since that time four more major union negotiations have succeeded, but each involved bodies within a single theological tradition.[15]

What the surveyors seldom noted was that the number of un-

14. C. C. Morrison, "The Ecumenical Trend in American Protestantism," *Ecumenical Review* 3/1 (October 1950) 1-13.

15. Surveys of church union negotiations may be found in H. Paul Douglass, *A Decade of Objective Progress in Church Unity 1927-1936* (New York: Harper and Brothers, 1937); Stephen Neill, *Towards Church Union 1937-1952* (London: SCM, 1952); and Ruth Rouse and Stephen C. Neill, eds., *A History of the Ecumenical Movement 1517-1948*, 2nd ed. (Philadelphia: Westminster, 1967), pp. 496-505. The journal *Ecumenical Review* carried updates on a roughly biennial basis from 1954 to 1974.

successful negotiations between 1910 and 1953 was twelve, precisely the same as the number that succeeded. That ratio proved true for the mergers in progress in 1952 as well. Furthermore, some of the mergers produced splinter groups that refused to follow the majority of their denomination into a union. For example, the merger of the Congregational Christian Churches and the Evangelical and Reformed Church in 1957 produced not only the United Church of Christ but also a continuing association of Congregational Churches.

The spirit of the 1950s, however, was an optimistic one. All the statistical indicators were up. Budgets were big and deficits small, people flocked to church, and steeples sprouted over every suburb. In 1960 a book appeared with the title *The Social Sources of Church Unity*, an intentional contrast to the title of H. Richard Niebuhr's *The Social Sources of Denominationalism*, which had been published about thirty years earlier.[16] Niebuhr's well-known argument asserted that denominations arose because of four powerful social determinants: class, region, race, and nationality. Robert Lee's title, on the other hand, intended to signal that the sociological tide had turned and that "the reduction of social difference among class, sectional, racial and ethnic lines" would be conducive to church unity. The book is interesting because it presents a different explanation for the history of ecumenical activity. According to Lee, the motivation for such activity is not intrinsic to the nature of the church, as Morrison's reference to the "Spirit of Christ" had implied. The impetus, rather, comes from without, from the culture and its underlying social currents. The glacier was replaced by an ice floe.

Just a few months after the publication of Lee's book, sociology became history. In December 1960, Stated Clerk Eugene Carson Blake invited Episcopalian Bishop James Pike to join him in persuading their respective churches to invite other denominations into a Consultation on Church Union (COCU). It was a sign of the temper of the times that this "Blake-Pike proposal" was accepted not only by Episcopalians and Presbyterians but eventually by nine Protestant bodies, including three black ones. By 1966 *Principles of Church Union* had been developed and by 1970 a *Plan of Church Union* was ready. After ten years of progress,

---

16. Robert Lee, *The Social Sources of Church Unity* (Nashville: Abingdon, 1960). A later study of the ecumenical movement that traces it to social needs ("functionalism"), rather than to theological imperatives within the tradition, is James R. Kelly, "A Sociological Perspective on the Ecumenical Movement," *Ecumenical Trends* 12/8 (September 1983) 118-24. For a broader review of sociological research on ecumenism, see Phyllis Goudy Myers and James D. Davidson, "Who Participates in Ecumenical Activity?," *Review of Religious Research* 25/3 (March 1984) 185-203.

the consultation felt so sure of success that it renamed itself the "Church of Christ Uniting."[17]

The decade of COCU's rise, however, brought other forces into play. Between 1960 and 1970 the United States suffered a series of crises that shattered the optimistic picture of increasing social unity. It was a decade that popularized the terms "polarization," "white backlash," and "generation gap." The sociological tide seemed to be flowing toward division. Membership in many Protestant denominations declined steeply, particularly in those bodies most active in COCU. Contributions toward the work of the National Council of Churches also dwindled as denominations struggled to cope with strong internal factions that opposed positions which the NCC took on the recognition of Communist China, racial integration, and U.S. participation in the Vietnamese War. Some of those internal tensions led to schism and the formation of new church bodies with strongly conservative outlooks. A census of religious bodies found twice as many new denominations being formed in the 1960s as in the 1950s.[18]

The 1960s also brought Roman Catholics into the ecumenical scene after years of Vatican opposition. Early in the century, Protestant efforts to bring Roman Catholics into the Faith and Order Movement were met by the uncompromising assertion that unity could come only through reunion with the See of Rome. At mid-century the papacy issued warnings and declarations that restricted Roman Catholic participation in the formation of the World Council and the National Council of Churches. Then, in 1964, the Second Vatican Council issued a Decree on Ecumenism that urged "all the Catholic faithful to recognize the signs of the times and to take an active and intelligent part in the work of ecumenism."[19] Within two years the National Conference of Catholic Bishops created a Committee on Ecumenical and Interreligious Affairs, which promptly set up a liaison with the NCC. Appropriately, Catholic

17. Eugene C. Blake, *A Proposal Toward the Reunion of Christ's Church* (Philadelphia: General Assembly Office of the United Presbyterian Church in the U.S.A., 1961). Paul A. Crow, Jr. and William Jerry Boney, *Church Union at Midpoint* (New York: Association, 1972).

18. J. G. Melton, *A Directory of Religious Bodies in the United States* (New York and London: Garland, 1977). For an interpretation of the divisive tendencies within Protestantism, see Dean R. Hoge, *Division in the Protestant House: The Basic Reasons behind Intra-Church Conflicts* (Philadelphia: Westminster, 1976). A factual summary of the work of the NCC from 1950 to 1975 may be found in Nathan H. VanderWerf, *The Times Were Very Full* (New York: NCCCUSA, 1976).

19. Walter M. Abbott, ed., *The Documents of Vatican II* (New York: Guild Press, 1966), p. 347 ("Decree on Ecumenism"). The effect of this decree on one Roman Catholic theologian is traced in Patrick W. Collins, "Gustave Weigel: An Uncompromising Ecumenist," *Journal of Ecumenical Studies* 15/4 (Fall 1978) 684-703.

79673

bishops recommended that observance of the "Christian Unity Octave" in January be combined with the Protestant tradition of the "Week of Prayer for Christian Unity," so that both groups would be united in prayer if not in structure.[20]

The active presence of Catholics on the ecumenical scene produced a major shift of emphasis in ecumenical efforts. Attempts at church union among Protestants seemed less compelling when measured against the vaster prospect of a general union of all Christians. At the same time, all ecumenists realized that doctrinal questions could not be swept aside in dealing with Rome, and serious doctrinal questions did exist. The way forward, therefore, would have to be slower and more thorough, with dialogue on a church-by-church, bilateral basis. "Bilaterals appear to fill an ecumenical gap for some churches," reported a Protestant ecumenist in 1972, "especially where specific controversial questions are major dividing factors. . . . Bilaterals appear to possess more weight and urgency than multilaterals for the churches involved."[21]

By the end of the 1960s, these growing bilateral dialogues, together with the increasing polarization in American society, had set the stage for a new chapter in ecumenical history. That is clear in retrospect, but at the time ecumenical leaders couldn't figure out exactly what was going on. A report to the National Council of Churches in 1969 said, "so much has happened, and yet at the same time, so little. . . . The churches do not have a clear enough idea of how the unity of the church should be expressed." The mood and perplexity recall the situation in the late 1930s. The accepted projections were not working out and no new path had been discovered. It was, said the report, a time of "crisis" in the New Testament sense—that is, a time of decision.[22]

A careful reading of the report makes clear that the decisions had already been made. The report notes that there seemed to be less "investment of money and manpower . . . in councils." The pace of church union negotiations also had slowed. Although the report lists six "union negotiations," a closer examination shows only one, the COCU project, actually moving toward union. In contrast to that meager list, the report

20. Cavert, *Church Cooperation and Unity in America,* pp. 32, 287, 291-92.

21. John Deschner, "Developments in the Field of Church Unity," *Ecumenical Review* 24/4 (October 1972) 451. For a survey of dialogues and articles about them, worldwide, see J. F. Puglisi, *A Bibliography of Interchurch and Interconfessional Theological Dialogues* (Rome: Centro Pro Unione, 1984).

22. "Crisis and Promise in the Ecumenical Movement," Fourth Annual Report to the General Board of the National Council of Churches from the Department of Faith and Order, Division of Christian Unity (1969, typescript), pp. 1, 4.

notes thirteen "interconfessional conversations" or dialogues.[23] The clearest signal of all that the tide had turned occurred in 1973, when the COCU *Plan of Union* failed to achieve approval from the participating denominations. Although the dream of church union among Protestants did not die, it certainly seemed less attainable.

"These are tough times for the ecumenical movement," wrote Robert McAfee Brown in 1969. "The excitement has worn off. . . . Again and again one hears the estimate 'Ecumenism has had it,' with the implication that the movement peaked somewhere around the end of Vatican II and has been going downhill ever since."[24] "Most of the members of the leadership network of the 1940's and the 1950's are now retired or dead, and no equivalent group has arisen to takes its place," lamented another ecumenist. He went on to suggest that ecumenism had lost its sense of "transcendence" and had become merely another feature of institutional Christianity, "suffering the same loss of credibility that attaches to church life generally. . . ."[25] Others blamed the problem on the institutional self-interest of denominations or on the failure to bring ecumenical urgency to the grass roots.[26]

The problem lay more in disappointed expectations than in reality.[27] Enchanted by the vision of an inexorable flow toward church union—at least among Protestants—many ecumenists felt frustrated by the turbulent waters of the 1970s. It is true that the NCC was under attack and that the COCU process broke up on the rocks of denominational caution, but although previous efforts for church union had also turned out to be premature they had provided stimulation for new plans. The Roman Catholic entry into the ecumenical stream was bound to create a new and confusing pattern for a while, but in a few years it would begin making its own contributions. And as far as grass-roots ecumenism was concerned, the impulses were already there—albeit coming from unexpected sources.

At the same time that leaders of "mainline" denominations were

23. Ibid., pp. 27-28, 22-26.
24. Robert McAfee Brown, "Personal Musings on the Changing Ecumenical Scene," *Journal of Ecumenical Studies* 6/2 (Spring 1969) 236.
25. Robert S. Bilheimer, "Let American Ecumenism Be Ecumenical," *Journal of Ecumenical Studies* 16/1 (Winter 1979) 202-03.
26. Cf. Donald P. Warwick, "Organizational Politics and Ecumenism," *Mid-Stream* 14/1 (January 1975) 293; Russell E. Richey, ed., *Denominationalism* (Nashville: Abingdon, 1977); Robert T. Handy, "Denominationalism and Ecumenism: Partners or Enemies?," *Ecumenical Trends* 10/1 (January 1981) 1-4; and Stephen Neill, "Ecumenism's Past and Present," *The Christian Century*, June 4, 1975, pp. 568-72.
27. "Sometimes, hopes have been unrealistically high. . . . We are only at the beginning of the movement toward unity." James K. Mathews, "Ecumenism at Mid-Passage," *Ecumenical Trends* 11/2 (February 1982) 29.

pondering the fate of COCU, lay members of those churches—and of other churches as well—were meeting together, praying together, and conducting common Bible study and worship. They were attending mass rallies where denominational differences melted away. They were caught up in the charismatic renewal movement, which was spreading throughout Protestant and Roman Catholic congregations after 1970.

The charismatic movement is usually traced to 1960, the same year that the COCU proposal was made, but the two movements operated at opposite levels of the ecclesiastical pyramid. COCU was initiated by a Presbyterian stated clerk and an Episcopalian bishop. It was front-page news from the beginning. It operated at the highest levels of church-to-church diplomacy. The charismatic movement arose in several local settings, unpublicized and half-secret for several years. It was not popular with mainline Protestant leadership and its acceptance in Roman Catholic circles was slow in coming. Although the movement seemed to spring up in congregational, that is, denominational settings, and although it has tended to end up in a variety of denominational renewal movements, there was a strong ecumenical phase in the 1970s, when the common experience of glossolalia swamped denominational differences for a time. The great charismatic conferences, such as that in Kansas City in 1977, were purposely designed to permit denominational workshops during the day—thus mollifying nervous bishops and church leaders—and then to gather everyone together for ecumenical rallies at night. Church bodies gave cautious approval to participation in the movement, but their official statements usually carried warnings about "elitism" and the loss of important denominational traditions. The movement did demonstrate, however, that "transcendence" was still a potent motivator toward ecumenism.[28]

The more traditional ecumenical movement also showed new strength toward the end of the 1970s as the forces that had been at work during the decade began to reveal their positive direction. Roman Catholic participation in ecumenical conversation on the national and international levels brought issues of faith and order into prominence. The Faith and Order Commission of the World Council of Churches had long been occupied with questions relating to ministry and the

---

28. Richard Quebedeaux, *The New Charismatics II: How a Christian Renewal Movement Became Part of the American Religious Mainstream* (San Francisco: Harper and Row, 1983), gives a friendly view. For the ecumenical discussion, see Michael Harper, "Charismatic Renewal—A New Ecumenism?," *One In Christ* 9/1 (1973) 59-65, and Peter Hocken, "Charismatic Renewal and Christian Unity," *America* 144/7 (December 1, 1979) 340-42. Denominational pronouncements are gathered in Kilian McDonnell, ed., *Presence, Power, Praise*, II (Collegeville, MN: Liturgical Press, 1980).

sacraments, and in 1982 it issued *Baptism, Eucharist and Ministry*, a document that asks member churches to say whether they can "recognize in this text the faith of the Church through the ages." Rather than announcing agreement on all details, the document offers broad statements that enable churches to compare their respective practices and beliefs. It is assumed that church bodies might be willing to recognize that, although other bodies differ from them in emphases, there is enough common ground to warrant recognition of the other bodies' ministries and sacraments. Thus "mutual recognition of ministries" becomes a new goal for ecumenical activity. It does not demand that denominations give up their identity, but it does open the possibility of intercommunion and exchange of clergy.[29]

COCU also found a way forward in the later 1970s through the concept of "covenanting." The theological idea of covenant had played a part in earlier doctrinal statements of the COCU denominations, but by 1981 it was seen as a paradigm for the process itself.[30] Instead of proposing immediate union on the basis of a definite plan, the participating churches agreed in 1984 to seek "mutual and formal recognition . . . of their respective members, churches and ministries," and then to move toward "acts designed to reconcile the presently differing forms of ministry, to enable regular eucharistic fellowship, and to create various interim bodies for common life and action at each level of the churches' life." The process might take ten to fifteen years, and the exact form of the eventual united church would be developed on the way. The key change from earlier proposals was the commitment to a process rather than to a formal structure.[31] Even if the process proceeded no further than the first step—mutual recognition of members, churches, and ministries—the ecumenical posture of participating churches would be significantly improved.

The covenant paradigm has also dominated restructuring efforts in the NCC. A process begun in the late 1970s produced a new

---

29. *Baptism, Eucharist and Ministry*, Faith and Order Paper No. 111 (Geneva: World Council of Churches, 1982). Cf. Jean M. R. Tillard, "Elements of Unity in Recent Ecumenical Discussion—A Roman Catholic View," *Mid-Stream* 18/4 (October 1979) 392-403. The entire issue of *Journal of Ecumenical Studies* 21/1 (Winter 1984) is devoted to "*Baptism, Eucharist and Ministry* and Its Reception in U.S. Churches."

30. Paul A. Crow, Jr., "The Covenant as an Ecumenical Paradigm," *Austin Seminary Bulletin* 96 (March 1981) 60-72. Gerald F. Moede, *Oneness in Christ: The Quest and the Questions* (Princeton: Minute Press, 1981); see also his "Response to Stuart G. Leyden," *Journal of Ecumenical Studies* 20/2 (Spring 1983) 280-83.

31. *Covenanting Toward Unity: From Consensus to Communion* (Princeton: COCU, 1985). The theological basis is given in a companion volume, *The COCU Consensus: In Quest of a Church of Christ Uniting* (Princeton: COCU, 1985).

Preamble and Purpose statement, which describes the council as a "community of Christian communions" that "covenant with one another to manifest ever more fully the unity of the church." The new concept asks for more participation by the member bodies in governance, funding, and interpretation, and at the same time proposes clearer lines of accountability from program units to the governing board. It shapes a more closely knit council at the same time that it leaves the door open for even greater unity when the member churches are ready for it.[32]

Looking back over the course of ecumenical movements in the United States, one is struck by the way in which they have come, wave after wave, never reaching the goal and yet never leaving the ecclesiastical landscape unchanged. Efforts at interchurch cooperation through agencies and councils have led to countless reorganizations and realignments, but the cooperation has increased. Visions of church union have beckoned denominations to consider ending their separate existence in order to form a larger whole, and, although none of those visions has yet become reality, the denominations have achieved internal mergers and have looked for ways to move closer to one another. Mutual recognition of ministries and sacraments among some denominations has been a substantial step in that direction. Furthermore, common spiritual experiences of laypeople across denominational lines have prepared the ground for further ecumenical efforts. Each wave makes it easier for the next to advance, and the tide appears to be rising.

32. Robert W. Neff and Candace Carman Weeks, "Next Steps Toward Community: An Inside View," *Journal of Ecumenical Studies* 22/2 (Spring 1985) 221-34.

6. Public Worship in Protestantism

James F. White

The past fifty years have seen momentous changes in the public worship of many of the Protestant churches in America. I shall pick up the account where Henry Sloane Coffin left it in 1935 in *The Church through Half a Century*,[1] although it is a quite different kind of history that I must survey. This is especially true because of the difficulty of doing justice to the full spectrum of Protestant worship in America. One has seven major liturgical traditions plus many ethnic, racial, and cultural styles within each of those traditions. At best I can only hint at the diversity present in American Protestant worship, a diversity ranging from the right-wing liturgical traditions, Lutheran and Anglican, to the central traditions, Methodist and Reformed, to the left-wing traditions, Free Church, Quaker, and Pentecostal.

Clearly, in American Protestantism, the majority tradition is the Free Church tradition. Unfortunately, little liturgical scholarship has been directed to the study of its development in America, particularly in its various sectarian expressions. This makes it a "soft" tradition when compared with a tradition whose development has been carefully documented and articulated, a "hard" tradition. The soft traditions are often vulnerable to being conformed to traditions that have benefited from liturgical scholarship, simply because there is no one to defend the values of an unstudied tradition. Such lacunae make it difficult to write a comprehensive history of worship in this period since some traditions are far less accessible to historical documentation than are others.

On the one hand, there are the right-wing traditions in which

1. New York: Scribner's, 1936; pp. 185-206.

service books such as *Lutheran Book of Worship*[2] and *Book of Common Prayer*[3] are mandatory and the degree of predictability for the words (rite) is high, although actions (ceremonial) can vary widely. In the central tradition, except for the sacraments, which usually follow a service book, the typical Methodist or Presbyterian Sunday service has no uniform structure and the degree of predictability is much lower. For the left-wing majority, the only predictability comes in the use of a hymnal (which may or not be denominational) and the Bible. Obviously, the higher the degree of predictability, the easier it is to chronicle developments, but, since the right-wing traditions are a minority, such an account is always only partial.

I shall trace the scene in Protestant public worship in America chronologically from 1935 to 1985. This time span seems to divide into three parts: the period of *aestheticism* from 1935 to 1945; the period of *historicism* from 1945 to 1965; and the period of *ecumenism* from 1965 to 1985. The only clue to future developments is to note the likely continuance of present-day tendencies and some of their probable consequences.

I. Aestheticism (1935-1945)

The first period represents the growing sophistication of American society and the tendency to substitute the experience of the beautiful for emotional outbursts. My home congregation decided, when it built its new gothic church, to forbid shouts of "Amen" during services, much to the consternation of some. But the buttoned-down emotions found alternate forms of expression in printed services, the splendor of stained glass, and choral music. Vested choirs replaced the gospel octet; prayers of confession were printed for all to read in unison; and the altar was safely fixed to the wall, near to God and away from people. For all except Pentecostals and Quakers, this period saw the triumph of that greatest liturgical innovator since Gutenberg, one A. B. Dick, a Chicago businessman whose stencil duplicator made every pastor an instant Cranmer when it came to preparing services.

The two great leaders during this era for much of central and left-wing Protestantism were Von Ogden Vogt (1879-1964) and Elbert M. Conover (1885-1952). Vogt's four books, especially *Art and Religion*,[4] advocated borrowing "from the materials of the past those trea-

2. Minneapolis: Augsburg, 1978.
3. New York: Church Hymnal Corporation, 1979.
4. New Haven: Yale University Press, 1921.

sures which are least burdened with abandoned concepts."[5] This encouraged an eclectic style of blending past treasures with present relevance, placing Darwin and Marx in stained glass, for example. Conover's influence was in church architecture. As director, after 1934, of the Interdenominational Bureau of Architecture, Conover advocated building gothic churches with divided chancels. His books, such as *Building the House of God*[6] and *The Church Builder*,[7] were widely used. Conover's legacy was scattered over the land as Methodists, Presbyterians, Congregationalists, and Baptists erected their own less expensive versions of the elegant gothic that Ralph Adams Cram (1863-1942) had popularized among Episcopalians.

Valiant efforts were made during this period to improve the quality of church music. Individuals like Archibald T. Davison of Harvard *(Protestant Church Music in America)*[8] led the way. The anthem became a well-established part of mainline church music. In black congregations, the gospel hymn was brought to new heights by Charles Tindley (1856-1933) and Thomas Dorsey (1899-   ).

Preaching tended to be topical, with great concern for relevancy. William Stidger in Boston typified the concern for "preaching to real life situations." Issues of pacifism were raised as war loomed ahead, and then preachers had to address the concerns of a nation at war.

There seems to have been little awareness among either Protestants or most Roman Catholics of the presence of a small group of liturgical pioneers whose work would help bring about a new reformation in worship, both Roman Catholic and Protestant. Men such as Virgil Michel (1890-1938), H. A. Reinhold (1897-1968), William Busch (1882-1971), Martin Hellriegel (1890-1981), Gerald Ellard (1894-1963), and Reynold Hillenbrand (1905-1979) were busy sowing the seeds on this side of the Atlantic for changes that would sweep across the face of American Christian worship after Vatican II.

For Methodists, the era produced the first *Book of Worship*, the first full service book since Wesley.[9] This 1945 volume, labeled "For optional and voluntary use," gathered together a variety of orders of service and materials for the church year. Much was borrowed from Anglican sources, but the use of the book was rather limited except for the official "Ritual." In similar fashion, the Presbyterian Church in the United States of America published a new edition of its *Book of Common*

---

5. *Modern Worship* (New Haven: Yale University Press, 1927), p. 29.
6. New York: Methodist Book Concern, 1928.
7. New York: Interdenominational Bureau of Architecture, 1948.
8. Boston: E. C. Schirmer Music Company, 1933.
9. Nashville: The Methodist Publishing House, 1945.

Worship in 1946, which was garnished by widespread borrowings from Anglican and Reformed churches and included a lectionary.[10] In a sense, these volumes show the direction in which the central and left-wing churches were leaning. Much of their borrowing from other traditions seems to have been motivated by fascination with the aesthetic quality of the materials borrowed.

II. Historicism (1945-1965)

The period after World War II saw major shifts in worship priorities among American Protestants. Worship as a parallel to the experience of the good, the true, and the beautiful was now simply not enough. Perry Miller once remarked that before the war he was an Emerson enthusiast; after leading the tank corps that liberated Buchenwald he became a Jonathan Edwards follower. The theological expression of this shift, forced on a whole generation by world history, was neo-orthodoxy. Once faith in humanity's innate goodness was shattered, something more sound had to replace it. This found expression in a period of historicism or neo-Reformation focus in worship. For twenty years, these trends tended to be dominant in what was written about worship and also shaped what was practiced in thousands of congregations.

The usable past that best suited the needs of this era was the Reformation of the sixteenth century, although Methodists got equal mileage out of the eighteenth century. We now realize why the worship of this era had such appeal. The heavily penitential language of the Reformation liturgies spoke directly to and for those who were bent on recovering the Christian doctrine of original sin. The most conspicuous part of Anglican morning prayer that Methodists incorporated into the second *Book of Worship* (1965)[11] was the penitential preface added by Cranmer in 1552. "Miserable offenders" may still have been a bit strong for Methodists, but the penitential tone was certainly there. Indeed, it is nearly impossible to persuade ministers who received their liturgical formation in the 1950s and early 1960s that they can dispense with a prayer of confession on any occasion, even weddings. Certainly the penitential aspect of worship received more than its due share of attention during this period.

10. Philadelphia: Publication Division of the Board of Christian Education of the Presbyterian Church in the United States of America, 1946.

11. Nashville: The Methodist Publishing House, 1965. (Note that the 1945 edition said on the title page, "For Voluntary and Optional Use"—a rubric that does not appear in the second [1965] edition.)

This was also the age of Sputnik. Americans came to feel insecure about trusting in military might alone. A much greater concern with the classic Christian faith became evident, especially as stated in the historic creeds. While the previous era delighted in impromptu affirmations of faith, frequently composed weekly, the period of historicism recovered the thrill of tradition. The Apostles' and Nicene Creeds once again became important parts of worship. Curiously, this concern with firm foundations did not yet translate into widespread use of a lectionary outside of the right-wing traditions. Lutherans became embroiled in controversy over the addition of a eucharistic prayer in the 1958 *Service Book and Hymnal*.[12] A clear break with American Lutheran tradition, it nevertheless involved the addition of an important creedal element to "The Communion."

Beyond these specific concerns, the liturgies of the Reformation and Wesleyan eras had intrinsic appeal. Probably the most representative book of this period was Bard Thompson's *Liturgies of the Western Church*, which provided ready access to the great Protestant liturgies from Luther to Wesley.[13] Among the Reformed, the Mercersburg School of the nineteenth century, which had recycled similar materials a hundred years earlier, was the subject of much scholarly attention. Presbyterians were busy rediscovering that Calvin and Knox had produced service books, and Methodists found that much of Wesley's warm heart was fueled by the cold print of his *Sunday Service*.[14] In essence, what was happening in the central churches and in some on the left-wing was that the dominant revivalistic order of worship, with its invariable three parts—preliminaries, sermon, harvest, was beginning to be challenged by alternatives. Services might still end with "An Invitation to Christian Discipleship," but there now were other historical patterns to follow than simply that of nineteenth-century evangelism.

Some evidence of the degree of change over two decades is found in the next generation of Methodist and Presbyterian service books. The second (and last) *Book of Worship* (1965) shows Methodists looking to Wesley for guidance in respect of his Anglican heritage. One of the compilers claimed that the 1965 revision of the eucharist was meant to be a "brisk version of [Cranmer's] 1549." This return to the Reformation era was a major feature of the book, which also added a lectionary, recovered portions of the psalter, and incorporated resources

12. Minneapolis: Augsburg, 1958.
13. Cleveland: World, 1961. (This book remained in print, with various publishers, for the next quarter-century.)
14. Cf. *John Wesley's Sunday Service of the Methodists in North America* (Nashville: United Methodist Publishing House, 1984).

for the church year. The language was still Elizabethan. The 1970 Presbyterian *Worshipbook* was largely completed by 1968.[15] It appeared late enough to adopt contemporary language but too early for inclusive language. Like the Methodist book, it did not anticipate most of the revisions of the era after Vatican II, although the brand-new ecumenical lectionary was included. Essentially the *Worshipbook* is a neo-Reformation book, making a valiant effort to achieve the weekly eucharist that Calvin had sought. The service also follows him in keeping the warrant (i.e., the words of institution) detached from the eucharistic prayer. In both books, the focus is much more on the sixteenth and eighteenth centuries than on the third and fourth. The usable past was to change rather drastically in a few short years.

In the 1940s important agents for the transformation of worship were still in embryonic form and were scarcely recognized as consequential. Associated Parishes, founded in 1947, became the spearhead for liturgical renewal among Episcopalians. Two years later, the 1949 General Convention authorized the *Prayer Book Studies* series which, in 1950, began to publicize the case for revision of the 1928 prayer book.[16] In 1946, William E. Slocum and Romey P. Marshall founded the Order of St. Luke among Methodists. We have already mentioned the Roman Catholic liturgical pioneers who had begun to plant for a great harvest that finally came in the 1970s.

Surely one of the most significant developments of this period was the growth of liturgical scholarship among American Protestants. This new phenomenon was reflected in the work of such men as Cyril C. Richardson, Massey H. Shepherd, Jr., Luther D. Reed, Arthur Carl Piepkorn, and others. Liturgical scholars were gradually appointed to seminary faculties, particularly of the Methodist seminaries, where they could help break the captivity to the familiar that so many seminarians brought with them. As early as 1955, the United Lutheran Church in America led the way in appointing the first full-time denominational worship executive, Edward Brown.

The 1950s and 1960s saw much attention given to congregational song (hymnody). Hymnbooks of this period tended to undertake the recovery of the best from the past. Instrumental and choral music were improved by nine schools of sacred music, including Westminster Choir College (established in 1926) and Union's School of Sacred Music (1928).

15. Philadelphia: Westminster, 1970 (*Services* edition); 1972 (*Services and Hymns* edition).

16. 32 vols., New York: Church Pension Fund/Standing Liturgical Commission, 1950-76.

The 1950s witnessed an enormous amount of church building, which became a billion dollar annual industry during this period. Many of these buildings were designed on the twin assumptions that Christian worship is basically unchanging and that the church occupies a dominant place in society. Both assumptions were to undergo serious questioning during the 1970s, but the buildings of this earlier period remain monuments to then prevailing opinions.

Preaching during this period, in many cases, moved to more impassioned pleas for social reform as the civil rights movement (and opposition to it) engulfed the attention of many congregations. Lectionary preaching was still only a little cloud on the horizon, although more denominations were now making lectionaries available. New exegetical tools, especially *The Interpreter's Bible*, gave the preacher improved resources for biblical study.[17]

III. Ecumenism (1965-1985)

No one, least of all Roman Catholics, was prepared for the hurricane of liturgical change that came in the wake of Vatican II. The last two decades have seen more liturgical change for Western Christians than have the past four centuries. For Roman Catholic worship, the Middle Ages came to an abrupt end on December 4, 1963, with the promulgation of the *Constitution on the Sacred Liturgy*.[18] Few Protestants suspected then that Vatican II had also written the agenda for Protestant liturgical change. A period of glacial change was transformed overnight into one of hurricane velocity.

The liturgical *Constitution* approved at Vatican II was the result of sixty years of scholarly and pastoral work. Yet the immediate response was anything but scholarly. The late sixties was a time of euphoria for ministers and priests, who acted like people released from long years of imprisonment. Common assumptions about worship were questioned and judged to be arbitrary. The organ was challenged by the guitar, stained glass by cloth banners, and the seated congregation by dancers.

In retrospect, much of this response seems to have been inevitable. It is now an accepted dogma that worship can and should change. But this was a new discovery in the late 1960s and proved most liberating. Much that now seems silly—the balloons and confetti, the wordy banners

17. 12 vols., New York: Cokesbury-Abingdon, 1951-57.
18. Collegeville, MN: Liturgical Press, 1963.

and placards—was part of a necessary experience of liberation before the work of reconstruction could begin. Clearly much of the impetus for change among Protestants was the excitement generated by Roman Catholics when they first realized that they, too, could be folksy. Nothing was as well publicized as their so-called underground Masses. The new folksong music with a beat delighted many, while textile art blossomed in churches. All these phenomena were contagious among Protestants. The spirit of the 1960s, stirred by an unpopular war, encouraged rebellion from established forms of office and ritual.

Something much more important was happening than was then apparent. We had actually moved into a new era in which it has become impossible to view worship in terms of the old isolated traditions. The period 1965-1985 is, above all else, the ecumenical era, with worship leading the way in breaking down many remaining juridical and theological barriers. Freed from old inhibitions, everyone shamelessly borrows from everyone else. Denominational hymnals, for example, have become an anomaly, the contents becoming more and more identical with each revision. If one's only criterion is finding the best hymnody available, denominational labels are no longer important.

Much of the post–Vatican II hurricane came as the result of the earlier and lesser storms of the liturgical movement. Whether one traces this movement back to Prosper Gueranger (1805-1875) in France, to Lambert Beauduin (1873-1960) in Belgium, or to a host of other liturgical pioneers, the liturgical movement set the stage for the post – Vatican II reforms, both Protestant and Catholic. In this country, one can trace to shortly after World War II the growing urgency of the vernacular for Roman Catholic liturgical reformers. Certainly this issue became the linchpin for the new reforms, although the *Constitution* itself was remarkably reticent beyond allowing the faithful at Mass "a suitable place . . . [for] their mother tongue," particularly in the readings, common prayer, and responses. The complete abandonment of Latin was hardly envisioned.

Key concepts in the *Constitution* have governed the reforms in many churches, especially a "full, conscious, and active participation," a "noble simplicity," a "richer fare" of Scripture, and indigenization. Whether any church has achieved much of the last-named phenomenon is questionable, although efforts have certainly been made. But participation, simplicity, and Scripture stand out as keynotes in all that liturgical reformers in the various western churches have attempted in recent years.

Vatican II mandated revision of all the Roman Catholic liturgical books, work that began in 1964 and was virtually complete with the publication of *de Benedictionibus*[19] in 1984 and *Caeremoniale Episcoporum*[20] the same year. By comparison, the Tridentine books took nearly fifty years (1568-1614) to complete. Unlike the Tridentine books, the new rites had great consequences for Protestants as well.

One of the most obvious changes was the adoption of a modern English vernacular when the stage of translation was reached. Until 1970, all Protestant service books were written in Elizabethan English. Long forgotten was that the Reformers had insisted on addressing God in the familiar second person, "Du" or "Thou," instead of in more formal terms. During the four ensuing centuries, the language of worship again became sacralized, just the opposite of what the Reformers desired. The 1970s saw much controversy over this issue. Eventually, Episcopalians were to compromise and publish Rites I and II in Elizabethan and contemporary English, with both traditional and contemporary collects. The Presbyterians led the way with a complete service book in contemporary language. Some of this material from the early 1970s now seems a bit flat, but it was probably necessary to get the theology straight before moving on to more lyrical language.

One Reformation pattern that did surface in the local liturgies of the late 1960s was a tendency to didacticism. One can readily spot the services of this time because they put into the mouths of the people lengthy theological or ethical statements. The compulsion to make worship "useful" led to didacticism, reminiscent of John Knox's tendency to pray a commentary on the Lord's Prayer.

Folk music became a widespread idiom as the pendulum swung further toward popular participation. Professionally trained church musicians felt shouldered aside by guitar-plucking teenagers. Often sung to rather simplistic lyrics, the music was sufficiently winsome to invite participation by anyone who could hum a simple tune. Various supplements were issued to augment denominational hymnals, but they were often outsold by private collections in paperback.

Such custodians of good music as Erik Routley (1917-1982) sought to channel the best of the music and texts into new hymnals. Monuments of this period are: *The Hymnal of the United Church of Christ* (1974),[21] *Lutheran Book of Worship* (1978), *The Hymnal 1982* (Episcopal),[22] and Routley's own product for the Reformed Church in America, *Rejoice in the Lord* (1984).[23] A new United Methodist hymnal will appear

---

19. Vatican City: Congregation for Divine Worship, 1984.
20. Vatican City: Congregation for Divine Worship, 1984.
21. Philadelphia: United Church Press, 1974.
22. New York: Church Hymnal Corporation, 1985.
23. Grand Rapids: Eerdmans, 1985.

in 1989. Each of these has perforce incorporated new musical idioms, including folk song, ethnic materials, and the more conventional texts of such modern hymn writers as Brian Wren and F. Pratt Green. These hymnals are distinctly political documents, trying to serve a wider variety of constituents than was ever contemplated in previous hymnals.

Enormous changes have also taken place in the architectural setting of worship. It became hard for anyone to justify altar-tables fixed against a wall when Roman Catholics had made them free standing. Once one had celebrated the eucharist facing the people, it was difficult to turn one's back to them again. There was a widespread move toward more centralized space, with the people gathered as closely as possible about pulpit, altar-table, and font. Participation thus became the key word in architecture as well as in rites. A new concern developed late in this period with "gathering space" and its effect on the process of coming together to form a community. Increasing attention was shown to the design of baptismal fonts so that (among pedobaptists) infant baptism by immersion would be possible, and the immersion of adults feasible in all cases.

Clearly a very significant characteristic of this period was the revision of liturgical texts by many of the major denominations. In several ways, this process was different from all previous ones. Certainly much of the revision of Protestant liturgical books was sparked by the revisions underway among Roman Catholics. The resources made available in Vatican City, and the priority given this process by Pope Paul VI, had assured that the Roman Catholic revisions would be the most careful in history. No other church could match the full-time paid staff and 800 consultants used in developing the Roman Catholic Sunday Mass lectionary, which was then simply revised and adopted by Protestants.

Behind the reforms was a vast body of scholarship in which the work of non-Roman Catholic scholars like Yngve Brilioth and Gregory Dix played important roles. More than any other document, the third-century *Apostolic Tradition* of Hippolytus helped shape the course of such liturgical revisions as the Roman Catholic eucharist and the 1980 United Methodist *An Ordinal*.[24] Since the same documents and the same scholarship were accessible to everyone, it is not surprising that the revised liturgies look alike. Ironically, the conservative Hippolytus sparked much liturgical change in the twentieth century by opposing it in the third.

Few churches participated in this process without constant

24. Nashville: United Methodist Publishing House, 1980.

awareness of what other churches were doing. And there were few inhibitions about borrowing whatever was considered superior. Episcopalians took from Lutherans the observance of Transfiguration as the last Sunday after the Epiphany, a practice dating back to Johann Bugenhagen. United Methodists adopted the Reformed custom of a prayer of illumination as practiced by Calvin. All made their own versions of the Roman Catholic Sunday lectionary. Far more than during any other period of history, worship was reformed through an ecumenical approach.

Much depended on when one entered this process and on when one went into print with hardbound books, thereby effectively stopping the process. Numerous issues arose, so that later entrants benefited from the proposals and the mistakes of the earlier arrivals. By the time that the decision to accept contemporary English had become common to all, new concerns had already arisen over the use of inclusive language in reference to humans and, eventually, to God. The process of Christian initiation (baptism, confirmation, and first communion) posed new issues. The books prepared by Methodists and Presbyterians in the 1960s perpetuated these as distinct rites by introducing services of "confirmation." In the 1970s attempts were made to reunite the process and (unsuccessfully) to eliminate the term "confirmation" altogether.

All churches entered upon liturgical reform with few or no options other than a standard form. Roman Catholics surprised everyone by authorizing, in 1967-68, four and eventually nine eucharistic prayers. Episcopalians produced six, Lutherans six (including solely the *verba*), Presbyterians eight, and United Methodists a total of twenty-two. Such a variety of anaphoras had disappeared in the West for nearly a thousand years. In almost every new rite, a variety of options was provided. Flexibility and adaptability became favored goals in modern liturgical revision.

As the seventies progressed, new questions of justice became ever more acute as it was increasingly realized that worship had often been a source of injustice. The exclusion of references to women and children and the pejorative use of such terms as "black," "blind," "old," and "child" led many to realize that worship was deeply involved in unwitting forms of social control. Even more important than language were the roles people played in the leadership of worship. Many congregations discovered that they had no good reason for having only middle-aged men serve as ushers or for hiring men as organists in large churches while expecting women to volunteer to do the music elsewhere. In Roman Catholic parishes women began to assist in distributing communion at a time when some United Methodist bishops were discouraging anyone but the ordained from such a role. As more and more women entered the ordained ministry in most Protestant churches, except the Lutheran Church—Missouri Synod, clerical garb frequently began to change from a black preaching robe with padded shoulders to the ancient and unisex alb. Efforts were made to understand worship in relationship to children's stages of development. The roles played in worship were opened to more age groups and to both sexes.

Language about humans was resolved, for the most part, in the seventies. God-language still remains hotly debated. United Methodists (1984) and Presbyterians have issued guidelines at the national level, but with little resulting consensus. The National Council of Churches' *An Inclusive Language Lectionary* has provoked much controversy, but little agreement, in its revision of Scripture.[25]

An important advance has been made in the deliberate attempt to include minority persons in the revising of liturgical texts and hymnals. Revision committees now are much more representative of all constituents of the church involved. No longer, for instance, can it be assumed that all American Presbyterians speak English as their first language. This new consciousness is perhaps most apparent in music and in the concern to include Hispanic, Asian, Native American, and black hymns in new editions of hymnals. This concern also insures that the folksy hymns of Bill Gaither will be represented in new hymnals just as surely as the more sophisticated Erik Routley works.

Thus many of the problems encountered, the methods employed, and the resulting rites were remarkably similar. In this period, worship increasingly became a source of unity among Christians rather than of disunity. Still, distinctive characteristics of each tradition persisted. It is instructive to look briefly at the chief denominational achievements in this era of liturgical revision.

In the Episcopal Church, the Standing Liturgical Committee was authorized as early as 1949 to commence revision of the 1928 *Book of Common Prayer.* Thirty years later, this action led to a new book, the fourth American *Book of Common Prayer.* Immediately noticeable is the book's increased length, from 622 pages in 1928 to 1,001 in 1979. If a consensus was reached in this process of revision, it is that there are equally acceptable alternate routes to the same destination. The new acknowledgment of pluralism may be the most distinctive feature of the final product.

Episcopal liturgical revision was aided by that church's distinguished liturgical scholars. The process was advanced by twenty-nine

25. 4 vols., Atlanta: John Knox, 1983-86.

volumes of *Prayer Book Studies* (1950-1976) containing both commentaries and proposed rites. Beginning with volume XVII, *The Liturgy of the Lord's Supper*, these became forms of the rites as eventually adopted.[26] The next volume, *Holy Baptism with the Laying-on-of-Hands*, proved too advanced and led to some retreats.[27] All the volumes display a deliberate effort to keep abreast of liturgical scholarship around the world. In this respect, the prayerbook given final approval in 1979 has inaugurated a new era, for it is not just a revision rooted in the Anglican tradition but endeavors to reflect both ancient classical and modern ecumenical Christian worship. *The Book of Occasional Services* provided additional seasonal, pastoral, and episcopal services.[28]

The Lutheran process was quite different. In the fall of 1966, at the initiative of the Missouri Synod, the Inter-Lutheran Commission on Worship was organized by the four main Lutheran bodies in this country and Canada. The ultimate goal was a joint service book, which was preceded by a series of trial services and hymns, the *Contemporary Worship* series.[29] Ten volumes were published, plus a notable booklet on eucharistic prayers, "The Great Thanksgiving."[30] The whole process was coordinated by a full-time staff, which also supervised the results of much trial use in parishes.

Some hard decisions had to be made. With regard to the lectionary, it was eventually decided to give priority to the ecumenical (i.e., Roman Catholic) lectionary in alliance with the other American churches rather than to follow European Lutherans in retention of the one-year cycle. Five eucharistic prayers were accepted, plus the *verba*, but some of the more radical proposals were rejected. A move to eliminate a separate rite for confirmation failed, but compromise left open the possibility of reuniting the process of initiation and provided for affirmation of baptismal vows by the lapsed. Daily services were provided and a joint Lutheran-Roman Catholic *Service of the Word* has recently been published.[31]

The result of twelve years of effort was the publication in 1978 of *Lutheran Book of Worship*, a combination service book and hymnal. It made music an integral part of the usual services, with a variety of stylistic options. On the eve of publication, the Missouri Synod withdrew from the process to publish its own *Lutheran Worship*,[32] although some

26. New York: Church Pension Fund, 1967.
27. New York: Church Pension Fund, 1970.
28. New York: Church Hymnal Corporation, 1979.
29. 10 vols., Minneapolis: Augsburg, 1970-76.
30. New York: Inter-Lutheran Commission on Worship, 1975.
31. Minneapolis: Augsburg, 1986.
32. St. Louis: Concordia, 1982.

of the synod's congregations use *Lutheran Book of Worship*. (For three Lutheran churches in the United States the LBW preceded and opened the way for organic union in 1988.) Further services appeared in *Occasional Services*.[33] Lutherans have been most deliberate in introducing new services to pastors in workshops and in significant publications such as *Manual on the Liturgy*[34] and *Commentary on the Occasional Services*.[35] One of the lessons of recent liturgical reform is that liturgical catechesis is almost as important as revision itself if new rites are to have intelligent use.

It was more difficult to involve United Methodists in liturgical revision, especially when the 1965 *Book of Worship* and the 1966 *Book of Hymns*[36] were still new. But by 1970, even those who had just been through eight years of labor on those volumes could be persuaded that a new era had dawned. The United Methodist services appeared in individual booklets, beginning with *The Sacrament of the Lord's Supper* in 1972.[37] The unexpected success of this service led to instituting the *Supplemental Worship Resources* series.[38] Successive volumes, usually with an introduction, commentary, and optional passages, appeared in the seventies and eighties. These included the initiation rites,[39] weddings,[40] funerals,[41] the lectionary,[42] and a collection of eucharistic prayers.[43] The five basic services were approved for trial use by the 1980 General Conference and were published in *We Gather Together*.[44] The same conference also approved *An Ordinal* "for Official Alternative Use."

Attention was also given to hymnody. Two collections of Hispanic music, *Celebremas* I and II, were published apart from the SWR

33. Minneapolis: Augsburg, 1982.

34. Philip H. Pfatteicher and Carlos R. Messerli (Minneapolis: Augsburg, 1979). Cf. Marilyn Stulken, *Hymnal Companion to the Lutheran Book of Worship* (Philadelphia: Fortress, 1981).

35. Philip H. Pfatteicher (Philadelphia: Fortress, 1983).

36. Nashville: Methodist Publishing House, 1966. (Originally published as *The Methodist Hymnal*.)

37. Nashville: Methodist Publishing House, 1972 (subsequently reissued); *El Sacramento de la Santa Cena: Un Texto Alterno, 1978; The Sacrament of the Lord's Supper: Revised Edition, 1981; A Service of Word and Table; Complete Text 1984 Edition*; and *Un Servicio de la Palabra y el Sacramento: Texto Completo Edición de 1984.*

38. 17 vols., Nashville: United Methodist Publishing House/Abingdon Press, 1972-88.

39. *A Service of Baptism, Confirmation, and Renewal* (Nashville: United Methodist Publishing House, 1976; rev. ed., 1980).

40. *A Service of Christian Marriage* (Nashville: Abingdon, 1979).

41. *A Service of Death and Resurrection* (Nashville: Abingdon, 1979).

42. *Seasons of the Gospel* (Nashville: Abingdon, 1979).

43. *At the Lord's Table* (Nashville, Abingdon, 1981).

44. Nashville: United Methodist Publishing House, 1980.

series.[45] A hymnal supplement appeared in 1982, preceded by a major collection of church music in the black tradition, *Songs of Zion,*[46] and followed by a collection of Asian-American hymnody, *Hymns from the Four Winds.*[47] Two volumes of services dealt with the Lent-Easter cycle and the Christmas-Epiphany cycle. Another provided services of *Blessings and Consecrations.*[48] A revised collection of eucharistic prayers was published in 1987.[49]

All these services have been provisional, many (such as the eucharist, 1972, 1980, and 1984) having gone through several generations of revision. The fruits of this process were harvested in 1985 with the publication of *The Book of Services,* the five basic services plus calendar, which are now part of the official "Ritual" and will likely comprise the worship section of the next hymnal, expected to be published in 1989. The hymnal will recover a fuller psalter, absent for fifty years.

All these services break with the previous strategy of simply revising within the Anglican-Methodist traditions, in favor of a much broader view of ancient and ecumenical Christianity. John Wesley's theology, however, does inform the Methodist works, offering a positive statement of the eucharist as sacrifice and emphasizing its pneumatological and eschatological aspects. Certainly Wesley, with his great respect for the *Apostolic Constitutions,* would have applauded the use of the much earlier *Apostolic Tradition* in framing eucharistic, baptismal, and ordination rites.

In the United Methodist Church, occupying the liturgical center, use of the new rites is not compulsory. The situation among Presbyterians is somewhat analogous, although in this case one must also take account of *The Directory for Worship,* revised for the United Presbyterian Church in the U.S.A. in 1961.[50] We have already noted the 1970 *Worshipbook* and its 1972 inclusion of a hymnal. The *Worshipbook* was not destined to have widespread use. It signaled the end of one era as much as the beginning of another.

In 1970, an Office of Worship and Music was created with a full-time staff. It is assisted by the Presbyterian Association of Musicians and the periodical *Reformed Liturgy and Music.* Until recently, Presbyterian liturgical scholars have been a rare breed. This, perhaps, accounts for the slowness of Presbyterians in entering the most recent period of liturgi-

45. Nashville: Discipleship Resources, 1979 and 1983.
46. Nashville: Abingdon, 1981.
47. Nashville: Abingdon, 1983.
48. Nashville: Abingdon, 1984.
49. *Holy Communion* (Nashville: Abingdon, 1987).
50. Philadelphia: Office of the General Assembly, 1962-63.

cal revision. However, these late arrivals have the advantage of profiting from the works and mistakes of others. In 1984, the first *Supplemental Liturgical Resource* appeared, namely, *The Service of the Lord's Day*,[51] followed in 1985 by *Holy Baptism and Services for the Renewal of Baptism*.[52] In 1986 volumes appeared on weddings and funerals, and one is soon expected on daily services.[53] Eventually, a new hymnal-service book may be produced in the 1990s.

The indebtedness of this latest series to the United Methodist services is obvious and is hardly surprising, since the Methodist volumes synthesize much study that is going on throughout western Christendom. Yet there are distinctive Reformed earmarks in the SLR series. In some of the eucharistic prayers, the words of institution follow the traditional pattern as part of the prayer; in others, they can be read separately as a warrant for the eucharistic action. The problems of inclusive language, surfacing too late for the 1970 *Worshipbook*, are faced clearly; language referring to humans and to God has been reconsidered, without abandoning the terms "Father," "Son," and "Lord."

The prospects are that with the completion of the Presbyterian services, the current period of liturgical revision will come to an end, perhaps for another generation to resume under different circumstances. Churches presently seem concerned with consolidation of the reforms already made.

IV. Some Results of Liturgical Revisions

Some important consequences are apparent in the revisions of the 1970s and 1980s. Clearly the most successful of the new liturgical books has been the lectionary. Published by Roman Catholics in 1969 for use beginning in the 1970 liturgical year, it was immediately picked up and revised by Presbyterians, Episcopalians, and Lutherans. In 1974, the Consultation on Church Union prepared a consensus (and fifth) version of the four versions then in use. This version was adopted, for a decade, by the United Methodist Church. The number of lectionaries was clearly a problem, even though the differences among them were minor. Ten years later, the Consultation on Common Texts published *Common Lectionary*.[54] Not only did it eliminate the discrepancies among

---

51. Philadelphia: Westminster, 1984.

52. Philadelphia: Westminster, 1985.

53. *Christian Marriage,* and *The Funeral: A Service of Witness to the Resurrection* (Philadelphia: Westminster, 1986).

54. New York: Church Hymnal Corporation, 1984.

the versions, but it also made a major advance by introducing a *lectio continua* pattern for the Old Testament lessons after the Day of Pentecost. It was immediately accepted by United Methodists and Presbyterians, and has been selectively used by Lutherans and Episcopalians. Appeals by the American hierarchy to Rome for its use among Roman Catholics have so far been unsuccessful.

The lectionary's greatest impact, of course, has been on preaching. It is now estimated that 65 percent of United Methodist clergy use the lectionary, an astonishing change from almost 0 percent ten years earlier. The consequences for preaching have been enormous, especially in encouraging a more exegetical approach. Commentaries based on the lectionary, such as Reginald Fuller's *Preaching the New Lectionary*[55] and the several series of *Proclamation* volumes,[56] have sold widely. It is significant that the lectionary includes an Old Testament lesson for each Sunday, except during the Easter season, and thereby incorporates thirty-eight books of the Bible (other than the psalter) whose use had been largely absent from Protestant worship in recent decades.

Anyone using the lectionary soon found that he or she had also entered into a much deeper engagement with the church year. Festivals such as the Baptism of Our Lord, Transfiguration, All Saints' Day, and Christ the King became integral parts of the annual cycle, and this development led to a greater number of special services such as Christmas Eve, Ash Wednesday, and Easter Vigil, which, although previously unobserved, are rapidly becoming part of the worship life of many congregations. These new occasions for preaching have led many preachers to a serious wrestling with problems of Christology. How, for example, does one successfully interpret the Transfiguration before one identifies all the approaches that do not work?

The lectionary has spread far to the liturgical left and is regularly used in some Southern Baptist seminaries. It has made unexpected inroads into the Church of the Nazarene, Church of the Brethren, and many others on the liturgical left. A grass-roots ecumenism has developed, with many priests and ministers doing exegesis and sermon preparation together. This highly successful ecumenical venture has been achieved without anyone organizing a national committee or setting up an office.

Another major development in recent years has been the charismatic movement. Originating early in this century among the culturally dispossessed, it sprang up among Roman Catholic college students in

---

55. Collegeville, MN: Liturgical Press, 1974; rev. ed., 1984.
56. Published by Fortress Press (Philadelphia).

the 1960s and thus broke into the mainline denominations. After initial panic on the part of many denominations, it has been accepted and even welcomed by Roman Catholic and Protestant leaders, with the possible exception of Missouri Synod Lutherans and Southern Baptists. Charismatics and noncharismatics have learned to live together in many congregations to their mutual enrichment.

Another development, more difficult to document but equally important, is the gradual move to greater sacramental life among many Protestants. Some of the steps Episcopalians have taken since the 1940s are now being taken by other Protestants, although without the same controversies over ceremonial. Some churches (except for those already having it weekly, such as Disciples of Christ or Church of Christ) are slowly moving from quarterly to monthly communion, and are then adding the great festivals. Some are also moving to the new weekly communion. United Methodist and Presbyterian service materials certainly encourage such moves.

The basis of the new sacramental life is a recognition of humanity's need for visible signs whereby to relate to other humans and, ultimately, to God. A new anthropology studies the importance of sign-acts, and raises questions about the sign-value of what we do together in worship. As a result much more attention is now being given to the quality of celebration. How can the acts of washing and eating attain their highest sign-values in baptism and the eucharist? This new sacramental emphasis has very important consequences for the conduct of worship, to say nothing of its architectural setting. This emphasis has been closely tied to preaching, and the unity of word and sacrament has been newly stressed.

Certainly one reason for increased use of the lectionary and for greater concern for the sacramental life is the new attention in many seminaries to the teaching of worship. Institutions such as Drew University, the University of Notre Dame, and the Graduate Theological Union in Berkeley have produced academically trained Ph.D. graduates in liturgical studies. Their teaching and scholarship have had significant impact on the formation of seminarians and on the church as a whole. Denominational worship staffs, largely a new phenomenon of the 1970s, have done much through workshops and publications to advance in more thorough and systematic fashion many of the changes already in progress.

It is difficult, of course, to determine the degree of change in many of the churches on the liturgical left. How much has Southern Baptist worship changed in the last fifty years? No one, it seems, knows. Probably the quality of music has improved. Certainly the newest

Southern Baptist hymnal gives reason to believe that this is the case. Some congregations have adopted the lectionary; most have not. A few have decided not to rebaptize those persons baptized as infants in other denominations. Quite a few baptize preschool children on occasion, and even more perform some kind of infant dedication. It is not unreasonable to suppose that many of the liturgical revisions that increasingly appeal to United Methodists and Presbyterians will also prove attractive to Southern Baptists.

At any rate, it seems safe to argue that much of what has happened in Protestant worship in recent years has been centripetal. The seven traditions, once so diverse, have heaped their riches into a common coffer. Without their covers, it would be difficult to identify the tradition of many service books by their contents alone. On the theological level, much of this coalescence was heralded in the World Council of Churches 1982 document, *Baptism, Eucharist and Ministry*.[57] That document reflects many of the new realities of worship that have been worked out, and lived with, in the Protestant churches of America during the past half-century.

57. Geneva: World Council of Churches, 1982.

7. Women and the Churches

Barbara Brown Zikmund

"One doesn't swear around women and preachers." This little piece of American folk wisdom contains an interesting message. It reflects the assumption that women and the churches play a civilizing and moralizing role in society. It also emphasizes the fact that the history of women and the history of religion in North America go together. Because women have been deeply involved in church work and because churches have both abused and blessed the gifts of women, any history of twentieth-century religion must examine the relationship of women and the churches. During the last fifty years, how have women influenced and been influenced by the church?

No one will deny that this has been a period of rapid and disruptive change, especially for women. The list of social, political, medical, economic, and ecclesiastical changes that have directly affected women seems almost endless. Nevertheless, it is possible to organize the material by examining five questions asked by women themselves as they have lived out their faith in the twentieth century: (1) How can we serve the church? (2) How do we live Christian lives? (3) Who are we as women? (4) What needs to be changed in the church? (5) Why bother with the church anyway?

Before exploring the various ways in which twentieth-century women have wrestled with these questions, one must put things i context. The 1920s was a decade of seeming emancipation for women. In 1920 the suffrage amendment was finally ratified and women could vote. Many people believed that society would now improve. The final push for women's suffrage argued that voting women would protect the home, voting women would preserve American values, voting women would support progressive reforms.

At the beginning of the suffrage campaign, the argument had been quite different. Giving the vote to women was seen as a matter of justice. If all persons were created equal, women had a "right" to vote. Equality was God-given. Equality was the foundation of American democracy. By the early twentieth century, however, the suffrage argument had shifted from one of justice to one of expediency. Instead of focusing upon basic rights and the similarities between men and women, advocates emphasized the differences between the sexes. Because of these differences, if women had the vote, society would benefit from the civilizing influence of women.

Once women could vote, therefore, they needed to determine how they would use it. At one extreme, radical feminists lobbied for individual freedoms and pressed for equality. At the other, church women looked for new ways to bring a special woman's touch to the organizational structures of life.[1] Within the churches this quest took an interesting twist. During the 1920s several denominations carried out reorganizations of their mission boards. For many years Presbyterian and Congregational women supported independent women's boards of missions, which had been founded to support unique women's ministries in the late nineteenth century. Now, in the 1920s, these boards lost their autonomy and were absorbed into denominational mission structures. It was an ironic development. Church women argued that women brought special gifts to the church, yet they cooperated in reorganization schemes that ultimately diluted their capacity to make special contributions to the church's mission.[2]

I. How Can We Serve?

It is not surprising, therefore, that one of the basic questions asked by women in the churches in the twentieth century has been, "How can we serve?"

---

1. Aileen Kraditor, ed., *Up From the Pedestal: Selected Writings in the History of American Feminism* (Chicago: Quadrangle, 1968), pp. 110-31.

2. Barbara J. MacHaffie, *Her Story: Women in Christian Tradition* (Philadelphia: Fortress, 1986), pp. 131-32. See Elizabeth Howell Verdesi, *In But Still Out: Women in the Church* (Philadelphia: Westminster, 1976) and Lois A. Boyd and R. Douglas Brackenridge, *Presbyterian Women in America: Two Centuries of a Quest for Status* (Westport, CT: Greenwood, 1983) for the story of Presbyterian women's boards. See also Priscilla Stuckey-Kauffman, "For the Sake of Unity: The Absorption of Congregational Women's Boards of Foreign Missions by the American Board, 1927, with Special Attention to the Women's Board of Missions for the Pacific" (M.A. thesis, Pacific School of Religion, 1985).

As more and more women moved into higher education, often in church-related schools, they searched for appropriate ways to serve the church. Roman Catholic women entered religious orders in great numbers, staffing important educational and health-related ministries.[3] Protestant women moved into more demanding volunteer positions in local church life. A few women took training as religious educators and created a new "profession" for women in the church, the "Director of Religious Education" (DRE).[4] Still others sought theological education and the full responsibilities of ordained clergy.[5]

Basically, however, fifty years ago when Christian women considered how they could serve the church, they were passive. Most women took for granted that they would spend the greater part of their lives as wives and mothers. To raise a family and to keep a Christian home was sufficient. Participation in church activities was part of that picture. Although black women and lower-class white women had more economic responsibilities beyond the home than did white middle-class women, volunteering at church remained the predominant expression of "women's work" at church during the first half of the twentieth century.

Some of the more liberal free church denominations (Congregationalists, Disciples, Northern Baptists, and Unitarians) had ordained women since the late nineteenth century.[6] Many women participated in the world evangelism movement, so that by 1929 women missionaries outnumbered men by two to one.[7] Deaconess orders gave women special opportunities for service at home.[8] During the 1920s and 1930s Methodists, Presbyterians, and Lutherans engaged in lengthy debates about the proper leadership roles of women in the churches, finally es-

---

3. See Lorine M. Getz, "Women Struggle for an American Catholic Identity," in Rosemary Radford Ruether and Rosemary Skinner Keller, eds., *Women and Religion in America 1900-1968: A Documentary History*, vol. 3 (San Francisco: Harper and Row, 1986), pp. 176-222. Also Mary Ewens, "Removing the Veil: The Liberated American Nun," in Rosemary Radford Ruether and Eleanor McLaughlin, eds., *Women of Spirit: Female Leadership in the Jewish and Christian Traditions* (New York: Simon and Schuster, 1979), pp. 256-78, and *The Role of the Nun in Nineteenth-Century America* (New York: Arno, 1978).

4. Dorothy Jean Furnish, "Women in Religious Education: Pioneers for Women in Professional Ministry," in Ruether and Keller, *Women and Religion in America*, vol. 3, pp. 310-38.

5. Barbara Brown Zikmund, "Winning Ordination for Women in Mainstream Protestant Churches," in Ruether and Keller, *Women and Religion in America*, vol. 3, pp. 339-83.

6. Barbara Brown Zikmund, "The Struggle for the Right to Preach," in Ruether and Keller, *Women and Religion in America*, vol. 1, pp. 193-241.

7. MacHaffie, p. 131.

8. One attempt to reevaluate the deaconess role is Elizabeth Meredith Lee, *As Among the Methodists: Deaconesses Yesterday, Today, and Tomorrow* (New York: The Methodist Church, 1963).

tablishing new specialized ministries designed especially with women in mind (Commissioned Church Worker, Certified Church Educator, Certified Lay Professional).[9] These lay ministries gave Christian women new alternatives to marriage, or at least appropriate ways to spend the premarriage years.

Yet during the Depression there was great societal pressure on women not to take jobs away from men with families. Although expanded education gave women new skills and aspirations, social custom continued to limit their opportunities. Between 1910 and 1940 the percentage of single career women declined. Women usually felt that they had to make a choice between career and marriage/family. Despite the suffrage amendment most Americans believed that the family, not the individual, was the basic unit of society, and anything that might jeopardize the family's future was questionable.[10]

II. How Do We Live?

This observation leads to a second question relative to the story of women and the church over the past fifty years: "How do we live our lives?"

Throughout American history the labor of women has been indirectly recognized. The old saying, "behind every great man is a woman," has not been taken lightly. During the twentieth century, however, women have struggled increasingly with the growing tension between home and workplace. Because the church has been historically linked to the family, women's relationship to the church has been part of this tension.

During the Depression years married women were discouraged from taking jobs outside the home, although the 1930s did produce a number of able single career women. With the beginning of the Second World War, however, everything changed. Suddenly, women were begged to take jobs. In order to serve God, family, and country, women were needed in the workplace. The old assumption that a Christian woman should choose between work/career and home was compromised.

Out of that experience many women came to value their independence and economic power. Even though church and society continued to insist that the homemaker role was primary and should not be jeopar-

9. MacHaffie, p. 134.
10. William Henry Chafe, *The American Woman: Her Changing Social, Economic, and Political Roles, 1920-1970* (New York: Oxford University Press, 1972), p. 10.

dized, women rationalized that they could do it all. Many middle-class white women stayed on the job after the war to provide "extra money" to help families buy a house or send kids to school. Lower-class and minority women worked as they always had. As a result, the number of women employed outside the home rose steadily from 1940 to 1960.[11]

Mainline Protestant churches and suburbanizing Roman Catholic parishes, however, tended to ignore these developments. While the postwar baby boom emphasized family values, women lived increasingly complex lives. The growth of suburbia made it more difficult for commuting husbands to be deeply involved at home or at church, so women adjusted. The 1950s were years of family life and church growth. For many women they were years of trying to find the right balance between home and work and church.

Social historians note that after 1945 women did not want to go back to prewar ways but that they also refused to let go of the homemaker ideal. They made great efforts to find new meaning in the traditional roles of wife and mother. Homemaking was glorified. Some working women rationalized that they did not have careers outside the home, only jobs. Others simply added new responsibilities and kept going. As a recent study of church women put it:

> . . . many of these women have new roles and they have kept the old roles as well. Rather than changing roles, they are assuming more roles and responsibilities. They are homemakers, wives, mothers, volunteers, and breadwinners. They do not want to let anybody down. If they drop some of their church activities, ask a neighbor to take over the car pool, or ask their husbands to make the next trip to the orthodontist, they feel guilty. They feel that they should do it all. And so when the stress begins to build up, they just try harder, do not complain, and cling to some satisfaction in being needed everywhere—at home, church and work.[12]

The churches were not totally insensitive to this situation. As the World Council of Churches took shape in 1948, a "Commission on the Life and Work of Women in the Church" launched a worldwide study of women's place in the church. The study noted that American churches channeled women's ministries through "separate women's lay organizations." In developing these independent organizations, American women were criticized for "becoming a church within a church" and also for being "theologically illiterate."[13]

11. Ibid., pp. 175-95.
12. Nancy J. van Scoyoc, *Women, Change, and the Church* (Nashville: Abingdon, 1980), p. 36.
13. An American study sponsored by a Counseling Committee of Women representing National Interdenominational Agencies was published for the Federal Council

During these years most American churches remained largely insensitive to women's plight. Conservative evangelicals emphasized that the husband should be the head of the family. Liberals reminded each other that they had probably expected too much of suffrage. As June Sochen said, "The Christian view of ultimate imperfection could become a respectable reason for sensitive people to avoid doing anything about real human problems."[14] Women had what Betty Friedan came to call "the problem with no name."[15]

For the twenty-five years from 1935 to 1960 the general pattern of women's relationship to American church life remained basically unchanged. A few people challenged ecclesiastical systems to give women more direct leadership opportunities in the churches. Catholic religious orders and Protestant women's organizations expanded their support for traditional expressions of church work for women. But, until the early 1960s, most churches failed to help women understand their situation or to embrace a new vision for their lives.

III. Who Are We?

A third question, therefore, began to gnaw at the consciousness of church women: "Who are we as women in the contemporary church and society?" Although this is ultimately a very theological question, women refused to let the question become too theoretical.

In the 1960s three developments set the stage for a new wave of feminism that slowly found its way into American churches. First, the increased ecumenical and cross-cultural activity of many American churches allowed women to compare themselves to women in other religious and cultural traditions. As so-called "younger churches" moved to give women more direct and valued roles in the church, American women felt their own limitations more keenly.[16]

Second, in 1963 the report of the President's Commission on Women revealed new facts about how women were actually living their lives and challenged some of the assumptions about women common

---

of Churches. See Inez M. Cavert, *Women in American Church Life* (New York: Friendship, 1948). The international report appeared as Kathleen Bliss, *The Service and Status of Women in the Churches* (London: SCM, 1952). The quotation comes from a reprint of a *Christian Century* editorial that appeared in *The Woman's Pulpit* 30 (July-December 1952) 2.

14. *Movers and Shakers: American Women Thinkers and Activists, 1900-1970* (New York: Quadrangle, 1973), p. 224.

15. *The Feminine Mystique* (New York: Norton, 1963).

16. Many of the "united churches" founded in the earlier twentieth century did ordain women. See *The Woman's Pulpit* 25 (October-December 1947) 8.

in the churches. When this new knowledge merged with the energy of the civil rights movement, women sought change.[17] The publication of *The Feminine Mystique* in 1963 gave popular visibility to women's concerns.

Third, the Second Vatican Council broadened traditional understandings of the church to give enhanced value to the laity. This eventually led Roman Catholic women to raise the question of women's ordination and to reshape the life and practice of women's religious orders.

The question of identity, or Christian vocation, stood at the heart of the new feminism. Women did not want to determine simply how to serve, to adjust, or even to measure up to the expectations of church, family, and society; they wanted freedom to be faithful to their Christian calling and to find fulfillment as led by the Spirit. This feminist vocational search often began with small groups of women exploring their own experiences, in what came to be known as consciousness-raising groups. In some denominations these meetings led to resolutions, task forces, special studies, and feminist resources. New groups or caucuses developed alongside traditional women's fellowships and altar guilds. Many church women became impatient with the unexamined patriarchal habits of the church.[18]

In 1964 a growing political consciousness led to the formation of the National Organization for Women (NOW). Four years later the NOW Task Force on Women and Religion passed a resolution urging that ecumenical enthusiasm for church unity not be "used as an excuse for not eliminating discrimination against women."[19] In fact, an increase in what Martin Marty has called "female submission theology" proved to be a much greater barrier in later efforts to eliminate sexism. In 1972, after many years of effort, Congress passed the Equal Rights Amendment (ERA). Seven years later, however, despite the efforts of many progressive church women, it still did not have the required number of state ratifications. By 1978 conservative churches, like the Southern Baptists and the Mormons, mobilized to stop the ERA. Even with an extension of the deadline, the ERA died.[20]

Within some churches, however, there were changes. A small number of Protestant denominations had ordained women in the

17. President's Commission, *The American Woman* (Washington, D.C.: U.S. Government, 1963).

18. MacHaffie, pp. 135-36.

19. *The Woman's Pulpit* 46 (April-June 1968) 2.

20. A good case study of the Mormon campaign against the Equal Rights Amendment is Sonia Johnson, *From Housewife to Heretic: One Woman's Struggle for Equal Rights and Her Excommunication from the Mormon Church* (Garden City: Doubleday, 1983).

nineteenth century, but by the 1960s there were still very few women clergy.[21] Holiness and Pentecostal groups, which originally had encouraged women's leadership, became more conservative.[22] By the 1930s the Methodists and Presbyterians had established new forms of female lay leadership and specialized ministries, but they still refused to give women equal status as clergy. Finally, during the period of church growth in the 1950s, Methodist and Presbyterian women were granted full clergy rights. Women ministers could fill empty pulpits and work as associates in larger urban churches.[23]

After 1960 those denominations which still did not ordain women felt new pressures. Lutherans with roots in Scandinavia were influenced by the liberalizing actions of their European cousins. The Lutheran Church in America ordained its first woman in 1970. By contrast, the conservative Missouri Synod still refused even to grant women equal lay rights.[24] Episcopalians remained bitterly divided on the issue into the 1970s, although the 1968 Lambeth Conference of Anglican bishops agreed that "there were no theological barriers to women priests." Finally, in 1974, a few sympathetic bishops proceeded with eleven irregular ordinations. Two years later the national governing bodies officially admitted women to the priesthood, provided a bishop was supportive.[25]

Out of all this ferment about ordination new ecumenical and ecclesiastical tensions developed. Women in the Orthodox churches insisted that their role in the church did not call for ordination.[26] Other churches hesitated to ordain women lest they jeopardize future ecu-

---

21. See Jackson W. Carroll, Barbara Hargrove, and Adair T. Lummis, *Women of the Cloth: A New Opportunity for the Churches* (San Francisco: Harper and Row, 1981) and Edward C. Lehman, Jr., *Women Clergy: Breaking through Gender Barriers* (New Brunswick, NJ: Transaction Books, 1985).

22. This is the conclusion of Letha Dawson Scanzoni and Susan Setta, "Women in Evangelical, Holiness, and Pentecostal Traditions," in Ruether and Keller, *Women and Religion in America,* vol. 3, pp. 223-65.

23. See Carroll, et. al., *Women of the Cloth,* Chapter 2. A more recent study of the Methodist situation is Harry Hale, Jr., Morton King, and Doris Moreland Jones, *New Witnesses: United Methodist Clergywomen* (Nashville: UMC Division of Ordained Ministry, Board of Higher Education and Ministry, 1980).

24. See Marjorie Garhart, "Women in the Ordained Ministry," Report to the Division for Professional Church Leadership, Lutheran Church in America, 1976; and Raymond Tiemeyer, *The Ordination of Women: A Report Based on Materials Produced through the Division of Theological Studies of the Lutheran Council in the U.S.A.* (Minneapolis: Augsburg, 1970).

25. See Emily C. Hewitt and Suzanne R. Hiatt, *Women Priests: Yes or No?* (New York: Seabury, 1973). For the period since women were ordained, see John H. Morgan, *Women Priests: An Emerging Ministry in the Episcopal Church 1975-1985* (Bristol, IN: Wyndham Hall, 1985).

26. See *Orthodox Women: Their Role and Participation in the Orthodox Church,* a re-

menical cooperation and mutuality or betray their loyalty to the Bible.[27] Catholic women continued to challenge the Vatican, which became more entrenched in its opposition to women priests.[28]

However, the pressures for change also brought some women together. By the 1970s female enrollments in theological seminaries began to rise significantly.[29] In 1975 1,200 people gathered in Detroit for an Ordination Conference to "call for action" within the Roman Catholic church.[30] Also in 1975 two evangelical Protestant women published a best-selling book on Christian feminism entitled *All We're Meant To Be*.[31] The World Council of Churches sponsored a consultation on sexism in Berlin (1974), and the United Nations declared 1975 "International Women's Year." Jewish and Christian women shared new scholarship on biblical authority. By the early 1980s global questions concerning women's economic, social, and religious situation were being examined by many international organizations, culminating with meetings in Strasbourg, France, and Sheffield, England, sponsored by the Commission on Faith and Order of the World Council of Churches, and in Nairobi, Kenya, to commemorate the end of the United Nations Decade on Women.[32]

---

port on the Consultation of Orthodox Women, September 11-17, 1976, Agapia, Romania (Geneva: World Council of Churches, 1977). See also an American Orthodox response to the World Council of Churches study on the Community of Women and Men in the Church, namely, Ecumenical Task Force of the Orthodox Church in America, *Women and Men in the Church: A Study of the Community of Women and Men in the Church* (Syosset, NY: Department of Religious Education, Orthodox Church in America, 1980).

27. *Baptism, Eucharist and Ministry,* Faith and Order Paper 111 (Geneva: World Council of Churches, 1982), highlights this concern. In 1984 the Southern Baptist Convention formally condemned the ordination of women. Cf. *New York Times,* June 15, 1984, p. 7.

28. See *Declaration on the Question of the Admission of Women to the Ministerial Priesthood,* published by the Sacred Congregation for the Doctrine of the Faith, 1976. Responses to this declaration are found in Leonard and Arlene Swidler, eds., *Women Priests: A Catholic Commentary on the Vatican Declaration* (New York: Harper and Row, 1977) and Carroll Stuhlmueller, ed., *Women and Priesthood: Future Directions* (Collegeville, MN: Liturgical Press, 1978).

29. William Baumgaertner, ed., ATS Fact Book on Theological Education 1985-86 (Vandalia, OH: Association of Theological Schools in the United States and Canada, 1986).

30. Anne Marie Gardiner, ed., *Women and Catholic Priesthood: An Expanded Vision—Proceedings of the Detroit Ordination Conference* (New York: Paulist, 1976).

31. Nancy Hardesty and Letha Scanzoni, *All We're Meant To Be* (Waco, TX: Word Books, 1975).

32. See two reports edited by Constance F. Parvey, *Ordination of Women in Ecumenical Perspective,* Faith and Order Paper 105 (Geneva: World Council of Churches, 1980) and *The Community of Women and Men in the Church: The Sheffield Report* (Philadelphia: Fortress, 1983).

IV. What Needs to Be Changed?

As women discovered new things about themselves and pursued the logic of discipleship within the Christian community, they also began to think differently about ministry and theology. They found themselves asking, "What needs to be changed in the church?"

Obviously, the push for ordination remained fundamental to many Christian feminists. As long as women were considered unfit for professional church leadership, many Christian women were deeply troubled. Although in recent years certain American denominations seem to be attracting more women than men to the ordained ministry, only about 5 percent of the world's clergy are women. Change, however, needed to be conceptual as well as organizational. For this reason, in the 1970s and 1980s, women began to rethink Christian theology. They did not simply contend that a few ecclesiastical laws required change; they called for changes in the basic understanding of the faith. These changes fell into three areas: understandings of authority, attitudes about the body, and a concern for language.

It is interesting that even while many feminists were calling for the ordination of women, other feminists were questioning the theological validity of ordination itself. Why does the church, the people of God, the priesthood of all believers, need ordination? If all are one in Christ, sacramental gifts rest upon every believer. In these discussions women examined assumptions about the permanence of ordination and the hierarchical implications of holy orders. Some feminists refused to wear vestments, to use titles, and even to seek ordination itself.[33]

Historically, women in the church have always looked to the authority of the Holy Spirit in their ministries because the authority of Scripture and tradition tended to limit their freedom. Consequently, it has been natural for contemporary women scholars to approach the authority of Scripture more contextually. Women asked, "How is my experience of the Gospel reflected in this particular Bible passage?" Many women have become convinced that the authority of "woman church" (that is, the experience of early Christian women) provides a new norm for biblical interpretation.[34]

33. See Norene Carter and Rosemary Radford Ruether, "Entering the Sanctuary: The Struggle for Priesthood in Contemporary Episcopalian and Roman Catholic Experience," in Ruether and McLaughlin, *Women of Spirit,* pp. 356-83; and Paul Jewett, *The Ordination of Women* (Grand Rapids: Eerdmans, 1980).

34. The works of Elisabeth Schüssler Fiorenza are most significant here. See her "Feminist Theology as a Critical Theology of Liberation," *Theological Studies* 36 (December 1975) 605-26, and *In Memory of Her: A Feminist Theological Reconstruction of Christian Origins* (New York: Crossroad, 1983).

These new understandings of authority began to be expressed by seminary women and to be reflected in the ministerial style of women clergy. Women in theological education wanted something other than an authoritarian educational model where the expert poured selected information into submissive pupils. They believed that good education was collaborative rather than competitive.[35] Women clergy tended to emphasize that a good pastor works among the laity as part of a ministry shared by the whole church. As one observer wrote, "women are more inclined to use the circle or rainbow as a model for ministry rather than the pyramid."[36]

A second area where women have argued that the church needs to reconceptualize its faith involves the relationship between body and spirit. For many years Christianity has perpetuated a hierarchical dualism, suggesting that the physical realities of life are less important than the spiritual. Perhaps because women have been more vulnerable due to their weaker bodies and their sexuality, Christian feminism has rebelled against such dualism. Women remind theologians that the central event of the Christian faith is the Incarnation, when God became flesh. To deny the importance and goodness of the "carnal" distorts Christianity.

Many of the major issues of the women's movement in the last twenty-five years have been body issues: birth control, rape, abortion, wife and child abuse, pornography, and homosexuality. These are topics that Christian theology has only begun to take seriously. Even the rising concern over ecology may be interpreted as a body issue, calling society to live within the physical realities of the earth's limited resources, rather than acting as if these realities are irrelevant.[37] Dealing with these body issues has been theologically demanding. Church women are bitterly divided. Most agree, however, that these issues cannot be ignored.

Third, women are concerned about language and symbols. Any

35. See the Cornwall Collective, *Your Daughters Shall Prophesy: Feminist Alternatives in Theological Education* (New York: Pilgrim, 1980).

36. MacHaffie, p. 142.

37. There are many books and articles on body issues. The writings of Beverly Wildung Harrison are especially useful. See her essay "Human Sexuality and Mutuality," in Judith L. Weidman, ed., *Christian Feminism: Visions of a New Humanity* (San Francisco: Harper and Row, 1984), pp. 141-57; *Our Right to Choose: Toward a New Ethic of Abortion* (Boston: Beacon, 1983); and *Making the Connections: Essays in Feminist Social Ethics*, ed. Carol W. Robb (Boston: Beacon, 1985). The writings of Elizabeth Dodson Gray, *Why the Green Nigger?: Re-Mything Genesis* (Wellesley, MA: Roundtable, 1979) and *Patriarchy is a Conceptual Trap* (Wellesley, MA: Roundtable, 1982), point out the relationship between this dualism and ecology. See also Susan Griffin, *Women and Nature: The Roaring Inside Her* (New York: Harper and Row, 1978).

time Christians do theology they are attempting an arduous, perhaps impossible task: they try to capture in words the transcendent realities of a living faith. For this reason, metaphor, art, music, and movement have long been used in Christian worship.[38]

Jews and Christians take language especially seriously, claiming that the Scriptures are "Word of God." They choose words carefully to develop theology. They build dogma on creedal statements made of carefully selected words. Over the last fifteen years women in the church have been extremely sensitive to the power of language. First, women realized that when the words "man" and "mankind" were used in reference to both men and women, women became invisible. Although language experts insisted that women were included in such generic words, in reality they were not. Psychological studies on language confirmed that people considered human and male attributes equivalent, whereas women and feminine characteristics remained secondary. So, if in Christ there is neither male nor female, the use of generic male language in the church was counterproductive.

Furthermore, women began to argue that the faith development of young girls was being distorted by the male bias of the language. Certain versions of the Bible exacerbated the problem by translating gender-neutral Hebrew and Greek words into sex-specific English. This was the case not only with language about human beings but also with language about God. Even though theologians recognized that God is beyond human gender, women noted that the language habits of the church presumed that God is male. Some women called this idolatry, because it literally made God in the image of men. They argued that it was time to move beyond God the "father."[39]

The inclusive language issue remains one of the most fundamental and troublesome concerns of women in the churches. In the early 1980s the National Council of Churches sponsored the development of *An Inclusive Language Lectionary*,[40] providing new translations of lectionary texts that are sensitive to the ways in which sexism, racism, and mil-

---

38. One of the earliest books to examine the importance of language in worship was Sharon and Tom Neufer Emswiler, *Women and Worship: A Guide to Non-Sexist Hymns, Prayers, and Liturgies* (New York: Harper and Row, 1974). See also Sallie McFague, *Metaphorical Theology: Models of God in Religious Language* (Philadelphia: Fortress, 1982).

39. The writings of Nelle Morton are important. Her essays published over several decades have been collected in *The Journey Is Home* (Boston: Beacon, 1985). Two recent responses to the language issue are Marjorie Suchocki, "The Unmale God," *Quarterly Review* 3 (Spring 1983) 34-49; and Diane Tennis, "The Loss of the Father God: Why Women Rage and Grieve," *Christianity and Crisis,* June 8, 1981, pp. 164-70.

40. *An Inclusive Language Lectionary: Readings for Year A, B, and C,* published for the National Council of Churches of Christ in the U.S.A. (Atlanta: John Knox; New York: Pilgrim; and Philadelphia: Westminster, 1983, 1984, 1985).

itarism distort biblical meaning. However, the old familiar words have been difficult to give up and adequate substitutes are not always available. New theological problems regarding the Trinity and Christology emerge when the old language is changed.

Church women do not all agree about the importance of inclusive language. Many have felt that the language issue has been overblown. Others, however, continue to believe that the words used to state the faith are never just a matter of taste, but should reflect the liberation promised in the Gospel.

V. Why Bother?

In all this ferment about the place of women in the churches and the attendant push to rethink issues of authority, the body, and language, many women (and men) have felt that it was not worth the effort. They have asked the ultimate question, "Why bother with the church anyway?"

In any reform movement there are always persons who become disenchanted or impatient. They generally forsake the critique and move on to other things. With women and the churches, however, this has not happened. Today there are serious feminists who continue to ask many of the same questions that women in the churches are asking. These feminists, however, consider themselves "post-Christian." They have little love for the church and refuse to worry about it. Instead, they seek to recover the religious insights of ancient goddess religions and to celebrate the sacrality of women. They believe that the patriarchal bias of Christianity is so deep and entrenched that the church cannot be redeemed.[41]

Christian feminists refuse to give up on the liberating power of the Scriptures and the promise of the church. They seek new ways to understand the normative authority of the Bible and to use interpretive principles to liberate God's word in Scripture and the church, believing that God has promised liberation to all creation. They find that when

41. The most well known post-Christian feminist is Mary Daly. Since the publication of her first book, *The Church and the Second Sex* (New York: Harper and Row, 1968), she has moved into a self-consciously post-Christian philosophy. See *Beyond God the Father: Toward a Philosophy of Women's Liberation* (Boston: Beacon, 1973); *Gyn/Ecology: The Metaethics of Radical Feminism* (Boston: Beacon, 1978); and *Pure Lust: Elemental Feminist Philosophy* (Boston: Beacon, 1979). See also Naomi B. Goldenberg, *Changing the Gods: Feminism and the End of Traditional Religions* (Boston: Beacon, 1979).

women's experience informs the interpretive task it is possible to discover new theologies and leave behind old oppressions.

Christian feminists and post-Christian feminists share common goals. They name the same oppressions and search for faithfulness in community. Both groups believe that only when the patriarchal repression of women and women's religious experience is replaced with faith and practice affirming a healthy relationship to the holy can the human religious spirit be free. They differ only because some of them still believe that the church is worth the bother.[42]

VI. Whither Women and the Churches?

Throughout American religious history the churches have depended upon women, and women have loved and lived for the church. It is possible to argue that women's contributions have uniquely shaped American churches.[43]

Between 1935 and 1985 women have tried to determine how to serve the church, how to live their lives, what it means to be a woman, what needs to be changed in the church, and why it is important. During this period women have drawn closer to the churches and, at the same time, have found new freedom from the churches.

Today American women are more directly involved in the governance and ministries of the churches than they were fifty years ago. Rising female seminary enrollments and the increasing acceptance of women clergy indicate that this trend will continue. Even where ordination is still denied, women are actively engaged in church leadership. Furthermore, women are also challenging some of the long-standing assumptions and practices of church life. Their participation will lead to transformation.

Some people fear that the church and its leadership will be devalued when women dominate the ministry, just as teaching and secretarial work lost stature when they became "women's jobs."[44] In the global context, however, the male hegemony in the church is far from over. Perhaps it will be possible for the church to benefit more equally from male and female clergy in the years ahead.

42. A recent collection of Christian feminist essays is Letty M. Russell, ed., *Feminist Interpretation of the Bible* (Philadelphia: Westminster, 1985).

43. Barbara Brown Zikmund, "The Contributions of Women to North American Church Life," *Mid-Stream* 22 (July-October 1983) 363-77.

44. This possibility was pointed out by Letty M. Russell, "Clerical Ministry as a Female Profession," *Christian Century* 96 (February 1979) 125.

At the same time that we note the greater visibility of women in professional ministries, it is important to recognize the ways in which women's lives are less involved with churches than they were fifty years ago. New life-styles, economic independence, time limitations, and value judgments have caused many women to leave the church, while the individualism of contemporary religion means that even women who consider themselves religious will not invariably look to the church for support.

As a historian of American religious institutions I am troubled by some of these trends, but I am also optimistic that the gifts of women will bring some new vitality into tired institutions.

8. A Half-Century of Jewish-Christian Relations

Gordon Tucker

St. Augustine, in the fifth century, wrote of the Jews that

> . . . they do not listen to what we say because they do not understand what they read. Certainly, if they understood what the Prophet, whom they read, is foretelling [here Isaiah 49:6 is quoted], they would not be so blind and so sick as not to recognize in Jesus Christ both light and salvation. Likewise, if they understood to whom the prophecy refers which they sing so fruitlessly and without meaning [here Psalm 18:5 is quoted], they would awaken to the voice of the Apostles, and would sense that their words are divine.[1]

In other words, to use another famous phrase, the Jews are like asses, carrying the Old Testament prophecies as if they were merely a burden, not understanding fully their significance. In an oddly similar vein, Moses Maimonides wrote in the twelfth century that Christians play an important role in God's messianic plans by enabling the Gentiles to embrace monotheism and thus to move a step closer to the future salvation.[2] Both of these statements, especially the Augustinian one, typify much of even the best of Jewish-Christian relations until very recently.

---

1. St. Augustine, *Adversus Judaeos*, 1:2, in *The Fathers of the* Church (New York: Fathers of the Church, Inc., 1955), vol. 27, p. 392 (translation by Sister Marie Liguori).

2. Moses Maimonides, *Mishneh Torah*, "The Book of Judges," Laws Concerning Kings, 11:4. The text referred to here appears only in early editions and manuscripts of the *Mishneh Torah*. See Abraham Hershman, ed., *The Code of Maimonides*, Book Fourteen ("The Book of Judges") (New Haven: Yale University Press, 1949), pp. xxii-xxiv.

I. Christian Views of Judaism: Established Patterns

Christian views of Judaism are of particular interest owing to the political and social domination that Christians exercised over Jews and Jewish communities for centuries in land after land. And even when those views conceded any legitimacy to Judaism, they did so for entirely instrumental reasons. That is, Judaism's legitimacy was construed as a background to Christianity, as a channel through which the idea of God and his Messiah could be developed sufficiently to allow a small first-century community to recognize the Son of God on earth. The heroic personalities of the Hebrew Bible, and all the laws, poetry, and narratives contained in it, were important because the community that told those stories, lived by those laws, and fought those wars, kept the religion of ancient Israel alive in a hostile world and thus enabled the Christ to change the nature of Israel and project it outward.

In other words, even in the most positive of Christian attitudes toward Judaism, only the perils and ultimate successes described in, for example, I and II Maccabees were considered significant, while Jewish perils and (rare) successes in the Christian era were of little note. Had Judah and his brothers failed, there might not have been a Jewish community to recognize the messianic prophesies that Jesus came to fulfill. On the other hand, had the Jewish community not produced great statesmen, physicians, poets, linguists, and liturgists in tenth- to twelfth-century Iberia, the divine economy, for Christians, would presumably have been unaffected. It is quite clear that this basic attitude led to a near-total disinterest in Jewish affairs and history beyond the Crucifixion (or, at the latest, the destruction of Jerusalem in 70 C.E.). And this, it must be repeated, represented the best of Christian attitudes toward Judaism. For many Christians throughout the ages the Hebrew biblical literature was of no moment at all or was even a negative influence on the true faith, since history had begun *de novo* (as the Julian and Gregorian calendars reflect) with the coming of Jesus.

Christian-Jewish relations remained in these established patterns for nearly two millennia. The conventional modes of thought manifested themselves in obvious but significant ways. "Dialogue" among Christians and Jews, if it occurred at all, was strictly a matter for the elite of the respective communities. Indeed, dialogue as we now know it did not exist; exchanges among the elite took the form of "disputations" or other types of polemic. Contact that might lead to greater mutual understanding among the masses was unimaginable. Indeed, the "theological instrumentalism" of the elite—their viewing Judaism or Christianity as a means toward some theological end—was mirrored in an instrumentalism among the masses, whereby Christians and Jews viewed one another simply as cooperative or competitive economic actors, providers of services, and so on (except when aroused to other passions by religious leaders). Accordingly, as the modern university developed, it was inevitable that Jewish literature would be studied and taught only within the context of the study of Christianity or of religion in general. The established conventions of Christian thought made it impossible to consider Judaism as an evolving civilization with its own historical continuity. The great histories of the western world reflected those conventions as well. Jewish significance was purely derivative.

In sum, it can be said that until the twentieth century relationships between Christians and Jews displayed a number of fairly constant features:

(1) They were mainly polemical and confrontational;
(2) They were marginal in the sense of taking place only at the level of the elite;
(3) Theologically, Christians and Jews tended *at best* to view one another as vehicles or instruments for a theological purpose understood purely in terms of the *observer's* religious system; and
(4) Judaism was not seen by the church or by Christians as having a continuous, evolving history extending from the ancient Israelites to the diaspora communities of medieval and modern times.

This background is essential for understanding just how thoroughly and fundamentally Christian-Jewish relations have changed in the United States during the last fifty years. The American churches, whose history Robert T. Handy has so outstandingly studied and explicated, have developed a relationship with their counterpart institutions in the Jewish world that, while hardly devoid of ambiguities and tensions, is unprecedented in Christian history. Some details of this novel relationship bear recording here, and they in turn will lead to some reflections on the causes of this development.

II. New Agencies for Dialogue: The Impact of Pluralism and Secularity

If we focus on institutions, we find that the past half-century saw either the creation or the flourishing of a wide range of offices and organizations whose existence we take for granted today. Among them are the

National Conference of Christians and Jews (founded already in 1927); the Secretariat for Catholic-Jewish Relations of the National Conference of Catholic Bishops; the Office of Jewish-Christian Relations of the National Council of Churches of Christ; and, on the international scene, the International Council of Christians and Jews, to name just a few. It is a commonplace today that every eighteen months there is convened in the United States a National Workshop on Jewish-Christian Relations, a gathering of enormous magnitude involving major representatives of all the churches as well as Jewish religious and communal leaders. Jewish-Christian dialogue on both religious and political issues is regularly sponsored by all of these agencies and by many national Jewish organizations, such as the Anti-Defamation League of B'nai Brith, the American Jewish Committee, and the American Jewish Congress. Virtually none of this activity was taking place prior to 1935.

Why is the dialogue between Christian and Jewish religious communities so advanced, relatively speaking, on the North American continent? The reasons for this phenomenon are undoubtedly diverse and complex, but at least one significant clue is to be gleaned from the following fact. Writing in 1986, Eugene Fisher, the executive secretary of the Secretariat for Catholic-Jewish Relations of the National Conference of Catholic Bishops, noted that "in the United States and Canada, dialogue is anything but a 'top-down' affair. Indeed, here it is rather the opposite. Local dialogue groups are often well advanced even of official statements, and thus they perform the service of testing and validating ideas in concrete fashion." Further, from the same report: "At any given point in time there may be between seventy-five and one hundred diocesan sponsored (or approved) Catholic-Jewish dialogue groups active throughout the country."[3] The facts concerning Jewish dialogues with the Protestant churches have not been considerably different.

The pattern of these Jewish-Christian relations in twentieth-century America thus stands in direct contrast to what was the long-standing historical experience of Jews with Christians on the European continent, where, as noted above, what religious contact there was took place on the level of the elite and in a polemical spirit. In North America there seems to be a much greater propensity among the clerical leaders, and even the laity, of religious communities to establish and nurture contacts that would foster greater mutual understanding and

---

3. Eugene J. Fisher, "Information Report on Catholic-Jewish Relations in the U.S.A.: Twenty Years After *Nostra Aetate*" (unpublished report of the Secretariat for Catholic-Jewish Relations, the National Conference of Catholic Bishops), pp. 4, 7.

respect. It is perhaps not too fanciful to suppose that this new pattern may be related to the distinctive American experience of these faith groups. Two aspects of that experience stand out as possible explanations for the flourishing of Jewish-Christian relations on contemporary American soil.

First, there is the freedom, openness, and mobility of this society, particularly in the period following the Second World War. The pluralism of mid-twentieth-century America is striking and pervasive. Both individuals and communities that, in other settings, could have passed one another by quietly, found themselves constantly encountering their opposite numbers. The high degree of social encounter and cooperation on the secular scene, from the public schools and business associations to the formation of political alliances, could scarcely stop short of greater curiosity about the religious beliefs and practices of sister communities, and of a willingness to take the relatively minor risks involved in exploring them. It goes without saying that this increased contact at all levels was particularly pronounced for some groups, such as the Jewish and Catholic communities, which shared certain experiences as fairly new immigrant ethnic groups.

A second important feature of the contemporary American setting is the constitutional secularity or, at least, neutrality of the official social and governmental structures, which means that no particular religious group enjoys dominance or any official status. Again, this fact stands in sharp contrast to the previous history of Jewish-Christian relations in continental Europe and Great Britain. More than that, the absence of dominance on the part of one or another religious group was, and is, accompanied by a sense among many religious groups that, with respect to the wider, secular society, they have a shared agenda and set of values that it is in their common interest to cultivate and jointly advocate. Time and again, on issues ranging from civil rights to antiabortion activism and immigration reform, different religious communities have joined forces to press religious points of view on a society whose government is debarred from reacting to such viewpoints reflexively and automatically. The Jewish community, despite its own significant degree of internal diversity, has often been a partner with one or another Christian community in such coalitions.

A striking institutional embodiment of these two characteristics of American society dates from 1938. In that year, on the very eve of World War II, Louis Finkelstein of the Jewish Theological Seminary of America, in New York, established an organization for the conduct of interfaith study and dialogue, which he called the Institute for Religious and Social Studies (IRSS).[4] It is noteworthy that he did not do this alone, but readily brought others into the enterprise from the outset, among them Henry P. Van Dusen, Harry Emerson Fosdick, Henry Sloane Coffin, and John Courtney Murray. Despite the fact that some of the leading "national figures" of Judaism, Catholicism, and Protestantism were involved in founding this new institute, it was not intended to be, nor did it become, simply a venue for dialogue among the elite. During its fifty-year history, the IRSS has provided instruction and support for ministers, priests, and rabbis, who, as it turned out, were quite enthusiastic about the possibilities for mutual acquaintance and joint efforts. It has also provided a place where Protestant and Catholic clergy could meet in conversation comfortably, and where the Christian clergy could learn more about Jewish interpretation of Scripture and Jewish practices.

What is perhaps most compelling about the institute's founding, however, emerges from a consideration of its novelty from the Jewish point of view. In the late 1930s Jewry was in a state of crisis that rivaled anything it had endured in its long history and that would soon surpass any catastrophe it had ever known. Two things would have characterized any similar crisis in past Jewish history. First, the Jewish community would turn inward, relying on its own strength and resources, not expecting or trusting anyone outside its circle to be of any help. Second, any attempt to make contact with the Christian community would prove fruitless; there would be virtually no sympathetic ear. In the United States, however, in 1938, there was a Jewish community that acted on an opposite instinct, with an opposite effect. As prospects for world Jewry grew darker in the late 1930s, the IRSS endeavored to *widen* the radius of Jewish conversation and to establish working relations with very unfamiliar allies, namely, the Protestant and Catholic clergy. This was unprecedented in Jewish history. Moreover, not only was the attempt novel, the response was as well. There *were* sympathetic ears, many in the Christian communities, who were quite willing to establish these heretofore unknown contacts with their Jewish counterparts.

To be sure, the IRSS did not specifically deal during the war years with the catastrophes befalling European Jewry, and it certainly did not serve as a means for providing aid to that devastated community. Still, the essential point is that the ongoing communication and the intellectual and spiritual contact between Jews and Christians in those crisis years followed no previous pattern. It was a unique historical phe-

4. The IRSS is today known as the Louis Finkelstein Institute for Religious and Social Studies, having been renamed in 1986 to honor its founder.

nomenon. Indeed, some years later, Abraham Joshua Heschel remarked that the special importance for him of dialogue with Christians was that it held out promise that never again in Jewish history would Jews face a crisis and have no one to turn to in the Christian communities.

Why was the typical historical relationship between Jews and Christians in time of Jewish crisis (that is to say, virtually no relationship at all) not followed in the United States in 1938 and thereafter? Surely the answer lies, in part, in the two characteristics of American society noted above. The IRSS could only have come about, and have taken the form it did, because the clergy and intellectuals whom Finkelstein assembled were leaders of communities that were not isolated one from the other. The pluralism of American life, which was especially pronounced in a metropolis like New York, meant that many points of contact in many different contexts had *already* been established among Catholic, Protestant, and Jewish communities and individuals. In such a setting, which had few precedents, it was not quite such a major step for religious leaders to form an organization that would formalize dialogue and study. This development serves to confirm Fisher's observation, cited earlier, that Christian dialogue with Jews is definitely not the result of pressure from the "top down." At any rate, it took a society with the open and pluralistic character of twentieth-century America to foster the creation of an institution such as the IRSS.

The second feature of American society—its essential secularity on the official level—was relevant as well. This situation makes it likely that religious leaders will see themselves as having a common agenda, which otherwise would not be promoted. When Finkelstein created the IRSS, he was not ignoring the impending world war and its attendant catastrophes. On the contrary, it was precisely his deep concern about these events that led him to reach out to Christian leaders who, he sensed, would have similar fears and concerns. Whether or not these pioneers in interreligious dialogue should have attempted to do more about the events themselves, and whether they could have succeeded even had they tried, remain open questions. What is clear, however, is that Finkelstein was right in approaching his fellow religious leaders, who together sought to lay a foundation for a society and a world that would not so easily drift into moral anarchy in the future. It is equally clear that the religious leaders who began dialogue in 1938 felt that they had an urgent common agenda, which, when properly developed through dialogue and study, would be of immense service to a society that might not otherwise attend to the perspectives and imperatives of the great monotheistic religions.

The IRSS was the first significant departure from the old pattern, but there have since been many similar endeavors. One of these deserves special notice since it represents another important institutionalization of the value of dialogue between Christians and Jews in the United States. This development, which began slowly some twenty-five years ago, is the interest displayed by seminaries of all faith groups in making provision for some kind of interreligious study or contact in their curricula. This interest shows how large the perceived stake in Christian-Jewish dialogue has become or, alternatively, how much it is taken for granted. It is simply assumed today, in a growing number of seminaries, that future clergy will pursue their calling or profession among their counterparts in other religious groups, and that an important, if not critical, part of their ministries will be the ability to understand, and hence to work with, those counterparts.

III. Some Results: New Attitudes, New Educational Ventures, New Theologies

The institutional vehicles for the furtherance of Christian-Jewish relations that have come into being since the 1930s have produced palpable effects, including altered attitudes among the "rank and file" of religious groups, new curricular proposals in universities and seminaries, and the development and articulation of new theologies. The first two results can be briefly summarized.

Although a relatively low sense of cultural isolation on the part of local churches and Jewish communities—a feature particularly prominent in America's cities—was certainly responsible in part for the first successful steps toward closer relations between Christians and Jews at all levels, attitudes at the local level were, in turn, affected by those enhanced relations. This change has been documented in some communities. For example, a survey of 400 American Catholic educators in 1982 produced the following percentages of affirmative reactions to these two statements:

(1) "Judaism still plays a unique role of its own in God's plan of salvation"—92 percent agreed;
(2) "The Jewish Covenant with God has never been revoked by God; the Jews remain 'people of God'"—85 percent agreed.[5]

It seems reasonable that such near unanimity among religious educators would be transmitted in significant measure to those whom they

---

5. Fisher, op. cit., p. 8.

serve (and, indeed, would in part *reflect* the latter's attitude as well). How sound that assumption is will be touched on presently.

Within Protestantism, perhaps the most striking emergence of positive attitudes has occurred in recent years among the most conservative groups. This phenomenon seems to be a further confirmation of the hypothesis that the low degree of social isolation in pluralistic America has helped Christian-Jewish relations flourish. For as evangelical Christians began to "come out" socially and politically in the last decade or so, they also began to seek and find common ground with Jewish communities with which they would normally have had little or no contact. American Jews, for their part, have exhibited similar tendencies. In community after community across the United States, Jews display less inhibition than ever before in making contact with Christians, while the traditional, real fear of Christian missionizing seems to have faded considerably. Today only the Orthodox Jewish community still refuses to discuss theological (though not other) matters with Christians, ostensibly on the ground that good theological fences make good neighbors. It can, in fact, be cogently argued that the best indication of the mutual positive turn in popular attitudes, and of the lowered level of suspicion, are the often frank and public *disagreements* that Jews and Christians now feel free to express.

The second result of closer and more normal contact between Christians and Jews, namely, changes in and enrichment of teaching about Christians and Jews in various settings, presents a somewhat more complicated picture. It is true that the developments of the past fifty years have resulted in many tangible advances in higher education. At universities during the last few decades, Jewish studies have achieved an autonomous status as a flourishing field of scholarship. Greater balance between Christian and post-biblical Jewish elements has also been achieved in the general humanities curriculum covering the intellectual history of western civilization. Professors who have thus reconceptualized their teaching and research have often had prior involvement in Christian-Jewish dialogue. We have already noted some of the interesting and positive developments in seminary education along these lines.

What is less pronounced, however, is the effect on religious education at the elementary and secondary school levels. There have been many laudable initiatives in the Protestant churches toward correcting negative attitudes about Jews in Christian religious teaching, and, after *Nostra Aetate,* much of value has been proposed by the Holy See and the American Catholic bishops as well. However, recent studies indicate that progress in elementary and secondary school curricula, and in textbooks, is much slower than is desirable.[6] This area of Christian-Jewish relations is receiving a good deal of deserved attention today.

Finally, there is the realm of theology, the third area affected by enhanced Christian-Jewish relations. There have been a number of very significant theological developments that are closely related, both as effects and as causes, to positive achievements in Christian-Jewish relations in general. Three such developments will be noted, without any pretension to completeness. They are: theological stances toward and concerning the State of Israel; the Jewish foundations of Christianity; and the status of the election of Israel.

First, the theological significance of the restoration of a Jewish presence to the Land of Israel and the emergence of the sovereign State of Israel. Increased contact and dialogue between Christians and Jews have raised, and have begun to resolve, important problems and points of tension relative to these events. It is not at all strange that the State of Israel, laden with such great emotional weight for the Jew, following two millennia of prayer for restoration and coming on the heels of the destruction of one-third of the world's Jews on a Christian continent, would be a potential source of interreligious friction and misunderstanding. What is a bit odd is that such tensions often arose in two seemingly contradictory ways. In part they arose owing to a Christian failure to understand the theological significance of the State of Israel for Jews. They have also arisen in equal measure because of a Christian ascription of what to Jews was the *wrong* theological significance to the Jewish state. The first difficulty arose because many Christians were unaccustomed to think of political collectives as having theological meanings and religious aspirations over and above those attaching to the individuals who compose such collectives. This view clearly could not square with the always communally based eschatology of Judaism. So the churches tended, and still tend on occasion, to view the restoration of Jewish sovereignty as an event that is politically rather than theologically important.

Reinhold Niebuhr, who was deeply involved in Christian-Jewish dialogue, already recognized and sought to correct this error in 1942, during the height of the Second World War. In "Jews After the War," he made a significant case for Zionism:

> Liberals characteristically assume [he asserted] that the Jewish problem was solved when Jews were guaranteed their rights as individual citi-

6. For a complete statement concerning these findings, as well as many others related to them, see Judith H. Banki, "The Image of Jews in Christian Teaching," *Journal of Ecumenical Studies* 21/3 (Summer 1984) 437-51.

zens. But there were *collective rights* too, such as the right of a people to exist and cultivate its unique identity.[7]

Although couched in political terms, these were telling theological words for their time. They are still relevant. The continuing contact between Judaism and the churches has kept this issue on the agenda and has brought about increased understanding on this theological point.

In 1986, for example, the secretary of the World Council of Churches' Consultation on the Church and the Jewish People wrote as follows:

> For too long the conflict of Israel with the surrounding Arab states and the Palestinians has been treated by the churches as a political problem with no genuinely religious component, when in fact it presents one of the most serious theological problems facing us today. . . . How do we reconcile the church's definitive identity with the Jewish people, of whom Israel is today the most tangible and powerful symbol, with the church's conviction that its place is on the side of the poor and dispossessed?[8]

To be sure, this statement undoubtedly raises other questions concerning the Palestinians' political status, but it is undeniable that Christian recognition of the theological importance of sovereignty for the Jewish community is an important step in the right theological direction.

At the same time, there has often been an ascription of theological significance to the State of Israel that makes Jews uncomfortable for other reasons. Typically, though by no means exclusively, this perspective has been advanced by evangelicals, who tend to speak of nothing *but* Israel's theological significance, one derived from a view of Israel as the fulfillment of a divine promise and so as a harbinger of the final consummation of history. This, however, is not the significance that Jews themselves ascribe to Israel, though increased understanding has come about in this matter as well. One evangelical Christian who has been particularly involved in dialogue with Jews noted in a recent essay that Christians unfortunately tend to understand Jerusalem in otherworldly terms, thereby obscuring the very rich worldly history of Jerusalem that is still being played out.[9] This insight marks an important theological advance that is obviously related to greater mutual understanding between Jews and Christians.

---

7. As quoted in Richard Fox, *Reinhold Niebuhr* (New York: Pantheon, 1985), p. 210 (emphasis added).

8. World Council of Churches, *Current Dialogue* 10 (June 1986) 11-12.

9. Marvin Wilson, "An Evangelical Christian View of Israel" (unpublished paper given at a conference at Gordon College in February 1985).

Both types of progress that have been sketched here have been summed up best by the Roman Catholic theologian Marcel Dubois:

> Certainly, time will still be needed before Christian theology, reflecting *from within* on the components of the Jewish consciousness—People, Torah, Land—reaches the point of understanding and justifying the link between the Jewish people and the land in which its history, its tradition, its wisdom, and its prayer are rooted for ever. We cannot correct twenty centuries of misunderstandings, mistakes, and tragedies in twenty years. Nevertheless, a new principle has been clearly defined, a principle which involves an outlook and an attitude, a principle which should be the foundation of our hope: "To understand the Jew as he understands himself."[10]

Another theologian who has been most concerned to "understand the Jew as he understands himself" is Paul van Buren, who in 1984 wrote as follows:

> A mighty reversal has come about in the long history of Israel. Twenty centuries of living under the dominion of foreigners have come to an end, and once more the Jewish people have taken on the responsibility of living their eternal covenant with all the social, political, and military consequences of being a people in control of the land which God has given them. I learned firsthand that there are Jewish theologians wrestling with the question of what God is up to in our time. And since the *goyim,* or at least the Gentile church, have seen and said that the ancient love affair between God and God's people Israel is still on, Christian theological education has an exciting agenda thrust upon it. The church can ignore it if it will, but to do so is to forfeit all claim to speak of the living God. We live in a time in which something vital is going on between God and the people of God. Since the church is bound to that same God by its Lord Jesus Christ, we should not be surprised that it, too, is being shaken into a new understanding of God's and its own relationship to the Jewish people.[11]

This statement says much about the need for a deeper Christian understanding of the reality of Israel and also introduces the next theological point, namely, Jewish and Christian understandings of the Jewish background of Christianity.

This area is yet another fertile field of theological inquiry emerging from Christian-Jewish dialogue. As noted earlier, one of the centuries-long conventions of Christian thought about Judaism was a refusal to view Judaism in the Christian era as a vibrant, organic unfolding of

10. Marcel Dubois, "Letter to Ze'ev Falk," *Immanuel* 17 (Winter 1983/84) 102.
11. Paul van Buren, "Theological Education for the Church and the Jewish People," *Journal of Ecumenical Studies* 21/3 (Summer 1984) 491.

pre-Christian Judaism. In other words, the Jewish tradition from, say, the period of the literary prophets to contemporary times was not seen as a continuously developing civilization, but merely as a development that reached a critical plateau in the first century and has somehow survived as an anachronism ever since. The reverse form of this pattern of thought, no less prevalent in traditional Christian theology, denied such continuity to Christianity itself. That is, Christianity was not seen as emerging gradually and organically from its Jewish background, but as a new beginning, a cosmic event that *fulfilled* what came before but was not *continuous* with it. This "theology of discontinuity" has also been challenged in recent times, largely owing to the increased quantity and quality of Christian-Jewish dialogue.

Briefly put, a recurring theme among a growing number of Christian theologians today is that the church must understand itself in its Jewish context, that Christology cannot ignore the Jewishness of Jesus, that Christian faith must take account of the continuous existence of a Jewish community that itself has grown and has rejected an essential Christian tenet in the name of *its* apprehension of God. One can again turn to Dubois for a concise description of this theological trend:

> . . . On each side, Jewish and Christian, we are now capable of recognizing, without evasion and without reticence, the Jewish identity of Jesus. That is also a new fact. We are no longer ashamed or afraid of this truth which, on both sides, we preferred to hide or to forget because we found it disturbing or without interest. In order to take hold of the humanity of Jesus, to understand the reality of the incarnation, Christian exegetes and theologians no longer hesitate to consider Jesus in the surroundings and the tradition from which he came according to the flesh. The title of a recent book suffices in its very conciseness to express this new attitude: *And the Word Became a Jew*. On the Jewish side, parallel progress can be observed in the direction of this objectivity. Without recognizing, of course, Jesus as Lord and Messiah, there is no longer any hesitation in recognizing in him a son of the Jewish people. Thus, in order to speak to me of Jesus, . . . [a] Professor of New Testament at the Hebrew University in Jerusalem sometimes says to me simply: "My teacher and your God." This admirable formula is full of significance and is, in any case, the expression of an astonishing progress in mental lucidity.[12]

Finally, attention must be directed to what is perhaps the most radical and far-reaching theological result of Christian-Jewish dialogue over the last half-century. Increasing numbers of Jewish and Christian

12. Dubois, op. cit.

theologians—taking up but going beyond a point that Franz Rosen-zweig addressed earlier in this century—have been teaching and writing about the "dual covenants." This theological stance reverses some nineteen-hundred years of Christian theology by affirming that God's covenant with the Jewish people is still in force, has not been abrogated. This affirmation is, of course, the ultimate theological corollary of the mutual respect that twentieth-century America has nurtured in its Christian and Jewish communities.

Of all the advocates of this approach to Christian theology (and it is in the Christian context that it is the most startling),[13] the most prominent is Paul van Buren. His words serve as the best introduction to and summation of this historic development:

> Israel's election to be a kingdom of priests, a holy nation, to be as Abraham's seed a blessing for all the nations, is clearly central to the Scriptures of Israel which the church from the beginning acknowledged as its Canon, but it has not been interpreted by the church as eternal. Rather, the church, in flat contradiction to other parts of its Canon—the assertion of the Apostle to the Gentiles that "the gifts and call of God are irrevocable" (Romans 11:29), and again, "you do not support the root but the root supports you" (11:18)—has read the story of Israel's election as a tale come to an end. It read its "Old Testament" as a story that had passed away, having been taken up, renewed and ultimately superseded by its "New Testament." Israel's election, on this reading, valid enough in what was to be called an "old dispensation," had been transferred to the church in a "new dispensation." Indeed, the church had become Israel!
>
> This reading of Israel's Scripture and our Apostolic Writings, however, has become a matter of debate in recent decades. Paul's words are being heard in the church for the first time in its history. Reversing eighteen centuries of its teaching, the church is now asserting officially that if Israel was once elected, its election endures. God's covenant with Israel, it is being argued, is eternal, for this is surely the message of Israel's (and the church's!) Scriptures. That is certainly what Israel has heard from those writings throughout its history. Now the church is beginning to hear this same word. If it does, then it has no choice but to acknowledge God's election of the present, living Jewish people. In that case, a Christian theology of Israel becomes a necessary part of the church's theological task.[14]

These are all major developments and they promise to set the

---

13. A Jewish thinker who explored this theological territory is Jacob Agus.

14. Paul van Buren, *A Christian Theology of the People Israel* (New York: Seabury, 1983), p. 22.

theological agenda for Jews and Christians for many years to come, fostering even more significant dialogue. To be sure, some pitfalls need to be guarded against. For one, an appreciation of the Jewish origins and foundation of Christianity does not in itself ensure an acceptance of Judaism's continued validity. To use a somewhat extreme analogy, Jews can uncover and acknowledge the Canaanite background of much of their Scripture and their ritual observances, but such scholarly activity does not preclude an absolute rejection of the legitimacy of Canaanite religion or (what is milder) a judgment that this "background" religion is utterly insignificant for Jews today. In part, of course, this response is due to the fact that Canaanite religion no longer survives; yet it remains true that an appreciation of origins does not in itself require recognition of the kind of "parallel validity" that van Buren envisions. Second, it is rather too easy for both Christians and Jews to say that the most important advances must be made in the area of Christian theology, that Christians must account for Judaism in their theology, but that Jewish theologians need not account for Christianity. That may be true in some logical sense, and it is empirically true that Christian theology has been the most guilty of unqualified rejections. But true dialogue requires that Jewish theology also confront and understand the eschatological claims that Christians make and live by.

Today's theologians are not unaware of these potential pitfalls. Even these cautionary words, however, taken in tandem with the trends that have been chronicled in this essay, suggest that the last fifty years of momentous progress in Christian-Jewish relations are only part of a "breaking story" that will yet determine much of the future of Christians and Jews, both as separate communities and as partners in the world they share.

9. Americans in World Mission: Revision and Realignment

William R. Hutchison

To a remarkable degree, perceptions of the missionary enterprise, after mid-century at least, varied with an observer's vantage point. Developments that to some appeared radical and cataclysmic, to others seemed glacial or virtually nonexistent.

Americans whose reference point was mainline Protestantism, for example, were likely to be impressed (or, perhaps more often, depressed) by the apparently huge decline, since the 1930s, in the foreign mission commitments of denominations that had thoroughly dominated the movement in the nineteenth century and the first half of the twentieth. The number of "career" personnel those churches sponsored had shrunk from about 10,000 to 3,000 between 1935 and 1980; and within the same bodies the ideologies supporting and surrounding missions appeared to have been altered by winds of change that had leveled many or most of the old landmarks.

Yet foreign observers, in Europe or Latin America as well as in "the lands beyond," were likely to see almost none of this—or to find little meaning in such data if aware of them. What they saw instead, from the mid-30s onward, was a vast *increase* in the number of American missionaries—from 11,000 to 35,000! Any altered rhetoric or programs that they could detect in some parts of this missionary force seemed more than counterbalanced by the traditional sounds and practices emanating from other sectors.[1]

1. The best source for recent comparative figures, and the best analysis of them, is Robert T. Coote, "The Uneven Growth of Conservative Evangelical Missions," *International Bulletin of Missionary Research* 6 (July 1982) 118-23. The data, analyses, and

What had happened was that, as the total mission enterprise (like other American ventures overseas) had grown dramatically during this half-century, the earlier dominance within it of "ecumenicals" over "evangelicals" had been more than reversed. In the rough but not unfair terminology that became standard in the 1960s, "ecumenical" designated the churches that traditionally had led the foreign mission effort and that now were associated through the National Council of Churches and its Division of Ministries (DOM). "Evangelical" stood for the churches and mission agencies affiliated through two other umbrella organizations, the IFMA and the EFMA ("interdenominational" and "evangelical" foreign mission associations), and for most of a large and growing number that were not affiliated with any federative body. So far as one accepted those categories, one could show that ecumenicals had exchanged their ten-to-one preponderance (in career personnel) of 1935 for a one-to-eleven position in the early 1980s.

The personnel figures, while they did not "lie," could not of course tell the whole of a very complicated story. That story was not simply a matter of some religious bodies getting out of the missionary business and of others taking their places. The oldline churches, for example, though they might no longer be organized for "foreign missions" or be employing many people called missionaries, undoubtedly had more of their people working abroad, in religious and quasireligious occupations, than ever before. At the same time, "evangelicals" overseas were such a varied lot that one needed immediately to look beyond bald figures to actual ideas and practices. It was true that, within the impressive evangelical force of 32,000 career missionaries (plus "short-termers" of all sorts), a good many did voice and enact the assumptions of nineteenth-century foreign missions. At the other extreme, however, were overseas workers of quite different description—evangelical social radicals, for example, and evangelical revolutionaries.

It is possible, so long as one has been alerted at the outset to these complexities, to describe the churches' international ventures, 1935 to 1985, by tracing the adjustments that ecumenicals and evangelicals made (or failed to make) to a changing world environment, and also by tracing their adjustments, or continuing maladjustments, to each other.

---

supporting evidence in the present paper are expanded in W. R. Hutchison, *Errand to the World: American Protestant Thought and Foreign Missions* (Chicago: University of Chicago Press, 1987), Chapters 6 and 7, Afterword.

I. Ecumenical Protestants Rewrite the Tradition

Ecumenicals and evangelicals, even as they developed their separate identities during these years, looked to and claimed the same sacred history, recent as well as ancient. Most evidently, the era whose highlight was the World Missionary Conference at Edinburgh (1910) figured as an apostolic age in relation to which later events were viewed as fulfillment or apostasy. For liberals the importance of Edinburgh— apart from its sheer magnitude and importance as an ecumenical event—lay in its having initiated a shift from "foreign missions" thinking to "world mission" thinking. At the very outset of the era, an Edinburgh subcommission on The Church in the Mission Field had warned that its own title was outmoded: "The whole world is the mission field, and there is no Church that is not a Church in the mission field. Some Christian communities are younger and some are older, but that is all the difference." Later in the same report the commissioners warned that even an older/younger dichotomy, with its potential for continued paternalism, was dangerous and should be seen, at most, as "transitional and not permanent."[2]

In the 1920s and 30s the apostolic succession, so far as the more advanced ecumenists were concerned, had been embodied in international student organizations (the Student Volunteer Movement, the YM- and YWCAs) that were increasingly committed to social reform and to cooperation in good works with non-Christian faiths. The saints of this tradition were such liberal missiologists as Daniel Fleming of Union Seminary (New York) and William Ernest Hocking of Harvard. Its "councils" were the great ecumenical assemblies that as early as the Jerusalem Conference of 1928 had generated a revised mission rhetoric highly suspect among conservatives.

The international student movement, nearly always the pacesetter for liberal ideas, in the 1920s had challenged the mission leadership to heighten their concern for social reform and world reconstruction, to lessen their preoccupation with personal evangelism, and to begin meeting other world religions in "humble dialogue." Fleming, the most prolific and probably the most influential of liberal missiolo₅. 's, in the same decade was urging that the "continents" for Christian outreach and Christian conquest were no longer Africa and Asia, but rather "the great transverse areas of human activity" such as industrialization, nationalism, materialism, racial injustice, war, and poverty.

2. World Missionary Conference, 1910, *Report of Commission II. The Church in the Mission Field* (Edinburgh: Oliphant, Anderson and Ferrier, 1910), pp. 4-6.

Fleming also went beyond the notion of humble dialogue between other faiths by in effect proposing a humbling dialogue between western Christians and what he thought were neglected elements in biblical tradition. In a provocative *Christian Century* article, "If Buddhists Came to Our Town," he asked whether Americans would wish, or even allow, persons of exotic faith to inject themselves in our society in some of the ways that had been habitual for western missionaries abroad. Would we, for example, want Moslems or Buddhists, even if they ran the best schools in town, to seek to alienate our children from what we consider the most important element in our culture? His answer, though modulated, was clearly that Americans of his time would by and large not accept any such arrangement. He proposed that Christians take their Golden Rule more seriously and apply it less selectively.[3]

William Ernest Hocking, who in the early 1930s directed a massive reconsideration of the theory and practice of foreign missions, endorsed such liberal recommendations and, with the aid and advice of collaborators like Fleming, added a few of his own. Most centrally and controversially, the "Laymen's Report" of 1932 urged Christians in their approach to other religions to press beyond dialogue to collaboration. The "continent" that Hocking, the idealist philosopher, yearned to conquer was materialism. The proposal in the Laymen's Report that most scandalized conservatives was that the religions of the world—more precisely, the best or reformist elements in each of them—should cease competing and instead unite in the desperate worldwide battle to sustain spiritual values.[4]

The moderates who in the 1930s directed most mission boards and interdenominational organizations agreed with conservatives that this was going too far. But these leaders, and the ecumenical movement with them, were nonetheless committed to numerous elements in the revised worldview that thinkers like Fleming were projecting. John R. Mott, the premier American statesman of both the missionary and the ecumenical movement, had himself proposed at the Jerusalem Conference that the whole vocabulary of "sending" and "receiving" churches be scrapped. In the 1930s, conservative retrenchments urged by the Dutch missiologist Hendrik Kraemer, though they impressed ecumenical leaders and helped stiffen their resistance to sheer collaborationism, did not win most of them over. If a normative American stance could

3. Daniel J. Fleming, *Whither Bound in Missions?* (New York: Association, 1925), pp. 135, 122-44; "If Buddhists Came to Our Town," *Christian Century* 46 (February 28, 1929) 293-94.

4. William Ernest Hocking, et. al., *Re-Thinking Missions: A Laymen's Inquiry After One Hundred Years* (New York: Harper, 1932), p. 23.

be identified amid the discussions of the 1930s, it was one reflecting neither Hocking's emphasis on the commonalities among world religions nor Kraemer's insistence on their radical discontinuity, but rather the longstanding liberal contention that Christ came to "fulfill" other faiths by building on what each had to offer. Edmund Soper, whose *Philosophy of the Christian World Mission* (1943) best represented this mediating position, allowed that his view "must be called that of [Christian] uniqueness together with continuity."[5]

As liberals, over the next two decades, moved beyond this "definite maybe" toward prescriptions akin to Hocking's, the usual procedure was not to renounce evangelistic aims but to subject them to radical redefinition. Unwilling, especially under fire, to eschew either "evangelism" or "conversion," the most ingenious and socially active of the ecumenicals called upon the image of a Christ who, above all, lived among and for others. They were inclined to view world mission as an active Christian presence throughout the world, and to define conversion less in individual terms than as the radical remaking of social structures. "Christian presence," as a paper of the World Student Christian Federation explained in 1964, "does not mean that we are simply there; it tries to describe the adventure of being there in the name of Christ, often anonymously, listening before we speak . . . , involved in the fierce fight against all that dehumanizes, ready to act against demonic powers, to identify with the outcast, merciless in ridiculing modern idols and new myths."

That Federation document, though it took pains to allow for personal evangelism, circumscribed both the methods and the message that had been common in the past. "Once we are there, we may witness fearlessly to Christ if the occasion is given"; yet "we may also have to be silent." Even the more vocal sort of "fearless witness" would have a different sound from that of traditional soul-saving. These innovators were convinced that the latter, in addressing human concerns, had persistently confused human (and in this case parochially western) remedies with divine remedies. More seriously and fundamentally, it had absolutized western ways of phrasing the issues to be addressed. For the future, the test of valid mission must be whether or not one, in entering the concerns of others, also accepts "their issues and their structures."[6]

The Uppsala meetings (1968) of the World Council of Churches

---

5. Rodger C. Bassham, *Mission Theology: 1948-1975* (Pasadena: William Carey Library, 1979), pp. 21-25; Edmund D. Soper, *The Philosophy of the Christian World Mission* (New York: Abingdon-Cokesbury, 1943), pp. 21-25.

6. Bassham, *Mission Theology*, p. 72.

became the focus for a broader form of the same idea: namely, that the world and not the church sets the agenda for mission. Norman Goodall, editor of the Uppsala documents, thought the delegates "not only recognized that . . . the world was writing the agenda for the meeting; the right of the world to do this was largely taken for granted and Uppsala tried to read the writing, understand it and respond to it." The world's programs were in no way to supersede God's program for humanity; rather they were (or at least contained) that program. What most marked the Uppsala assembly, according to Goodall, was "its preoccupation—at times, almost, its obsession—with the revolutionary ferment of our time, with questions of social and international responsibility, of war and peace and economic justice, with the pressing, agonizing physical needs of men, with the plight of the underprivileged, the homeless and starving, and with the most radical contemporary rebellions against all 'establishments,' civil and religious."[7]

The most persistent and wide-ranging exponent of this kind of thinking was Johannes Hoekendijk, a Dutch theologian and ecumenical activist who since 1965 had been Professor of Missions at Union Seminary in New York. Hoekendijk, a member of both the European and the American "study groups" that prepared working papers for Uppsala, applied the traditional term "evangelism" to a conception of the church's role that struck many contemporaries as decidedly untraditional if not heretical. From Hoekendijk's point of view, however, it was the evangelical tradition that had been guilty of heresy. "Evangelism," as refracted and distorted through the assumptions of modern culture in the West, in the main had constituted a response not to God's call for renewal but to some very human apprehensions about the church's loss of its central place in society. The word "evangelize," he complained, had too regularly been a "biblical camouflage of what should rightly be called the reconquest of ecclesiastical influence." It had, moreover, been used to excuse the practice of "preparing" mission grounds for evangelism by imposing something called Christian civilization—which in reality was western civilization.

The resulting missionary tradition was one that, Hoekendijk insisted, "cannot guide us any longer." Where it had succeeded at all, it had succeeded not in planting seeds of Christian life, but in transplanting fully formed stalks of German Lutheranism, or Dutch Catholicism, or bourgeois Methodism. Hoekendijk, enthusiastically planting his own seeds for the constructive formulations of the 1960s, pled in

---

7. Norman Goodall, ed., *The Uppsala Report 1968* (Geneva: World Council of Churches, 1968), p. 17.

1950 for an evangelism that would express itself through flexible structures capable of direct action in society. The precedent from Christian tradition would be the diaconate; the model in the secular order was the laboratory. The church must go where the need is, and once there it must operate experimentally.[8]

The term—"go-structures"—that Uppsala delegates adopted for this model of the church was perhaps less than attractive, but it did make the point: liberals were inveighing against a static "waiting church" that merely sits, preening and perfecting itself, inviting others to come in on the church's terms or not at all. The *bête noire*, or foil, was a "parish system" seen as immobile, self-centered, and introverted. The parish, Hoekendijk thought, was "an invention of the middle ages [that is] completely inadequate and unfit to give expression to the life of a community which believes that Christ and this modern world are bound together." Challenging commitments to "church growth" that modern evangelicals (partly because of assaults like Hoekendijk's) were seeking to revive and strengthen, the advance party of the 1960s went so far as to question the propriety of bringing converts into the existing churches. Hoekendijk, with characteristic acerbity, called it a scandal that people should be so induced "to adapt themselves to the various patterns of the present chaos of denominations." The church, instead of promoting individual conversions to inflexible and unresponsive social structures, should bestir itself to promote conversion "on the corporate level in the form of social change."[9]

II. Conservative Backlash

The advance reports for the Uppsala assembly, published together in 1967 as *The Church for Others and the Church for the World*, marked a high point of antitraditional thinking among ecumenicals, and by the same token served as an unusual provocation to stronger evangelical opposition. After protests about these documents from conservatives (many of whom soon withdrew from World Council affiliation), "church

8. Johannes Hoekendijk, "The Call to Evangelism," in Donald McGavran, ed., *The Counciliar-Evangelical Debate: The Crucial Documents 1964-1976* (Pasadena: William Carey Library, 1977), pp. 44-54.

9. World Council of Churches, *The Church for Others and the Church for the World* (Geneva: WCC, 1967), pp. 18-19, 76; Hoekendijk, "Christ and the World in the Modern Age," *The Student World* 54 (1961) 81; "Notes on the Meaning of Mission(ary)," in Thomas Wieser, ed., *Planning for Mission* (New York: United States Conference for the World Council of Churches, 1966), pp. 46-47.

growth" advocates gained a hearing in the assembly's deliberations. The final Uppsala Report, reflecting those exchanges, conceded that the church is the structure within which "the signs of the new humanity are experienced" and affirmed that Christians find their true life in the church's life of word, sacrament, and fellowship. "The growth of the Church . . . both inward and outward" was acknowledged to be of urgent importance.

But such statements might have been printed in a separate section labeled Minority Opinions. One spokesman for those opinions characterized the final Uppsala report as a patchwork quilt whose seams remained visible. That was apt; it was also evident that some of the vital interests of the conservatives never so much as made it into the quilt.[10]

Among these, certainly, was the traditional missionary emphasis on personal evangelism. Just before the assembly, Professor Donald McGavran of Fuller Seminary had asked in print, "Will Uppsala Betray the Two Billion?" From his point of view the Uppsala working groups had not only maligned the church; they had utterly ignored the multitudes who "live and die in a famine of the Word of God more terrible by far than the sporadic physical famines which occur in unfortunate lands." In view of this alleged neglect, he found the ecumenicals' use of terms like evangelism and mission obfuscating if not downright dishonest.

It seemed to conservatives that once again, as so often in the past, modernists with dubious Christian credentials had stolen the evangelicals' rhetorical clothing and were trying desperately to wear it. McGavran observed that while the word "mission" was repeatedly used in the preliminary Uppsala documents, its meaning was *"nowhere* that of communicating the good news of Jesus Christ to unbelieving men in order that they might believe and live." Liberals, he complained, were appropriating words that had had settled meanings for at least 250 years and without warning or explanation were forcing these words to bear radically different freight. Though McGavran said his readers would have to judge whether or not this constituted a "pious fraud," he did not leave them without guidance in making such judgments. Nor was he to be satisfied by the concessions embodied in the final assembly document. Uppsala *had* betrayed the Two Billion.[11]

If liberals could be accused of stealing some parts of the tradition—carrying them off to their theological tailor shops to be altered beyond recognition—it had to be conceded that they left other parts

---

10. Goodall, *Uppsala*, p. 29; Bassham, p. 83.
11. McGavran, pp. 233-37.

untouched. Much of the nineteenth-century rhetoric, methodology, and martyrology was simply abandoned. That abandonment made evangelicals the more avid about asserting their own rights of inheritance. "Seeking an identity," as Rodger Bassham puts it, through an emphasis on explicit contrasts between their positions and those of the liberal churches, McGavran, Carl F. H. Henry, and others stressed evangelicals' direct filial relations to the Edinburgh Conference, its rhetoric, and its ebullient spirit. A Chicago meeting of evangelicals in 1960 sought to rehabilitate the Watchword that had fallen into disuse in the 1920s—"The Evangelization of the World in This Generation"—and that venerable slogan was featured six years later in the ringing peroration of their Wheaton Declaration. Similarly, despite the severely negative connotations that had come to be attached to the term "proselytism," the Wheaton delegates sought to refurbish that conception.[12]

While some of these "affiliated" or mainstream evangelicals, as well as zealots on the far religious right, seemed bent on perpetuating western paternalism, such aims could not easily be attributed to the evangelical effort as a whole. The statistics of missionary deployment made it plain that evangelicals felt called upon to "proselytize" for the faith not merely in the Third World but among Catholics in France and Brazil and among the heathen in Darkest America.

That evangelicals were seeking converts in the supposedly Christian West could prompt other troublesome questions, for example about latent (or even blatant) anti-Catholicism. It was nonetheless essential, when one sought to evaluate the "evangelical surge" in missions, to be aware that in the mid-70s American Protestant bodies were reporting 400 missionaries in Germany, nearly 400 in France, 2,000 in Brazil, 750 in Colombia, 200 in Spain, over 100 in the United Kingdom. Forty-three percent of North American Protestant overseas personnel were serving either in Latin America (36 percent) or in Europe. While some of these were attached to ecumenical agencies such as Church World Service, incomparably more were evangelists and workers for conservative groups. The northern Presbyterians in 1975 were sending only about one-sixth of their missionary personnel to these regions, but for Southern Baptists the figure was two-fifths, and a number of conservative agencies listed more missionaries in Europe than in Asia and Africa combined.

Such deployments could suggest the alleged American propensity for trying to convert other Christians to American Christianity; but they also lent some credence to the evangelicals' claim that they, as

12. Bassham, pp. 277-78, 210-11.

much as the liberals, were thinking in "world mission" rather than tradi-tional "foreign mission" terms.[13]

In at least one further respect, however, evangelicals could be seen as looking enthusiastically backward, and not so much to Edin-burgh as to a pre-Edinburgh era: they sought to reinstate Christ's Great Commission ("Go into all the world and preach the Gospel") as a suffi-cient justification for missions. Such mainstream missionary leaders as Robert E. Speer, early in the century, had refused to ground the mis-sionary rationale on the Great Commission, which they saw as an over-used and simplistic form of biblical literalism that had, moreover, masked too much aggression or insensitivity in the past. But evangelical rhetoric in the 1960s laid enormous emphasis on the license allegedly provided by Christ's last command, and occasionally did so with more than a touch of the old heedlessness and *ex parte* argumentation. John R. W. Stott of London opened the first of three addresses on the Great Commission by asserting that "in the last resort, we engage in evange-lism today not because we want to or because we choose to or because we like to, but because we have been told to. The Church is under orders. The risen Lord has commanded us to 'go,' to 'preach,' to 'make disciples'; and that is enough for us." And Billy Graham's keynote address used much the same language: "If there were no other reason . . . the command of Christ would be enough! It is not optional—we have no choice."

Graham also rang the changes on a number of objections to lib-eralism and ecumenism regularly voiced by evangelicals: the liberals' "syncretistic" search for points of unity with other world religions; their "universalist" persuasion that Christ is somehow present in all peoples and societies, so that all will be saved; and their dangerous move from a spiritual to a secular conception of the church's task. He charged that evangelism had been thoroughly transmuted into a concern for educa-tion, social reform, and "evangelization of the structures of society." But Graham's depiction of the "liberal establishment" was a good deal less lurid than others commonly heard. Eugene Smith, a WCC observer at the evangelicals' Wheaton Conference of 1966 (his observer status was a comment in itself), came away appalled at the virulence of conserva-tive indictments. "The distrust of the ecumenical movement within this group," Smith reported, "has to be experienced to be believed."[14]

13. Edward R. Dayton, ed., *Mission Handbook: North American Protestant Ministries Overseas,* 11th ed. (Monrovia, CA: Missions Advanced Research and Communication Center, 1973), pp. 437ff.
14. Carl F. H. Henry and Stanley Mooneyham, eds., *One Race, One Gospel, One Task: World Congress on Evangelism, Berlin, 1966,* 2 vols. (Minneapolis: World Wide Pub-

III. Adjustments on the Right

Yet even at this early and militant stage the new evangelicalism was not simply a carbon or continuation of the old. The Watchword and the Great Commission had been reasserted among evangelicals, and with them the potential for renewed tribalism and condescension; but the old attendant rhetoric, involving active depreciation of other faiths and revelations, seemed notably absent. The primacy of personal over social evangelism had been trumpeted; but it was also clear that many evangelicals were seeking new and more serious modes of accommodation between that firm commitment and liberal-to-radical social programs. The nineteenth century had been reinstated; but this included the nineteenth century of Rufus Anderson and Henry Venn, mission leaders who had fashioned the classic case for indigenization.

To be sure, such attempted adjustments not only pale against the backdrop of vehemence concerning ecumenical Christianity; they could also seem mere gestures toward modern social problems, or self-serving attempts to improve the image of evangelicalism's past performance. Billy Graham, at Berlin, ran through the obligatory references to great social reformers whose work had been initiated by conversion to Christ. Many others did the same, until at length a black evangelist retorted that whatever the situation may have been in nineteenth-century England, evangelicalism in his own lifetime had meant passivity in social matters, a tacit support of the status quo, and evasive pleas that one cannot change human hearts by legislation. William Pannell complained that "frankly I am a bit weary of hearing that Lord Shaftesbury and Wilberforce effected social change in England." Legislation, another black delegate added, "did for me and my people in America what empty and highpowered evangelical preaching never did for 100 years."[15]

Despite such expressions of skepticism about evangelical "adjustments," and also because of them, the balance between evangelism and social action did change, and with some rapidity. As the evangelical contingent, like its liberal opposite number, held its meetings increasingly in nonwestern locations, and sometimes drew more Third World delegates than the ecumenicals did, western evangelicals heard pleas for change more compelling than those they had been hearing, and in general resisting, from western or white-American colleagues. At the

---

lications, 1967), 1:37, 24-26. Smith is quoted in Denton Lotz, "'The Evangelization of the World in This Generation': The Resurgence of a Missionary Idea Among the Conservative Evangelicals" (Ph.D. dissertation, University of Hamburg, 1970), p. 301.

15. Henry and Mooneyham, 1:28; Bassham, pp. 225-28.

Lausanne meeting of evangelicals in 1974, the strident voices against a church-growth or convert-counting emphasis were those of Latin Americans. René Padilla, for example, warned that "there is no place for statistics on 'how many souls die every minute,' if they do not take into account how many of those who die, die victims of hunger." Samuel Escobar added that spirituality without involvement in social, economic, and political concerns is mere religiosity.[16]

Evangelicals of Europe and North America were also affected, however, by accelerating appeals from within their own ranks, particularly from younger adherents involved in the antiwar and civil rights movements. A 5,000-delegate Congress on Evangelism at Minneapolis in 1969 focused on social issues and found itself (to the distress of many participants) defining evangelism to include the social witness. The organization named Evangelicals for Social Action, the magazine called *Sojourners*, and a "Chicago Declaration" of 1973 all represented the emergence and growing influence of what Rodger Bassham refers to as "a small but disciplined and articulate [radical] group." As part of the same process, evangelicals developed a less alarmed and more discriminating reaction even to fairly extreme ecumenical formulations such as *Church for Others.*

Thus John R. W. Stott was not alone in considering, by the time of the evangelicals' Lausanne meeting in 1974, that his views had altered in the preceding eight years. The ecumenicals' insistence that "the church is mission" he still considered an overstatement. But he clearly spoke for many others in accepting the shift in focus signified by terms like *missio dei* (i.e., this is not the church's mission, fundamentally, but God's), and by admonitions to turn the church "inside out" in response to the world's agenda. As Stott now saw the matter, Christ commanded believers to follow his living example, and this example was one of service in and to the world. The divine commission, therefore, "must be understood to include social as well as evangelistic responsibility, unless we are to be guilty of distorting the words of Jesus." Stott now conceived social action and evangelism to be partners. "As partners the two belong to each other and yet are independent of each other. Each stands on its own feet in its own right alongside the other. Neither is a means to the other, or even a manifestation of the other. For each is an end in itself."[17]

---

16. Bassham, p. 237.

17. Ibid., pp. 271-74: J. D. Douglas, ed., *Let the Earth Hear His Voice: International Congress on World Evangelization, Lausanne* (Minneapolis: World Wide Publications, 1975), p. 68; John R. W. Stott, *Christian Mission in the Modern World* (Downers Grove, IL: Inter-Varsity Press, 1975), p. 23.

In a number of other respects, too, "affiliated evangelicals" by the mid-70s were sounding less like strident opponents of the ecumenicals, more like a centrist or mediating party. Some, not content with an emphasis on indigenization, supported the notion, common in ecumenical circles, that a moratorium on western missionary activity and financing might be called for in some parts of the world. Though still on guard against such traditional menaces as syncretism and universalism, many embraced the possibility of sympathetic dialogue with persons of other faiths. Less was said, as time went on, about a prescriptive and sufficient Great Commission. In all these areas, an attitude of penitence—not merely on behalf of conservative evangelicalism, but more generally with respect to Christian action in the world—had to a large extent replaced the triumphalism of just a decade earlier.[18]

IV. New Consensus, or Old Dissensus?

With mainstream evangelicals conceding a number of important points to the ecumenicals, and with the latter making equally visible efforts to incorporate more personal evangelism into their programs, talk of a "new consensus" in the late 1970s was more than a benign exercise in wishful thinking. Ecumenicals and organized evangelicals had indeed developed large areas of agreement and were justified in expecting to stress them and build upon them. Yet those who yearned for such an outcome were bound to be sobered by the evident dissensus between these parties and the mission agencies on the religious far-right. For every evangelical who joined Dr. Stott in concessions to ecumenical arguments, there were several on the far right to take their places in promoting mission attitudes close to those of the imperialist era. Robert Coote in 1982 published the results of a study that showed mainstream evangelical missions as well as those of the ecumenicals losing ground, statistically, to the "unaffiliated." The EFMA and IFMA ranks had swelled in twenty years by about 3,000 missionaries, largely because former "ecumenical" agencies had changed associations. But the numbers in the "unaffiliated" category had shot up in the same period from 7,000 to 17,000, both because of new ventures and recruiting and because various agencies had found even the mainstream evangelical organizations too liberal.[19]

To assume that all "nonaffiliated" agencies and their workers

18. Bassham, pp. 141-42, 235-44, 332-33.
19. Coote, "Uneven Growth."

were conservative or fundamentalist would be incorrect, though most were such, quite avowedly. Still less would it be safe to suppose that all were perpetuating an older cultural imperialism; now, as in the past, some of the most theologically conservative mission groups outdid all others in "going native" and blending with the local culture. Yet David Stoll's conclusions about Wycliffe Bible Translators, one of the largest of the nonaffiliated groups, could doubtless be applied to many others, particularly if phrased in Stoll's carefully balanced way. The work of the Translators, he wrote, though "organized as an intrigue, . . . is clearly an evangelical intrigue with its own jealously guarded objectives. The deeper problem is the group's naiveté, its capacity for looking the other way and serving dictatorships, if that will serve the Great Commission."

The nonaffiliated were, sometimes by intention and sometimes not, carrying the torch for the more conservative methods and ethnocentric assumptions of the past, and it was the ubiquity and visibility of such groups that, above all, caused casual observers to doubt whether "American missions" had changed appreciably over a half century—or a century and a half! It could seem, simply as a matter of everyday observation, that the spectrum of American attitudes and practices was similar to what foreign nationals or their parents had known earlier in the century. The old adage seemed to apply: "Plus ça change, plus c'est le même chose."[20]

Not infrequently, Americans and others who felt they had left traditional foreign missions behind took a similar, and in this case a highly alarmed, view. In fact, where a new consensus did seem to have developed between ecumenism and important segments of evangelicalism, one of its marks was a poignant sense of frustration. Had American Protestantism come this far in relating to the world only to be upstaged by oldstyle cultural and religious imperialists? The dilemma was not unlike those that mainline Protestants were experiencing at home. Unable to preach the message or imitate the methods of religious extremists, such Protestants were forced, in both domestic and foreign settings, to watch somewhat helplessly as religious extremists succeeded in persuading many that theirs were the normative expressions of Protestant Christianity and American values.

Yet in the overseas situation, as at home, the actual reach and effectiveness of right-wing ideologies were easily exaggerated. Ecumenical Christianity abroad, for example, even if one were not to consider

---

20. David Stoll, *Fishers of Men or Founders of Empire? The Wycliffe Bible Translators in Latin America* (London: Zed Press, 1982), p. 86; Edward R. Dayton, "Current Trends in North American Protestant Ministries Overseas," *Occasional Bulletin of Missionary Research* 1 (April 1977) 2-7.

the substantial numbers of its lay representatives in "secular" serving agencies, occupied a position significantly stronger than might be suggested by the one-to-eleven imbalance in American missionary personnel. In 1980, more than 40 percent of Japanese Protestants belonged to bodies that found themselves able to affiliate with the World Council of Churches. For India, the figure was 60 percent.[21]

V. Prospects

As one looked to the future, the truly important question was not which faction—ecumenicals, affiliated evangelicals, or independents—would send out the most workers or would most successfully promote its version of Christian outreach. The overriding question was the degree to which overseas Americans, whatever their theological loyalties or group affiliations, could divest themselves of the tribalism and condescension of earlier eras.

The answer would depend in part upon the fate of more general American conceptions concerning that society's place in the world. The Christian triumphalism that many still considered a measure of faith and commitment would probably submit to further revision only to the extent that an ingrained American and western triumphalism was also revised.

In the late 1970s, in the wake of the Vietnam and Watergate experiences, liberal internationalists had dared to hope that such revision was indeed occurring, and at an unprecedented rate. It was common in those years to propose that Americans, long accustomed to thinking of themselves as a uniquely chosen people, were prepared to face the modern world without "the comforting notion of a special purity in the national heart." A self-styled Chosen People were coming to accept their real-world status as *goy b'goyim*—a people among peoples.[22]

Renewed national assertiveness in the 1980s, even if interpreted as a rear-guard action, made such projections more doubtful; by the mid-80s observers at home and abroad were less prone to speak of either an American or an American Christian acceptance of equal status among the peoples of the earth. Yet xenophobic turns in opinion

---

21. David B. Barrett, *World Christian Encyclopedia* (Nairobi: Oxford University Press, 1982), pp. 419, 370.

22. Conor Cruise O'Brien, "Innocent Nation, Wicked World," *Harper's* (April 1980) 33; Sacvan Bercovitch, "The Rites of Assent: Rhetoric, Ritual, and the Ideology of American Consensus," in Sam B. Girgus, ed., *The American Self: Myth, Ideology, and Popular Culture* (Albuquerque: University of New Mexico Press, 1981), p. 35.

and policy were unlikely to halt what Sacvan Bercovitch called the "encroachments of history" upon traditional American claims to innocence and privileged treatment. In the longer run, in fact, they might simply provoke new encroachments—new pressures upon Americans to accept their real-world status.

If more realistic attitudes could be expected to flourish anywhere, one might confidently look for them in the context of a world Christianity in which the West's dominance, numerically and otherwise, appeared to have ended definitively. American attitudes and the American churches had, in reality, come a long way since the 1930s. Further maturing along the same lines, whether produced by an internal dynamic or by the pressures of history, would mean that the modern-day American missionary would at last be perceived less as a chaplain to the old imperialism, more as someone intent on maintaining Christian effectuality within the new religious and cultural pluralism.

10. American Church History from a Third World Perspective

Kosuke Koyama

The theme of this paper challenges us to a much needed understanding ing of the interaction between the history of the American church and that of the third world churches. It suggests the need for an "interchurch history" reflecting the ecumenical nature and scope of the church itself.

Theologically, the concept of mutuality is fundamental to the church's ecumenicity. Historically, however, the perspective of "third world church history from the viewpoint of the western church" has prevailed. In general, the churches in Asia, Africa, and Latin America have been planted by the western churches. One must not forget, however, the continuing presence of ancient churches in the third world and the significant eastward progression of the Christian faith during the church's early history. One of the striking facts of global church history in our time is that the West's predominance is being challenged by the third world churches. We are witnessing a shift of Christianity's center from the traditional Atlantic West to the vast regions of Asia, Africa, and Latin America.[1] Such radical historical change demands a new perspective from which to interpret the global significance of Christianity for the whole of humanity. What, then, does *American* (i.e., United States) church history look like from the perspective of the third world?

---

1. Among the 1,200 delegates at the famous World Missionary Conference in Edinburgh (1910), there were only 17 Asians. Among the 2,600 bishops at the Second Vatican Council (1962-65), 1,318 were from the third world. Among the 847 delegates at the Sixth General Assembly of the World Council of Churches (1983), 369 were from the third world. For useful background information, see K. M. Panikkar, *Asia and Western Dominance* (London: Allen & Unwin, 1953).

I. "The West (North) Teaches; the East (South) Learns"

This paper views the American church since 1945 in the light of the liberation of humanity from all kinds of oppressive powers. I find significant the following declaration from a 1979 conference of the Ecumenical Association of Third World Theologians: "In our countries today, there can be no truly indigenized theology that is not liberational."[2] Gustavo Gutiérrez has likewise written: "To 'remember the poor' (Gal. 2:10) means in Latin America to keep in mind the overwhelming majority of the population."[3] It is from such a standpoint of concern for liberation that the third world church sees the American church.

A perceptive treatment of American church history and the "third world" appeared at the beginning of this century in Presbyterian mission executive Robert Speer's two volume work, *Missions and Modern History* (1904), with its significant subtitle: *A Study of the Missionary Aspects of Some Great Movements of the Nineteenth Century*.[4] This ambitious undertaking covered twelve "great movements," all but two related to Asia, beginning with the Taiping Rebellion in China (1850-64). According to Speer, each of these movements, which in aggregate influenced the life and destiny of 1 billion people, is "intelligible only as we understand its missionary relations."[5] In his view, "the whole Western movement upon Asia is revolutionary and subversive" and its central impact is moral and religious in nature.[6] Speer approvingly quoted a statement of "a modern historian" that Adolf Harnack had previously cited in his well known book, *What Is Christianity?*, namely: "The image of Christ remains the sole basis of all moral culture, and in the measure in which it succeeds in making its light penetrate is the moral culture of the nations increased or diminished."[7] Speer maintained that this

2. From the text of the Ecumenical Association of Third World Theologians meeting at Wennappuwa, Sri Lanka, January 1979. See *Irruption of the Third World: Challenge to Theology*, ed. Virginia Fabella and Sergio Torres (Maryknoll, NY: Orbis, 1983), p. 81.

3. Gustavo Gutiérrez, *We Drink from Our Own Wells* (Maryknoll, NY: Orbis, 1984), p. 124.

4. Robert E. Speer, *Missions and Modern History: A Study of the Missionary Aspects of Some Great Movements of the Nineteenth Century*, 2 vols. (London: Revell, 1904).

5. Ibid., p. 8.

6. Ibid., p. 669. Cf. p. 670: "Western civilization, with whatever shortcomings, is Christian civilization, and it should not conceal its religious character in advancing upon the East." (I personally remember that in 1945, right after the war, General Douglas MacArthur, the Supreme Commander of the Allied Powers, appealed from Tokyo to the American people to send "as many missionaries as possible" to teach Japanese the Christian morality.)

7. Ibid., p. 677. Speer commented: "The figure of Jesus Christ has been the greatest contribution to the idea of education in all lands; whether he was recognized as

Christian moral training is precisely what the western commercial "trades" could not impart to the East (third world). Therefore, Christian missions have "indisputable and absolute right of precedence" over the commercial trades.[8] The moral impact of the Christian mission is to be seen above all, said Speer, in the "great movements" of the (Asian) peoples. "The first stirrings of the new life" were thus given by the Christian mission.[9]

Speer's outlook reveals the American church's traditional self-understanding of its relationship to the religious and moral life of the peoples of the vast third world and of the churches planted among them. That self-understanding, in short, is this: "The West (North) teaches; the East (South) learns." This "missionary truth," which in fact has been promulgated for 500 years and upheld by millions of faithful Christians in America as well as in the East and the South, is now being challenged by what has happened in history since the end of World War II. Humanity's positive appreciation of the remarkable western contributions to science and technology is now counterbalanced by a seriously negative appraisal that this same science and technology have led the whole world into the catastrophic dead end of unremitting cold war between the superpowers and into the imminent possibility of global nuclear holocaust. The old "missionary truth" cannot remain unquestioned and intact against the background of such recent historical events.

II. Tension between the Concepts "America" and "Church"

Before proceeding, I must say a few words about my understanding of "American church history" in the present context. One must surely invest much time and energy, over many years, in order to master this subject and profit from its study. Expert knowledge of American church history, however, is possessed by an extremely limited number of third world Christian scholars. Nevertheless, there is a pervasive experience of Christian America in the third world. Accordingly, third world church historians who know American church history are charged with a

---

perfect man or savior of mankind, it challenged the foundations of traditional culture." Cf. Adolf Harnack, *What Is Christianity?*, trans. T. B. Saunders (reprint ed., New York: Harper & Row, 1957), p. 123. (The "modern historian" was not identified.) See also M. M. Thomas, *The Christian Response to the Asian Revolution* (London: SCM, 1966), p. 88.

8. Speer, op.cit., p. 685.

9. Ibid., p. 691.

special responsibility to mediate between this knowledge and their own people's *experience* of "Christian America."

Basically, such mediation may take the form of two possible approaches to the relationship between "America" and "church." The first approach assumes that little if any real tension exists between these two concepts: the mighty nation America is a Christian nation, and it has consistently supported the Christian mission abroad with both material and spiritual resources. Here American church history is understood as the history of a vigorous, generous, missionary-minded Christian nation. America is a Christian Benefactor. Theologically, the nation America symbolizes the grace of God in world history. Think of the countless schools, particularly schools for the education of women, and the hospitals (leprosariums) that the American "foreign" mission, as the expression of the nation America, has established throughout the world in the last 100 years![10]

A second approach takes a very different tack. It recognizes imperialistic, exploitative forms of behavior in the empire America, and it urges the American churches to exert efforts to check, by the power of Christian teaching and example, American capitalism's brutal exploitation of Latin America (to cite but one instance of such behavior). Theologically, American church history is here viewed in light of a biblical critique of national idolatry. In solidarity with the oppressed millions in the third world, the third world church voices the prophetic words of judgment against a profit-seeking capitalist "Christian" America: "Woe to him who builds his house by unrighteousness" (Jeremiah 22:13).[11]

The third world experience of American church history *combines*

---

10. The Americans built not only hospitals and schools. The post-war Constitution of Japan, promulgated in 1947 at American insistence, was one of "Christian" America's most positive examples of international behavior. Article IX reads: "Aspiring sincerely to an international peace based on justice and order, the Japanese people forever renounce war as a sovereign right of the nation and the threat or use of force as a means of settling international disputes. / In order to accomplish the aim of the preceding paragraph, land, sea, and air forces, as well as other war potential, will never be maintained. The right of belligerency of the state will not be recognized." Thus Japan's 100 million people, through their Constitution, have experienced the "soul" of America and her religion.

11. The following statement by Eunice Santana de Velez may stand as one illustration, among innumerable cases, of America's dominating power: "In Puerto Rico we are born into colonialism, we think colonialism, we speak colonialism, we behave colonialism, we study colonialism, we eat colonialism, we breathe colonialism, we live colonialism, we die colonialism. And it is only within that context that we can understand Puerto Rico, its people and what happens within this country." From *The Christian Rural Mission in the 1980's: A Call to Liberation and Development of Peoples,* published by the National Council of Churches of Christ in the USA (New York, 1979), p. 52.

these two interrelated viewpoints, neither of which is to be treated lightly. Robert Speer was right in pointing out that the core significance of American Christianity, in the context of its global expression, is located in its moral and religious impact. Proclaiming the supremely moral name of Jesus Christ, building schools and hospitals abroad to meet human needs, and voicing words of criticism against one's own nation's idolatrous exploitation of others are all concrete expressions of Christian faith and life in the eyes of humanity and, particularly, of people in the third world. These concrete expressions have much to do with the themes of liberation theology, though this connection between theology and behavior is often ignored by those who have never visited mission hospitals in the remote parts of the world.

In brief, the attention of the third world church is focused upon the relationship between the Christian church in America and the nation America as it affects the quality of human life in the third world. As has been suggested, the complicating factor in this relationship is that the nation America, like any nation, can behave immorally, and that a sizable number of American churches can support (or acquiesce in) such immoral behavior, doing so even "theologically." In addition, one must not overlook the prevalence of a "privatized" Christian faith in the third world churches themselves.

III. American Church History in the Critical Time of "Reorganization of World History": Two Opposing Views

The Old Testament scholar Gerhard von Rad has characterized the prophet Jeremiah as one who perceived that God was engaged in a "reorganization of world history" in his time.[12] This dramatic phrase may be properly applied to our own time. A venerable missiological tradition—extending from the great sixteenth-century Jesuit missionary Francis Xavier to John R. Mott, one of the most distinguished missionary names in modern American church history—came to a critical moment of Christian self-examination when two opposing interpretations of world history were presented at the First Assembly of the World Council of Churches in Amsterdam in 1948.[13] These interpretations were advanced, respectively, by John Foster Dulles, an American Pres-

12. Gerhard von Rad, *Old Testament Theology*, 2 vols., trans. D. M. G. Stalker (Edinburgh/London: Oliver & Boyd, 1962-65), 2:208.
13. See *The Church and the International Disorder*, ed. W. A. Visser 't Hooft (New York: Harper, 1948).

byterian layman, and Josef L. Hromádka, a Czech theologian. In this debate, the tensions between the two approaches to "American church history from a third world perspective" were brought clearly, if indirectly, to expression.

Christian dedication to "God's greater glory" *(ad majorem dei gloriam)*, through the propagation of Christian morality and the vision of world evangelism (Xavier, Mott, Speer), animated Dulles's address:

> If Christian churches do not produce the needed vision, what can we expect but that mankind will stumble? . . . The need is for more effective political use of moral power. The moral law, happily, is a universal law. . . . It was Christians most of all who wanted a world organization which would depend primarily on moral rather than physical power.[14]

Dulles warned the assembly of a Soviet leadership that insists that change in history "can only be effected by violent means."[15] His remarks were given added weight by the great prestige attending the recent victory of the Allied Powers over Nazi Germany and Imperial Japan. By contrast, Hromádka declared:

> The basic issue of our times, both in national and international life, is far more than freedom and democracy. It goes beyond the categories of capitalism and socialism, liberalism and communism. . . . The whole of the civilized human race is sick, and none is justified to claim a monopoly of means and medicines for the cure of the disintegrated international order.[16]

Quoting Romans 3:12, Hromádka warned the assembly "against any effort to identify the Church of Christ with a definite political cause or to use her against any international power bloc."[17]

Both eminent Christians, Dulles and Hromádka, understood that world history is now being reorganized; but they differed sharply in their interpretation of what "America" in its depth, that is, American church history, means to the world. Dulles underscored the special moral quality of Christian America that would be beneficial to the postwar world, while Hromádka insisted on the perspective of the Gospel, which judges all nations.[18] Though Hromádka was from the so-called second world, this dramatic confrontation at Amsterdam uniquely displays the unavoidable tensions, and ambiguities, which today inform the third world's perspective on American church history.

14. Ibid., p. 113.
15. Ibid., p. 100.
16. Ibid., pp. 115ff.
17. Ibid., p. 117.
18. See ibid., pp. 73-142.

In my view, the self-critical Christian world today is not responding directly to John R. Mott's call for "the evangelization of the world in this generation." It is responding, rather, with a penetrating examination of the first-world Christian church, emphatically of the American church, which issued that earnest missionary call. What Mott passionately stood for throughout his life has not been eliminated from the Christian awareness of history. It is now beginning, rather, to express itself in a different form. The Christian dedication to evangelism, say the new critics, must be seen in light of the third world church's scrutiny of the (American) Christian world's moral contradictions. This scrutiny implies a fundamental reorientation of missiology in our time. And this reorientation, in turn, has been profoundly influenced by the advent of liberation theology.

In theological language, one may suggest that the contrast between Dulles and Hromádka is one between a *theologia gloriae* and a *theologia crucis*. To be sure, while one may make such a distinction in theology, the actual course of history itself does not support such a neat, unqualified distinction. Perhaps this is the reason why *both* Christian interpretations of history remain challenging and relevant. In any event, for the last forty years both the American church and the third world church have experienced the serious inner contradictions that beset the idea and the reality of "Christian America."

IV. The Black Christian Critique of the American Contradiction

In the 1960s, Americans' awareness of their nation's moral contradictions was deepened and enlarged by the events associated with Martin Luther King, Jr., the great civil rights leader. Likewise, the third world began to reappraise American church history in the light of the stirring words spoken by this frequently imprisoned Baptist preacher. One of his most memorable utterances, for the third world church, had to do with the global implications of what America was doing in Vietnam:

> We were taking the black young men who had been crippled by our society and sending them eight thousand miles away to guarantee liberties in Southeast Asia which they had not found in southwest Georgia and East Harlem. So we have been repeatedly faced with the cruel irony of watching Negro and white boys on TV screens as they kill and die together for a nation that has been unable to seat them together in the same schools. So we watch them in brutal solidarity burning the

huts of a poor village, but we realize that they would never live on the same block in Detroit.[19]

With these few simple words, King relentlessly exposed the tragic inner contradictions within pious and racist America, which was trying to "guarantee liberties in Southeast Asia" while denying them at home. The geographical scale on which he exposed this contradiction spanned 8,000 miles, reaching right into the third world of Vietnam. To the third world church "Vietnam" is the most recent expression of the American "manifest destiny." America sends missionaries wherever there is a moral problem. America sends troops wherever there is a military problem. King's pronouncement of judgment upon a racist America thus implicitly pronounced judgment on the American doctrine of manifest destiny and thereby joined America's future with that of the third world. (This linkage, indeed, was a work of the third world *within* the first world.) There can be little doubt that the third world church perceived the finger of God, which casts out demons, at work in the person of the black civil rights leader. His poignant words, quoted above, gave the third world church an eloquent example of "historical" exegesis of the biblical faith in this critical time of the reorganization of world history.

The story of the struggle for civil rights in the 1960s is perhaps the most important "Christian message" that has ever come from America to the third world. Among many important contributions, it gave the third world a theology that God is not "white."[20] To hazard a generalization: with Martin Luther King, Jr. *(theologia crucis)*, not with John Foster Dulles *(theologia gloriae)*, American church history has become extremely relevant to the third world. America, that is, is perceived no longer as a morally secure Christian America, but as an America that struggles to achieve social justice by overcoming racism. Since the "King event" in American history, the Gospel of Christ preached by Americans must necessarily touch upon the truth about America's spiritual contradiction. In this specific sense, then, America has truly become a "chosen" nation.

19. "A Time to Break Silence," speech delivered at Riverside Church, New York, April 4, 1967; printed in *A Testament of Hope: Essential Writings of Martin Luther King, Jr.*, ed. James M. Washington (San Francisco: Harper & Row, 1986), p. 233.

20. See *Black Theology: A Documentary History, 1966-1979*, ed. Gayraud S. Wilmore and James H. Cone (Maryknoll: Orbis, 1979), p. 46. I consider this book to be one of the most significant for the third world church to have come from America. The vast majority of third world peoples are "colored" (I am thinking of Asians in general). It is important to know that they themselves are very much "color prejudiced."

V. America as "Cain"

The Roman Catholic bishops in Latin America, after Vatican II, presented their liberation theology ("Let my people go!") on two historic occasions: first, in 1968, at the Second General Conference of Latin American Bishops in Medellin, Columbia; and, second, in 1979, at the Third General Conference of Latin American Bishops in Puebla, Mexico. Meanwhile, in 1976, the National Council of Churches' Division of Overseas Ministries received "An Open Letter to North American Christians" from the main Protestant religious leaders in Latin America. Here are two key paragraphs from this letter:

> Friends and fellow Christians, it is time that you realize that our continent is becoming one gigantic prison, and in some regions one vast cemetery; that human rights, the grand guidelines of the Gospel, are becoming a dead letter, without force. And all of this in order to maintain a system, a structure of dependency, that benefits the mighty privileged persons of your land and of our land at the expense of the poor millions who are increasing throughout the width and breadth of the continent.
>
> If in the past you felt it to be your apostolic duty to send us missionaries and economic resources, today the frontier of your witness and Christian solidarity is within your own country. [Through] the conscious, intelligent and responsible use of your vote, . . . you must ask yourselves if you will or will not be "your brother's keeper" in these lands of America, from which the blood of millions of Abels is clamoring to heaven.[21]

Thus, from the standpoint of the third world church, the American nation and an American Christianity that supports its national policy are looked upon as a murderous "Cain."

One of the signers of the letter, the Cuban Sergio Arce, had reflected in 1970 on the themes of "ecumenism and bourgeois individualism" and "ecumenism in capitalist societies." He pointed out that any ecumenism not based on "the biblical concept of the human being as an essentially social being" cannot be a Christian ecumenism.[22] He spoke of a "revolutionary ecumenism" that is "on the secular paths of our revolutionary world, our revolutionary Cuba, by lending our hands on the cane plantation, sweating together in the open air, in the trench of socio-economic-political obligation fulfilled, and the duty that is in-

---

21. See *Christianity and Crisis*, October 18, 1976, p. 231.
22. Sergio Arce, *The Church and Socialism: Reflections from a Cuban Context* (New York: Circus Publications, 1985), p. 75.

cumbent on us as human beings and as Cubans."[23] His remarks implied that "America as Cain" is an international expression of a popular "privatized Christianity" in America, one that evades the biblical passages that refer to the social responsibility of Christians. Frequently, the Reformation doctrine of "justification by faith alone" has been used to argue against Christian "social action." Privatized Christianity promotes oppression, namely, in the words of Pope Paul VI at the Medellin Conference, the "systems and structures which cover up and favor grave and oppressive inequalities."[24] The realization that the privatization of Christian faith can make a "Cain" of a Christian America is a message that provokes painful and confusing debates in America itself and even in the third world church. I say "even in the third world church" advisedly, since the majority of third world churches also understand the Christian faith "personally" (privately) without much attention to its social implications. American evangelists who fly into the third world in waves, and who engage in saturation bombing with "the Gospel" in order to save "lost billions," invariably preach this privatized Christianity.

Tragically, the world is divided between a Cain zone and an Abel zone. In the Cain zone, people are dying from overeating, while in the Abel zone they die from starvation. Unfortunately, every Abel zone also has its own Cains ("Herods") who (most of them are Christians) exploit and torture their people with the permission of the "Emperors" (who are often also Christians). The report of the 1983 meeting of the Ecumenical Association of Third World Theologians, in Geneva, is titled "Doing Theology in a Divided World." Third world theologian Philip Potter writes as follows:

> In the Third World, theology has to be done in a context of the most tragic and devastating history of domination, exploitation, and destruction that humanity has ever known and perpetrated. For the last nearly five hundred years, and particularly since the industrial revolution of the eighteenth century, Europe and later North America, and the outposts of Europe in South Africa, Australia, and New Zealand, joined in this century by Japan, have been engaged in a massive onslaught on the peoples, lands, and resources of the Third World. Although slavery had been practiced in many parts of the world, the slave trade of the seventeenth to the nineteenth century conducted by Europe from Africa to the Americas and the institution of slavery represented a new demonic phenomenon in history, the effects of which still remain, not least in the

23. Ibid., p. 82.
24. As quoted by Joseph Gremillion, *The Gospel of Peace and Justice* (Maryknoll: Orbis, 1976), p. 18.

form of white racism. These events took place around the time of the Renaissance, the Reformation, and Counter-Reformation in Europe, and were accelerated in the era of the Enlightenment of the eighteenth century and the French Revolution in the name of liberty, equality, and fraternity.[25]

These words disclose to the world at large the contradiction (sin) of western Christendom over the last five centuries, going back to a time even before the discovery of America. Our present perspective, stretching from Francis Xavier to Mott-Speer, to Dulles-Hromádka and to Sergio Arce, must be located in the larger framework of this tragic history.[26] The moral contradiction pointed out by Martin King during the Vietnam War has, in fact, been operative for 500 years. Third world theologians urge and demand that the world, particularly the Christian world, acknowledge the grave importance of this historical perspective. In short, according to Potter, the West has been "Cain" to the rest of the world for the past five centuries: a gigantic accusation leveled by the vast third world humanity against the dominant religion of the Atlantic world, Christianity.

The devastating experience of slavery and colonialism, which were perpetrated for centuries by western Christian masters, has made the third world church suspicious of the Christian doctrinal view of history as linear. Western imperialism, which refashioned Christian eschatology, has made good use of this linearism. The drive of human greed has an efficient linear thrust. The third world church mistrusts the American idea of a "linear" manifest destiny. The image of history as "zigzag," though awkward, would be truer to the viewpoint of a third world church existing among brutalized peoples. History as "zigzag" is an image in keeping with God's steadfast love (*hesed* in the Hebrew

25. *Doing Theology in a Divided World,* ed. Virginia Fabella and Sergio Torres (Maryknoll: Orbis, 1985), p. 11.

26. Philip Potter's critical notice of the recent joining of Asian Japan to the group of western exploiters requires us to trace the history of the rise and fall and revival of Japan during the last one hundred years. The fanatical Pacific War (1941-45, continuous from the 1931 China War), inspired by Japan's devotion to her parochial gods, came to its catastrophic end with the nuclear incineration of two cities. Supported by the good will of the victors, Japan stepped into the new era of the post-war Constitution. In the language of this Constitution, Japan moved from her paralyzing parochialism ("this world is for my glory") to emancipating universality ("this world is for the glory of all the peoples"). The best portion of the spiritual heritage of the western Enlightenment—that is, translated into theological language, the concept of "the Universal God"—was enshrined in the Preamble of the post-war Japanese Constitution. Today, in her life of ancient spirituality and modern scientific technology, Japan must engage in self-criticism in the light of "the Universal God." She must not return to the doctrine of "the weak and beggarly elemental spirits" (Gal. 4:9), which once utterly destroyed her.

Bible) that accompanies humanity's sinful course *(theologia crucis).*[27] The image of history as rectilinear suggests far too smooth a progression *(theologia gloriae)* to be true to human experience. "Cain" works against "Abel" with high efficiency. Colonialism was one of the most efficient operations ever engaged in by one part of humanity against another. Look at the efficient "straight lines" (what could be *more* efficient?) that colonial masters drew on the African map, dividing the peoples.

VI. Questions Put to American Church History by the Third World Church

The third world church is struggling to find an authentic apostolic and catholic identity in its own historical context. It is too soon to say that it has found this identity by establishing solidarity with the oppressed masses, though in my judgment it is only by moving in this direction that the third world church can attain and display apostolicity before its own people. To be sure, there is as much confusion and ambiguity in its life as in the church life of the first world. The extremely complex intertwinement of the first and third worlds, for all their good and evil, is the reality of the human condition today. "Test the spirits to see whether they are of God" (1 John 4:1). In the process of searching for its own Christian identity, the third world church puts a number of questions to the American church and thereby indicates how it perceives the history of that church. Among the issues at stake in this questioning are the following:

a. The cosmological and the eschatological

The religious experience of humanity may be expressed in a paraphrase of Psalm 121: "My help comes from heaven and earth." Salvation is cosmologically experienced. Against this general background comes the affirmation that "My help comes from the Maker of heaven and earth," which implies that salvation is to be experienced eschatologically. In church history the cosmological has been subordinated to the eschatological. That this subordination must not be accepted without careful

27. One must ask which view of history—the linear, the cyclic, or some other—can best express the *hesed-agape* of the biblical God. Such questioning will take us deep into the "Christ and culture" issue. The Indian Jesuit Samuel Rayan holds that salvation history "lies beyond linear and cyclic thought-patterns and must be described in non-geometrical, positively personal terms." See *Asian Christian Theology, Emerging Themes,* ed. Douglas J. Elwood (Philadelphia: Westminster, 1980), p. 125.

theological examination is suggested by the third world's long and profound religious history (Hinduism, Buddhism, Taoism).[28] The eschatological loses its saving power when it is separated from the cosmological. Church history must be brought into dialogue with the general religious history of humanity. American church history is being evaluated by the third world church from the viewpoint of this concern, which focuses our attention, in particular, on the history of American missionary experience in the lands of the eastern religions.

b. A wider concept of church history

The religious conviction of "ethical monotheism" is at the center of American church history. The third world church, existing in a polytheistic religious environment, has inherited this conviction. The great thesis that there is One God who is concerned about the maintenance of social justice in the world is expressed in the three Semitic faiths: Judaism, Christianity, and Islam. The ethical monotheism that "unifies" these faiths is of special importance for the theology of the third world church. Christianity, understood in a "broader" sense, can comprise the three Near Eastern faiths. Seen from this angle, the value of American church history for the third world church is found in the history of American Christianity's experience and propagation of ethical monotheism. The question facing the third world church is whether this ethical monotheism has given more *shalom* to humanity than has natural polytheism.

c. American military culture

The Hindu doctrine of "retribution" (action-reaction, *karman*) is widely accepted as an everyday truth in the religious and cultural traditions of India and, broadly, of Asia. American military culture today operates largely in congruence with this doctrine. At the center of this culture is a commitment to "the balance of terror"—nuclear deterrence—to maintain "peace." This position is, in emotional and philosophical terms, more in line with the Hindu doctrine of *karman* than with the Christian doctrine of grace. Indeed, the idea of "balance" as the ultimate principle for resolving the problem of evil is what *karman* means. It was only in May 1986 that the bishops of the United Methodist Church in America, opposing the majority "Christian" trend, rejected this retributive doc-

---

28. On the relationship between the cosmological and the eschatological, see my book *Mount Fuji and Mount Sinai* (Maryknoll: Orbis, 1985).

trine of deterrence and called upon American Christians to return to the Christian doctrine of a new possibility of grace in history.[29]

The vast amount of its resources that America has poured into military preparedness expresses its confidence in the doctrine of *karman*. The American military culture of retribution has thus produced its peculiar dehumanization. The religious tradition in which the essential value of humanity is defined as the "image of God" has been replaced by a tradition whose anthropology is based on *karman*. The third world church is not contending that the doctrine of retribution has little or no value. It *does* maintain that there is a discrepancy between the doctrine of retribution and the "sublime morality of Christ."

d. American denominationalism

One of the most destructive experiences of the third world church relates to the denominational divisions it has inherited from the Christian missions of the West. Western denominationalism has often been compared to the Indian caste system by both Christians and non-Christians. In fact, for the last three decades, a number of Asian nations have been reluctant to grant visas to western missionaries on the ground that Christian missions increase divisions in their national life. American religious culture has largely been built upon particular denominational traditions and experiences of the Christian faith. However, in the judgment of the third world church, such acceptance of denominationalism cannot go unchallenged.[30] Still, one must not overlook the fact that the third world churches have received substantial financial help through the system of American denominationalism. Here both the third world church and the American church encounter a painful ambiguity.

e. Patriotism in a Christian America

Christianity has imparted to humanity the concept of a loving God whose love is directed to the whole of humanity. Examined from this perspective of universality, patriotism may readily involve a narrow

29. The general spiritual and political orientation of American Christian rightist groups is expressed in these words of the Rev. Jerry Falwell: "The sad fact is that today the Soviet Union would kill 135 million to 160 million Americans, and the United States would kill only 3 to 5 percent of the Soviets because of their antiballistic missiles and their civil defense" (*Listen America!* [New York: Bantam Books], p. 85). Here an influential American church leader graphically displays his adherence to the doctrine of *karman*.

30. See Fabella and Torres, eds., *Irruption of the Third World: Challenge to Theology*, p. 40.

parochialism, even a psychology of self-righteousness. The human feeling of devotion to one's own nation must be brought under the judgment of the universal God. From the viewpoint of the third world church, which all too often stands at the receiving end of the destructive impact of American patriotism, recent American church history (particularly since the inception of the deadly cold war between the superpowers) must be assessed in its relationship to the history of American patriotism.

f. "Hiroshima" in a Christian America

Two cities, Hiroshima and Nagasaki, were destroyed by American nuclear attack in 1945. With this event, the possibility of cosmic genocide by nuclear weapons entered human history. How, during the past four decades, has American church history treated "Hiroshima"? In this regard special importance attends "A Pastoral Letter on War and Peace, the Challenge of Peace: God's Promise and Our Response," issued by the National Conference of Catholic Bishops in May 1983. American Christians are charged with the gravest responsibility on earth today. The future of humanity, of all living beings and the earth's biosphere itself, may depend upon how the American churches influence their nation's government. Is it possible to reinterpret recent American church history in the light of this awesome responsibility?

PART TWO

The Changing Theological Disciplines

11. Professionals and Pedagogues: A Survey of Theological Education

Glenn T. Miller

Pluralism has long been the glory and the shame of American religion. While pluralism nurtured such religious values as tolerance and individual self-determination, it also promoted separatism, the waste of resources, and the reduplication of religious efforts and institutions. Theological education has reflected this dark side of American pluralism. Whenever a denomination, religious movement, or theological oddity aspired to respectability, its leaders established a school to transmit their faith to new generations. Once a school exists, the laws grant it conditional immortality and the institution continues after the original reasons for its genesis have become outmoded. Consequently, the history of American theological schools is a series of institutional crises in which schools seek new self-understandings to replace older orthodoxies. From 1935 to 1950, the belief that theological schools primarily trained professional ministers eased many transitions.[1]

---

1. "Profession" and "professionalism" are, admittedly, loaded terms that mean different things to different people. The literature on the subject is vast. I have found the following useful in understanding professionalism and professional education: Burton Bledstein, *The Culture of Professionalism: The Middle Class and the Development ʿ Higher Education in America* (New York: Norton, 1976); "The Professions in America," *Daedalus* 94 (1963) 647-860; Everette C. Hughes, *Education for the Professions of Medicine, Law, ʾheology, and Social Welfare* (Berkeley: Carnegie Commission on Higher Education, 1973); William J. MacGlothlin, *Patterns of Professional Education* (New York: Putnam's, 1960) and *The Professional Schools* (New York: Center for Applied Research in Education, 1964). For specific applications to theology, see Jackson Walter Carroll, "Seminaries and Seminarians: A Study of the Professional Socialization of Protestant Clergymen" (Ph.D. dissertation, Princeton Theological Seminary, 1970), and James Gustavson, "Theological Education as Professional Education," *Theological Education* 5 (Spring 1973) 187-93.

GLENN T. MILLER

I. Professionalism

In 1934, William Adams Brown and Mark A. May published *The Education of American Ministers* in four volumes.[2] The study was an attempt at reform. Surveys were an established means of educational change. The most successful surveys were the searching examinations of medical education by Abraham Flexner. His *Medical Education in the United States and Canada* (1910) and *Medical Education in Europe* (1912) evaluated existing American medical institutions according to the high standards of the university-related schools.[3] Medical educators quickly drew the right conclusions from these studies. The training of physicians, which had often been conducted in private (for profit) schools with inadequate lab and clinical facilities, became centered in university-related schools with nearby research hospitals and laboratories. While the effects were never as dramatic, law school surveys also helped reorder that profession's educational procedures.[4]

The new Brown-May survey followed an earlier survey, *Theological Education in America,* prepared by Robert Kelly in 1924.[5] Kelly's findings were so bleak and depressing that the leaders of the major schools, who maintained that Kelly, an outsider, did not understand seminaries, demanded that a new study be undertaken by a theological educator. The Conference of Theological Schools (an organization founded in 1918 for discussion of the question of the seminaries' relationship to the post–World War I situation)[6] commissioned the new study. John D. Rockefeller's Institute of Social and Religious Research agreed to pay for the research if the seminaries agreed to use its results. Brown and May were not only to issue a statistical study of theological education; they were also to promote needed change.[7] If sponsorship by theo-

2. William Adams Brown and Mark A. May, *The Education of American Ministers,* 4 vols. (New York: Institute of Social and Religious Research, 1934). Hereafter referred to as Brown-May.

3. Abraham Flexner, *Medical Education in the United States and Canada* (New York: Carnegie Foundation, 1910); *Medical Education in Europe* (New York: Carnegie Foundation, 1912).

4. Robert Stevens, *Law School: Legal Education in America from the 1850's to the 1980's* (Chapel Hill: University of North Carolina Press, 1983), especially Chapters 6 and 7.

5. Robert Kelly, *Theological Education in America: A Study of One Hundred and Sixty-One Theological Schools in the United States and Canada* (New York: Doran Company, 1924).

6. The conference first met at Harvard, August 13-16, 1918.

7. The best account of the process of moving from the Brown-May study to the establishment of the A.T.S. is David Blaine Cable, "The Development of the Accrediting Function of the American Association of Theological Schools, 1918-1938" (Ph.D. dissertation, University of Pittsburgh, 1970).

logical schools aided the study, it also limited the results. Brown and May (unlike Flexner) could not use standards beyond the reach of the existing schools. Brown personally believed that theological education needed a university setting to train religious leaders adequately, and in *Theological Education* (1914) and *The Case for Theology in the University* (1938) he vigorously defended that position.[8]

Brown-May's thesis was simple: theological schools exist to train ministers and the schools ought to reorganize themselves around this task. Brown wrote:

> It [the task of ministerial education] is to furnish the minister with the knowledge he needs to understand his . . . task and to develop the skills which will enable him to discharge it effectively under the particular conditions which confront him as a Protestant minister in the United States. . . .[9]

Accordingly, the seminaries and divinity schools ought to derive their standards from the work expected of their graduates. Just as medical and legal schools saw practice as the best guide to preparation, so theological schools ought to emphasize the acquisition of specific skills.

Although little agreement existed on the theological interpretation of ministry, Brown-May discovered a consensus about what ministers did. The survey listed five areas: worship leader, evangelist, teacher, pastor, and administrator.[10] Although a present-day educator might divide Brown's pastor into counselor and social action advocate, Brown's description of the parish ministry is still valid.

In part, Brown and May were successful because they articulated a widely shared understanding of theological schooling. Traditionally, Protestants believed that theology was a "university" discipline built on its own logical foundations. Ministers were trained in this discipline. Throughout the nineteenth century, the conviction grew that theological education needed a new justification. The older understanding was reversed. Now the purpose of theology was to produce ministers. As early as Friedrich Schleiermacher's *Brief Outline of the Study of Theology*

---

8. William Adams Brown was the leading expert on theological schools in the United States. In addition to the survey, he published *Theological Education* (New York: Macmillan, 1914); *The Case for Theology in the University* (Chicago: University of Chicago Press, 1938); "A Century of Theological Education and After," *Journal of Religion* 6 (July 1926) 363-83; "The Common Problems of Theological Schools," *Journal of Religion* 1 (May 1921) 282-95; and "The Seminary of Tomorrow," *Harvard Theological Review* 12 (April 1919) 165-78. Brown's vision of theological education was based on his liberal understanding of the continuity between all areas of human knowledge and achievement. He was America's best theorist of theological education in the twentieth century.

9. Brown-May I, 196.

10. Brown-May I, 196-208.

(1811; rev. ed., 1830),[11] advanced theological opinion stressed church service as the reason for study. The progressive optimism of such innovative American university presidents as William Rainey Harper, of the University of Chicago, gave this ideal a new-world flavor.[12] The widespread popularity of progressive education contributed to a willingness to see action as the measure of reflection. The religious situation in the 1930s also made this reversal compelling. The conflict between fundamentalists and modernists, although moderated after the Scopes Trial (1925), continued, and the Conference of Theological Schools, predominantly liberal in composition, wanted to retain the loyalty of such conservative seminaries as Princeton and Southern Baptist. By defining theological education as ministerial education, Brown and May found a standard that all might share.

Brown-May's equation of theological education with ministerial preparation influenced, directly and indirectly, the most important changes in theological education from 1935 to 1985. The transformation of theological education from a virtually all-male preserve in 1935 to a more sexually integrated enterprise in 1985 was partially related to the professional model. Although the feminist movement, liberation theology, and the turmoil of the 1960s influenced the change, professionalism eased the transition. Since ministry was a job and women could be trained to do that job, little reason existed to exclude them from either the training or the profession itself. Another illustration of the equation's direct influence was the merger or grouping of small seminaries in a particular location. Since few of these cooperating institutions agreed theologically (and almost all underestimated the problems of cooperation), the professional understanding of theological education held together fragile unions.

II. Accreditation

Rockefeller commissioned the Brown-May study with an agreement that the seminaries would form an association with reasonable standards of accreditation.[13] The need was acute. In 1935, more than 144 seminaries (no one knows the exact number) existed. These schools were plural-

11. Friedrich Schleiermacher, *Brief Outline of the Study of Theology* (Edinburgh: T. & T. Clark, 1850).

12. William Rainey Harper, "Shall the Theological Curriculum be Changed and Why?," *American Journal of Theology* 3 (January 1899) 45-66.

13. This section is deeply indebted to Cable's study (see note 7). See also Earl Barker, "Accreditation of Theological Schools," *Peabody Journal of Education* 14 (January 1937) 169-77.

istic in curriculum, standards for administration, library holdings, teaching staff, and degree structure. The college degree as prerequisite to seminary study, perhaps the oldest American standard, was rarely attained. Only one of every three ministers had both college and seminary training.

Seminary accreditation was both similar to that in other professional schools and different at the same time. While the standards of medical and law schools were ultimately guaranteed by the state (for example, the bar examination in law and the board examination in medicine), seminaries operated without governmental regulation. The mundane problems of transfer of credits and standardization of degrees, which encouraged colleges and universities to form voluntary accrediting associations, were less pressing for seminaries. Seminary programs were self-contained, and the few transfers were easily handled on an individual basis. Two factors further complicated the problem. First, the historical accidents that had created a school gave it a specific identity or character which it believed had to be preserved. Second, each church jealously guarded admission to its own ministry.

Brown-May's identification of theological and ministerial education provided a way for the better seminaries to cooperate without abandoning their identities or their relationships to particular churches or theologies. In 1934, the Conference of Theological Schools became an accrediting agency. Lewis Sherrill, a Harvard religious educator, was elected executive secretary and commissions on standards of admission and accreditation were appointed.[14] In 1936, the conference changed its name to the American Association of Theological Schools in the United States and Canada (later the Association of Theological Schools) and adopted standards for seminaries based on the results of the Brown-May survey. The new standards affirmed four points: (1) the seminaries were to concentrate on the Bachelor of Divinity degree, which was to be awarded only to college graduates; (2) all schools were to have at least four faculty members; (3) each school was to have adequate financial resources (from endowment and other sources) to support its program; and (4) each school had to maintain a library commensurate with its published curriculum. Procedures, analogous to those of other accrediting bodies, were established to determine whether the standards were attained or not. Initially, only forty-four schools were able to satisfy the association that they had met the standards, and all but sixteen of

14. Lewis Sherrill's sense of substantial progress is attested in "American Association of Theological Schools," *Christian Education* 20 (February 1937) 207-10, and "The Status of Theological Education," *Christian Education* 19 (February 1936) 219-30.

these received notations for some failures (particularly in the area of nongraduate admissions). The development of the standards was to be progressive. From time to time, the Association was to raise the benchmarks and to urge its members to meet the higher marks.

Many factors (few associated with education) encouraged the steady expansion of the number of accredited institutions. The most important was government. During the Second World War, the armed forces set requirements for the chaplaincy analogous to those for other professional (specialized) members of the officer corps. Just as a degree from an accredited law or medical school was required for doctors and lawyers, so an accredited seminary degree was required for chaplains. Also, from 1946 to the early 1970s, the Veterans Administration subsidized the education of men and women in service. These actions made accreditation almost necessary. Although military careers were popular during the "cold war," the new revenues were the key to change. More potential ministers could now afford theological education, and a sufficient pool of college graduates was available to permit seminaries to limit their nongraduate enrollments. In turn, churches raised their standards. Many denominations, including the popularly based Methodists and American (Northern) Baptists, made seminary a requirement for full ordination.

The A.T.S. expanded to meet the increasing number of schools seeking accreditation. A grant of $250,000 from the Sealantic Fund (John D. Rockefeller, Jr.) in 1955 financed the first full-time director, Charles L. Taylor, and established an office. During the 1950s and 1960s, the association grew to include most of the nation's Protestant schools (including the evangelical schools), and, by the 1980s, new Protestant schools routinely sought the association's blessing. Perhaps the best measure of the success of the A.T.S. was the number of seminaries also accredited by secular agencies.

After Vatican II (1962-65), Roman Catholic institutions began to apply for membership. By and large, American priests had been educated in schools that continued the educational traditions of seventeenth-century France. These schools emphasized theological uniformity and priestly formation, a program of regimented piety that shaped the young priest's religious character. Jesuit schools, which stood outside this tradition, shared many of the same concerns, although with more stress on dutiful and obedient scholarship. While some modification of existing standards was necessary to accommodate the radically different style of theological education practiced in Catholic institutions, their admission and standardization were smooth. The professional understanding of theological education thus created a shared community of values between rival confessions.[15] Protestants and Catholics learned from each other. Catholic seminarians became less cloistered and were enrolled in field education and modern counseling programs, while Protestant students placed a new value on spirituality and religious growth.

In the course of fifty years, then, accreditation became the accepted norm for theological schools. Theological education now had clear standards (if still low compared to schools of law, medicine, and social work). Further, accreditation encouraged the creation of a community of theological educators who discussed common problems, hopes, and expectations. The journal *Theological Education* (first published in 1964), and the association's annual meetings, provided a forum. In addition, the association became a conduit for faculty research and development.

The significance of the association can be underestimated. Accreditation and discussion of issues were not dramatic events; years were required for either to have an effect on an institution or a system of schools. The best evidence for the influence of accreditation was the Niebuhr-Williams-Gustafson report, *The Advancement of Theological Education,* published in 1957. The book's title was significant. Compared to the problems detailed by Brown-May in the 1930s, theological education had advanced, despite the work's caution that there was "little basis for complacency."[16] The schools had corrected many serious flaws and were ready to lead the church in new directions. The concept of the "pastoral director," which the authors (perhaps mistakenly) believed was emerging in their time, offered one new possibility, as did the increase in the size of Protestant congregations. To be sure, many of the changes advocated by the association were related to larger patterns in American education. All schools, for example, have demanded more education for their teachers; all professions have tightened entrance requirements; degrees have become more valued by society at large. Still, the A.T.S.'s achievement has been substantial. Accreditation produced a common understanding of theological education and a method for

15. John Tracy Ellis, ed., *The Catholic Priest in the United States: Historical Investigations* (Collegeville, MN: St. John's University Press, 1971); pp. 94-97 detail some of the changes as Ellis saw them. Most interesting is the emphasis on college graduation and counseling, both marks of the "professional" understanding supported by the A.T.S.

16. H. Richard Niebuhr, Daniel Day Williams, and James Gustafson, *The Advancement of Theological Education* (New York: Harper, 1957), p. 200. See also Niebuhr and Williams, eds., *The Ministry in Historical Perspective* (New York: Harper, 1956) and Niebuhr, Williams, and Gustafson, *The Purpose of the Church and its Ministry: Reflections on the Aims of Theological Education* (New York: Harper, 1956).

evaluating the quality of that education. If the schools still reflected the pluralism of new-world religion, they possessed some common characteristics as well.

Graduate theological education might have adopted a system of accreditation without the professional model. After all, the Bible schools and colleges, which resisted earlier efforts at standardization, eventually established an accrediting agency.[17] But, as events unfolded, the widespread acceptance of the identification of theological education with ministerial preparation sped and aided the process. Patterns of cooperation were established that crossed confessional and party (liberal, conservative, fundamentalist) barriers, which might otherwise have proved impassable. Evangelicals and Roman Catholics obviously differ on many issues, but they agree on the value of a common professional standard for their clergy. Ironically, theological education, historically divisive among American Christians, has been one of the few areas in which practical ecumenism has partially succeeded.

III. The Minister as a Helping Professional

The professional approach to theological education shaped the most successful ministerial specialty: counseling. The understanding of the minister as an advisor on life's way had many origins. American religious liberalism was dissatisfied with traditional pastoral care. In *The Christian Pastor and the Working Church* (1914), Washington Gladden promoted the "minister as friend," who, he hoped, might replace the traditional authoritarian pastor who examined families about their souls.[18] The new discipline of religious education, established by 1914, combined progressive education, an appreciation of human development, and theology into a workable approach to personal problems. The example of successful ministers helped make counseling part of the accepted definition of the pastor. Harry Emerson Fosdick in the North, and Theodore Adams in the South, incorporated counseling into their ministries. Both Adams and Fosdick consulted psychologists and psychiatrists, served their churches as counselors, and,

17. See Virginia Brereton, "Protestant Fundamentalist Bible Schools, 1882-1940" (Ph.D. dissertation, Columbia University, 1981); also Herbert Cocking, "Bible School Accreditation by the North Central Association, 1970-1980" (Ph.D. dissertation, University of Michigan, 1982). Many of the problems that seminaries faced in the 1930s were characteristic of the Bible colleges and schools in the 1950s and 1960s.

18. Washington Gladden, *The Christian Pastor and the Working Church* (New York: Scribner's, 1914), especially Chapter 7, "The Minister as Friend."

more importantly, used psychological insights in their widely imitated preaching.[19]

The "revival" of the 1950s increased interest in counseling by combining traditional theology with the belief that religion promoted mental health. "See your minister, priest, or rabbi" became one of the stock responses in such newspaper columns as "Dear Abby." Popular religious personalities, including Fulton Sheen, Billy Graham, and Norman Vincent Peale, repeated the same message. If any single understanding of ministry came to be shared by ministers and their publics, it was that the clergy were members of a "helping" profession, one closely related to—although different from—psychology and social work.

Counseling influenced the daily work of ministers in different ways. For most, counseling was another duty alongside weekly worship and parish administration. Others took new paths. The chaplaincy, a ministry that originated in the medieval church, was expanded to include hospitals, prisons, and industrial plants as well as the more traditional military services. Some ministers set themselves up in "private practice" as pastoral counselors, and financed their work by fees or by support from an ecumenical network of congregations. Seminaries naturally responded to the interest in pastoral psychology. By the late 1950s, serious work in counseling became a mark of a good seminary. The pressing question concerned how this was to be done. Although many institutions relied on the traditional classroom, others incorporated some type of "clinical" experience into their programs.

The new clinical programs had a long history, beginning in the late nineteenth century. Graham Taylor, who taught at Hartford and Chicago, placed his students in different ministries and rigorously supervised their work. By monitoring student employment, Taylor hoped to transform the church work used by students to finance their studies into an opportunity for learning.[20] George Coe, of New York's Union Seminary and, later, of Teacher's College—Columbia University, used a similar method derived from progressive education.[21] The most im-

---

19. Robert Moats Miller, *Harry Emerson Fosdick* (New York: Oxford University Press, 1985), especially Chapter 15, "On Being a Real Person: A Protestant Preacher as Confessor and Counselor." On the influential ministry of Theodore Adams of Richmond's First Baptist Church, see John Carlton, *The World in His Heart* (Nashville: Broadman Press, 1985).

20. Graham Taylor, "Field Work: Its Educational Value and Relation to the Financial Aid of Students," in *Christianity Practically Applied* (New York: Baker and Taylor, 1894) II, 428-41.

21. George Albert Coe, "The Theological Seminary: The Laboratory Method in the Department of Religious Education," *Religious Education* 7 (October 1912) 420-24. Also "The Education of Ministers," *Religious Education* 5 (December 1910) 454-57.

portant beginning,[22] however, came in the 1920s when William A. Keller (Cincinnati), Richard Cabot (Boston),[23] and Anton T. Boisen (Worchester, Mass.)[24] began experimenting with hospital situations in the training of ministers.

The new approach had its greatest impact after 1930. In 1931, Philip Giles was appointed to the recently united Andover and Newton Theological Schools as a professor of clinical training, a tenure that lasted until 1953. Working from this base, he established a string of training centers that served the New England schools. At the same time, Helen Flanders Dunbar established centers in the middle states. In 1935, Seward Hiltner began his long career in pastoral psychology, exploring new methods of instruction and their theological implications; in 1945, Wayne Oates began his noteworthy program in Louisville, Kentucky.

Between 1935 and 1980, the practitioners of clinical pastoral training clarified its methods, theology, and relationship to the seminaries. Clinical education occurred at sites distant from the host school. A skilled counselor could only supervise a few students. A successful program thus required the coordination of a number of separate sites, each with its own personnel. The new discipline might have developed as a paraecclesiastical and paraseminary movement. This did not happen, perhaps because of the deep devotion to the churches on the part of such seminary-related clinicians as Wayne Oates, John Billinski, and Seward Hiltner, and—above all—owing to the post–World War II success of the seminaries in establishing themselves as the preferred means of ministerial preparation. By 1967, after a long process of refinement, the various groups offering clinical training accepted a common set of standards for supervisors. The relationships with the seminaries, usually through professors of counseling (pastoral care), were also clarified at this time. In effect, counseling developed its own system of accreditation and evaluation.

The methods of clinical training were both obscured and clarified

---

22. The best treatment of the rise of the clinical training movement is Edward Thornton, *Professional Education for Ministry: A History of Clinical Pastoral Education* (Nashville: Abingdon, 1970). See also E. Brooks Holifield, *A History of Pastoral Care in America* (Nashville: Abingdon, 1983). An even broader perspective is provided by John T. McNeill, *A History of the Care of Souls* (New York: Harper, 1951).

23. Richard Clarke Cabot, a medical doctor, was perhaps the clearest of the original clinical advocates about the purposes of the new program. Significantly, he often linked clinical training with ethics. See John Oliver Nelson, "Richard Clarke Cabot and the Development of Clinical Education" (Ph.D. dissertation, University of Iowa, 1970).

24. For an interesting account of Boisen, see Henri Nouwen, "Anton T. Boisen and Theology through Living Human Documents," *Pastoral Psychology* 19 (September 1968) 49-63. Cf. A. T. Boisen, "Period of Beginnings," *Journal of Pastoral Care* 5 (January 1951) 13-16.

by the use of the language of medical education by the movement's leaders.[25] Beneath the verbiage was the belief that an intense period of work under a supervisor, in a controlled situation (usually a hospital), enriched by peer interaction and response, was the best method to develop counseling skills. It was not so much learning by experience as it was education through evaluated performance. As in some secular programs, the counseling of the students was part of the program. Young counselors learned to help others by helping themselves. Similar insights, of course, lay behind the less well-defined efforts at field education, but the failure of field education to develop sufficiently clear standards (and perhaps its continuing function as a form of financial aid) made it less successful.

The importance of pastoral care in the overall development of post–World War II theological education encouraged some theologians to discuss the issues raised by counseling. In the 1950s and early 1960s, Paul Tillich used modern psychology as one of the principal elements in his "method of correlation." More directly related to clinical training were the studies of Gordon Jackson and John Cobb, who applied process metaphysics to pastoral psychology.[26]

The pastoral psychology movement was, of course, directly related to the professional understanding of theological education set forth in the Brown-May study. Counseling was an important element in a twentieth-century minister's vocation. But the clinical movement was also an implementation of the ideal of professional education. If "profession" implies the demonstrated capacity to perform a designated task, pastoral psychology was the one area of ministerial education where professionalism was more than a vague slogan. The pastoral psychologists convincingly demonstrated what a truly professional model of education might entail and thereby challenged theological schools to be more honest in their rhetoric.

IV. The New Doctors

If the pastoral care movement enabled seminaries to produce students who embodied the belief that the ministry is a "helping profession," the professional definition of seminary education enabled many schools to

---

25. James Ashbrook, "Limitation of the Older Medical Model in Training Pastoral Counsellors," *Journal of Pastoral Care* 22 (December 1968) 232-34.
26. Gordon Jackson, *Pastoral Care and Process Theology* (Washington, D.C.: University Press of America, 1981). John B. Cobb, *Theology and Pastoral Care* (Philadelphia: Fortress, 1977).

survive the 1970s and 1980s. When the long struggle in Vietnam ended, many seminaries were financially strapped and out of kilter with their wealthy patrons. Further, the counterculture movement, a source of meaning for some faculty and students, slowly disintegrated. Within colleges and universities, students became more vocationally oriented, and many observers noted a turn to the political right.

The mainstream seminaries saw themselves as embattled institutions, for both good and bad reasons. The financial crisis was substantial and interest in the ministry, especially among white males, was apparently declining. While increased enrollment of women and minorities and a trend toward second career decisions eased the crisis, the schools remained in a tight situation and needed to attract new students. To be sure, evangelical seminaries were growing, but, in some ways, their growth created similar problems. Money had to be found to support their increased size and to pay their increasingly professional faculty.

At the same time that seminaries faced their crisis, ministers were experiencing serious status anxiety. This uneasiness could be dismissed with a quip. Ever since the second generation of Puritans, some Americans have bewailed the declining power of old ideals and institutions, particularly the church and its ministry. But new or old, the feeling of unease was real. One manifestation was the widespread dissatisfaction with the degree nomenclature. As late as the 1960s, ministers received a second bachelor's degree for a longer period of study than that of their peers in other helping professions, and that degree was not understood by the general public. A professional, in the popular mind, held at least a master's degree. Despite some traditionalist wringing of hands, the degree became Master of Divinity.

The change in the name of the degree was only a beginning. American Christians, particularly in middle-class congregations, often sought men with doctoral degrees for their pulpits, and many clergymen sought doctorates to advance their careers. Those who lacked the time, the money, or the academic skills to earn the degree believed that they were second-class ministers whose career advancement was effectively blocked.

Theological educators were more willing to hear this complaint than in the past. Many, including those employed by the A.T.S., saw the limits of the existing master's program. The three-year program was educationally sounder in its purely academic courses than in its expressly professional components. Academic theology could be taught in the traditional three-hour lecture or two-hour seminar format, and the round of examinations and papers insured a measure of mastery. But this same format did not serve the professional fields well. How, for example, could the limited experience available in a three semester-hour course in preaching or religious education provide a sufficient basis for a successful ministry? At best, the student did one or two small projects. Even with field and clinical education (not required at all schools), the program was too theoretical to insure professional competency. Since a fundamental rethinking of the master's program was improbable, if for no other reason than faculty politics, something new was needed.

The doctor of ministry degree attempted to develop a new student market for theological schools, to satisfy the clerical desire for the status of a doctorate, and to provide a means for more in-depth professional training.[27] By the early 1970s, the majority of seminaries offered the new program. At the heart of the new degree was a period of professional experience under intense personal supervision, followed by the planning, execution, and report of a specific project in ministry. Considered in terms of its intellectual and educational values, the new program was promising. At last ministers, like their counterparts in other professions, might have their early performance carefully scrutinized and their professional development monitored, while contributing to a data base constructed from thousands of project reports.

Unfortunately, many Doctor of Ministry programs were instituted with indecent haste. In their effort to attract students, seminaries established training centers far from their home base (with its library and personnel resources) and, occasionally, overworked their teaching faculties by an excessive load of new doctoral candidates. Perhaps more serious was the fact that the new programs learned little from either clinical training's success or field education's failure. The key element in any effective program of vocationally based education is the quality of the supervisors, but no national body sought to certify the D.Min. supervisors, to monitor programs of training for them, and to

---

27. Literature on the D.Min. (both published and unpublished) is far too extensive to give more than a few important references to the development of the new structures. See H. B. Adams, "Doctoral Studies for Pastors: In-service Doctoral Programs," *Christian Century* 82 (April 28, 1965) 560; "Patterns of Continuing Education: The S.T.D. at San Francisco," *Theological Education* 1 (1965) 223-25; "Advanced Pastoral Studies: A New Need," *Encounter* 26 (Summer 1965) 340-48; and "D.Min. Degree After Ten Years: A Symposium," *Christian Century* 93 (February 4-11, 1976) 96-111. See also James Forrest Cobble, "The Influence of the Doctor of Ministry Program and Its Expanded Clientele on the Program Content, Instructional Practice, and Perceived Mission of McCormick Theological Seminary" (Ed.D. dissertation, University of Illinois at Urbana-Champaign, 1981). Cobble has the most extensive bibliography that I have found on the D.Min. program.

establish accepted norms of what constituted good supervision. Often the supervisor was simply one who had performed a particular ministry well. Similar observations should be made about the lack of appropriate norms for the evaluation of projects and project reports. The faculties of the various seminaries were not trained to administer the new degree and were provided with few guidelines for its implementation.

The D.Min. experience may be still too new to be assessed accurately. Most major shifts in theological education require several generations of teaching and learning before they become effective. The teaching of social ethics, for example, originated at Andover Seminary in the 1880s, but it did not become a necessary part of the curriculum until the 1930s in liberal schools, and even later in more conservative institutions. The future of the D.Min. remains open, but ultimately the future of the professional understanding of the seminaries and divinity schools may rest on its success or failure.

V. Roads Not Taken

The professional understanding of theological education has provided seminaries with needed guidance in the twentieth century. In addition to the developments sketched above, a plethora of new curricula, "parish-based" theological proposals and experiments, and plans of student evaluation (Readiness for Ministry) were all shaped by some variation on the basic theme of education for ministry. One may say, with only slight exaggeration, that the professional understanding of ministry has provided theological education with what little coherence and sense of purpose it has had. But, as is true of most decisions, the adoption of a professional understanding of theological education excluded other possibilities.

a. The orphaning of theology

Whatever else was true of theological education before the twentieth century, it was education in theology. The demands of the discipline, or, after the eighteenth century, the disciplines, provided the coherence and structure for what was taught. Although Edward Farley may be guilty of some romantic nostalgia in his picture of the synthesis of affective and scholarly elements in classical *theologia*,[28] the fact remains

28. Edward Farley, *Theologia: The Fragmentation and Unity of Theological Education* (Philadelphia: Fortress, 1983).

that theological schools were the house of theology, shaped by its demands and serving the will of its practitioners.

The most striking fact about theological education during the past fifty years has been its comparative independence from theology. Ironically, between 1935 and 1985 American Protestant theology attained its highest level of achievement since the Puritans. In addition to the work of such greats as Reinhold and H. Richard Niebuhr and Paul Tillich, process, liberation, and feminist theologies have made significant contributions to the understanding of Christianity. The better neo-evangelical theologians, especially Carl F. Henry, have shown the continuing vitality of American conservative thought. Yet none of these theologies or theologians shaped the theological curriculum or set the seminaries' academic agenda. Theological schools have been comparatively indifferent to the educational implications of theological study. To be sure, theology was often done in seminaries by various professors, but their work did not significantly change the institutions in which they worked. A historian can recount the story of the previous fifty years of theological education with little reference to theological issues.

At the same time, the seminaries generally lost their leadership in the academic study of religion. Since the 1950s, religion departments have expanded in the nation's secular universities and have certainly attained parity with the theological schools, and probably have surpassed them, as centers of religious scholarship.[29] Much of the creative work in such areas as American religious history, Ancient Near Eastern studies, and world religions is done under their auspices. They have also begun to make their presence felt in the broad area of philosophy of religion (a term originally applied to traditional apologetics, which I use to refer to all nondogmatic or nonconfessional theology).

The location of religion departments in secular contexts has not made them secular in comparison to seminaries, which presumably demand "commitment." A course in New Testament in a state university is similar in many respects to the equivalent course in a seminary and students bring their own "ultimate concerns" to any religion course.

---

29. Seminary educators have understandably not wanted to give much attention to this issue. See Robert T. Handy, "Theological Seminaries and Graduate Education in Religion," *Council on the Study of Religion Bulletin* 7 (December 1976) 6-7; E. J. Jurji, "The Role of the History of Religions in College/University/Seminary Curricula," in *Ex Orbe Religionum*, ed. Kees W. Bolle and others (Leiden: Brill, 1972); E. Thomas Lawson, "Implication for Theological Education in Seminaries of the Study of Religion in the University," *Theological Education* 3 (Spring 1967) 396-402; David Schuller, "University Religion Departments: Challenge to Theological Seminaries," *Asbury Seminarian* 21 (October 1967) 20-23; and Randolph C. Miller, "The Discipline of Theology: Seminary and University," in *Does the Church Know How to Teach?*, ed. K. Cully (New York: Macmillan, 1970).

Part of the illusion of secularity comes from the accelerated development of courses in the history of religions (comparative religions, world religions, etc.), and from an emphasis on the particular character of religious experience (or the religious dimension of experience) as the object of study.

No inherent reason exists for university domination of the study of religion. Both the history of religion and the study of religious experience have had a long history in divinity schools, and the changing currents of student and faculty interest should reinstate them. Individuals who are familiar only with their own faith necessarily have a superficial understanding of that faith. Moreover, the increasing religious complexity of the United States means that future ministers must be more involved in dialogue with other religions than most are at present.

The seminaries' loss of intellectual leadership may be the most serious problem confronting the schools in the 1980s and 1990s. This observation is more fundamental than the typical and somewhat carping theme of the sad state of faculty research that can be found in Brown-May, Niebuhr-Gustafson-Williams, and almost every other serious discussion of "what's wrong with the seminary?" The declining intellectual role of the seminaries threatens the churches' place in the larger society and, ultimately, their capacity to enlist the best men and women in their service.

b. Isolation from culture

The existence of successful religious studies departments and the seminaries' loss of a monopoly on the public discussion of religion may reflect a deeper structural problem. Self-standing seminaries were an accident of history, not a product of reason. In the early nineteenth century, the seminaries' physical separation from other institutions of higher education did not materially affect their curriculum or their place in the world of letters. However, when the university evolved in the later nineteenth century, physical separation began to have significant consequences. Theologians were not present for many important cultural discussions and they were not pressed by colleagues to deal with various significant issues. Ironically, the university-related divinity schools (with the partial exception of Chicago) were often as unrelated to the ongoing life of the university as were the self-standing seminaries.[30] By 1935, the problem had become acute; by 1985, a crisis.

---

30. For a kinder critique of the university-related schools, see George Lindbeck, *University Divinity Schools: A Report on Ecclesiastically Independent Theological Education* (New York: Rockefeller Foundation, 1976).

Isolation from advanced theoretical studies, of course, may have little impact on the day-to-day life of a congregation, and the leaders of seminaries may argue, with good conscience, that they are doing something else. Such arguments may also be superficial. The professional understanding of theological education provides theological educators with too easy an identity. If seminaries exist to train ministers, then little more has to be said about their place in the ecology of learning. The schools are useful because they are used. Further, the schools' professionalism reflects accepted American values. Americans hope that their jobs will attain the status of a profession, and such marks of professionalism as increasing specialization, continuing education, and evaluation are part of our society. The problem here arises from the nature of religious commitment. Religion claims to give a coherent and meaningful interpretation of all reality, and religious leaders must be able to articulate the most basic understandings of life available within a culture. Unlike accountants, hairdressers, and other professionals, who may or may not see their jobs as part of a whole, ministers by virtue of their office look beyond everyday existence to life's abiding structures and values. If religion loses its claims on the depths of the common life, it loses its specifically religious component and becomes one of many partial views of human experience (not that it becomes irrelevant, only quaint).

The seminary's isolation from American higher culture has been most apparent in the area of science and technology. For good or ill, America is an advanced technological society and there is little chance that it will soon return to bucolic bliss. Any serious listing of the achievements of the American people in the last fifty years will focus on their scientific and technical progress, and the next fifty years will probably continue this pattern. The minister can no longer adequately advise couples about marriage without some knowledge of the advanced technologies used in limiting family size, and many serious ethical dilemmas are related to medical technology's capacity to extend biological life almost indefinitely. Ironically, the American minister who graduated from a first-rate department of religion and a good seminary may be more able to converse with a Hindu sage than with a local computer club, a researcher in electronics, or a modern biologist. Unless the church's witness is to be reduced to moralistic admonitions, sustained conversation with the technocratic leaders of our culture is imperative.

c. The community

Seminaries have been concerned with social issues since 1880, and the period between 1935 and 1985 was no exception. Seminary professors and students (at least in liberal schools) were participants in utopian plans for society spawned by the Depression. The careers of noted Christian ethicists, such as Reinhold Niebuhr, were almost a parable of the intellectual's struggle for a voice in the social arena, while other noted ethicists, such as James Luther Adams, pioneered new analyses of American social and political life.

The radicalism of the 1960s lasted longer in many theological schools than in the society as a whole and had a measurable impact on particular schools. Some, like New York's Union, attempted to combine youthful radicalism, institutional change, and academic study into a different model of the seminary. By its modeling of social justice in such areas as admissions, governance, hiring, and worship, Union hoped to point the way to a new order. Other seminaries accepted parts of the new model, especially in the fields of Afro-American studies and feminist theology and history. All in all, theological schools became different as a result of these changes. More women and blacks can be found on faculties and in the student body. Theological instruction is more responsive to student needs and desires, and schools are more aware of the ethical ambiguities of the older style of doing business.

Yet, although the historian cannot document a negative, most seminaries have not been profoundly changed by the new ethics. Most of the adjustments have been cosmetic (the addition of new courses and instructors) and the various "theologies of" continue to have the character of a fad. Despite their prophetic claims, the seminaries remain about fifteen years behind the society as a whole in finding ways to deal with contemporary social issues. Whereas other professions have passed the stage of debating whether this or that group ought to be admitted, theological schools continue the patterns of militancy characteristic of the early stages of social change. Something is seriously wrong somewhere. And just as the professional model can justly claim some credit for some seminary successes, so it must also bear partial blame for this outstanding failure.

A survey of the seminary literature from Brown-May to the present suggests that, in the last analysis, the adoption of the professional model militated against the consideration of other alternatives. No matter what else seminaries might wish to be, they have existed primarily to prepare individuals for professional life. Professionalism was the one (and perhaps only) nonnegotiable item in the self-awareness of theological educators. Just as they had to set aside the demands of theology as an organizing center for their institutions, so they likewise had to set aside the possibility of living on the edges of social change. Individual professors might participate fully in intellectual life; individual professors might debate the social and political issues; but their institutions remained locked in a single interpretation of their role.[31]

VI. Concluding Very Unscientific Postscript

> *When philosophy paints its grey on grey and the evening sets in when all cows are black, then the owl of Minerva takes flight.*
>
> —Hegel

To write the history of one's own time is always risky. The subtle and real movements of spirit, often submerged in the wealth of contemporary data, are never fully exposed to view. Possibly a future historian, less involved in the mundane world of our present affairs, will identify other commitments (perhaps Readiness for Ministry, Congregational Studies, or the merger of many small schools into centers for theological education) as true dawnings of the next chapter in the corporate history of theological education.

Nonetheless, if I may be permitted to enter the troubled waters of spirit, when a movement becomes aware of its own dynamics, radical change may then be in the offing. The last half-decade has seen new reflections on the meaning and character of theological education by thinkers as subtle as Ronald Hough, John Cobb, and Edward Farley.[32] As we become increasingly conscious of the extent to which the professional understanding of seminary education has dominated theological existence, the onset of the decline of professionalism may be posited. Perhaps it is already dead (at least as an object of loyalty) and only the wake and funeral remain. The dark night in which all cows are black, after all, is the prelude to a new dawn in the unfolding of common life. No historian, patently, can write the story of the future, but can only recall the abiding pattern of death and resurrection (as characteristic of institutions and ideas as of individuals) and witness to the Spirit that makes all things new.

The editors have challenged me, as indeed they should anyone who sees a movement or period ending, to sketch an alternative to the

31. Broad generalizations cry out for refutation, and there have been some creative attempts to struggle with the issues on a theological rather than an institutional level, e.g. Letty Russell, "Tradition as Mission: Study of a New Current in Theology and Its Implications for Theological Education" (Th.D. dissertation, Union Theological Seminary, New York, 1969).

32. Ronald C. Hough and John B. Cobb, *Christian Identity and Theological Education* (Chico, CA: Scholar's Press, 1985).

present pattern. I am not a systematic theologian, but I judge that a truly theological curriculum for the twenty-first century is not impossible and ought to be attempted. I understand a theological curriculum to be one that delineates, as accurately as possible, the nature of the Christian faith. I believe that such a curriculum would rest on a tripod of three elements: (1) a thorough introduction to the study of religion and religious experience; (2) an examination of the history and tradition of the church catholic; and (3) an in-depth study of our present (and foreseeable) cultural context.

The assumptions behind these suggestions are obvious. Christianity is a religion both in dialogue and in competition with other religions. Unless one is to believe that Christianity fell from the blue, one needs to understand religion and religious experience in order to understand our common faith. But each historical body is unique. Christianity must be studied on its own terms and from its own classic documents. Like all religions, moreover, Christianity exists only within a particular context, which it both changes and is changed by. No living religion can escape incarnation and change. To understand what Christian faith actually is in the present historical situation, one must understand that situation thoroughly, using all available tools.

A curriculum based on these principles would almost necessarily have to be taught in a university-related school, where the resources for in-depth analysis are available. Nor would such a curriculum pretend to prepare anyone to do the "job" of the minister. The most it could do is to produce sensitive, informed interpreters of the Christian faith who understand its grandeur and its weakness.

12. The Bible and American Protestantism

Edwin S. Gaustad

Prophecy is risky business. In 1915 Charles Foster Kent declared, "The older dogmatic, theological interpretation of the Bible, with all its conflict and sectarianism, has passed into history."[1] A full two generations after those words were written, history showed few signs of having emptied itself of dogmatism or conflict or schism with respect to the Bible. Yet the Yale Divinity School professor, looking back on a generation of archaeological discovery, literary analysis, linguistic sophistication, cooperative translations, and widely accepted critical conclusions, had grounds for his bold assertion.

The last two decades of the nineteenth century had witnessed an explosive surge in biblical studies, a surge of such magnitude as to promote developments more far-reaching, more foundation-shaking, than anything occurring in the study of Scripture during the previous millennium. The ninth edition of the Encyclopedia Britannica, appearing in the late 1870s, summarized even as it popularized much of the revolution then occurring. Organized in New York City in 1880, the Society of Biblical Literature gathered together the American notables who would dominate the new science and the new history as these pertained to the study of the Bible. An English Revised Version of the Bible appeared in 1885 (with an American counterpart in 1901), which, among other things, called public attention to the many scholarly advances made between the 1611 King James translation and that undertaken nearly three centuries later. In the 1890s an avalanche of biblical scholarship virtually buried an eager if bewildered public: concordances,

1. *Religious Education* 10 (1915) 327.

dictionaries and encyclopedias, historical geographies, and critical commentaries. The whole idea, as Samuel Driver pointed out in his *Critical and Exegetical Commentary on Deuteronomy* (1895), was to bring the English reader "abreast of the best scholarship and knowledge of the day."[2] That was a large task, and one not carried out easily or without stormy controversy.

For the closing decades of the nineteenth century also saw much of this scholarship being viewed not as the ally of the Christian church but as its enemy. Taking the most negative connotation of the term, many Protestants in Europe and in Britain, no less than in America, saw "critical" scholarship as precisely that: destructive, negative, corrosive. Its effect was not to purify faith and commitment but to destroy both. Protracted and painful heresy trials, that of Union Seminary's Charles Augustus Briggs in 1893 being all too typical, muted the excitement of new discovery and marred the ability of churchmen and scholars to work steadily together. American higher education was already in process of passing out from under denominational control, that process now being accelerated by a widening gap between the biblical specialists in the universities and the biblical interpreters in the pulpits. In the struggles of the sixteenth-century Reformation, Protestantism had cast its lot with Scripture and not with Tradition. Now, as the twentieth century approached, that firm foundation of authority seemed under attack as never before.

To the academic mind, however, the path ahead seemed unmistakably clear: more manuscript discoveries, more linguistic skills, more truth unfolded, more scholarly alliances formed and allies won. Dogmatism and sectarianism would necessarily yield to forces like that. Professor Kent, in 1915, no doubt reasoned as did many others. Life, however, is never as neat as logic. The messy facts are that when Robert T. Handy began his own college career two decades later, Protestantism in America had never been so deeply divided, so bitterly recriminatory, so prone to further separations and condemnations. "Fundamentalists" excoriated "Modernists" and vice-versa, while millions of churchgoers took refuge in local loyalties or found much of the fury and fire beyond their ken. The question of who within Protestantism was faithful and who perfidious was almost exclusively a question of attitudes toward the Bible. In looking, therefore, at the fifty-year period between 1935 and 1985, we cannot escape the storms but will endeavor to move through them to a better understanding of the Bible's place in American Protestantism.

2. S. R. Driver (Edinburgh, 1895), p. xi.

I. Protestant Scholarship and Biblical Translation

In the first half of the twentieth century, Protestants took the lead in biblical study in the United States, just as they led in anxious opposition to much of what went on in that realm. Harvard, Yale, Union, Princeton, and Chicago represented the outstanding centers of biblical investigation, while the presidents of the Society of Biblical Literature during this period included such Protestant notables as William Rainey Harper, Henry Preserved Smith, Ernest DeWitt Burton, C. C. Torrey, Edgar J. Goodspeed, Shirley Jackson Case, Burton Scott Easton, James Moffatt, Frederick Grant, Henry Cadbury, Morton Scott Enslin, E. C. Colwell and many more. The decade of the 1930s saw the launching of an ambitious translation project that would bear fruit in the forties and fifties: the Revised Standard Version (the RSV New Testament appeared in 1946, the Old in 1952). Greeted by both public acclaim and public outcry, this version survived to see the former overwhelm the latter as, very gradually, the profound attachment of the English-speaking world to the King James Version loosened.

One of the several significances of the RSV was that it represented an earnest effort to bridge the gap between academic scholarship and ecclesiastical utility. With deliberate and sensitive concern, the translators managed to create a Bible that was faithful to scholarly demands at the same time that it met liturgical needs. The RSV was intended to be a Bible for the whole Protestant community, not the esoteric text of an erudite few. Scholars engaged in this epochal revision included Lutherans, Baptists (Northern and Southern), Presbyterians, Congregationalists, Methodists, and Harry M. Orlinsky of the Jewish Institute of Religion. Such ecumenicity in preparation augured well for breadth in adoption, not only throughout the Protestant community but, years later, in the worshiping communities of Roman Catholics and Jews as well. After 1965, for the first time in English-speaking Christendom, Roman Catholics and Protestants could, with official blessing, read and worship with the same Bible.

Just as the whole Bible was readied in 1952, a Methodist printing house, Abingdon Press, launched its ambitious twelve-volume project, *The Interpreter's Bible,* which printed passages from the King James and the RSV in parallel columns at the top of pages that supplied both critical and expository commentary. As George A. Buttrick explained in his preface to this large work:

> The King James Version is not only a devotional classic in its own enduring right, which in majestic cadence worships God in the beauty of holiness, but is so inevitably true in many of its translations as almost

to have added new power to the original word. For this reason, and because it is so hallowed in memory, it is placed first on each working page. The Revised Standard Version stands alongside it because, by the general consent of scholars, it is the most accurate revision of the King James Version; and one which, moreover, has been intent on preserving the priceless values of the Tyndale-King James tradition.[3]

A decade later, the same publishing firm issued the four-volume *Interpreter's Dictionary of the Bible*. Both major undertakings were quite successful in reaching a wide public and in sharing responsibly and effectively the results of biblical study in general, and of the scholarship that went into the Revised Standard Version in particular.

Once it was clear that the monopolistic hold of the King James Version was broken and that biblical scholarship could be widely shared, the publishing world along with the Protestant world responded accordingly. Under the direction of the American Bible Society, a fresh translation (rather than a revision) of the New Testament appeared in 1966, the Old Testament a decade later. This effort, Today's English Version, was less concerned to maintain the Tyndale-King James tradition than so to use the English language as to awake, attract, and impress. Words should be simple, idioms should be current, and, above all else, meaning should be clear. According to Keith R. Crim, Today's English Version "has been especially popular among children and young people, new Christians, and people who use English as a second language."[4] Appealing to a somewhat more conservative constituency, the New International Version, issued in 1978 under the auspices of the International Bible Society, also took advantage of the latest manuscript discoveries, even as it sought to eliminate archaic and difficult English expressions.

The work of such broadly based committees virtually assured the translators (and the publishers) that their efforts would not go unnoticed or unappreciated. The cost of such undertakings is enormous and thus daunting to the individual entrepreneur. Yet, personal sallies into the thicket of biblical translation also met with success in the United States. At the University of Chicago, Edgar J. Goodspeed produced the New Testament in what he frankly called an "American Translation," arguing that since the New Testament was itself written not in formal and classical Greek but in the popular dialect of the people, so it should be presented in the twentieth century in the language of the public at

---

3. *The Interpreter's Bible*, 12 vols. (New York and Nashville, 1951-57), 1:xvii-xviii.
4. See Chapter 2 of Ernest S. Frerichs, ed., *The Bible and Bibles in America* (Atlanta and Philadelphia, 1987).

large. Joined by his colleague J. M. Powis Smith, who took responsibility for a similar translation of the Old Testament, Goodspeed could welcome a complete *American Bible* in 1931. Since this work preceded the RSV by two decades, it bore the brunt of much public criticism for "tampering" with the King James Version and for making a heretofore uninformed American audience suddenly aware that an entire revolution had occurred in the textual study of the Bible. Despite the criticism, however, the freshness and clarity of the translation made this Bible a significant publishing success, as the translation of James Moffatt had proved to be in both Britain and America in the 1920s.

Many later private translations appeared in the "Handy era," some designed for special denominational audiences and many for children or for adults with reading difficulty. Some chose to follow particular manuscript traditions, such as early Syriac, while others went beyond translation to interpretation, a fascinating example of the latter being Clarence Jordan's *Cotton Patch Version . . . A Colloquial Translation* with a southern accent (1963-70).[5] Still others took steps, particularly with respect to those portions of Scripture used in public worship, to eliminate needlessly masculine-dominated, sexist language.

In much of this work, the northeastern "establishment" of liberal Protestantism took the lead. But in the 1960s and 70s, more conservative Protestants moved boldly into the field. The formation of the Institute for Biblical Research in 1970 was one such index and the 1978 New International Version, noted above, was another. A whole generation of evangelicals and conservatives, fresh from the nation's best graduate schools, joined with British counterparts and immigrant denominations of European background to lend their strength to biblical investigation and translation. As Mark Noll has pointed out, the period from the mid-1930s to the mid-1970s marked a "return" of evangelicals to the scholarly community. Scholarship was, once again, a valued commodity and education a worthy goal. Under leadership provided by such men as Bruce Metzger, George Ladd, Everett Harrison, and Earle Ellis, the successors to the stormy days of modernist/fundamentalist battles moved to "take their stand within the contemporary stream of philosophical, theological, and critical thought."[6] This boded well, not alone for biblical translations but for the vitality and cohesion of American Protestantism as a whole.

5. Ibid.; see Chapter 3 by Harold P. Scanlin.
6. The words are George Ladd's, quoted in Mark A. Noll, *Between Faith and Criticism* (San Francisco, 1986), p. 121. Attention should also be called to the fifty-two-volume biblical commentary projected by Word Books (Waco, TX).

II. Biblical Authority and Denominational Life

What was being done to and with the Bible by scholars in the first half of the twentieth century filtered down to pulpit and pew in such a way as to cause much searching of heart and testing of institutional loyalty. As early as 1924 Harry Emerson Fosdick, in his popular *Modern Use of the Bible,* tried to keep preacher and people abreast of what was happening so as to allay suspicions and keep lines of communication open. He argued that higher criticism (though he deplored the term) "restores to us the whole Book. It gives us a comprehensive, inclusive view of the Scriptures and enables us to see them, not piecemeal, but as a whole . . . , as a unified development from early and simple beginnings to a great conclusion."[7] But what had required several years of rethinking on Fosdick's part naturally demanded similarly prolonged reevaluation at both the denominational and the parish level.

We shall select within American Protestantism three denominations for a more detailed examination of the issues at stake and the resolutions sought or achieved or missed: the Presbyterians, the Lutherans, and the Baptists. Biblical orthodoxy, a hallmark of American Presbyterianism, was of course the central issue in the C. A. Briggs trial noted above. But from the founding of Princeton Seminary in 1812, Presbyterian scholars had held to that standard with a scholarship and tenacity that could not readily be matched. The names of Hodge, Warfield, Thornwell, and Dabney call that solid tradition to mind, a tradition of "scholastic Calvinism" joined with Scottish Realism that reigned without significant challenge for a century. In the late 1920s, however, tensions that the general assembly could not ignore developed between those who emphasized "inerrancy" and those who thought that such language damaged rather than enhanced the Bible's authority for faith and life. The report of a special commission in 1927 "broke the grip of the old Princeton Theology in the North and allowed a place for theological diversity and cultural pluralism in the church."[8]

But if the commission's report was intended to bring peace, it failed in that goal. Princeton Seminary was reorganized in 1929; the leading supporter of the "inerrancy" position, J. Gresham Machen, departed; and in 1936 a small but bitter schism resulted in the creation of

7. H. E. Fosdick, *The Modern Use of the Bible* (New York, 1926), pp. 11-12.

8. Jack B. Rogers, "Biblical Authority and Confessional Change," pp. 131-56 in a special issue of *Journal of Presbyterian History* (59/2: Summer 1981) devoted entirely to "Presbyterians and Biblical Authority." I am much indebted to this issue, especially to the Rogers article; quotation is from p. 134.

the Orthodox Presbyterian Church. In southern Presbyterianism unity was maintained until the 1970s, when about 250 congregations withdrew from the Presbyterian Church U.S. to form the Presbyterian Church in America. Again, the question of "inerrancy" was at issue. The influx of neo-orthodoxy into both North and South in the 1940s and 50s helped for a time to soften the differences, as both liberal and conservative factions found biblical theology more congenial and traditional doctrine more meaningful. But the center did not hold with sufficient strength to prevent all division, and even when divisions did not occur, tensions remained to surface when church mergers took place (as in 1958 and in 1983) or when confessional modifications were introduced (as in 1967 and in 1976).

The Westminster Confession of seventeenth-century England had long been authoritative for Presbyterians in America and was widely influential beyond that single denomination. It could not and would not be lightly dismissed. The protracted deliberations of both northern and southern branches of Presbyterians, the many drafts, the careful revisions, the elaborate mechanism for voting—all this spoke to the importance as well as the delicacy of the task of writing a new confession of faith in an era when consensus could hardly be assumed. Some theologians were convinced that the sixteenth-century Reformation creeds represented a better starting point for revision than did a product of the civil and religious strife of seventeenth-century England. Others were concerned that the biblical scholarship of recent decades not be inhibited or thwarted by cries of biblical "inerrancy." Some referred the phrase "Word of God" primarily to Christ, while others referred it chiefly to the Bible. The tensions of the 1920s had not gone away by the 1960s. As a result the northern church's confession of 1967 constituted something of a "political compromise" with respect to biblical authority: "The one sufficient revelation of God is Jesus Christ, the Word of God incarnate, to whom the Holy Spirit bears unique and authoritative witness through the Holy Scriptures, which are received and obeyed as the word of God written." Some of those responsible for the revision took comfort in the capitalized "Word" when referring to Christ, the lower case "word" when referring to the Bible.[9]

In the southern branch during the 1970s, a new Declaration of Faith addressed the same distinction between the "living Word of God" (i.e., Christ) and the "written Word of God" (i.e., the Bible). In an effort to show that this was more than mere wordplay or typographical

9. Ibid., p. 143.

nicety, a commentary accompanying the 1976 Declaration explained as follows:

> We must say of Christ that he is God himself with us, but we cannot say that of Scripture. We can worship Christ but we cannot worship the Bible. Jesus Christ is the Word of God in a more direct way than the Bible. Nevertheless, once we are clear about this, we must say that the Bible too is the Word of God.[10]

In the process of redefining the central articles of faith, differences long ignored or papered over required discussion and debate, even if the result were further political compromise rather than perfect unanimity. Few Christian creeds, however, are expressions of the latter—studied ambiguity being an ancient and, one assumes, even honorable tradition. The long anticipated reunion of Presbyterians in America, consummated at last in 1983, only made more urgent the theological task of finally getting beyond, in the words of Fuller professor Jack B. Rogers, "the stalemate of the fundamentalist-modernist controversy regarding the nature and function of Scripture."[11]

Historically, Lutherans have argued more about the nature and meaning of fidelity to major creedal formations, such as the Unaltered Augsburg Confession, than about the "inerrancy" and authority of the Bible. Still, the same forces of modernity that pressed upon other branches of American Protestantism also hit home among Lutherans— though not with full force until the 1970s. Prior to that cataclysm, the *Lutheran Church Quarterly* had addressed rather calmly in the 1930s and 40s the understanding of revelation, the sense in which the Bible is the Word of God, and "The Place of Biblical Criticism in a Lutheran Seminary."[12] In the latter paper, presented to theological professors of the United Lutheran Church meeting at Springfield, Ohio, in 1937, Henry Offermann declared that biblical study posed many problems which could not in good conscience be ignored. "The God whom I serve is a God of truth, and he wants me to serve him in spirit and in truth." Therefore, all such problems "have to be examined anew in accordance with the best scientific methods that modern scholarship can offer." Criticism has the advantage of inviting further criticism, of correcting itself as it goes. Lutherans in America have "hitherto assumed an attitude of aloofness, if not of actual hostility, to the labors of Biblical criticism," but, Offermann argued, this must no longer be the case. The Lutheran

10. Ibid., p. 145.
11. Ibid., p. 151.
12. See *Lutheran Church Quarterly* 10/2 (April 1937); 17/3 (July 1944); and 10/4 (October 1937).

church is not some fringe sect, not some unevangelical group that regards the Bible as a lawbook, not some timid voice afraid that it "may offend the weak." We cannot fight modern battles clothed in the armor of a medieval knight. So biblical criticism and modern scholarship, it was forthrightly argued in 1937, must be firmly and boldly taught in the Lutheran seminary.[13]

Thirty years later, voices lost their calm and seminaries their serenity as the question of biblical authority took on unexpected urgency in the Lutheran Church—Missouri Synod. In 1968 Robert H. Smith, then a professor at Concordia Seminary in St. Louis, compared various Lutheran views of the Bible, concluding that all were agreed that Scripture is the sole normative authority for Christian faith and life. Differences arose between those Lutherans loyal to the scholastics of the seventeenth century (remember the Presbyterians above?) and those loyal to the reformers of the sixteenth. Said Smith: "The 'scholastics' have taken the phrases 'verbal inspiration' and 'inerrancy' as their 'shibboleths.' The 'confessional' or 'evangelical' group points out that these words should not be regarded as necessary, (1) partly because they were never used by Luther and the Lutheran Confessions, and (2) partly because they distort the teaching of Luther and the Confessions, unless guarded with extreme care."[14] A small cloud on the horizon billowed into a dark storm.

By 1972 the president of the Missouri Synod, Jacob A. O. Preus, had ordered an investigation of the faculty at Concordia, an investigation that the Lutheran editor of *Dialog* characterized as a medieval inquisition. "The Missouri Synod has hereby sunk to the lowest level of theological thinking in the history of Lutheranism in America. . . . None of us ever dreamed that one of the major Lutheran traditions in the world would tear itself apart on questions that once animated the minds of fundamentalists in the 1920s." What is being demanded, said the editor, is a false unity, a conformity that is more biblical than the Bible, "because in the Bible we know there is no unity of doctrine, no single line of interpretation, no one theology. . . ."[15] When Preus was asked in 1974 to identify the crux of the dispute at Concordia, he answered directly: "The authority of the Bible." John Tietjen, president of that seminary until dismissed early in 1974, countered that the real issue was power: the denomination was caught in a power play in which the issue of bib-

---

13. *Lutheran Church Quarterly* 10/4:404, 405, 406-07, 408. Similarly positive and relaxed views of higher criticism may be found in the same journal, 13/1 (January 1940), and in *Lutheran Quarterly* 2/3 (August 1950).

14. *Lutheran Forum* 2/10 (October 1968) 13.

15. Carl E. Braaten in *Dialog* 11/4 (Autumn 1972) 250-51.

lical authority was the smokescreen but control of all of the synod's institutions the reality. Once such power was no longer challenged or checked, then the entire Missouri Synod could be remolded and refashioned to conform to the ideological and theological standards of a few.[16]

Biblical authority continued to be the slogan, however, as those in authority sought to separate the "Bible believers" from the "Bible doubters." And so schism struck in the mid-1970s when over 100,000 members of the synod withdrew in protest to form the Association of Evangelical Lutheran Churches, then a decade later to participate in the merger of the two remaining major Lutheran bodies: the American Lutheran Church and the Lutheran Church in America. Charles Foster Kent would not understand.

For Baptists, schism came both early and late, early for the Northern or American Baptists and only in the present moment for the Southern Baptists. The issue of biblical authority was an underlying theme in the 1933 separation of the General Association of Regular Baptists, as well as in the 1947 creation of the Conservative Baptists Association of America, while in the stresses of the Southern Baptist Convention in the late 1980s biblical authority overrode every other consideration— except, once again, power. While not as confessional as either Presbyterians or Lutherans, Baptists have from the seventeenth century onward adopted creedal formulations. But no single creed ever attained such authority in itself as to become the major arena of battle; rather, the case among Baptists, North and South, has been one of loyalty to the New Testament as the "sole authority for faith and practice." Baptists have asserted this biblical authority along with an emphasis upon "the priesthood of the believer," thereby granting, at least in theory, the right of every church member to arrive at his or her own interpretation. Not surprisingly, this principle, when actively practiced, made for a wide variety of views, but that was not the way it was supposed to work out. All have a right to interpret, but all should agree.

Much of Baptist quarreling and separating has transpired under the banner of a biblical literalism that emphasized millennial expectations, especially the dispensationalist scheme popularized by J. N. Darby in England and by Cyrus Schofield in America. But the complexities and mysteries and charts of this eschatology played havoc with the familiar sloganeering of "private interpretation." As Timothy Weber has wryly noted: "In the final analysis, there is something incongruous about fundamentalists who say they can read the Bible by themselves,

16. See *Christianity Today*, October 25, 1974, for the views of J. A. O. Preus; *Christianity Today*, April 11, 1975, for the views of John Tietjen.

then pore over Schofield's notes in order to discover what the text really means." One baneful consequence of this scholastic fundamentalism was an intolerance for multiplicity as well as an inability to account for it. "Fundamentalists have quarrelled with each other," Weber observed, "nearly as much as they have quarrelled with their enemies," a fact that accounts for many of the schisms in Baptist life in America, black and white, North and South.[17]

In recent years, Baptists in the North made a more conscious effort to show how history and culture have altered the ways in which the Bible was interpreted throughout Christian history at large and within Baptist history itself. In two informative articles, Norman Maring in 1958 carefully reviewed "Baptists and Changing Views of the Bible, 1865-1918," concluding that "the inadequacy of traditional formulations seems clearly demonstrated." What was also clearly demonstrated was the ceaseless splintering of the Baptist family into segments that no longer talked to each other, no longer sought synthesis or grounds of mutual understanding.[18] In 1962, James R. Branton wrestled with the authority of the Bible in an article which concluded that the Holy Spirit "speaking in the Bible and interpreting it in the living tradition of the church is the true source of authority," especially as that Spirit is identified in the life and ministry of Jesus Christ.[19] And in 1966 Robert T. Handy himself wrote on the relationships between Scripture and tradition with a view to rescuing "tradition" from its outcaste state and to placing Scripture in its historical and ecclesiastical context. Quoting Albert Outler, Handy observed that "The Word of God in Scripture is the constitutive tradition of the Christian community." Sensitive to the persisting tensions between Protestants and Roman Catholics on the relative merits of Scripture and tradition, Handy saw "much more common ground than once would have been dreamed possible." The discussion has not ended, but much of the ground has shifted.[20]

In the South, Baptists found their own ground shifting under them as tensions between pietists and scholastics, between "moderates" and "conservatives," polarized. The dismissal in 1963 of a professor from a Southern Baptist seminary for writing a book on Genesis that acknowledged some of the critical problems involved in interpreting

17. See the excellent chapter by Conservative Baptist Timothy P. Weber, "The Two-Edged Sword: The Fundamentalist Use of the Bible," in a book of high quality and much utility edited by Nathan O. Hatch and Mark A. Noll, *The Bible in American Culture* (New York, 1982); quotations are from pp. 114, 116.

18. *Foundations* 1/3, 4 (July, October 1958).

19. *Foundations* 5/2 (April 1962).

20. *Foundations* 9/2 (April-June 1966).

that book pointed to difficult times ahead. A "Baptist Faith and Message Fellowship" kept watch for any signs of creeping liberalism, especially with respect to the Bible. By 1980 a political program for taking over the leadership of the Southern Baptist Convention in the name of "inerrancy" had begun, with year by year increments of power over seminaries, home and foreign mission boards, and all major committees within the convention. In 1984, convention President James T. Draper identified "the dramatic shift away from biblical authority" as the crux of the tension between parties and wings. Priesthood of the believer and soul competency are cherished beliefs, Draper acknowledged, but such claims "cannot be a license to promote nonbiblical views without restraint in our cooperative efforts." What we now have with respect to the Bible, he argued, is not historical and literary criticism, but destructive criticism, substituting reason for revelation, situation ethics for propositional ethics, human relativities for divine absolutes.[21]

Where all this will end for the Baptists, or the Lutherans, or the Presbyterians, or for Christianity in America is far from clear. The "Handy era," beginning a decade after the Scopes trial, three and one-half decades after the Briggs trial, five and one-half decades after the formation of the Society of Biblical Literature, might have become, following Professor Kent's timetable, one of harmony and fellowship and theological maturation. This has not turned out to be the case. Liberals have confessed to an overfondness for modernity, an overconfidence in the scientific method, an overcommitment to the notion of inevitable human progress, sometimes sinking so low, Fosdick wrote long ago, that they acted as though the ultimate compliment to be paid to Almighty God was that some scientist somewhere believed in him.[22] Reinhold Niebuhr condemned a soft-headed, sentimental liberalism that forgot about sin, guilt, depravity, and the need for redemption. After Holocaust and Hiroshima, modernists were far less sure that they had uncovered the secrets by which a kingdom of God could be brought to earth. At the same time, biblical critics who had been regarded as leaders in weaning thousands away from the Bible indulged in an orgy of "rediscovery" of that book. From mid-century down to the present, critical scholars were engaged in *Rediscovering the Bible* (Anderson), *The Rediscovery of the Bible* (Neil), *Rediscovering the Parables* (Jeremias), *Rediscovering the Teachings of Jesus* (Perrin), *Rediscovering the Teaching of the*

21. James T. Draper, Jr., *Authority: The Critical Issue for Southern Baptists* (Old Tappan, NJ, 1984), pp. 99, 42-43.
22. Cited in Robert T. Handy's balanced and thoughtful article, "Fundamentalism and Modernism in Perspective," *Religion in Life* 24/3 (Summer 1955) 381-94.

Evangelists (Rohde), *Rediscovery of Apocalyptic* (Koch), and *Rediscovering Paul* (Petersen). Alleged apostates had found their way home.

On the other side, Mark Noll has recently written, conservatives owe it to themselves, and to their churches and to the academic community, "to prune the lush but eccentric interpretations that thrive among evangelical Bible-believers." He added:

> Readings of Scripture based on arcane numerological tabulations, derived from word studies in the King James Version, featuring flights of allegorical fantasy, advanced with transparent intent to justify social, political, or economic hobby horses, or teased by legerdemain from the apocalyptic visions of Ezekiel and Revelation—all should be a scandal to the student of Scripture. And since these aberrations appear most frequently among evangelicals, it is the duty of evangelical scholars to correct them whenever possible. Not to do so offers critics of their scholarship an excuse for ignoring responsible evangelical work. Much more important, not to do so dishonors the Scriptures.[23]

Although in business interlocking directorates may not be the grandest of ideas, in American Protestantism a joining together of the liberal and the conservative wings in common scholarly pursuits may be able to give the body Protestant good health and new life. "Come, let us reason together. . . ."

III. The Bible and Protestant Culture

In the earlier centuries of America's history, Protestant domination meant, most conspicuously, a stamping upon the culture of biblical language, biblical motifs, biblical history, and biblical counsel. The Bible constituted the common frame of discourse and, more often than not, the ultimate court of appeal. When pilgrims left an old land for a new, they followed the example of Abraham who, by God's guiding hand, had done the same. When later migrants moved west across the Mississippi, it was to the tune of "Jordan's Stormy Banks" that they, like Israel of old, crossed into the promised land. When slaves were emancipated, both the whites who preached and the blacks who sang knew that this freedom had been anticipated in the demand of Moses to Pharaoh: "Let my people go." Manifest Destiny was biblical destiny: "This land shall be your possession before the Lord." Jurists, governors,

---

23. Mark A. Noll, *Between Faith and Criticism,* p. 194. In a note, Noll bemoans the fact that the best selling Bible-related book of the 1970s, Hal Lindsey's *The Late Great Planet Earth,* paid no attention to biblical scholarship, conservative or liberal (p. 238 n. 11).

and presidents, no less than preachers, never needed to explain the context of a biblical quotation; the surrounding circumstances could be assumed, as could the force of authority that went with it. Whether or not what Robert Handy has called the "Second Disestablishment" has succeeded in dethroning the Bible in the national culture, it clearly has not disestablished that book from an enduring centrality in Protestant culture.[24]

In the last fifty years, the unresolved problems of the relationship between religion and education have cried out more stridently for solution. Protestants, who have often treated the public schools as their very own, have been shocked to discover that not everyone approved of Bible reading, praying, and hymn singing, all of these regularly having an identifiable Protestant cast. When, in 1962 and 1963, the United States Supreme Court rendered decisions that made it more difficult to maintain Protestantism's casual and traditional alliance with the public schools, great numbers of Protestants were both offended and outraged. Calls for amendments to the U.S. Constitution (joined with attacks on the Supreme Court) became one measure of the pervasive displeasure. That the Court not only permitted but actually encouraged the study of the Bible—as opposed to its devotional use—appeased few of those who regarded the book more as an object to venerate and protect than as one to read and reflect upon.[25] Some Protestants turned away from the public schools to start their own parochial schools, a venture that often has been thought of as primarily a Roman Catholic one.

In higher education, so long a denominational province, secular and public institutions gathered increasing millions of young people into their ever-widening fold. Mainline Protestantism reacted by trying to secure a toehold on the edge of great state campuses or by promoting the study of religion within the secular university. More conservative Protestants reacted by turning away from the university itself in order to establish Bible institutes, or by tightening control on the denominational colleges. In all of this, the Bible remained central to the tensions and to the controversies, if less central to the educational enterprise itself.[26]

With respect to social reform, the Bible kept its centrality, some-

---

24. Robert T. Handy, *A Christian America: Protestant Hopes and Historical Realities* (New York, 1971; rev. ed., 1984); see especially Chapter 7.

25. See Martin E. Marty's 1980 address to the Society of Biblical Literature, "America's Iconic Book," in Gene Tucker and Douglas A. Knight, eds., *America's Iconic Book* (Chico, CA, 1982), pp. 1-23.

26. See David L. Barr and Nicholas Piediscalzi, eds., *The Bible in American Education* (Philadelphia, PA and Chico, CA, 1982).

times as an ally for change and other times in league with those who opposed change. If not the determinative factor in reform movements in this country, it was rarely regarded, by any side, as irrelevant to the reform under consideration: war and peace, labor and management, race and civil rights, feminism and gender equality, liberation and revolution. In a thoughtful reflection on the Bible's place in America's reform movements, Ernest Sandeen has written:

> Apologists for the Bible have frequently cited its influence for good in transforming human institutions, but . . . there is little evidence that the Bible exerts this kind of influence independently of other cultural forces. . . . Women in ministry are both criticized and supported on the strength of the Scriptures. Accommodation, toleration, nonviolent social action, and separatism are all advocated by black ministers on the authority of the Bible. . . . Whatever impact the Bible has had upon social reform, its effect is not predictable, one-dimensional, certainly not magical.[27]

One might in fact argue that often it is social reform which has an impact on the Bible. In the Social Gospel movement, for example, the prophets of ancient Israel were swiftly elevated to a prominence they had not enjoyed before. More recently, in the feminist movement within Protestantism, one clear effect upon the Bible has been a more rigorous scrutiny of biblical translation with respect to its conscious or unconscious exclusiveness of language. No major reform movement in the Protestant culture, and very probably in the American culture at large, is prepared to ignore the Bible—its commandments or its prohibitions, its precedents or its silences. If the Bible does lend itself to an alliance, it proves—even in a "secular" age—still to be a powerful ally, as Martin Luther King so dramatically demonstrated.

At another level, the Bible continues to infuse its themes and its dreams into American art, music, and literature. "Even when people had preserved a sense of the Bible's authority over against culture," Giles Gunn observed, "they have not been able to resist thinking in its images, speaking in its language, feeling in its forms."[28] Thus in "high" art and "folk" art, one finds the Testament of Scripture competing with that other great source of artistic inspiration in the American experience, the Testament of Nature. Music of biblical imagery and power has to some degree moved out of the churches "into the concert hall and opera

27. See Ernest R. Sandeen, ed., *The Bible and Social Reform* (Philadelphia, PA and Chico, CA, 1982); quotation is from Sandeen's introduction, p. 8.

28. Giles Gunn, ed., *The Bible and American Arts and Letters* (Philadelphia, PA and Chico, CA, 1983), p. 2.

house" in recent years. "If, as has sometimes been argued, America is moving into a post-Christian era, one of the results is that the Bible has begun to be accepted into the general culture as a cultural artifact transcending its purely religious setting and interpretation."[29] A paradox indeed, if as the Protestant ethos wanes, a biblical ethos waxes, with a sort of atmospheric universality. So also in modern American fiction, "traditions reach forward to affect even those who would spurn them." While ecclesiastical superstructures may crumble, novelists have consciously or otherwise carried on their dialogue with modernity "in forms continuous with those in biblical narratives." They have had recourse to biblical modes—such as the jeremiad, or saga, or parable, or apocalypse—"to explore and illumine" a perplexing and confounding contemporaneity, utilizing those literary forms that are so firmly fixed in the traditions of western civilization and in the reservoir of the American experience.[30]

In the realm of politics, it is easy to dismiss the frequent appearance of biblical language and sometimes even biblical theology as nothing more than the crassest sort of political utilitarianism: to give the crowd its scriptural bread and its spiritual circuses. But as James T. Johnson has pointed out, it sometimes represents a struggle to find something to hold together a society so noisily heterogeneous, so manifestly pluralistic. If American culture does cohere, "one element helping to sustain that cohesion remains a common set of symbols, imagery, values, assumptions, and expectations rooted in the Bible." [31] In the field of constitutional law, Edward Gaffney, Jr., sees an important dialectic as having existed between biblical religion and such central principles as freedom of expression, life in community, and limits on authority. Beyond these specifics, however, Gaffney argues that biblical tradition cannot be eliminated from the way in which America "tells her tale . . . without a significant loss of cultural identity and purpose."[32] On the other hand, the devil does quote Scripture, we are told, so that behind all biblical clothing, whether in politics or economics or ethics, one must search for the biblical truth.

As we enter the closing years of the second millennium of the Christian era, Protestants have reason to reflect upon their place in

---

29. Edwin M. Good, "The Bible in American Music," ibid., p. 153.

30. Rowland A. Sherrill, "The Bible and Twentieth-Century American Fiction," ibid., pp. 79-81.

31. James T. Johnson, ed., *The Bible in American Law, Politics, and Political Rhetoric* (Philadelphia, PA and Chico, CA, 1985), p. 5.

32. Edward McGlynn Gaffney, Jr., "The Interaction of Biblical Religion and American Constitutional Law," ibid., pp. 81-105.

human history no less than in American history. With a peculiar commitment to the Bible, they may be forgiven for sometimes thinking that their place in history will also determine the Bible's ultimate place as well. On the American scene, it may be that, as the polls suggest, Protestants revere the Bible more than they read it. Yet, what other book comes close to being read as much? Moreover, even those who do not read it hear it in sermon and song, see it in art and architecture, contend with it in education and reform, and find themselves shaped by it in ways too subtle to trace. The Bible has not been dislodged from a unique place in Protestant private devotion, another subtlety that may prove far more significant than its undisputed ratings in bestsellerdom. If one could write a history of the "use and abuse" of the Bible in the last fifty years or in the last 500, in both cases "abuse" would likely be the longer section. Yet that much abused, much pounded upon, much burned, much misapplied and misquoted book has survived, almost intact. If longevity and endurance were the only test of inspiration, that particular quarrel would be over.

13. American Catholic Biblical Scholarship

Gerald P. Fogarty, S.J.

For American Catholics the dawn of the twentieth century brought heady days. From 1905 to 1908 the *New York Review,* published at the New York archdiocesan seminary at Dunwoodie, sought to keep its readers abreast of what was happening in biblical criticism and other areas of theology.[1] One of the seminary's professors, Francis Gigot, S.S., had already in 1901 published the first volume of his *Special Introduction to the Study of the Old Testament,* wherein he openly embraced the source theory of the Pentateuch's composition. In 1906, rather than submit his second volume to the special censorship demanded by his French superiors, he and four other Sulpicians on the faculty withdrew from their congregation.[2] The Dunwoodie seminary was at the time involved in ecumenical exchanges with Union Theological Seminary, where the renowned biblical scholar, Charles Augustus Briggs, was deeply interested in the biblical question in the Roman Catholic church. In 1906 Briggs collaborated with Baron Friedrich von Hügel, an English Catholic exegete, in critiquing the Pontifical Biblical Commission's decision on the Mosaic authorship of the Pentateuch.[3] Briggs subsequently became the spokesman for liberal Catholic scholars in publicizing the witch hunt against suspected modernists. Further south, at the Catholic University

---

1. Michael J. DeVito, *The New York Review (1905-1908)* (New York: The United States Catholic Historical Society, 1977).

2. Sulpician Archives, Baltimore, Gigot to Dyer, Dunwoodie, February 13, 1905; Dyer to Gigot, February 23, 1905. E. R. Dyer, *Letters on the New York Seminary Secession* (Baltimore, 1906), pp. 54-67.

3. Charles A. Briggs and Baron Friedrich von Hügel, *The Papal Commission and the Pentateuch* (London: Longmans, Green, 1906).

of America in Washington, D.C., a brilliant young Dutch exegete, Father Henry Poels, was forced to resign his post in 1910 because he could not swear that, in conscience, he believed that Moses wrote the Pentateuch.

This early American Catholic biblical scholarship and the rapprochement between Catholics and Protestants could have provided the basis for mature American Catholic biblical studies by the 1930s. Unfortunately, the condemnation of modernism in the century's first decades curtailed any such development. Catholic biblical scholars took as their starting points not the findings of critical scholarship but papal encyclicals and other Roman statements. While Leo XIII had seemed to encourage a relatively broad approach in *Providentissimus Deus* (1893), under Pius X the Pontifical Biblical Commission, which he had founded in 1903, became increasingly conservative. In 1906, in the first of a series of decisions pertaining to the critical-historical method, the commission declared that scholars must teach that Moses was substantially the author of the Pentateuch—a decision that provoked the open exchange of letters between Briggs and von Hügel. Then, in 1919, Benedict XV issued his *Spiritus Paraclitus,* which held that Scripture must be viewed as recording actual history in the scientific sense.[4]

Catholic scholars were not only bound by Roman decisions in their biblical interpretation; professors of Scripture were also required to obtain their degrees either from the Biblical Commission or from the Pontifical Biblical Institute. Leo XIII had announced the intention to found an institute directed by priest-scholars chosen from among both the diocesan clergy and the various religious orders. He informed the great French Dominican, Marie-Joseph Lagrange, that he was to be one of the professors. When Pius X opened the Biblical Institute in 1909, however, he placed it under the exclusive direction of the Jesuits. Under its first rector, Leopold Fonck, S.J., the institute set as one of its goals the rejection of the historical method, particularly as espoused by Lagrange and his École biblique in Jerusalem.[5] Both the Roman decisions and the mentality of the early Biblical Institute exemplified a particular type of Thomistic theology that was incapable of dealing with the historical method necessary for a scholarly understanding of Scripture. Thus Catholic study of Scripture in America, as elsewhere, became increasingly isolated from the mainstream of biblical studies. The Catholic biblical scholarship that had existed at the beginning of the century was

---

4. Benedict XV, *Spiritus Paraclitus,* in *Rome and the Study of Scripture* (St. Meinrad, IN: Grail Publications, 1962), pp. 53-55.

5. See *Père Lagrange: Personal Reflections and Memoirs,* trans. Henry Wansbrough with a foreword by Pierre Benoit, O.P. (New York: Paulist Press, 1985), pp. 94, 143-53.

either forgotten or had gone underground. In the 1930s, change seemed unlikely.

Illustrative of the state of this scholarship in the 1930s was the early work of Michael J. Gruenthaner, S.J., the first native-born American to obtain his doctorate from the Biblical Commission. While finishing his degree, he wrote "The World of the Old Testament and Its Historicity," a chapter in the multivolumed *European Civilization: Its Origin and Development,* published by Oxford University Press in 1934. Gruenthaner's "chapter" was a 466-page paraphrase of the Old Testament, which he treated as a scientifically historical account.[6] One reviewer commented that, "ignoring both modern criticism and modern knowledge, it might have been written by a devout pre-Voltairean."[7]

While Gruenthaner's work represented what Catholics were actually publishing on biblical questions, there was an underground tradition that kept alive—if not public—the more progressive attitude of the early part of the century. In 1928 Edward Arbez, S.S., joined the faculty of the Sulpician Seminary in Washington. Already in 1907-08, while teaching at St. Patrick's Seminary in Menlo Park, California, he had used Gigot's *Special Introduction to the Old Testament,* by then suspect in conservative circles. In his classroom lectures he had also used creative ways to get around the literal interpretation of the Biblical Commission's decisions and he alerted his students to the problems of contemporary scholarship.[8] Yet he cautioned them not to repeat his words outside the classroom. Thus, in the early thirties, unless one had been paying close attention to classroom lectures in certain parts of the country, American Catholic biblical scholarship, like other areas of the church's intellectual life, appeared to be aloof and set apart. All this was to change dramatically through an event not directly connected with biblical scholarship as such.

In January 1936 Bishop Edwin Vincent O'Hara of Great Falls, Montana, summoned Scripture professors to meet at the Sulpician Seminary in Washington. Chairman of the American bishops' committee on the Confraternity of Christian Doctrine (CCD), the agency that oversaw catechetical instruction, O'Hara called on the professors to

---

6. Michael J. Gruenthaner, "The World of the Old Testament and Its Historicity," in *European Civilization: Its Origin and Development,* 7 vols., ed. Edward Eyre (Oxford: Oxford University Press, 1934), 1:501-965.

7. *Times Literary Supplement,* December 13, 1934, p. 897. The reaction to Gruenthaner's fundamentalism was so intense that his chapter was omitted from subsequent editions of Eyre's work.

8. Sulpician Archives, Baltimore, Arbez, "Notes on Genesis," "New Testament Lecture Notes," "Notes on Isaiah." Interview with Msgr. Erwin J. Becker, Santa Rosa, CA, August 10, 1983. Arbez was Becker's professor at Menlo Park.

provide a new Catholic translation of the New Testament in order to update the Douay-Rheims translation then in common use in English-speaking countries. Though the bishops in England had used the Greek text for the Westminster translation of the New Testament, the American translation was to be from the Vulgate so that it could be used in Sunday Masses for the vernacular reading of the liturgical pericopes, in keeping with the norms issued by the Biblical Commission in 1934.[9]

The professors who first gathered to plan the translation of the New Testament also arrived at another decision that had more far-reaching importance. They voted to meet again in conjunction with the annual meeting of the CCD to be held in New York in October 1936. They accordingly invited all priests teaching Scripture to attend. Bishop O'Hara appointed Arbez to preside at this October meeting of scholars, who, in turn, voted to form the Catholic Biblical Association (CBA), elected the first officers, and directed them to draw up a constitution and bylaws.[10] In April 1937 the officers and O'Hara met at the Sulpician Seminary to draw up the constitution. By that date, the association already had eighty-three members. After drafting a constitution, the officers decided that the first formal meeting of the CBA would be held in conjunction with the annual meeting of the CCD in St. Louis in October 1937.[11] At this point, however, the CBA was still only nominally a scholarly organization. The bylaws, for example, stipulated that membership was open to all Catholics, without specification of scholarly qualifications.[12] Because it was originally founded to provide a translation of the Bible, it was closely connected with the CCD. In the future, there would be tension between the scholarly and the catechetical purposes of the organization, but, for the moment, there was at least an impetus for the re-emergence of American Catholic biblical scholarship.

At the first formal meeting of the CBA, most of the papers presented were concerned with the translation project. The title of one, however, was provocative. Romain Butin, S.M., professor of Semitic languages at Catholic University, spoke on "Some Evidence of Revision of the Hebrew Text in Ancient Times." His nuanced presentation on the meaning of the Mosaic authorship indicated that some vestiges remained of the more scholarly tradition of the beginning of the cen-

---

9. *Acta Apostolicae Sedis* 26 (1934) 315.

10. Archives of the Catholic Biblical Association (hereafter abbreviated as ACBA), "Plan for the Organization of a Scriptural Section of the Confraternity of Christian Doctrine," and "The Catholic Biblical Association of America, Minutes of Organization Meeting," New York, October 3 [1936].

11. ACBA, Minutes of the Meeting of the Officers, April 11, 1937.

12. ACBA, Bylaws.

tury.[13] Although his position was hardly radical and was well within the norms set by the Biblical Commission's decision on Mosaic authorship, Butin had so nuanced that decision that he appeared willing to consider subsequent redactions. Whatever future contributions he may have made to biblical scholarship, however, were cut off when he was killed in an automobile accident in December, two months after delivering his address.

At its first meeting the CBA took a further step that would directly promote scholarship—the founding of the *Catholic Biblical Quarterly (CBQ)*.[14] But, again, the CBA was ambivalent about its goals. The officers subsequently decided that the journal was to be "both technical and practical so as to appeal to the biblical scholar and to the Priest and educated layman—helpful to the Leaders of the Confraternity of Christian Doctrine."[15] The first issue of *CBQ* appeared in January 1939. The first editor was Wendell S. Reilly, S.S., professor of Scripture at St. Mary's Seminary in Baltimore.

In the spring of 1941, the Confraternity edition of the New Testament was published. It was the CBA's first joint venture into the biblical field. While it met with virtual silence from the scholarly world, it precipitated controversy within the American Catholic church over the issue of changing the familiar English style of the Douay-Rheims Bible. Moreover, the first printings contained a letter commending the work from Cardinal Eugene Tisserant, president of the Biblical Commission.[16] The publication of Tisserant's letter and the changes in English style provoked a prolonged controversy with Charles Callan, O.P., editor of *Homiletic and Pastoral Review* and, at that time, the only American consultor to the Biblical Commission. Callan first wrote to Bishop O'Hara to object to the changes in English usage and "to declare that no word of the Commission so far uttered is to be construed into meaning a formal approval by that authoritative Pontifical body of the Confraternity New Testament as it now stands."[17] Next, he succeeded in having

---

13. Romain Butin, S.M., "Some Evidence of Revision of the Hebrew Text of the Pentateuch in Ancient Times," *Proceedings of the Catholic Biblical Association of America: First General Meeting, St. Louis, Missouri, October 9 and 10, 1937* (n.p., 1937), pp. 16-18.

14. *Supplement to the Catholic Biblical Quarterly* 1 (1939) 8-12.

15. ACBA, Results of the Deliberations of the Executive Board of the Catholic Biblical Association, April 24, 1938.

16. *The New Testament of Our Lord and Savior Jesus Christ, translated from the Latin Vulgate: A Revision of the Challoner-Rheims Version, Edited by Catholic Scholars under the Patronage of the Episcopal Committee of the Confraternity of Christian Doctrine* (Paterson, NJ: St. Anthony Guild Press, 1941).

17. Archives of the Diocese of Kansas City (hereafter abbreviated as ADKC) 117, Callan to O'Hara, Hawthorne, NY, December 8, 1941.

Tisserant complain of the translation and "recommend a serious revision," to be entrusted to Callan himself.[18]

O'Hara had been anticipating some response from Callan and he had already mustered the support of the other bishops who composed the committee on the CCD, notably Archbishop John T. McNicholas, O.P. Not only was McNicholas widely regarded as the foremost theologian among the bishops, but he was also, like Callan, a Dominican. O'Hara designated McNicholas to draft the bishops' response to Tisserant. In addition, O'Hara obtained the support of Archbishop Amleto Cicognani, the apostolic delegate. McNicholas's letter denied Callan's competence as a biblical scholar and his suitability to carry out the revision proposed by Tisserant. McNicholas concluded by stating that the members of the episcopal committee never considered Tisserant's letter to be an explicit "approval" of the translation. The committee, rather, had merely taken his letter as "encouragement" and would omit it from future printings of the Confraternity New Testament.[19] The episcopal committee dated its letter June 27, 1942, and forwarded it to Cicognani, who promised to add his own letter "urging the viewpoint manifested by the Bishops."[20] Responding on October 14, Tisserant acknowledged "the unquestioned privilege of the Episcopal Hierarchy" to procure suitable vernacular translations of Scripture and stated that the commission's "recommendation" of Callan "was intended simply as a suggestion."[21]

These setbacks did not end Callan's efforts to thwart the dissemination of the CCD translation. Early in 1944, Callan and John A. McHugh, O.P., assistant editor of *Homiletic and Pastoral Review*, renewed the attack. The occasion was the publication of the Biblical Commission's clarification of its earlier decision concerning the translation of the pericopes used at Mass. The commission stated explicitly that while these pericopes were to be translated from the Vulgate, this decision did not preclude translations into the vernacular from the original languages.[22] Although, as will be seen, this clarification was the impetus for the CBA to abandon the translation of the Bible from the Vulgate and to begin afresh from the original languages, Callan and McHugh editorialized that the commission's statement made it obvious that the

18. Ibid., Tisserant to O'Hara, Rome, April 17, 1942.

19. Ibid., Episcopal Committee of the CCD to Tisserant, n.d., n.p. (draft).

20. Ibid., Cicognani to O'Hara, Washington, June 29, 1942. Cicognani gives the date of the bishops' letter as June 27, but in the letter of Tisserant, cited below, the date was given as June 23. There is no dated copy of the original.

21. Ibid., Tisserant to O'Hara, Rome, October 14, 1942 (copy).

22. *Acta Apostolicae Sedis* 35 (1943) 270-71.

CCD translation could not be used in the liturgy. There then followed a series of letters to the editor of *Homiletic and Pastoral Review*, signed "Amator Evangelii," probably Callan himself, which charged the translation with heresy for its rendering of certain passages.[23] Gruenthaner, who had become the editor of *CBQ* in 1942, answered these charges in *American Ecclesiastical Review*, which rebuttal O'Hara then ordered distributed to every bishop and priest in the United States.[24] Despite this public action by the hierarchy, "Amator" still published one more letter.[25]

Callan's attacks were unfounded, but they did illustrate some of the problems any new vernacular version would encounter in gaining acceptance. He had chosen to focus only on the Biblical Commission's response concerning the relationship between the liturgical texts and the Vulgate. By contrast, the CBA focused on the commission's encouragement for translations from the original languages, which proved to be but the beginning of an entirely new orientation in Catholic biblical scholarship.

American Catholics in the early forties were ill prepared for any change in the approach to the study of Scripture. In its second number for 1943, the *CBQ* published three articles commemorating the fiftieth anniversary of Leo XIII's encyclical, *Providentissimus Deus*.[26] None of these gave any indication that there was a change in the offing. In September 1943, however, Pius XII published his own commemoration of *Providentissimus Deus*, in which he signaled revolutionary changes in the Catholic approach to the study of Scripture. His encyclical *Divino Afflante Spiritu* was a clarion call for Catholic exegetes to return to the critical method largely abandoned in the early part of the century. "Being thoroughly prepared by the knowledge of the ancient languages and by the aids afforded by the art of criticism," said Pius, "let the Catholic exegete undertake the task, of all those imposed on him the greatest, that, namely, of discovering and expounding the genuine meaning of the

---

23. Amator Evangelii, "Communications from Our Readers," *Homiletic and Pastoral Review* 44 (1944) 449. See also "Amator Evangelii," ibid., pp. 616-19.

24. Michael J. Gruenthaner, S.J., "An Unfounded Charge of Heresy," *American Ecclesiastical Review* 110 (1944) 415. ADKC, O'Hara to Gruenthaner, Kansas City, June 27, 1944 (copy); O'Hara to Lilly, Kansas City, June 27, 1944 (copy).

25. Amator Evangelii, "Communications from Our Readers," *Homiletic and Pastoral Review* 44 (1944) 807-12.

26. Anthony J. Cotter, S.J., "The Antecedents of the Encyclical Providentissimus Deus," *CBQ* 5 (1943) 117-24; Richard T. Murphy, O.P., "The Teachings of the Encyclical Providentissimus Deus," ibid., pp. 125-40; Stephen J. Hartdegen, O.F.M., "The Influence of the Encyclical Providentissimus Deus on Subsequent Scripture Study," ibid., pp. 141-59.

Sacred Books."[27] The pope, then, had virtually reversed the thrust of *Spiritus Paraclitus.*

Yet even before the publication of *Divino Afflante Spiritu,* the first small signs of change had appeared, notably in the type of education the new generation of American Catholic scholars would receive. In September 1942, Robert J. O'Callaghan, S.J., enrolled in the Oriental Seminary of Johns Hopkins University. He was the first of a series of young Catholic scholars who went to Hopkins to study under William F. Albright for all or part of their linguistic education before going to Rome to do the the the requisite licentiate in Scripture.[28] He was soon followed by William Moran, Frederick Moriarty, S.J., Francis McCool, S.J., Raymond E. Brown, S.S., and Joseph A. Fitzmyer, S.J.—to name but a few. Albright's contact with this handful of students soon developed into a professional relationship with the CBA. In 1944, he was invited to address the CBA's annual meeting, his subsequent lecture being the first article by a non-Catholic scholar to be published in *CBQ.*[29] The CBA also voted to make him an honorary life member, the first time a non-Catholic had been admitted to the association in any capacity.[30]

Albright's relationship with Catholic biblical scholars involved much more than honorary membership in the CBA. In September 1947, when he went on an archaeological expedition, he arranged for Father Patrick Skehan, professor of Semitic languages at Catholic University, to take over his courses in Aramaic and Syriac at Hopkins.[31] This arrangement took on great significance in the years to come, though its impact on Catholic scholarship was gradual. Not only was there direct contact between Catholics and Protestants—the beginning of ecumenism, but Catholic and Protestant scholars were now receiving the same type of education from the same professors.

A glance through the pages of *CBQ* for the latter half of the 1940s indicates the continuing preoccupation of the CBA with the translation project and also shows the association's ongoing ambivalence about its purposes. Was it primarily to be a scholarly or a catechetical organization? Nevertheless, with ecclesiastical encouragement, critical methods were gradually assuming a larger role at CBA meetings. This would lead

27. Pius XII, *Divino Afflante Spiritu,* no. 23 in *Rome and the Study of Scripture,* p. 92.

28. W. F. Albright, *Bulletin of the American Schools of Oriental Research* 134 (April 1954) 4.

29. William F. Albright, "The Old Testament and Canaanite Language and Literature," *CBQ* 7 (1945) 5-31.

30. "Annual Meeting, 1944," *CBQ* 7 (1945) 102-04.

31. Archives of the Catholic University of America, Skehan Papers, Albright to Skehan, Baltimore, September 13, 1947.

to growing tension between biblical scholars and theologians. In 1948, Edward Siegman, C.P.P.S., of Precious Blood Seminary in Carthagena, Ohio, called for a "readjustment of the attitude [in textbooks on dogmatic theology] which uses Scripture for controversy and loses the idea of the living spirit of Scripture." He proposed that the traditional scholastic method of doing theology "might be balanced with a presentation that would begin with the scriptural data and [thereby] arrive at the [doctrinal] thesis."[32]

Though making no direct allusion to it, Siegman's position reflected a continuing shift in the Vatican's attitude toward Scripture studies. On January 16, 1948, the Biblical Commission had written to Cardinal Suhard of Paris to state that its earlier decisions on the composition of the Pentateuch were "in no way opposed to further and truly scientific examination of these questions according to the results obtained during the past forty years." The commission left open the question of what *type* of history was contained in Genesis and only entered the caveat that, in the eyes of some, the denial that Genesis narrated history in the strict sense was tantamount to denying that it narrated history at all.[33]

Although the Biblical Commission's letter to Suhard had been published in *CBQ*, it was not mentioned at the CBA meeting in 1948. The following year, however, the issues implicit in the letter came to the fore at the CBA's meeting in Emmittsburg, Maryland. In a paper on "Polygenism and Exegesis," John L. McKenzie, S.J., professor of Scripture at West Baden College, Indiana, argued that according to both *Divino Afflante Spiritu* and the commission's letter, polygenism (i.e., the plural origin of the human race) was not clearly ruled out of legitimate Catholic exegesis. His paper sparked one of the first heated debates at a CBA meeting. Attacking McKenzie for speaking of Adam and Eve as "representative figures," Gruenthaner charged that next he would speak of a "collective Christ." Siegman reminded Gruenthaner that St. Paul had already used similar language in speaking of the Mystical Body. Gruenthaner, however, had the last word, even if it did not promote scholarly discussion. He rejected McKenzie's paper for publication in *CBQ*.[34]

In retrospect, the heated discussion at Emmittsburg represented the maturing of American Catholic biblical scholarship. Gruenthaner still took what he perceived to be official church teaching as his starting

32. "Annual Meeting," *CBQ* 11 (1949) 4.
33. Denzinger-Schönmetzer, *Enchiridion Symbolorum* (hereafter abbreviated as DS), 3862-64.
34. "Annual Meeting," *CBQ* 12 (1950) 1. Interview with John L. McKenzie, August 3, 1983.

point for the interpretation of Scripture. In this, he had not advanced beyond his disastrous "chapter" published over a decade before. McKenzie, who had been one of his students, represented the new approach of discovering precisely what truth Scripture was presenting. Their argument, in fact, was almost a replay of the drama at the beginning of the century, when the official church reacted against both historical criticism of the Bible and theories of evolution. At that time, the Holy See condemned modernism. In 1950, as will be seen, Pius XII issued his encyclical *Humani Generis*.

In the meantime the CBA, outgrowing its original ambivalence, became intent on making its journal truly scholarly. At its annual meeting in St. Louis in 1950, the officers, without forewarning, demanded Gruenthaner's resignation as editor of *CBQ*, replacing him with Edward Siegman.[35] During Siegman's editorship from 1951 to 1958, the *CBQ* was transformed into the scholarly journal that so many of the association's members were now demanding. But the cost of the transformation was high, for over the next decade the CBA ran afoul of the older entrenched theology, which seemed to gain renewed impetus from Pius XII.

On August 12, 1950, Pius issued *Humani Generis*. Aimed primarily at the "new theology" then developing in France, the encyclical rebuked those theologians who sought to abandon the scholasticism so long approved by the church in favor of theological pluralism, who blurred the distinction between nature and grace, and who even acknowledged that truth could exist outside the confines of the Roman Catholic church. In what pertained more directly to Scripture scholarship, it dealt with three issues that were now becoming controversial. First, it spoke of "the sources of divine revelation," which were to be found "in the Sacred Writings and in divine 'tradition.'"[36] Second, while not denying the possibility of evolution, it condemned polygenism, for this would contradict the doctrine of original sin inherited "from the sin truly committed by the one Adam."[37] Finally, it cautioned those in historical disciplines who asserted that the first eleven chapters of Genesis were merely a figurative and not, in any true sense, a historical account.[38]

---

35. Robert North, S.J., "A Frontier Jerome: Gruenthaner," reprinted from *American Ecclesiastical Review* 148 (May-June 1963) 24. Interview with John L. McKenzie, August 3, 1983; interview with Msgr. Francis J. Rossiter, March 14, 1983; Archives of the Congregation of the Most Precious Blood, Carthagena, Ohio, Siegman to Oberhauser, Washington, January 31, 1951.

36. See DS 3886.

37. DS 3897.

38. DS 3898. For one interpretation of the context of *Humani Generis* within the history of Thomism, see Gerald A. McCool, S.J., *Catholic Theology in the Nineteenth Century: The Quest for a Unitary Method* (New York: Seabury, 1977), pp. 257-60.

The CBA took little heed of the new encyclical until its annual meeting in 1952, when two scholars—John L. McKenzie, S.J., and Roderick A. F. MacKenzie, S.J., of Regis College in Toronto—presented papers that were accused of deviating from the teaching of *Humani Generis*.[39] Both papers, nevertheless, were published in *CBQ*. *Humani Generis* was also the occasion for the first change in the CBA's constitution. Immediately after the debate on MacKenzie's paper, the members voted to insert a new clause in the constitution, setting out the primary purpose of the CBA.[40] Adopted at the CBA meeting in 1953, it stated that the association's main purpose was now "to devote itself to the scientific study of the Bible and to such branches of learning as are connected with it, in conformity with the spirit and the instructions of the Catholic Church, which the Association acknowledges to be the only divinely appointed custodian and authoritative interpreter of the Holy Scriptures."[41] The new clause was taken almost verbatim from *Humani Generis*.[42]

Despite the cautionary words now coming from Rome, the CBA began showing new boldness in its approach to scholarship. Under Siegman's editorship, the *CBQ* published a series of articles by David Stanley, S.J., of Toronto, which applied form criticism to the New Testament and alerted his readers to the recent discoveries of Catholic and Protestant scholars in France and Germany.[43] Still, the new Catholic appreciation for historical criticism was slow in gaining acceptance. When, on September 30, 1952, the 500th anniversary of the Gutenberg Bible, the CBA published the first volume of its translation of the first eight books of the Old Testament from the Hebrew, the introduction to Genesis still reflected a conservative orientation. "The Pentateuch," it said, was "substantially the work of Moses," which constituted "a closely knit literary unit and was originally conceived as one work written for a single purpose," but was later "divided . . . into five parts or books."[44] Only gradually did the CBA fully embrace the new scholarship, as new members, trained in historical method, began to take positions of leadership in the organization.

39. "Annual Meeting," *CBQ* 14 (1952) 352-53.

40. Ibid., p. 353.

41. "Constitution," *Supplement to the Catholic Biblical Quarterly* 16 (1954) 5.

42. See DS 3987.

43. Robert J. North, "American Scripture Century," *American Ecclesiastical Review* 150 (1964) 337.

44. *The Holy Bible, Translated from the Original Languages with Critical Use of All the Ancient Sources by Members of the Catholic Biblical Association of America, Sponsored by the Episcopal Committee of the Confraternity of Christian Doctrine* (Paterson, NJ: St. Anthony's Guild Press, 1952), p. 1.

Between 1955 and the first session of the Second Vatican Council in 1962, the church witnessed the replay of a drama first enacted at the turn of the century. In the earlier period, the question of religious liberty came up in the context of the movement known as "Americanism," condemned by Leo XIII in 1899. In 1907, in the context of modernism, biblical criticism was condemned by Pius X. At first glance, the two condemned positions seemed unrelated, but both had been attacked by the same conservative theologians. At issue was the perennial nature-grace dispute, now shaped by the church's fight against rationalism. In response to arguments for religious liberty and for an optimistic view of the potentiality of human nature, the church made grace rare. In response to assertions that Scripture gave evidence of a series of redactions, the church wished to limit divine inspiration to the original—preferably known—author.[45] In the 1950s, the issues remained virtually the same, but this time the Jesuits, unlike their predecessors, were on the progressive side. John Courtney Murray, S.J., professor of dogmatic theology at Woodstock College in Maryland, began addressing the question of religious liberty in 1943. He soon ran afoul of Joseph C. Fenton, editor of *American Ecclesiastical Review*. Fenton represented the type of Thomistic theology that was dominant since the end of the nineteenth century and that had as its leading exponent Alfredo Ottaviani, who was named a cardinal and secretary of the Holy Office in 1953. In 1955, Murray received word from his Roman superiors that the Holy Office was looking askance at his work and he ceased publication.[46]

Biblical studies, however, seemed to be untouched. The papers at the CBA's meetings became increasingly technical, though some were directed to a more general public. The neuralgic questions of the Bible's inspiration and the relationship of Scripture and tradition were not yet of serious concern to the American scholars. The translation project, rather, continued to occupy a major part of their attention (the CBA translation of both the Old and New Testaments was still far from completion). Clearly, American Catholic biblical scholarship would not break from its conservative past without some sign from Rome.

The sign came from no less authorities than Athanasius Miller,

---

45. See my "American Catholic Approaches to the Sacred Scripture," in Nelson H. Minnich, Robert B. Eno, S.S., and Robert F. Trisco, eds., *Studies in Catholic History: In Honor of John Tracy Ellis* (Wilmington, DE: Michael Glazier, 1985), pp. 104-08.

46. See Donald E. Pelotte, S.S.S., *John Courtney Murray: Theologian in Conflict* (New York: Paulist Press, 1975), pp. 51-54; and my *Vatican and the American Hierarchy: 1870-1965* (Stuttgart: Hiersemann Verlag, 1982; Wilmington, DE: Michael Glazier, 1985), pp. 380-82.

O.S.B., secretary of the Biblical Commission, and Arduin Kleinhans, the under-secretary. They chose an unusual way of giving this sign to the scholarly world. Reviewing a new edition of *Enchiridion Biblicum*, the official collection of church pronouncements on Scripture, Miller in *Benediktinische Monatschrift*, and Kleinhans in *Antonianum*, announced the virtual repeal of the commission's earlier decisions. Whenever the commission's decrees "propose views which are neither immediately nor mediately connected with truths of faith and morals," they stated, "it goes without saying that the scholar may pursue his research with complete freedom and may utilize the results of his research, provided always that he defers to the supreme teaching authority of the Church."[47]

Siegman published both of these reviews in the January 1956 issue of *CBQ* and added his own commentary. He reminded his readers that, on the one hand, Pius X had stated that the Catholic scholar was "bound in conscience to submit to the decisions" of the commission and could not "escape the stigma both of disobedience and temerity nor be free from grave guilt" if he "impugns these decisions either in word or writing." On the other hand, said Siegman, "since the decisions are not infallible and hence are revocable, as all Catholic theologians teach," was it not now possible and permissible for the scholar to "trust the indications that the decisions have been tacitly revoked?" Siegman was a bit too optimistic as to what "all Catholic theologians" taught on this matter, as he would soon discover.[48] He concluded his commentary with some remarks on the binding force of the commission's earlier decision about the historicity of Genesis 1–3. In light of *Divino Afflante Spiritu* and the Biblical Commission's letter to Cardinal Suhard, he argued, Pius XII in *Humani Generis* had reaffirmed "the Catholic's obligation to interpret Genesis 1–3 as implying the unity of the human race, but admits the probability that the narratives of the creation of Adam and Eve are to be understood metaphorically."[49]

Siegman's was one of the first statements in *CBQ* about metaphorical interpretations of Genesis 1–3—an issue directly related to inspiration and inerrancy. In September 1956 the CBA cautiously approached these matters at its annual meeting in Buffalo, the last time the association met in conjunction with the CCD, its parent organization. The program consisted of fifteen papers on messianism in the Bible. The topic seemed innocuous enough, but the treatment given it provoked

---

47. Edward F. Siegman, C.P.P.S., "The Decrees of the Pontifical Commission: A Recent Clarification," *CBQ* 18 (1956) 24.
48. Ibid., p. 23.
49. Ibid., p. 49.

disagreement. All the subjects under discussion—e.g., whether Isaiah 7:14 is to be treated as a messianic prophecy literally or typically, whether Deutero- and Trito-Isaiah each had one or multiple authors—would have been avoided by earlier American Catholic scholars.[50] Even so, the Americans had yet to address directly the issue of inspiration. This was to be the principal topic at the CBA's 1957 meeting.

R. A. F. MacKenzie, the president of the CBA, devoted his presidential address to "Some Problems in the Field of Inspiration." "Instead of 'the inspired author' of a given book or pericope or phrase," he counseled, "we should accustom ourselves to speak of 'the inspired authors.'"[51] The charism of inspiration, therefore, should be considered not individually but collectively, for "theologically, the viewpoint from which the work of the various part-authors must be examined is that of the completed canonical book."[52] Other papers addressed similar themes, which would have been foreign to Catholic scholars of a generation earlier. The minutes of the meeting, however, record no debate on the issue.

Nineteen fifty-eight was a year of transition for the CBA and its journal. Siegman had received a sabbatical leave from Catholic University and he intended to use it to obtain an S.S.L. from the Biblical Institute, which was now in the forefront of the new Catholic exegetical movement. He was succeeded as editor of *CBQ* by Roland Murphy, O.Carm., professor of Old Testament at the university. Not only would Murphy continue the orientation of the *CBQ* begun under Siegman; he would also be the helmsman for the CBA through the storms that soon broke out. For several years, clouds had been building on the horizon. At Catholic University, Fenton had been personally attacking Siegman. In 1959 he gained support from Archbishop Egidio Vagnozzi, who had replaced Cicognani as apostolic delegate.

Vagnozzi lost little time in displaying his attitude toward biblical scholarship. In January 1960 the Paulists began publication of a series of pamphlets on the Bible. The first to appear was an introduction to the Pentateuch by Niel J. McEleney, C.S.P., the editor of the series; the second was on Genesis by John L. McKenzie. The series had the *imprimatur* of Cardinal Francis Spellman, Archbishop of New York. Vagnozzi protested to Spellman and asked him to withdraw his *imprimatur*. Spellman, who had long been at odds with the delegate, was not about to tolerate this intrusion into his authority. Summoning McEleney and

---

50. "Annual Meeting," *CBQ* 19 (1957) 94-96.

51. R. A. F. MacKenzie, S.J., "Some Problems in the Field of Inspiration," *CBQ* 20 (1958) 7.

52. Ibid., p. 8.

Myles J. Bourke, then a professor of Scripture at Dunwoodie, he first gathered their views and then wrote Vagnozzi a forceful letter in which he repudiated the delegate's competence either to judge biblical scholarship or to request an ordinary to withdraw his *imprimatur*.[53] Nevertheless, Vagnozzi continued his intrusions into biblical scholarship, whether directly or indirectly.

Beginning early in 1959, biblical scholars came under attack from Fenton in *American Ecclesiastical Review*. In accusing them of violating the church's *magisterium*, he totally ignored Pius XII's *Divino Afflante Spiritu*, the Biblical Commission's letter to Cardinal Suhard, and other more recent Roman decisions.[54] He next implied that they were guilty of modernism.[55] In the summer of 1961, his journal became even bolder in its criticism of the new Catholic biblical scholarship, publishing two articles on this topic. Particularly offensive was one by Fenton's assistant editor, John L. Murphy, who argued that if the Catholic biblical scholar wanted "that charitable understanding urged by Pius XII, it would possibly be more prudent and would help matters no end if he himself would state in as clear a manner as possible the relationship of his data to Catholic theology."[56] These two articles were not isolated criticisms. Vagnozzi attacked several new theological developments in a speech at Marquette University in the summer of 1961. He reserved some of his sharpest criticism for biblical scholars who introduced "interpretations of Catholic teaching which would often appear to be contradictory to what had been believed not only in the last century but in the preceding centuries as well."[57]

These challenges to American Catholic biblical scholarship were but reflections of a battle then raging in Rome over the same issue. The Pontifical Biblical Institute was now under attack for the liberal views of some of its professors. Well aware of the ties between the American and Roman situations, the CBA had already in 1961 published its support of the Biblical Institute.[58] Here began a controversy that would con-

---

53. Interview with Niel J. McEleney, C.S.P., April 5, 1983; interview with Myles J. Bourke, March 9, 1983.

54. Joseph C. Fenton, "The Case for Traditional Apologetics," *American Ecclesiastical Review* 141 (July 1959) 407-11. See also Francis J. Connell, C.S.S.R., "Answers to Questions," *American Ecclesiastical Review* 140 (January 1959) 36.

55. Joseph C. Fenton, "The Priest and the Ascetical Cultivation of the Faith," *American Ecclesiastical Review* 142 (March 1960) 196-98.

56. John L. Murphy, "The Teaching of Schleiermacher, Part II," *American Ecclesiastical Review* 145 (July 1961) 30-31. See also Gerald T. Kennedy, O.M.I., "Scripture Revisited: Second Look at the Matter," *American Ecclesiastical Review* 145 (July 1961) 8-9.

57. Archbishop Egidio Vagnozzi, "Thoughts on the Catholic Intellectual," *American Ecclesiastical Review* 145 (August 1961) 74-75.

58. ACBA, Ernest Vogt, S.J., "Pro-Memoria sugli attachi contro il Pontificio Insti-

tinue into the first session of Vatican II in 1962. These unofficial attacks on biblical scholarship, moreover, seemed to be getting official sanction.

On June 20, 1961, the Holy Office, in agreement with the cardinal members of the Biblical Commission, issued a *monitum*. It mixed praise with admonition. It warned about widespread "judgments and opinions . . . which gravely imperil the exact historical and objective truth of Holy Scripture, not only in the case of the Old Testament, as Pope Pius XII had cause to lament in *Humani Generis,* but also in the case of the New Testament, involving even the words and events of the life of Christ." Scholars were to treat the sacred books with "prudence and respect" and "should keep before them at all times the doctrine of the Fathers and their way of thinking together with the *magisterium* of the Church, so that the consciences of the Faithful be not troubled nor the truths of Faith damaged."[59] The timing of the *monitum* in the midst of preparations for the Second Vatican Council and in the wake of assaults on biblical scholarship caused some consternation among members of the CBA.

At the meeting of the CBA late in the summer of 1961, the president, Robert Krumholtz, attempted to place the *monitum* within the context of its basic praise for biblical scholarship, while it warned of the dangers of popularization. In the papers that followed, however, there was little indication that the biblical scholars were in retreat. Barnabas Mary Ahern, O.P., for example, defended the value of form criticism in interpreting the Gospels.[60] When the scholarly part of the meeting was concluded, the CBA began its business session, which proved to be one of the most interesting in the association's history.

The session began quietly enough with a proposal to limit attendance at meetings only to scholars who were competent in the biblical field—a significant change in the CBA's original constitution, which had opened meetings to all Catholics, but one that would not consume the energies of the members at this point.[61] Then, from the floor, John L. McKenzie offered a resolution that he called a "Declaration against Defamation." It was a rebuttal to the charges made in *American Ecclesiastical Review.* Monsignor Patrick Skehan had already unsuccessfully attempted

---

tuto Biblico"; "Pontificum Institutum Biblicum et recens Libellus R.mi. D.ni. A. Romeo," *Verbum Domini* 39 (1961) 3-17; and [Roland E. Murphy] "The Close of a Controversy," *CBQ* 23 (1961) 269.

59. *CBQ* 23 (1961) 465.

60. ACBA, "Summaries of the Papers for 1961 Meeting."

61. ACBA, "Paraphrased Record of the Discussion at the Business Session of the Twenty-Fourth General Meeting of the Catholic Biblical Association of America, Thursday, August 31, 1961," pp. 1-4. The change was officially adopted at the meeting in 1962.

to have the executive board of the CBA adopt a similar resolution. The discussion that followed was the most heated in the CBA's history. Present in the audience was John L. Murphy, the author of one of the offending articles, who attempted to defend the journal's pastoral responsibilities to its readership—principally clergy. The scene which then unfolded could have been from a script for a made-for-television movie, with Skehan and Murphy alternating at the podium. When Skehan argued that dogmatic theologians, like Fenton, have "as much an obligation to read biblical arguments as scripturists have to be clear in their presentation," and urged the passage and publication of the resolution, the minutes record that "there was spontaneous applause."[62] The resolution was finally passed by an overwhelming majority. Included in it were specific references to the volumes and pages of *American Ecclesiastical Review*, including Vagnozzi's speech at Marquette.[63]

The scene now shifted to the editorial offices of the *CBQ* on the campus of Catholic University. Roland Murphy, the editor, was preparing the publication of the resolution when he received a summons to see Archbishop Vagnozzi, who asked him not to publish it. Since Vagnozzi had no jurisdiction over Catholic publications, Murphy ignored his request. The next day, Archbishop Patrick A. O'Boyle of Washington summoned Murphy. O'Boyle, who did have jurisdiction, initially wanted the resolution shelved altogether, but Murphy worked out a compromise, according to which the resolution was published, though without any specific reference to *American Ecclesiastical Review*.[64] This action, however, did not end Vagnozzi's overt opposition to biblical scholars. He was also instrumental in having Siegman, who had returned to Catholic University in 1959, dropped from the faculty for health reasons.[65]

On the eve of Vatican II, American Catholic biblical scholarship seemed to be losing the ground it had gained over the previous twenty years. Only two Americans were consultors to the Biblical Commission—Callan, who was to die in 1963, and John E. Steinmuller, a former professor of Scripture at the Immaculate Conception Seminary in Huntington, New York. In the meantime, the battle continued in Rome. When

62. Ibid., pp. 8-9.
63. Ibid., pp. 9-10.
64. ACBA, Murphy to members of the editorial board, Washington, September 25, 1961; Murphy to O'Boyle, Washington, September 20, 1961 (copy), with O'Boyle's final wording attached; see *CBQ* 23 (1961) 470. See also John L. McKenzie, "American Catholic Biblical Scholarship," in John J. Collins and John Dominic Crossan, eds., *The Biblical Heritage in Modern Catholic Scholarship* (Wilmington: Michael Glazier, 1986), pp. 115-32.
65. Archives of the Congregation of the Most Precious Blood, Siegman memorandum, n.d.

the first session of Vatican II opened in the fall of 1962, the bishops found before them a schema on the "sources of revelation." It was a prime example of the prevailing confusion between official church teaching and theological opinion. As Hubert Jedin had pointed out in 1957, the Council of Trent had avoided speaking of Scripture and tradition as two separate sources of revelation.[66] Nor was this the common teaching in the Catholic church in the United States prior to the Thomistic revival of the mid-nineteenth century.[67] Little wonder that at the first session of Vatican II, the biblical scholars locked horns with the Theological Commission, presided over by Cardinal Ottaviani, which had prepared the schema. They argued, however, from their study of Scripture and from their concern for ecumenism with Protestants, not from their knowledge of what the Council of Trent had actually taught. Toward the end of the session, Barnabas Mary Ahern addressed the American bishops on the deficiencies of the schema and on the need to consider the various types of literary forms in both the New and the Old Testaments. When he had concluded, Vagnozzi patronizingly rose to refute him.[68]

When the schema was brought to a vote, 1,368 bishops, a number less than the two-thirds majority needed for approval or rejection, voted against the text and 822 voted to retain it for further debate. At this point, Pope John XXIII intervened and withdrew the schema from discussion. He entrusted the drafting of a new text to a "mixed commission" to be composed of members of the Theological Commission under Ottaviani and of the Secretariat for Promoting Christian Unity, presided over by Cardinal Augustin Bea, S.J., a biblical scholar and former rector of the Biblical Institute. In many ways, the submission of the schema on revelation to a mixed commission was the beginning of the end of the school that held to two separate sources of revelation. But the conservatives did not immediately give up the fight.

Late in the pontificate of John XXIII, two of the Pontifical Biblical Institute's professors—Stanislaus Lyonnet, S.J., and Augustin Zerwick, S.J.—had been prohibited from teaching seminarians. During the summer of 1963, R. A. F. MacKenzie was named rector of the institute, which was now under renewed attack. When, in March 1964 he finally had an audience with Paul VI, he brought up the question of the two professors. The pope expressed complete surprise and instructed Car-

66. Hubert Jedin, *A History of the Council of Trent*, 2 vols., trans. Dom Ernest Graf, O.S.B. (St. Louis: Herder, 1961), 1:52-98.
67. See Fogarty, "American Catholic Approaches to the Sacred Scripture," pp. 92-93.
68. Vincent A. Yzermans, *American Participation in the Second Vatican Council* (New York: Sheed and Ward, 1967), p. 104.

dinal Bea to conduct an investigation. Within a short time, both professors were restored to their full teaching posts. Meanwhile, at its annual meeting in the summer of 1963, the CBA voted to admit both Lyonnet and Zerwick to honorary life membership. It also elected as president John L. McKenzie, who was a particular target of Vagnozzi's attacks.[69] Both actions were evidence that the CBA was feeling bolder in its defense of Catholic biblical scholarship.

Although the reinstatement of Lyonnet and Zerwick ended the overt attacks on biblical scholars, the official teaching of the Catholic church on Scripture remained intact. On November 18, 1965, Vatican II officially promulgated its dogmatic constitution on revelation, *Dei Verbum*, which declared that "sacred tradition and sacred Scripture form one sacred deposit of the Word of God, which is committed to the Church."[70] The exegete was encouraged to use all the tools of criticism but also to recognize "the marvelous 'condescension' of eternal wisdom." The constitution then drew an analogy between the human and divine elements in Scripture and the two natures of Christ: "for the words of God, expressed in human language, have been made like human discourse, just as of old the Word of the eternal Father, when he took to Himself the weak flesh of humanity, became like other men."[71] The constitution also addressed the issue of providing vernacular translations "in cooperation with the separated brethren," so that "all Christians will be able to use them."[72]

The CBA had already anticipated the council's encouragement of ecumenical cooperation in translating the Bible. At its annual meeting in 1965, the CBA decided to assign the books that had not yet been translated to Protestant scholars.[73] A year before, the editors of the translation had also begun cooperating with the bishops' committee on the liturgy, revised by Vatican II, to provide translations of the readings in the new liturgical lectionary. The new readings were to be used for the first time on the First Sunday of Advent in 1964.[74] The initial translations of some of the texts, however, created a number of problems. For example, the CCD edition had translated Luke 24:6 as "He is not here, but has risen." The new translation read: "He is not here; he has

69. Ibid., p. 96. Interview with William Moran, March 17, 1983; Moran, now professor of ancient Near Eastern languages at Harvard University, was then a professor of the Pontifical Biblical Institute.

70. *Dei Verbum*, no. 10, in Walter M. Abott, S.J. and Joseph Gallagher, eds., *The Documents of Vatican II* (New York: America Press, 1966), p. 117.

71. Ibid., no. 13, p. 121.

72. Ibid., no. 22, p. 126.

73. "Meeting of the Catholic Biblical Association," *CBQ* 27 (1965) 409-10.

74. "Meeting of the Catholic Biblical Association," *CBQ* 26 (1964) 470.

been raised up." Some Catholics saw this as diminishing Christ's divinity. Although the editors continued their work of revision, and, in 1970, published the *New American Bible,* American Catholic scholars have recognized that the NAB, too, was inadequate. In 1987 a new revision of the New Testament was published.

Translating the New Testament into contemporary English had been the occasion for arousing American Catholic biblical scholarship from its dogmatic slumber. While the NAB represented a milestone in the translation project, perhaps of greater significance was the *Jerome Biblical Commentary (JBC),* for this work showed the maturity of Catholic biblical scholarship in the United States. Begun in 1962, while the first schema on the "sources of revelation" was still under discussion at Vatican II, the *JBC* was consciously the work of Catholic scholars alone, because, as the editors explained, "there remains a feeling or suspicion both within and without the Roman Catholic Church" that cooperation between Catholic and non-Catholic biblical scholars "represents a private endeavor of only a few and that it is without any official backing in the church. The question of *the* Catholic interpretation of the Bible constantly reappears. It seemed to the editors that the best way to expose the misunderstanding implicit in this question was to produce a commentary written entirely by Catholics."[75]

The publication of the *JBC,* however, did not end all controversy over biblical scholarship in American Catholicism. Despite the encouragement given to scientific criticism by papal statements and by Vatican II, some of the old controversies still remain. On the one hand, conservatives seek to impose on biblical scholars the conclusions of an aprioristic theology. On the other, some liberals misconstrue the findings of biblical scholars to argue against church doctrine.[76] Nevertheless, as a group, Catholic biblical scholars have moved to the forefront of their field and several have been elected president of the Society of Biblical Literature. Looking back to the 1930s, they would find it difficult to discern any basic similarity between the older scholarship and the present Catholic approach to the study of Scripture. Still, the story of Catholic biblical scholarship during the last half-century is only a part of the larger story of Catholic theology in its gradual move away from its nineteenth-century battle with rationalism into its twentieth-century acceptance of historical-critical thinking.

75. Raymond E. Brown, S.S., Joseph A. Fitzmyer, S.J., and Roland E. Murphy, O.Carm., eds., "Editors' Preface," *The Jerome Biblical Commentary* (Englewood Cliffs, NJ: Prentice-Hall, 1968), p. xviii.

76. Raymond E. Brown, S.S., *Biblical Exegesis and Church Doctrine* (New York: Paulist Press, 1985), pp. 59-65.

14. Theology: Ephemeral, Conjunctural and Perennial

Gabriel Fackre

Twentieth-century surveys of contemporary theology teach more than they intend.[1] One lesson is the tendency for chroniclers to announce the arrival of a new theological era. Another is the ease with which the author's own world defines the limits of the data examined. Today's hermeneutics of suspicion makes us more aware of these things. However, it does not guarantee immunity from the same temptations. In this overview, finitude and sin surely will be discernible to the critical reader and the all-seeing Eye.

To help with the occupational hazards of theological chronology we make use here of a theory of varying rates of historical change developed by French students of culture (Braudel, Chaunu, Furet).[2] Adapting their analysis of three differently paced interacting planes to this half-century of theology entails: (1) an "ephemeral" theological history of short periods; (2) a longer "conjunctural" history shaped by Enlightenment premises and processes; and (3) a "structural" history characterized by barely perceptible movement and virtually perennial features.[3]

---

1. That includes the better ones, such as Daniel Day Williams, *What Present-Day Theologians Are Thinking* (New York: Harper, 1952) and Lonnie D. Kliever, *The Shattered Spectrum* (Atlanta: John Knox, 1981).

2. Fernand Braudel, *On History*, trans. Sarah Mathews (Chicago: University of Chicago Press, 1980), pp. 25-54, 91-104, *passim*; Pierre Chaunu, "L'histoire serielle Bilan et perspectives," *Revue historique* 243/2, 297-320; François Furet, "L'histoire quantitative et la construction du fait histoire," *Annales: Economies, sociétés, civilisations*, January-February 1971, 63-75.

3. "Systematic theology" is the subject proper of this essay, but understood in its broader sense.

On the doorstep of this era (1932) H. R. Mackintosh observed that "one striking feature of modern theology is its swiftness of movement."[4] The following five decades continued and increased this celerity. Thus we shall organize our commentary according to the dominant facts of an ephemeral theological scene. Within the kaleidoscope of twentieth-century theology, however, there are persisting conjunctural theological features traceable to the Enlightenment stress upon human autonomy. We fix here upon its expression in the will to technological mastery of the natural environment, which, in turn, raised sky-high the stakes of the human prospect. Horst Symanowski caught its theological significance: "Luther's question . . . 'How can I find a gracious God?' . . . unleashed crusades and started wars. . . . But how many people today are awakened to rise and seek an answer to this question? . . . Another question does drive us around, unsettles us, agitates whole peoples . . . 'How can I find a gracious neighbor?'"[5] With new capacities for radical evil or good in human hands, the theological problematic moved from the vertical to the horizontal: from alienation of the sinner from the righteous God to the estrangement of rich and poor, black and white, male and female, young and old, East and West. While other quandaries persist—Luther's anxiety (and that of medieval Christianity) over *sin*, patristic struggle with *ignorance* and *death*—the riveting question of our epoch is human *suffering*, personal and social. Suffering and its theological response, hope, are defining aspects of conjunctural history during this fifty-year era.[6]

"Christ and culture" is a persisting issue of theological structural history.[7] How does the Christian community remain both faithful and fruitful, relating to its age but not capitulating to it? Hence the perennial struggle to honor both text (tradition) and context (modernity), church and world, identity and vitality. We shall take note of this issue as it weaves its way through both ephemeral and conjunctural tracts of time.

I. 1935-1948

Our initial tract stretches to the year of the first assembly of the World

4. H. R. Mackintosh, *Types of Modern Theology* (London: Nisbet, 1937), p. 2.

5. Horst Symanowski, *The Christian Witness in an Industrial Society*, trans. George H. Kehm (Philadelphia: Westminster, 1964), p. 35.

6. On the varying Christian questions-answers, see Paul Tillich, *Systematic Theology* I (Chicago: University of Chicago Press, 1951) 48-49.

7. As in Claude Welch's study, *Protestant Thought in the Nineteenth Century*, Volume II: *1870-1914* (New Haven: Yale University Press, 1985).

Council of Churches.[8] A famous exchange between Karl Barth and Reinhold Niebuhr at this Amsterdam meeting reminds us of the giants in the land and the point of view with which they were associated.[9] In this country the theological foci and terms of argument were largely determined by the American version of the movement variously described as neo-Reformation, dialectical, crisis, or neo-orthodox theology.[10]

The belltower rope that Barth stumbled upon sounded a summons heard across the Atlantic. The principal representative in this country of biblical and classical Christian retrieval was Reinhold Niebuhr,[11] himself, however, a sharp critic of aspects of Barth's thought.[12] With him on a broad (very broad) neo-orthodox front can be included his brother, H. Richard Niebuhr, Edwin Lewis, the later Walter Marshall Horton, John MacKay, and Francis P. Miller.

Reinhold Niebuhr taught a theological generation to confront the imperial will in the depths of the self and in the structures of society, one discernible by honest introspection and shrewd social analysis, but finally known for what it is before the holy God who exposes our sin on the cross. Pride expresses itself either as apathetic retreat from responsibility or as an arrogant will to power over others, each cloaked in the garment of self-righteousness. The sovereign God sets limits to our personal and collective megalomania, history being strewn with the debris of proud nations and societies. And the *hubris* of individuals founders on either the Charybdis of fanaticism or the Scylla of despair. Answering hope cannot be found in the moralisms of "Jesusology," but in the word of the cross and resurrection. Albeit communicating through myth, the Scriptures yield the profoundest truth about who God is, who we are, where we are going, and what we must do. "Christian realism" teaches us to battle for justice by the organization of social power rather than by reliance on moral suasion, and to live with lowered historical expectations.[13]

8. This longest and, arguably, most formative period prompts the more detailed attention here.

9. For Niebuhr on Barth at Amsterdam, see "We are Men Not God," in *Applied Christianity*, ed. D. B. Robertson (New York: Meridian Books, 1959), pp. 168-74.

10. However inadequate the latter term (as much remarked upon), we shall employ it in conjunction with two parallel terms referring to other revisionist moves of the time, namely, neo-liberalism and neo-naturalism.

11. Numbered among these representatives were George Richards, Douglas Horton, Wilhelm Pauck, and Elmer Homrighausen.

12. See, for example, *Applied Christianity*, pp. 147-67, 175-96.

13. Themes elaborated in a rich Niebuhrian literature, reaching its high point with *The Nature and Destiny of Man*, 2 vols. (New York: Scribner's, 1941, 1943). Choice selections appear in *The Essential Reinhold Niebuhr*, ed. Robert McAfee Brown (New Haven: Yale University Press, 1986).

While neo-orthodoxy set the agenda, some walked out of the theological "meeting," others never attended, and many dissenting votes were cast: witness the minority caucuses—liberal, neo-liberal, and neo-naturalist; those restive with the agenda itself—fundamentalists, new evangelicals, and confessional orthodox; and those absent on other business—traditional Roman Catholics and Eastern Orthodox.

"Unrepentant" liberal Protestant theology continued here and there to voice its assertions of confidence in human goodness and historical progress.[14] More numerous were the chastened liberals who abandoned too optimistic estimates of human nature and history and spoke of the Christ of Calvary and Easter as well as of Galilee. Such neo-liberals included Niebuhr's Riverside Drive neighbors Harry Emerson Fosdick, John Bennett, Henry Pitney Van Dusen, and Henry Sloane Coffin. Others in this broad category (very broad) were James Luther Adams, Edwin Aubrey, Edwin Dahlberg, Georgia Harkness, Nels Ferré, and *Christian Century* editor Charles Clayton Morrison. Neo-liberals were critical of neo-orthodoxy, home-grown or European, defending liberalism as an attitude of open inquiry, stressing ethical imperatives, arguing for long-term historical hope, and finding a larger place for human experience (rational, moral, mystical) in theological method.

Keeping company with the latter in their attack on neo-orthodoxy were the neo-naturalists, continuing the "Chicago School," preeminently Henry Nelson Wieman and also colleagues Bernard Loomer and Bernard Meland. Neo-naturalists were more radical than neo-liberals in their transmuting of the divine Other into a creative process and Jesus into one of many manifestations of the universal "source of human good,"[15] and were more conservative in their grounding of hope less on human effort and more on metaphysical confidences.

Concurrent with the "neos," considering them all doctrinally suspect, were theologians of confessional orthodoxy occupied with the exposition of Reformation confessions and catechisms. A representative figure was Louis Berkhof, whose 1932 systematics was widely used in conservative seminaries.[16]

A vocal dissenting tradition was the growing evangelical phenomenon. Its momentum came initially from the fundamentalist movement of the early decades of the century (J. Gresham Machen).[17] But

14. See the book of that self-declared "liberal at bay," Julius Seelye Bixler, *Conversations with an Unrepentant Liberal* (New Haven: Yale University Press, 1946).

15. Henry Nelson Wieman, *The Source of Human Good* (Chicago: University of Chicago Press, 1946).

16. Louis Berkhof, *Systematic Theology*, 4th ed. (Grand Rapids: Eerdmans, 1939).

17. J. Gresham Machen, *What is Christianity? and Other Addresses*, ed. Ned B. Stonehouse (Grand Rapids: Eerdmans, 1951).

there were also first signs of another kind of conservative evangelicalism, adumbrated in the slender 1947 volume of Carl Henry, *The Uneasy Conscience of Fundamentalism,* stressing the social import of evangelical faith.[18]

Another meeting room was that of Roman Catholic theology. Here a long-standing Catholic scholasticism prevailed, albeit with exploratory moves along the neo-Thomist lines of a Jacques Maritain and Etienne Gilson. The theology of the manualists, guided by a rigorous construal of the dogmatic tradition and by a watchful magisterium (with fresh memories of the modernists), was the order of the day. However, an essay on religious freedom by an American Jesuit, John Courtney Murray, in the early 1940s, suggested important new directions to come.[19]

Behind yet another partition stood Eastern Orthodoxy. Here a traditionalist temper was also widespread, appearing in a patristic rather than a scholastic framework. Yet such "innovators" as Nicholas Berdyaev and Sergei Bulgakov were read within American Orthodoxy as well as by a larger public.

How did these various and changing (ephemeral) theological positions relate to the conjunctural question of suffering and hope? American neo-orthodoxy, whatever its diatribes against the Enlightenment, developed as a theological response to the commanding issue of human suffering, a response that was radicalized by the rise of totalitarianisms, the ravages of World War II, the Jewish holocaust, and the atomic bomb. Neo-orthodoxy, liberalism, neo-liberalism, and neo-naturalism were all responses to an epochal challenge experienced *in extremis.* Indeed, Reinhold Niebuhr's well-known doctrine of sin grew out of encounter with the incalculable pain inflicted by collectivities and with the need for social power to check their *hubris.*[20] Those who did not accept this agenda, or who were in attendance at a meeting elsewhere, continued inherited traditions that focused on one or another of the classical questions couched in traditional form. Yet they did so not without attention to human suffering and with a growing awareness of its social, economic, and political aspects.

The Church Against the World (1935), by H. Richard Niebuhr, Wilhelm Pauck, and Francis Miller, struck the note that was to characterize the neo-orthodox position on the structural issue of Christ and culture.

---

18. Carl F. H. Henry, *The Uneasy Conscience of Fundamentalism* (Grand Rapids: Eerdmans, 1947).

19. John Courtney Murray, "Freedom of Religion: The Ethical Problem," *Theological Studies* 4/2 (June 1945) 229-86.

20. Reinhold Niebuhr, *Moral Man and Immoral Society* (New York: Scribner's, 1932).

While historical context was not ignored, the *way* it was addressed was by insistence on the integrity of a Christian faith and church free of the corrupting ideologies of the hour. In this bellwether work, H. R. Niebuhr catalogued the isms that had taken the church captive—capitalism, racism, nationalism—and traced them to a foundational anthropocentrism, which he countered with a theocentrism grounded on Jesus Christ.

Those at the "theological meeting" who contested the dominant neo-orthodoxy also attacked the isms. But liberals, neo-liberals, and neo-naturalists looked instead to the capacities within human nature, or to immanent processes of cosmic history, to meet the challenges. Here context counted more than text.

Protestant orthodoxy, conservative evangelicalism, traditional Roman Catholicism, and Eastern Orthodoxy were allied in their rejection of modernity. On that basis we might place them formally on the text side of the text-context polarity. Yet their articulation of the ancient text was regularly in the language of a later age and its values, or was influenced implicitly by the assumptions of the present age, so that context often functioned more actively than acknowledged.

II. 1949-1962

Paul Tillich's *The Protestant Era* (1948) was a volume that symbolized both an ending and a beginning.[21] Ending, as it bears on matters theological in the United States, meant that a developing pluralism and secularity lowered the cultural profile of mainline Protestant institutions and its opinion-molders. Beginning signified the growing acceptance of the premise that Protestant theology could not be undertaken without incorporating fundamental features of the secular and pluralist landscape. While neo-orthodox influence continued strong during much of this period,[22] it was the messenger of endings and beginnings who emerged as a key figure.[23] Tillich, the theologian of culture, helped form a generation more interested in discerning how religion is the substance of culture than in setting the church against the world.[24]

---

21. Paul Tillich, *The Protestant Era* (Chicago: University of Chicago Press, 1948).

22. Niebuhr acknowledged some changes in his own thinking in *Man's Nature and His Communities* (New York: Scribner's, 1965).

23. Tillich, of course, had been writing for decades and was often (wrongly) associated with neo-orthodoxy. In my periodization, I choose to treat his work relative to its special American *kairos*.

24. The frequency of Tillich's name as "major mentor" in *A Dictionary of Systematic Theologians in North America*, ed. Thor Hall (Waterloo, Ontario: Council on the Study

Tillich's *Systematic Theology*, along with his occasional writings, expatiated upon God as being-itself, ripe historical moments as times of *kairos*, revelation as occasions in human experience of "miracle" and "ecstasy," the fundamental options of "heteronomy," "autonomy" and "theonomy," and theology developed by the "method of correlation."[25] The "world situation" to which the Christian answer is addressed was interpreted from within a philosophical tradition that extended from Schelling and Kierkegaard to Heidegger; was fed by the artistic and literary perceptions of Picasso, Sartre, and Camus; and was refined by the insights of depth psychology and religious socialism. Here one confronted "estrangement," "separation," "non-being" in a world evocative of anxiety and dread. The Christian answer to non-being is New Being found in Jesus as the Christ, the New Testament picture of one overcoming alienation in a self-emptying unity with the divine ground. The conjunctural question of historical suffering was now described in existential categories.[26] Yet the diagnosis appeared to shift the terms of the question from the historical plane to an ontological "dimension of depth," reflecting a post-war mood of despair, while the answer was phrased in therapeutic terms in which Christian hope seemed to be more a matter of coping than of historical action.

Other expressions of American existential theology were found in explicitly Kierkegaardian writings of the time; in a growing Heideggerian coterie that included both the followers of a demythologizing Bultmann and of a post-Bultmannian new hermeneutics; in the emergence of a therapeutically oriented theology (Seward Hiltner and David Roberts); and in a trend in the "theology of culture" that drew heavily on artistic and literary resources. Concomitant developments in Roman Catholic theology focused on the defense of the personal in a dehumanized world and saw the growing American influence of Karl Rahner's "transcendental anthropology." Extensive sociological commentary on post-war depersonalization found its way into theories of church mission for mobile, corporate, and suburban America. Theological rationale stressed an ecclesial *koinonia* that gave John and Jane Doe back their faces and their names.[27]

All these tendencies recognized and responded to the epoch's

---

of Religion, 1977), attests to his considerable influence, especially on those trained during this period.

25. Paul Tillich, *Systematic Theology*, 3 vols. (Chicago: University of Chicago Press, 1951-63).

26. And therein it was distinguished from the questions posed during other epochs in which the issues of sin/forgiveness, death/life, ignorance/truth came to the fore.

27. James Hoffman, *Mission: U.S.A.* (New York: Friendship, 1956).

encounter with suffering and its quest for hope, thus occupying the context side of the perennial text-context problem. But there were also the text-oriented theologians described (critically) by James Barr, who held that "Historians of theology in a future age will look back on the mid-twentieth century and call it the revelation-in-history period."[28] Here was a theological countercurrent that maintained neo-orthodoxy's emphasis on historic identity, namely, the American "biblical theology movement." Its leading representatives were Protestant biblical scholars—among them G. Ernest Wright, Bernhard Anderson, James Smart, James Muilenburg, Reginald Fuller, and Paul Minear, joined by Roman Catholics John MacKenzie, Roland De Vaux, and Bruce Vawter—who pointed to revelatory events in the history of Israel and Jesus Christ. They held that the authority of Scripture rested not on revealed propositions but on the witness therein to the deeds of God in a singular "holy history." Thus the Bible's engaged and earthy Hebrew mentality stood in sharp contrast to the abstract dispassionate Greek mindset and idiom. While the heritage was thus stressed by "biblical theology," the Enlightenment established the terms of its appropriation. The conjunctural problematic made its appearance in the focus on history and on the deliverance from misery and oppression wrought by God in it, one to be discerned in our own history and sought by our own involvement in the moil and toil of the times.

Concurrent with the biblical theologians, and sometimes allied with them, were other custodians of Christian identity. In their number were those who declared, "Let the church be the church!" A blossoming liturgical renewal movement and a recovered sacramentality in Protestant thought,[29] ecclesiologies that viewed the church as "the realm of redemption,"[30] and a church extension missiology that encouraged plantings in the new American suburbias all exemplified this churchly direction. These developments addressed the depersonalization of the day and the attendant hunger for community, and thus represented an ecclesial response to the era's coping/hoping issues.

Little noted in mainstream theology was the growing strength of a "new evangelicalism." Its intellectual bastions were Wheaton College,

28. James Barr, "Revelation through History in the Old Testament and in Modern Theology," in *New Theology No. 1*, ed. Martin E. Marty and Dean G. Peerman (New York: Macmillan, 1964), p. 62.

29. Renewed attention was given to John Williamson Nevin and Philip Schaff, nineteenth-century theologians who began a liturgical cum ecumenical movement in the seminary of the German Reformed Church at Mercersburg, Pennsylvania. Cf. James Hastings Nichols, *Romanticism in American Theology: Nevin and Schaff at Mercersburg* (Chicago: University of Chicago Press, 1961).

30. J. Robert Nelson, *The Realm of Redemption* (Chicago: Wilcox and Follett, 1956).

the newly founded Fuller Theological Seminary, and the recently launched periodical *Christianity Today*. A key figure in all these institutions was Carl F. H. Henry. While loyal to distinctively evangelical tenets, he helped pioneer a new direction by stressing rational argument for faith (a new apologetics), by rejecting the acerbic separatism of fundamentalist forebears, and by declaring the need for an evangelical ethics. Allies in these projects included Gordon Clark, J. Oliver Buswell, Edward John Carnell, and Bernard Ramm.

As suggested by the American anthology *Modern Catholic Thinkers* (1960),[31] Roman Catholic theology in this country still relied heavily on European giants. John MacKenzie, John Murray, Martin D'Arcy, and editor Robert Caponigri were the few locals represented in the volume. Many of the writers, American and otherwise, hinted at the fresh breezes soon to blow in their church. A window was cautiously being raised, yes, but in the fifties it was raised in a household of faith that was still wary of too much worldliness. Like most of the other theological developments in this period, both currents and countercurrents, Roman Catholic theology did not put itself forward into the fray in order to change the world.[32] The hope that it espoused in the face of suffering was represented by Teilhard de Chardin's famous figure of daylight at the end of a mine tunnel that made it possible for trapped workers to escape—a symbol of passive survival rather than of active change of the earth's very contours. To bring the mountains low and lift the valleys high was an image whose time was yet to come.

III. 1963-1970

"The sixties" evoke intense partisan interpretations. Some see it as the fanciful time of flower children, political and religious. Others believe it was the death knell of a 2,000-year tradition of belief. We take another tack with a clue from Roger Shinn. Writing of Union Seminary in the civil rights year of 1963, he said: "For many of our students the time has come to break the prolonged mood of introspection, . . . the fashionable revelling in anxiety. . . . [They] learned instead to march and sing. This has been the time when the American ear, long attuned to confused noises, heard the clear strains of

31. *Modern Catholic Thinkers: An Anthology*, ed. A. Robert Caponigri (New York: Harper, 1960).

32. Indeed, the first Roman Catholic president-to-be, John F. Kennedy, was at pains to prove to a Texas Protestant ministerium that he fully accepted the separation of church and state.

'We shall overcome some day!'"[33] Mainstream theology did take a significant turn, symbolized by that year's March on Washington with its memorable speech by Martin Luther King, Jr. ("I have a dream"). Dream, hope, vision, promise became key words for the period's future-oriented theologies. Their American architects drew on European thinkers Jürgen Moltmann and Wolfhart Pannenberg but adapted them to the American scene. So were heard the new songs of an Easter that "opened the future" and an Eschaton that makes us restless with the things that are.

While theoretical expositions of the theology of hope/future appeared (Carl Braaten, Robert Jenson, Kenneth Cauthen), it was "hope in action" that proved most compelling.[34] Action toward the future focused on the "secular city" and "the celebration of its liberties."[35] In a best-selling book, Harvey Cox amplified the sound of a growing chorus of theological voices that rejoiced in urban and secular graces and called visionaries to keep company with the "incognito Christ" at work in the struggles of "being" (war), "having" (poverty), and "belonging" (race).[36] The local church was attacked for its parochialism, inward-looking pieties, and suffocating sacramentalisms. The watchword of this kind of "secular theology" became "Join God where he is at work—in the world," with its reiterated texts: "God so loved the world," "You are the light of the world," "Go into all the world. . . ."

A group of younger American theologians, including Cox, constituted as The WCC North American Working Group on the Missionary Structure of the Congregation, gave these ideas early form. It produced a variety of popular writings complete with models drawn from the civil rights and peace movements, campus ministry, coffeehouse ministry, industrial chaplaincy, and local church renewal. (Active members were Colin Williams, Robert Spike, Gibson Winter, Andrew Young, Letty Russell, Gerald Jud, Michael Allen, Jitsuo Morikawa, Robert Raines, and some not so convinced about the "new ideology," such as Markus Barth.[37]) The Dutch missiologist J. C. Hoekendijk was much

33. Roger L. Shinn, *Union Seminary Tower*, Fall 1963, p. 3.

34. See the influential book by Hans J. Margull, *Hope in Action*, trans. Eugene Peters (Philadelphia: Muhlenberg, 1962).

35. Harvey Cox, *The Secular City: A Celebration of its Liberties and an Invitation to its Disciplines* (New York: Macmillan, 1965).

36. The social ethicist Gibson Winter's characterization.

37. The raw material of the Working Group is found in the mimeographed series *Concept* (Blue and Red), ed. Thomas Wieser, Department on Studies in Evangelism, WCC. For a review of the published literature associated with these figures, see Gabriel Fackre, "The Crisis of the Congregation: A Debate," in *Voluntary Associations*, ed. D. B. Robertson (Richmond: John Knox, 1966), pp. 275-97, 427-32.

quoted,[38] and behind him stood the giant figure of Dietrich Bonhoeffer. Bonhoeffer's writings, especially *Letters and Papers from Prison* (1953), and his personal example left the decisive mark on this as well as other forms of American secular theology. It was Bonhoeffer who invited "participation in the sufferings of God in the world" and who issued the call to humanization and the plea for a servant church and for the recovery of Old Testament earthiness. A revolution of rising expectations gave impetus to the conjunctural problematic, with the accent on a mobilizing hope. Concomitantly, the structural question received a clear answer: "Let the world set the agenda!" The church was seen to be a "postscript" to God's humanizing work, a "church for others" living in obedience to the "Man for others" (again, Bonhoeffer).

Roman Catholic theology struck out along similar lines. Pope John XXIII's call to "open a window" to let in fresh breezes from the outside seemed to harmonize with Bonhoeffer's emphases. Responses took different form: involvement in and interpretation of prophetic movements (the Berrigan brothers, Thomas Merton); "the servant church" challenging the perpetuation of institutionalism in ecclesial models (Avery Dulles); a stress on a future-oriented Kingdom of God as root metaphor (Richard McBrien); a pressing of "the participatory" that questioned hierarchy.

"God—the problem": so declared Gordon Kaufman on his way to an understanding of theology as essentially an act of the human imagination.[39] This kind of secular theology fixed upon the epistemological question posed by Bonhoeffer's "coming of age" and "god of the gaps" ideas. Its most radical expositors were the "death of God" theologians: William Hamilton, for whom secularity required deicide but made room for loyalty to the human Jesus; Thomas Altizer's mystical modalism cum atheism; and Paul van Buren's secular Christology as a Wittgensteinian "language game."[40] The eclectic and more church-connected proposals of J. A. T. Robinson won an American audience for his replacement of both "the God up there" and "the God out there" with a "divine depth dimension" manifest in Jesus of Nazareth.[41] The problem of God also received attention from a "process theology" rooted in the thought of Alfred North Whitehead, with philosophical

38. J. C. Hoekendijk, *The Church Inside Out,* trans. Isaac Rottenberg (Philadelphia: Westminster, 1966).

39. Gordon D. Kaufman, *God the Problem* (Cambridge: Harvard University Press, 1972).

40. Thomas J. Altizer and William Hamilton, *Radical Theology and the Death of God* (Indianapolis: Bobbs-Merrill, 1966); Paul van Buren, *The Secular Meaning of the Gospel* (New York: Macmillan, 1963).

41. J. A. T. Robinson, *Honest to God* (Philadelphia: Westminster, 1963).

interpretation by Charles Hartshorne and theological applications made by Daniel Williams, Schubert Ogden, and Langdon Gilkey. John Cobb and his Claremont colleague David Griffin put Whiteheadian thought in touch with world religions and helped to formulate a process Christology, process theodicy, process ecclesiology, and process ethics.[42]

Also responding philosophically to secularization were American and Canadian Roman Catholics: Gregory Baum (deity as the "divine becoming"), Leslie Dewart (God as the presence of the future), Gabriel Moran (in revelation theology), and Bernard Lonergan (whose work on theological method had worldwide influence).[43] Teilhard's thought also gained increased prominence in American Catholic circles and beyond (especially in relation to a new field of studies, "futurology"), as did that of Karl Rahner (whose *Theological Investigations* were in process of translation into English).

While the proliferation of secular theologies dominated the scene, the sixties also saw the continuing growth of conservative evangelical theology. Carl Henry was again active on the apologetic front, joined by H. D. MacDonald, Harold J. Brown, Gordon R. Lewis, and Roger Nicole, all of whom challenged secularizing tendencies, especially on the issues of revelation and Scripture.[44] Orthodox Protestant theology was equally adamant in rejecting the overall secular trend, especially the death of God theology. And mainline Protestant thought often treated "Christian atheism" as a transient media event. It connected secularity with issues of social change and ecclesial reform but remained unwilling to reduce Christ to human proportions, to substitute coffeehouse or metropolitan ministries for the local church, and to eliminate moral codes. (James Gustafson, Martin Marty, Gordon Cosby, Robert Raines, and George Webber were writing influential books.[45])

"Earth Day" in April 1970 may be taken to mark the close of "the sixties" in both cultural ferment and theological focus. Still change-oriented in temper, but with a somewhat different constituency, the ecology movement saw little to celebrate in the secular city and viewed its "can do" aggressiveness as the foe. Environmental activists, however,

---

42. A representative work of this period was John B. Cobb, *A Christian Natural Theology* (Philadelphia: Westminster, 1965). W. Norman Pittenger anticipated the rash of process doctrinal restatements; cf. *The Word Incarnate* (New York: Harper, 1959).

43. Kindred to the radical responses among Protestants was Leslie Dewart's *The Future of Belief: Theism in a World Come of Age* (New York: Herder, 1966).

44. For a review of evangelical apologetics, see Gordon R. Lewis, *Testing Christianity's Truth Claims: Approaches to Christian Apologetics* (Chicago: Moody, 1976).

45. Typical of the "yes, but" writing was Robert Raines, *The Secular Congregation* (New York: Harper & Row, 1968).

found themselves in alliance with former social radicals now seeking the elusive light in Aquarian experimentation and other extrahistorical ventures that marked the decade to come. But not all the warriors for peace and justice left the barricades. As the cultural and ecclesiastical polarization deepened in the late 1960s—"hardhats" vs. "hippies"—advocacy positions hardened and the rhetoric escalated from "humanization" to "revolution." Resistance in middle America and the summer soldiery of white liberals prompted many poor, black, and other marginalized people to rely more and more on their own resources and to claim their own terrain. Thus, in some cases, a harder line activist theology was joined to the softer mien of the earth mystic at the threshold of the seventies.

IV. 1971-1979

What Harvey Cox described as a series of experiments in communicating the Gospel, some commentators saw as a barometer of acculturated American theology.[46] In this decade Cox's *Feast of Fools* (1969), *Seduction of the Spirit* (1973), and *Turning East* (1977) reflected in one way or another the neo-mystical and Aquarian trends along with developing theologies of play, pluralism, and personal story. The social setting for the "new mentality" was often the weekend retreat, the summer conference, and the house church—each with its "intense group experience" or "religious happening." Often members of the clergy, wounded in the humanization struggles of the sixties, found their way to these occasions, which sometimes involved joining the ranks of "ex-pastors"[47] or a turn toward ministry mentored by a Rollo May, a Carl Rogers, or a rediscovered Carl Jung.

"World religions" moved increasingly to the fore during this decade under countercultural impulse, the growth of nonsectarian religious studies programs in universities, and heightened awareness of religious pluralism. Thus emerged the "pluralist theology" of transatlantic teacher John Hick, who challenged Christian particularities in *The Myth of God Incarnate* controversy, promoting in their place a "global"

---

46. The counterculture of the day was described by the Berkeley Ecological Revolutionary Movement as made up of "Gnostics, Hip Marxists, Teilhard de Chardin Catholics, Druids, Taoists, Biologists, Witches, Yogins, Bhikkus, Quakers, Sufis, Tibetans, Zens, Shamans, Bushmen, American Indians, Polynesians, Anarchists, Alchemists, . . . all communal and ashram movements." Quoted in *The Lancaster Independent Press*, February 14, 1970, p. 2.

47. Gerald Jud, *Ex-Pastors* (Philadelphia: Pilgrim, 1970).

faith.[48] A similar openness to religious truth beyond the circle of Christian particularity could be found among Roman Catholic theologians in the writings of Thomas Merton, Raymond Panikkar, and those influenced by the "anonymous Christianity" motif of Karl Rahner, yet without Hick's programmatic syncretism. So, too, a developing Asian-sensitized theology had its impact (Kosuke Koyama). Forms of "story-telling" theology, which stressed effective encounter through symbol, metaphor, and myth with dimensions of reality inaccessible to cerebral and discursive modes of interpretation, were a species of this genus (Sally McFague).

Drawing attention to "unthematized" commonalities in human experience, yet seeking linkage with Christian tradition, were various experiential theologies of the seventies. The debates in Roman Catholic "fundamental theology" were a showcase of the same: students of Karl Rahner following a transcendental-existential method, Lonerganians grounding the argument for faith in religious conversion, David Tracy correlating "limit situations" with primordial experiences of trust expressed in classic texts, and Edward Schillebeeckx showing how hunger for hope finds its fulfillment in an eschatological prophet experienced by his followers as the risen Lord.[49]

Schillebeeckx's suffering/hope program illustrates the unremitting power of the conjunctural question. All of the theologies mentioned, however unsecular their predispositions, were addressed to this issue, magnified as it was by awesome means at hand to shape the future. Yet, with notable exceptions (among them Cox and Schillebeeckx), the hoping often led "in and down" rather than "out and ahead" into history. For the latter, we must return to a parallel trajectory in this decade.

Just as one black pastor set the tone for much of the American hope theology of the sixties, so another sounded the trumpet for the newer "liberation theology." But this time change was heralded not by the dream of Martin King but by the anger of James Cone. As cultural resistance to social goals mounted so did the frustration of aggrieved minorities, and with it came the choice for separatism and confrontation. Cone's *Black Theology and Black Power* (1969), *A Black Theology of Liberation* (1970), and *God of the Oppressed* (1975) were anticipations of soon-to-be-familiar phrases and themes: "option for the poor," "epistemologi-

---

48. Illustrated by Hick's attempt to blend the eschatologies of various world religions in his *Death and Eternal Life* (New York: Harper & Row, 1976).

49. The massive exegetical studies of Schillebeeckx, *Jesus* and *Christ* (New York: Seabury, 1977, 1980), were much commented upon in Roman Catholic journals.

cal privilege of the poor," "hermeneutics of suspicion," "orthopraxis," "solidarity with the oppressed," and "Christ the Liberator," as developed in Latin American liberation theology and related movements. Yet the prophetic spirit was always bonded to black piety and a christological center. In-house disagreement there certainly was among black theologians (J. Deotis Roberts, Joseph Washington, Gayraud Wilmore, Major Jones, C. Eric Lincoln, George Kelsey, Preston Williams, and the still vital Howard Thurman and Benjamin Mays), but the oppression/liberation themes were shared.[50] Sensitized by black theology, large segments of the theological reading public gave respectful attention to the prolific Latin American theologians, especially Catholic theologians Gustavo Gutiérrez and Juan Luis Segundo and their Protestant counterparts, José Míguez Bonino and Rubem Alves, for whom salvation is inextricably bound up with social-economic-political liberation. Evangelical theologians in minority communities drawn to the liberation movement, among them Orlando Costas and Tom Skinner, were at pains to disengage the justice struggle from ideological frameworks and to connect personal with social salvation.[51]

During this period feminist (liberation) theology gained significant momentum in association with a wider women's movement. Mary Daly, in *The Church and the Second Sex* (1968), challenged sexism from within the tradition, but in *Beyond God the Father* (1973) and *Gyn/Ecology: The Metaethics of Radical Feminism* (1979) she issued an extra-Christian feminist manifesto that met the social "rape" of women by the theological "castration" of God and sought to gather female communities of protest outside the range of male hegemony. Meanwhile, another Roman Catholic theologian, Rosemary Radford Ruether (*Liberation Theology*, 1972) relentlessly exposed the body-mind dualisms of white male theology, attacked hierarchy in all its forms, and encouraged women to participate in ecclesial communities of liberation. Letty Mandeville Russell, with experience in an East Harlem ministry, worked along parallel lines, identifying a Jesus tradition of liberation/shalom/partnership (*Human Liberation in Feminist Perspective*, 1974) and leading efforts to render theological language inclusive (*The Liberating Word*, 1976). Phyllis Trible, using methods of the new literary criticism, demonstrated the possibilities of a feminist reading of Scripture in *God and the Rhetoric of Sexuality* (1978).

Conjunctural-wise, liberation theologies were unambiguously

---

50. See J. Deotis Roberts, *Liberation and Reconciliation: A Black Theology* (Philadelphia: Westminster, 1971).

51. Orlando Costas, *The Church and Its Mission* (Wheaton, IL: Tyndale House, 1974).

addressed to the problem of human suffering, confronting it from one or another framework of historical hope. Structural-wise, they were contextual theologies, holding that every school of thought is formed from within a social location and that all responsible theology is inseparable from the victim's struggle.

The Institute for Advanced Christian Studies, founded "to contain the secular tide that engulfs contemporary culture," was one indicator of the counter-presence and power of American evangelicalism in this period.[52] Here text was emphasized, indeed *the* Christian text, with evangelical energies concentrated on affirming the Bible's authority in the face of the perceived cultural accommodations of other theologies. Yet there was also an in-house "battle for the Bible" that pitted "inerrantists" against "infallibilists."[53] Noteworthy were the durable Carl Henry's six-volume *God, Revelation and Authority* (1976-83) and Donald Bloesch's two-volume systematics, *The Essentials of Evangelical Theology* (1978-79). Expanding church constituencies ("the evangelical empire"), not unrelated to the culture's quest for identity (neo-pietism paralleling neo-mysticism), gave a widening audience to evangelical theology.

The resurgence of a more traditional point of view was also to be seen among Roman Catholics, with both American supporters of Cardinal Ratzinger and other authors (Michael Novak) attacking liberation theology, challenging innovators Küng and Schillebeeckx, and questioning the effects of Vatican II on Catholic faith. Not aligned with this theological right were Roman Catholics like Avery Dulles and Raymond Brown, who affirmed *aggiornamento* but defended traditional landmarks in Scripture and Catholic doctrine.[54] This latter "centrism" had its counterpart in Protestant circles, as evidenced by a renewed interest in the lore of the Christian community, a plea for in-depth study of Scripture and Christian doctrine in congregations, and a revival of systematic theology in seminaries.

Some advocates of return to roots insisted on equal attention to fruits. This both-and view showed up in missiology, where efforts were made to bring Word and deed together, especially by evangelical activists such as Ron Sider, Jim Wallis, and feminist Virginia Ramey Mol-

---

52. Carl F. H. Henry, *Confessions of a Theologian* (Waco: Word Books, 1986), p. 341.

53. Harold Lindsell's *The Battle for the Bible* (Grand Rapids: Zondervan, 1976) was the opening salvo.

54. Avery Dulles, *Models of the Church* (Garden City: Doubleday, 1974); Raymond E. Brown, *The Critical Meaning of the Bible* (New York: Paulist, 1981). Centrist Eastern Orthodoxy, committed to the Tradition yet ecumenically open, continued the work of ecumenist Georges Florovsky, as in the writings of John Meyendorff, Timothy Ware, and Stanley Harakas.

lenkott. Veteran theologian Albert Outler gave impetus to the search for inclusivity by bringing together evangelicals, ecumenicals, and charismatics in important Notre Dame colloquia.

While standing on the textual side of the perennial structural question, all these tradition-oriented movements continued to address the conjunctural concern. The quest for identity was carried on to fortify the believing community in its struggle with the suffering inflicted or threatened by modernity and was carried out with a hope that invited historical action.

V. 1980-Present

At the turn of the decade *New York Times'* stories began to appear describing a new political constituency, "the religious Right." Exercised about abortion, homosexuality, pornography, the Equal Rights Amendment; supportive of nuclear buildup, tough anti-crime measures, and anti-Communist foreign policy; pressing for a "creationist" alternative to evolutionary teaching in school textbooks and a return of prayer to public schools, the "Moral Majority" helped to elect a new president and Congress and thus significantly changed the American political map. Giving leadership was a group of "political fundamentalists," a few of whom—Jerry Falwell, Pat Robertson, Jim Bakker, James Robison— were seen regularly and funded munificently by millions of television devotees. Theologically, these new faces and newly vocal multitudes (together with less politically active figures with their own television, radio, and paperback following—Jimmie Swaggart, Oral Roberts, Rex Humbard, Hal Lindsey) constituted a "neo-fundamentalist phenomenon,"[55] reading current events through the glasses of an apocalyptic premillennialism and a polemical view of inerrancy. What made this fundamentalism "new" was the application of its dispensational view of history to a specific political agenda, with a "secular humanism" demonology worked out by theoretician Francis Schaeffer and popularizer Timothy LaHaye, and a "reconstructionist" turn given by postmillennialist R. J. Rushdoony.[56]

Its cultural consequences impossible to ignore, neo-fundamentalism increasingly influenced the theological agenda, evoking sharp retort from the mainstream theologies. While its religious zeal appeared

---

55. A variation on Falwell's *The Fundamentalist Phenomenon: The Resurgence of Conservative Christianity,* ed. Jerry Falwell with Ed Dobson and Ed Hindson (Garden City: Doubleday, 1981).

56. R. J. Rushdoony, *The Institutes of Biblical Law* (Nutley, NJ: Craig Press, 1973).

to be a sea change from the recent secularity, neo-fundamentalism can justly be viewed as itself a secularization of faith[57] and, accordingly, as yet another response to the Enlightenment-informed conjunctural question. The reality of personal sinfulness, apocalyptic hope, and a sure knowledge gained from inerrant Scripture were all espoused to make life more livable in this world, protecting believers from its present dreads and anticipated holocausts. Indeed, one of its most popular permutations was a "health and wealth gospel" that promised adherents personal happiness and financial gain. By the mid-80s, the corruptibility of purveyors of this "have it all" theology had exposed the flaws in a view that failed to take seriously its own admonishments of sin and finitude, suggesting one of the lessons we must finally draw from all reductionist responses to conjunctural issues.

The explicit structuralist textuality of neo-fundamentalism had its counterpart in other, very different movements "back to basics." Protestant churches and their theologians were having second thoughts about quick responses to cultural trends insufficiently tested by Christian distinctives. A "Yale theology" appeared, represented by George Lindbeck's study of doctrines as the rules of Christian speech,[58] with the narrative theology of colleague Hans Frei in the background, and by a cluster of Yale graduates writing on the integrity of the Christian community's liturgical, catechetical, and ethical life. This "postmodern" and "antifoundationalist" posture criticized the secular and existentialist modes of theology for appealing uncritically to universal experiences, for acceding to the conventional wisdom of the academy, and for dissolving Christian singularities. As part of a wider movement often self-consciously representing families of faith—for example, books by Calvinist Nicholas Wolterstorff, Lutheran Ronald Thiemann, Roman Catholic Francis Schüssler Fiorenza—and often related to a parallel "canonical approach" to biblical studies by Brevard Childs,[59] this neo-confessional theology struck these notes: (1) "Here I stand" against the stream; (2) Be faithful to the texts of our tradition; and (3) Speak out of our ecclesial identity (whose importance was sometimes based more on "cultural-linguistic" arguments than on claims to objective truth).

57. This is the thesis of my *The Religious Right and Christian Faith* (Grand Rapids: Eerdmans, 1982).

58. George A. Lindbeck, *The Nature of Doctrine: Religion and Theology in a Postliberal Age* (Philadelphia: Westminster, 1984).

59. Nicholas Wolterstorff, *Reason Within the Bounds of Religion* (Grand Rapids: Eerdmans, 1984); Ronald F. Thiemann, *Revelation and Theology: The Gospel as Narrated Promise* (Notre Dame: University of Notre Dame Press, 1985); Francis Schüssler Fiorenza, *Foundational Theology: Jesus and the Church* (New York: Crossroad, 1986); Brevard Childs, *The New Testament as Canon* (London: SCM, 1984).

Parallel moves toward owning and clarifying one's heritage could be found in striking convergence documents on the reviving ecumenical scene, notably the American *COCU Consensus* (1985) and the text of the World Council of Churches' Faith and Order Commission on *Baptism, Eucharist and Ministry* (1982). There was also revived interest in neo-orthodox figures: a Barth boomlet among evangelicals and study of his work by pastors' groups, and a biography of Reinhold Niebuhr and republication of his selected writings.[60] Evangelicals remained a strong presence, but with increasing signs of diversity: a vigorous "high church" wing emerged, a radical evangelicalism questioned the culture more aggressively in social protest and communitarian experiments, and an ecumenical evangelicalism reached out to mainliners.

The contextual trends of the seventies continued as a strong countercurrent in the eighties, often with a heightened mood of "overagainstness." Third World liberation theology made advances owing to the intensification of Latin American political struggles as affected by Reaganism and to a growing Hispanic population in the United States. Feminist theological leaders (Elisabeth Schüssler Fiorenza, Phyllis Trible, Letty Russell) applied their hermeneutics of suspicion and reconstruction ever more rigorously to Christian charters and spoke increasingly of "woman church" with its own canon of feminist experience and, for some (e.g., Rosemary Ruether), its goddess traditions.[61] "Peace theologies" gained prominence under the impetus of nuclear threat (Gordon Kaufman, Susan Thistlethwaite), as did a "public theology" (Max Stackhouse, Richard Neuhaus) with a broader cultural interest and apologetic intent.[62] Pluralist theologies more actively questioned Christian particularity in the name of "theocentrism," as in Paul Knitter's *No Other Name?* and Paul van Buren's antisupersessionist writings on Jewish-Christian reality.[63] Earlier process, existential, secular, and narrative theologies continued to have followings, with their formulations now responding to newer themes, especially those of a her-

---

60. Richard Fox, *Reinhold Niebuhr: A Biography* (New York: Pantheon, 1985), R. M. Brown, ed., *The Essential Reinhold Niebuhr*.

61. Elisabeth Schüssler Fiorenza, *In Memory of Her: A Feminist Reconstruction of Christian Origins* (New York: Crossroad, 1983); Letty M. Russell, ed., *Feminist Interpretation of the Bible* (Philadelphia: Westminster, 1985); Rosemary Radford Ruether, *Womanguides: Readings Toward a Feminist Theology* (Boston: Beacon, 1985).

62. Gordon D. Kaufman, *Theology for a Nuclear Age* (Philadelphia: Westminster, 1985); Susan Thistlethwaite, ed., *A Just Peace Church* (New York: United Church Press, 1986); Max Stackhouse, *Public Theology and Political Economy* (Grand Rapids: Eerdmans, 1987); Richard John Neuhaus, *The Naked Public Square: Religion and Democracy in America*, 2nd ed. (Grand Rapids: Eerdmans, 1986).

63. Paul F. Knitter, *No Other Name?* (Maryknoll, NY: Orbis, 1985); Paul van Buren, *Discerning the Way: A Theology of Jewish-Christian Reality* (New York: Seabury, 1980).

meneutical turn. In all these theologies, whether taking their cues from text or context, the conjunctural problematic of suffering and hope continued to be formative.

The notes of inclusivity and collegiality that had been faintly sounded in the seventies grew stronger during the eighties. Ecumenicals and evangelicals found themselves allied on some issues, given the withering of earlier stereotypes, and their encounters intensified. Intra- and inter-liberation exchanges also increased (as in J. Deotis Roberts's *Black Theology in Dialogue* and Guillermo Cook's *The Expectation of the Poor*, the latter written from an evangelical-liberation perspective).[64] And, as previously noted, documents of ecumenical convergence gained respectful hearings.

Inclusivity also meant doing theology in the round. Systematic theologies began to flourish again in the late seventies and continued apace in the years following. The move beyond *ad hoc* and "theology and . . ." writings to fuller coverage of the traditional *loci* could be found all along the spectrum. Evangelical theologians produced single and multi-volume works (Donald Bloesch, Dale Moody, Millard Erickson),[65] while feminist Rosemary Ruether covered the classical topics.[66] And there were works by those speaking for confessional families (Carl Braaten and Robert Jenson—Lutheran, Richard McBrien—Roman Catholic, James McLendon—Baptist),[67] as well as works of a more ecumenical purview.[68]

VI. Some Concluding Observations

The application of the French historians' scheme to this most recent era of Christian theology suggests at least three matters for self-examination.

(1) While a theology insulated from its historical context is much

---

64. J. Deotis Roberts, *Black Theology in Dialogue* (Philadelphia: Westminster, 1987); Guillermo Cook, *The Expectation of the Poor* (Maryknoll, NY: Orbis, 1985).

65. Donald Bloesch, *The Essentials of Evangelical Theology*, 2 vols. (San Francisco: Harper & Row, 1978-79); Dale Moody, *The Word of Truth* (Grand Rapids: Eerdmans, 1981); Millard J. Erickson, *Christian Theology*, 3 vols. (Grand Rapids: Baker, 1983-86).

66. Rosemary Radford Ruether, *Sexism and God-Talk: Toward a Feminist Theology* (Boston: Beacon, 1983); one also notes the unflagging interest in Gustavo Gutiérrez's *A Theology of Liberation* (Maryknoll, NY: Orbis, 1971).

67. Carl E. Braaten and Robert W. Jenson, eds., *Christian Dogmatics*, 2 vols. (Philadelphia: Fortress, 1984); Richard P. McBrien, *Catholicism* (Minneapolis: Winston Press, 1981); James Wm. McLendon, *Systematic Theology: Ethics* (Nashville: Abingdon, 1986).

68. Geoffrey Wainwright, *Doxology* (New York: Oxford University Press, 1980); Gabriel Fackre, *The Christian Story*, 2 vols. (Grand Rapids: Eerdmans, 1984, 1987).

to be deplored, does "responsiveness" require the striking ephemerality of teaching that marks this half-century? The fine line between relating to a time and capitulating to it seems regularly to be transgressed as legitimate concerns become the occasion for entirely new theologies. Taking this world and this time seriously might better assume the form of a secular-sensitive Christian doctrine than of an acculturated "secular theology." And lively consciousness of the oppressed and disenfranchised is far better served by a liberated classical faith than by a "liberation theology" that knows only its own issues and talks only to its own people. The struggle against reductionism would also have its effects on our personal self-definitions. Preference would be accorded the adjectival neo-orthodox/existential/evangelical/process/feminist *Christian*, thereby preserving the key noun for one's *fundamental* identity. Thus a learning from this period must be a reeducation in the durabilities and a self-criticism of our American taste for theological fashions. Moreover, this struggle against the transient is related to the need to be at home with the "Christ against culture" mode of theological structural history.

(2) Theology that turns its back on the human consequences of technological advance in the Enlightenment epoch, failing to face the horrors of its abuse in war, tyranny, and oppression, is faithless. Christian theologians who believe in the Incarnation will be in solidarity with society's victims and strive mightily to harness technology's positive potential to human healing. The Gospel *is* good news to the poor. But must the commanding conjunctural issue of historical suffering and hope obscure the claimant questions of death, error, and sin? In Christian faith, penultimate hope is grounded in ultimate hope, and error demands the quest for truth. Most of all, the heart of the good news is the Word that the world's controversy with its Creator is over in the deed done in Jesus Christ. The Christian story turns on the redemption of the world from sin, as that was wrought in a Person and Work.

(3) The variety of theological views throughout this era testifies to American initiative and creativity. Does its protean character obviate the need for collegiality? Does diversity preclude unity? For all the pro forma theological criticism of individualism, the number of private orthodoxies strewn through this half-century belies the rhetoric. Consider these wise words from Hugh T. Kerr, Jr., coming at the end of a long tenure as editor of *Theology Today*. Commenting on the pervasiveness of "single issue theology," he asks: "What is the locus of single issues within the grand theological orbit of the Bible as a whole, of Christian tradition, past and present, and of the universal church everywhere? The kind of symmetry that theology was once supposed to imply may not be a viable option among theologians in our day, but it still must

be true that any portion of the gospel belongs within the implicative network of the whole of God's plan and purpose. Advocates of single issues tend to avoid such wider theological ramifications. Why?"[69] How desperately we need a Corinthian word about the many parts making their contribution to the one Body. How much we need to move beyond our single issue imperialisms toward a truly inclusive, catholic theology.

69. Hugh T. Kerr, Jr., "Editorial: Trademarks of Theology," *Theology Today* 42/4 (January 1987) 469.

15. Religion and Science

Wayne Proudfoot

From Puritan devotional piety to the present day, religious thought in America has always had an empirical component. Attention to the religious interpretation of experience has motivated interest in physics and psychology, in the laws that govern natural phenomena and in how we perceive those phenomena. Jonathan Edwards, Ralph Waldo Emerson, and William James were deeply interested in and conversant with the methods and results of science. Each developed sophisticated theories of perception. James proposed that theology be replaced by a science of religions in which the varieties of religious experience would be classified into types and the relevant implications drawn for philosophy and psychology. Following James, liberal religious thinkers in the first half of the twentieth century tried to clarify the status of religious beliefs and experience in the light of the successes of science, to address their conflicts, and to invoke the authority or the results of science in support of particular interpretations of religion.

At present, attention to the experiential component of religious thought and to the issue of the relation of science to religion seems to be in eclipse. A consensus holds that the rules governing statements and practices in religion and in science differ to such an extent that it is naive to imagine that the relation between scientific statements and religious beliefs could ever be one of conflict or support. Direct comparison or contrast would be evidence of an illegitimate confusion of categories. This defense of the autonomy of religious belief with respect to science is itself a way of addressing the relation between the two domains. If successful, it precludes at the outset any conflict between religious statements and other beliefs about the world. Changes in those beliefs occasioned by increases in our knowledge of some aspect of nature or culture need not require alterations in religious belief.

One of the chief issues for religious thinkers and theologians since the eighteenth century has been the relation of science and religious belief. This generalization is as true of those thinkers who claim to have no use for apologetics, and who hold that science and religion are completely different and unrelated activities and realms of discourse, as it is for those who attempt to reinterpret religious claims in the light of contemporary science. The argument that the beliefs and practices of science are radically different from and unrelated to those of religion is itself an apologetic move designed to obviate any conflict between the method and results of science and the claims of the theologian. The issue, however, is not so easily laid to rest.

The aim of scientific inquiry is to provide increasingly more adequate descriptions and explanations for the phenomena of our experience. Though considerable debate remains about how the adequacy of descriptions and explanations is to be assessed, appeal to realities or forces beyond the natural world is ruled out as illegitimate. This is not as great a restriction as it might seem, because the boundaries of the natural world are constantly being redrawn by the results of scientific inquiry. But theologians have traditionally claimed that God is independent of and prior to the world of nature, and that any ultimate explanation of particular events in the world, or of where we have come from and where we are going, requires reference to God as Creator and Governor. When scientific inquiry begins to yield explanations that conflict with those in the religious tradition and that make no appeal to anything beyond the natural, the question arises as to what is the explanatory role of religion and, especially, the cognitive status of religious belief.

The problem is not that science has arrived at the truth. Many of the beliefs about the world that were held 200 years ago have been revised or discarded. We have every reason to think that our descendants will look back at the physics and biology of the late twentieth century from a perspective shaped by different concepts and beliefs. Nevertheless, the process of scientific inquiry and theory construction has proven eminently successful in practice, includes resources for its own correction and improvement, and rules out reference to the traditional objects of religious belief and practice.

Science has probably never attained as much prominence and prestige in any society as in the United States during the years 1935-1985. By the beginning of this period the foundations of contemporary physics had been laid. The theory of relativity and quantum mechanics combined with evolving models of the atom to set the stage for the experimental and theoretical exploration of elementary particles that has occupied much of contemporary physics. The revolution in biology that followed the analysis of the structure of DNA is more recent. While psychology and the social sciences cannot claim such dramatic successes, for reasons that distinguish their method and subject matter from those of the natural sciences, they have also flourished during this period as never before. Space exploration and medical technology are only two of the areas in which the results of scientific study have captured the popular imagination.

Although the content of science has undergone great development during this period, the strategies employed by religious thinkers have not changed very much. Scientific advances have, of course, affected theology in a number of ways. Archaeology, philology, and linguistics have greatly altered our understanding of ancient texts. Anthropology and the other social sciences have enabled us better to understand the cultures in which traditional religious thought and practices were situated. But the several different positions on the relations of religious belief and practice to the growth and increasing adequacy of our scientific knowledge of the universe that are represented in American religious thought in our period are not new or specific to America, though they do represent the range of options available.

Six positions can be distinguished. The first three select particular ways in which science and religion can affect one another. The last three argue for the logical independence of the two activities and deny that either can properly affect the other. These six positions may be briefly delineated as follows:

(1) Science can be subordinated to religious belief. We often relegate this standpoint to the realm of traditional and now antiquated controversy over the heliocentric universe or Darwinian evolution; yet the dispute over "creation science" and the resurgence of theological fundamentalism are recent phenomena.

(2) Religious belief can be revised in the light of modern science and a conception of God can be formulated employing resources from the current state of our knowledge about the universe.

(3) The scientific method can be applied to religious experience, belief, and practice, as was advocated by William James.

(4) Religious thought and practice can be distinguished from science by reason of their concern with questions of meaning, value, and human purpose, each of which is beyond the reach of scientific description and explanation.

(5) Religious language, concepts, and belief are completely dif-

ferent from and independent of the language and practice of science. One can argue on theological grounds, or by analysis of the tacit grammar that governs the use of concepts and evidence in the two spheres, that they have different aims and rules and do not impinge upon one another at all.

(6) A stress on the autonomy of religious belief can be combined with attention to certain parallels between religious and scientific inquiry.

Each of these positions calls for further explanation and evaluation.

(1) Theologians have been anxious to avoid the mistakes of the past, especially those in which theology was permitted to dictate to science. Controversies from the time of Galileo down to the Scopes trial in 1925, in which ecclesiastical or biblical authority was set over against scientific theory, have led most modern religious thinkers to eschew any such authoritarian use of doctrine. Recently there has been a revival of interest in creationism, which represents the biblical account of creation as a scientific theory and defends it against evolutionary theories. This revival is important for historians of Christianity in the United States and for an understanding of the alienation of large segments of American society. Like fundamentalism more generally, it is a response to the threats of modernity to traditional values. The number of persons who sympathize with the subordination of science to religious doctrine, though they might not subscribe to creationism, seems to have grown recently and they have become bolder in the articulation and defense of their position. But this position is not and cannot be a plausible alternative to an enlightened understanding of both religion and science.

(2) The prime example of using the content of modern science to formulate a theology is process theology, which derives in part from the metaphysics of Alfred North Whitehead.[1] Though others, notably Charles Hartshorne and his students, have modified Whitehead's thought and have drawn on various strands in the history of philosophy and theology to formulate a neoclassical theism, the rapprochement with modern science and the categories that inform process thought come chiefly from Whitehead's work.[2] His major statement, *Process and Reality*, was published in 1929. Though process theology claims the authority of a conception of God and the world that is informed by con-

---

1. See especially Alfred North Whitehead, *Process and Reality* (New York: Macmillan, 1929).
2. For a statement of neoclassical theism, see Charles Hartshorne, *Man's Vision of God and the Logic of Theism* (New York: Harper, 1941) and *The Divine Relativity* (New Haven: Yale University Press, 1948).

temporary physics and mathematics, the categories by which it is structured are unaffected by the advances in physics and biology since at least 1930. There are other arguments that can be made in support of process thought, but much of its prestige comes from its presumed accord with modern scientific theory. It is hard to escape the conclusion that this prestige derives largely from the fact that Whitehead was a mathematician and logician who turned his attention to metaphysics. His rather idiosyncratic speculative system does not adequately express the state of physics even as it was half a century ago.

(3) William James proposed applying the scientific method of inquiry to religious experience, just as we do to other forms of experience. His radical empiricism was an attempt to expand the empirical method beyond what he saw as a reductive concentration on sense data and the allegedly simple components of experience. His *Principles of Psychology* (1890) is a remarkable synthesis of experimental results, introspective analysis, and sophisticated philosophical reflection. It remains a text from which psychologists and philosophers continue to learn. James urged the exploration of experience in all of its complexity and regarded the study of religious experience as an important part of the study of human nature. He proposed that a science of religions replace philosophy of religion and theology, hoping that *The Varieties of Religious Experience* (1902) would be a substantial contribution to such a science.[3]

Through his teaching and writing, James promoted a number of psychological investigations of religious experience and mysticism.[4] Others tried to heed his advice to set theology on a scientific foundation. In 1919, Douglas Clyde Macintosh of the Yale Divinity School published *Theology as an Empirical Science*.[5] In this and subsequent writings he sought to adapt his understanding of the method of scientific inquiry to theology.

Macintosh claimed to have developed a science of religions, building on James. He meant to draw not upon the content of contemporary physics or psychology but on the empirical methods of scientific investigation, in order better to understand religious experience and its implications for theology. Like James, he thought that philosophy of re-

---

3. William James, *The Varieties of Religious Experience* (New York: Longmans, 1902), pp. 430-57.

4. Among the more important were Edwin D. Starbuck, *The Psychology of Religion* (New York: Scribner's, 1900); James H. Leuba, *A Psychological Study of Religion* (New York: Macmillan, 1912); Edward S. Ames, *The Psychology of Religious Experience* (Boston: Houghton Mifflin, 1910); and James B. Pratt, *The Religious Consciousness* (New York: Macmillan, 1920).

5. Douglas C. Macintosh, *Theology as an Empirical Science* (New York: Harper, 1937).

ligion and theology should be replaced by empirical investigation of the varieties of religious experience. He subscribed to what he called a critical monistic realism with respect to the objects of our experience, including religious experience.[6] He held that the object of theology exists independently of our consciousness, and that knowledge of the existence and nature of this object is accessible through reflection on experience in general and religious experience in particular.

We now know more clearly than Macintosh did that science is not an empirical matter in his simple sense. The investigator does not merely observe the varieties of religious (or any other) experience and study them with the aim of making inductive inferences about the world. In the very act of identifying an experience as religious, both the one who has had that experience and the analyst have already assumed certain concepts and theories about the world. To claim that this is a theory-neutral empirical procedure is naive. Much has been written about this issue in science, and it applies with at least equal force to a science of religions. James's volume is a classic, full of insights, but it is not an example of the science of religions that he hoped it would be.

Once again, as in the case of Whitehead, it was not so much the details of scientific method that Macintosh brought to theology as the prestige of association with that method. In a festschrift for Macintosh published in 1937, the editors wrote: "Professor Macintosh's treatment of the problem of religious knowledge has been fruitful in our time because of his success in aligning the problem itself with the most powerful of the intellectual currents of the day. The scientific method is now acknowledged to be the method by which knowledge must come. Professor Macintosh has applied it to religion."[7]

Each of the positions examined thus far emphasizes the contributions that can be made by the mutual engagement of science and religion, stressing either what religion has to offer science or what the application of scientific results or methods means for the doing of theology. The most influential thinkers during the past half-century, however, have emphasized the differences between religion and science, their autonomy and independence, and have held that religious assertions have little or nothing to do with scientific claims. Though it is sometimes denied, these are also responses to the conflict between science and religion. A claim for the radical independence of religious belief and practice from science precludes any conflict between them.

6. Douglas C. Macintosh, "Experimental Realism in Religion," in D. C. Macintosh, ed., *Religious Realism* (New York: Macmillan, 1931), pp. 307-409.

7. Julius S. Bixler, Robert L. Calhoun, and H. Richard Niebuhr, eds., *The Nature of Religious Experience* (New York: Harper, 1937), pp. xi-xii.

(4) Religion is often distinguished from science on the ground that it addresses questions of meaning and value that exceed the limits of science. The aim of scientific inquiry is to describe and to explain, but it cannot answer normative questions. Religious issues arise at the limits of scientific understanding. This distinction can be drawn in several different ways.

Paul Tillich spoke of faith as the state of being ultimately concerned and argued that problems of meaning and value are intrinsic to the human condition. Anxiety arises over the contemplation of our own death, the threat of meaninglessness, and the experience of guilt.[8] Tillich described this as an ontological anxiety, which, unlike ordinary fears, cannot be laid to rest by developments or assurances within our experience. It is, rather, a profound existential concern that gives rise to questions that point beyond the human condition. The proper object of ultimate concern transcends and undergirds the world of our experience, the world that science describes and explains. The biblical account of creation in Genesis 1–3 may appear to be a statement about how the world came into being. In fact, however, it is a mythical or symbolic expression of a particular type of faith, an affirmation of God as the ground of our being. Theological statements are misconstrued if they are thought to make scientific claims. They are symbolic statements that are addressed to existential questions that arise from our condition as finite beings. "God created the world" is not a cosmological theory; it is an expression of trust in a ground of our being that transcends the polarities that characterize our experience.

A similar position can be stated in a manner that is free of Tillich's ontological commitments. The anthropologist Clifford Geertz, following Max Weber, has described religion as a set of cultural symbols that formulate conceptions of a general order of existence in the face of the anxiety that arises from the threat of meaninglessness or uninterpretability at the limits of our analytic capacities, our powers of endurance, and our moral insight. Our inability to explain things that cry out for explanation, to make deep or chronic suffering bearable, and to make moral sense of what happens to us gives rise to a need for some assurance that our experience is interpretable, even if we cannot comprehend it. "Bafflement, suffering and a sense of intractable ethical paradox are all, if they become intense enough or are sustained long enough, radical challenges to the proposition that life is comprehensible and that we can, by taking thought, orient ourselves effectively within

---

8. See Paul Tillich, *Dynamics of Faith* (New York: Harper, 1957) and *The Courage to Be* (New Haven: Yale University Press, 1952).

it—challenges with which any religion, however 'primitive,' which hopes to persist must attempt somehow to cope."[9] Religion addresses the problem of meaning, not the problems of description and explanation that science addresses. Religious questions arise at the limits of our interpretive capacities.

Theologians have employed existentialism, as did Tillich, as well as phenomenology and hermeneutical philosophy to further characterize this differentiation between the problems of meaning and value that are the concern of religion and the interests in description and explanation that motivate scientific inquiry.

(5) The most influential position on the relation of religious practice and belief to scientific inquiry and theory during the past fifty years has been an insistence not only on their difference but on their radical independence. In theological circles, this stance was largely a result of the impact of Karl Barth's neo-orthodox theology in this country, especially after the Second World War. Barth declared that Christian faith is concerned solely with the Word of God, which is grounded in God's revelation in Jesus Christ, and that it is completely unrelated to anything that can be inferred from human experience, including, and perhaps especially, religious experience.[10] In Barth's strongest statements of this point, what Kierkegaard called the "infinite qualitative difference" between man and God was applied also to the relation between the Word of God and all human words.[11] Theology is proclamation of and witness to the Word of God; its only relation to the method and results of science, or to any other human inquiry, is one of complete otherness. In a more considered statement, Barth described the biblical account of creation as a narrative that cannot be assimilated to scientific accounts on the one hand or to symbolic or mystical expressions on the other. It is "saga," which is neither myth nor theory.[12]

Some thinkers have endeavored to show the radical difference between religious beliefs and scientific statements, and their mutual independence, by analyzing the tacit grammatical rules that govern the proper use of concepts and linguistic expression in religious life and in scientific inquiry. Both Norman Malcolm and Paul Holmer have appealed to Ludwig Wittgenstein's remarks about the ways in which lin-

9. Clifford Geertz, "Religion as a Cultural System," in *The Interpretation of Cultures* (New York: Basic Books, 1973), p. 100.

10. For Barth's comments on religion, see Karl Barth, *Church Dogmatics*, I,2, trans. G. T. Thompson and H. Knight (Edinburgh: T. & T. Clark, 1956), pp. 280-361.

11. See Barth, *Church Dogmatics*, I,2, pp. 242-79.

12. Barth, *Church Dogmatics*, III,1, trans. J. W. Edwards, O. Bussey and H. Knight (Edinburgh: T. & T. Clark, 1956), pp. 42-94.

guistic practices are situated within, and given point by, the particular forms of life that are informed by those practices.[13] They have argued that religious doctrine can be understood only from within a religious life, and that theistic claims can be properly construed only from within the life and practices where those claims have a point. The aims and practices of science, it is claimed, are completely different from those of religion; hence there can be no relation of conflict or support between the two domains. The statement "God created the world" means one thing in a religious context and something quite different in a scientific context.[14] Creationism, accordingly, has nothing to do with the proper expression of faith in God the Creator.

Recently, several theologians at Yale have employed Barth's concept of saga and the philosophical analysis of the grammatical rules governing religious doctrine to argue that religious language is chiefly narrative—a linguistic form that differs from the descriptive and explanatory language of science and of our ordinary claims about the world. Hans Frei has drawn on Barth's discussion of saga as well as on H. Richard Niebuhr's idea of revelation as the story that mediates the life-understanding of an individual or a community—a story that is an internal history as distinct from an external history or biography.[15] This story or narrative is the chief form of biblical witness; it is the paradigm for the language of the Christian community; and it is completely different from the language employed in scientific inquiry.

George Lindbeck has drawn on the work of Wittgenstein and Geertz to argue for what he calls a "rule theory" of religious doctrine.[16] He claims that religion is similar to a language in that both are compre-

---

13. See Norman Malcolm, "Anselm's Ontological Arguments," in *Knowledge and Certainty* (Ithaca: Cornell University Press, 1963), pp. 141-62; Paul Holmer, *The Grammar of Faith* (San Francisco: Harper and Row, 1978).

14. Friedrich Schleiermacher made a similar point in 1830, when he said that the proposition expressed by a sentence in theology differs from the proposition expressed by the same sentence in philosophy: "Our dogmatic theology will not, however, stand on its proper ground and soil with the same assurance with which philosophy has so long stood upon its own, until the separation of the two types of proposition is so complete that, e.g., so extraordinary a question as whether the same proposition can be true in philosophy and false in Christian theology, and vice versa, will no longer be asked, for the simple reason that a proposition cannot appear in the one context precisely as it appears in the other: however similar it sounds, a difference must always be assumed." Friedrich Schleiermacher, *The Christian Faith*, trans. H. R. Mackintosh and J. S. Stewart (Edinburgh: T. & T. Clark, 1928), p. 83.

15. Hans Frei, *The Eclipse of Biblical Narrative* (New Haven: Yale University Press, 1974) and *The Identity of Jesus Christ* (Philadelphia: Fortress, 1975). H. Richard Niebuhr, *The Meaning of Revelation* (New York: Macmillan, 1941).

16. George Lindbeck, *The Nature of Religious Doctrine* (Philadelphia: Westminster, 1984).

hensive interpretive schemes. Theology and doctrines function as the grammatical rules of the language of religion, regulating what can and cannot properly be said within a particular context, but not making any first-order statements about the world. "Just as grammar by itself affirms nothing true or false regarding the world in which language is used, but only about language, so theology and doctrine, to the extent that they are second-order activities, assert nothing either true or false about God and his relation to creatures, but only speak about such assertions."[17] Religious doctrine and theology cannot, therefore, conflict with the theory or practice of science. A religion is a system of interpretation that is identified by the story or narrative that distinguishes it from other interpretations, and its truth is constituted by the skillful application of this narrative to novel experiences. Lindbeck's proposal is another attempt to obviate such conflict by arguing for the logical independence of religious belief from our scientific beliefs about the world. The concepts of rule and story are used to differentiate religious statements and commitments from factual claims.

(6) While accepting the distinction between religious practice and scientific inquiry, a number of writers have noted certain parallels between the two pursuits, underscoring the autonomy of religious interpretation yet pointing to various similarities. Already in 1913, in *The Problem of Christianity*, Josiah Royce called attention to numerous parallels in the practices of the interpretive communities of religion and science.[18] Both aim at creative and comprehensive interpretations designed to make sense of our experience; both require fidelity to a community and its aims; and both build on assumptions and proceed according to rules that must finally be accepted on faith. H. Richard Niebuhr followed Royce in claiming to discern in the practice of science the fidelity to a larger community and the loyalty to a more comprehensive ideal that are marks of the radical faith that is at the heart of monotheism.[19]

Historical and philosophical analysis has shown that science is not the straightforward inference from simple empirical data that D. C. Macintosh seemed to suppose it was. All data are theory laden. The investigator selects certain data according to his or her interests and constructs models, paradigms, and theories to make sense of that data, while trying to remain open to experiences that might subject these interpretive frameworks to criticism. Ian Barbour and others have examined the

17. Lindbeck, p. 69.
18. Josiah Royce, *The Problem of Christianity*, 2 vols. (New York: Macmillan, 1913).
19. H. Richard Niebuhr, *Radical Monotheism and Western Culture* (New York: Harper, 1960), pp. 78-89.

role of the imaginative construction of models and theories in scientific and religious inquiry and have pointed to numerous parallels as well as differences.[20] Some theologians have appealed to the work of Michael Polanyi and his description of the "tacit faith" that is presupposed by the scientific enterprise.[21] As was true in the case of Whitehead, it is difficult to escape the conclusion that much of the authority that Polanyi holds for theologians derives not so much from the substance of what he says as from the fact that a scientist has endorsed the idea that scientific inquiry and practice assume a stance of faith, and that there might be parallels between the tacit faith of science and religious faith.

It is important to see that each of these six positions aims to address the threat posed to religion by the successes of science. Even those writers who deny any apologetic interest are speaking to this issue. The problem, however, remains a difficult one. The prevailing strategy, which seeks to detach religious belief and practice from our understanding of the world, becomes implausible in its extreme forms. Values cannot serve as guides to action unless they are somehow connected with our beliefs about how the world is to be properly described and explained. At the very least, value terms are inapplicable if certain factual terms fail to apply.

The need to proclaim the independence of scientific inquiry from religious authority, and of religious understanding and practice from the prevailing scientific theory, conflicts with the need to anchor religious claims in factual ones. Answers to the problem of meaning and narratives that guide and shape our lives cannot be detached from our beliefs about the world if those answers and narratives are to orient us religiously and morally. Clifford Geertz is surely correct in viewing the function of religious symbols as one of welding together a worldview and an ethos, a way of describing and explaining the world and a set of guides for action.[22] Hence it would be incorrect to represent a worldview and an ethos as two separate systems that are entirely independent. In fact, the relations between them are pervasive and complex.

---

20. See Ian Barbour, *Myths, Models, and Paradigms* (New York: Harper and Row, 1974); Charles Coulson, *Science and Christian Belief* (London: Oxford University Press, 1955); Harold Schilling, *Science and Religion* (New York: Scribner's, 1962).

21. Michael Polanyi, *Personal Knowledge* (Chicago: University of Chicago Press, 1958). For the use of Polanyi for theology, see Thomas H. Langford and William H. Poteat, eds., *Intellect and Hope* (Durham: Duke University Press, 1968).

22. "What sacred symbols do for those to whom they are sacred is to formulate an image of the world's construction and a program for human conduct that are mere reflexes of one another. . . . Such symbols render the worldview believable and the ethos justifiable, and they do it by invoking each in support of the other." Clifford Geertz, *Islam Observed* (Chicago: University of Chicago Press, 1971), p. 97.

Thus it will not do to proclaim the radical independence of religious belief and practice from scientific inquiry.

The American religious tradition from Edwards to James, with its focus on experience and nature and its welcome of the practice and results of scientific inquiry, ought to provide resources for a reassessment of the relation between religion and science. Neither the proclamation of the radical independence of each nor the yoking of theology to a particular scientific theory is adequate. The past fifty years have produced much exciting work in the history and philosophy of science, dispelling the naive view of scientific inquiry as simple induction from empirical data. The complex interactions between scientific advances, popular beliefs about the world, and religious commitments that have been uncovered and mapped in earlier periods are surely at work in America today, but contemporary theologians and philosophers of religion have not managed to capture that complexity in their statements of the relation between religion and science. They have been too preoccupied with apologetic concerns to address those questions in a more sophisticated way. Perhaps here, as elsewhere, the researches of the historian will point the way toward a more adequate clarification of the conceptual issues.

16. The Church as Educator: Religious Education

William Bean Kennedy

During a half-century of what Martin Marty calls glacial change in American society and religion, the church in its educational work both reflected and contributed to such ground shifts as were occurring.[1] A new field and profession in the twentieth century, religious education in the mid-30s was still experiencing euphoria from its heyday in the previous decade. By 1930 religious education had become a major program in most congregations, with elaborate organizational support. It had also become an established discipline in theological schools, building its speciality chiefly on progressive education and psychology.[2]

Philip Lotz and L. W. Crawford, editors of the first of six survey volumes on religious education that appeared from 1931 to 1984, wrote of the "remarkable expansion" of "one of the youngest members of the educational family" since 1900 and claimed that

> There is in its veins the rich blood of achievement, for religion and education are so closely associated and bound up with all process and de-

---

1. This essay uses the word "church" in the singular to denote the church universal and to distinguish it from the many communions and local congregations, no one of which can exclusively claim to be "church," but to which all belong.
2. Allen J. Moore, "Religious Education as a Discipline," in *Changing Patterns of Religious Education*, ed. Marvin J. Taylor (Nashville: Abingdon, 1984), p. 95. This volume is the sixth in a helpful series of survey volumes. Previous ones include: Philip H. Lotz and L. W. Crawford, eds., *Studies in Religious Education* (Nashville: Cokesbury, 1931); Philip H. Lotz, ed., *Orientation in Religious Education* (New York: Abingdon-Cokesbury, 1950); Marvin J. Taylor, ed., *Religious Education: A Comprehensive Survey* (New York: Abingdon, 1960); M. J. Taylor, ed., *An Introduction to Christian Education* (Nashville: Abingdon, 1966), M. J. Taylor, ed., *Foundations for Christian Education in an Era of Change* (Nashville: Abingdon, 1976).

velopment that without the aid of these two adequate reasons for civilization, causes for its growth and development would be difficult to find.[3]

In 1950 Lotz wrote that religious education was "increasingly achieving the central place that it deserves in the life and work of the Church."[4] But others were raising serious questions.

Georgia Harkness, writing in 1931, affirmed that improved pedagogy had helped mitigate a growing antagonism of social mores to religious values, but she also noted "a feeling of depression" about the goals and content of religious education.[5] In 1976 Marvin J. Taylor, who edited the four survey volumes from 1960 to 1984, observed,

> In the mid-sixties we were still in the reflected glow of mainline Protestantism's post–World War II "success story." Educational participation was still on the increase, although the curve had begun to flatten out considerably. The profession of religious education still had reasonably clear bench marks for self-analysis. Much of that has been altered in the past decade. Both Protestant and Roman Catholic Christianity here in the States as well as abroad have experienced the pivotal uncertainties accompanying significant change. In many ways this book reflects these new realities.[6]

The half-century thus saw the new field move from excitement and euphoria to depression and confusion, from certainty about its self-understanding and mission to uncertainty and a fresh search. To explore this story, basic questions must be asked about how the church during these fifty years understood and practiced its education. These include questions of aim (why pursue religious education?), of strategy (how? when? and where?), of content (what to teach?), and of participation (who is involved?).

I. The Question of Aim: Why Pursue Religious Education?

An important goal statement was assembled by Paul H. Vieth in 1930 when he listed seven objectives, each of which began: "Christian religious education seeks to foster ['develop,' 'effect'] in growing persons. . . ." A revised statement of objectives emerged from the coopera-

---

3. Lotz and Crawford, *Studies*, p. 5.
4. Lotz, *Orientation*, p. 5.
5. Harkness, "An Underlying Philosophy for Religious Education," in Lotz and Crawford, *Studies*, p. 58.
6. Taylor, *Foundations*, p. 5.

tive work of many denominations in the National Council of Churches in 1958. This statement began: "The supreme purpose of Christian education is to enable persons to become aware of the seeking love of God as revealed in Jesus Christ, and to respond in faith. . . ." Notice the modest verbs: "seeks to foster" and "to enable." The editor of *Lumen Vitae* put it more theologically: "the aim . . . is to work with grace in the awakening or the increase of that faith which justifies us."[7] As author of an introductory book for a new United Church of Christ curriculum, Roger L. Shinn wrote that the aim was "to introduce persons into the life and mission of the community of Christian faith," thus adding to participation in and appropriation of the heritage the importance of training in mission.[8]

A significant tension exists between the local and the larger contexts of religious communions. Human beings experience their religion in local settings, through the intimacy of family life, the interpersonal relationships of a congregation, and the ongoing traffic of people in ordinary social and business activities. These local relationships, however, are enmeshed in networks of larger structures that strongly influence how the experiences of life are understood and interpreted. Religious and educational systems are part of these larger societal structures. As such they function as mediating institutions between the national and global structures and the local situation. Although the aims of religious education have tended to focus on the individual in the local community of faith, the communal nature of personhood and the educative tension with the larger church (and the global society) were to be increasingly emphasized in the latter part of the half-century. Such tension increased as the ground shifted toward a more obvious pluralism in North American life. The predominant ideological image of "American" as white, Anglo-Saxon Protestant, and male began to be challenged by the radical diversities of race, culture, religion, class, and gender.

Religious minorities soon realized that their education needed particularistic intensification. Jewish education, traditionally seeking Jewish religious survival amid other cultures, found deeper commitment to that aim after the Holocaust. Roman Catholics, who during these decades were moving into the mainstream of North American religious life, became aware that their parochial school strategy left more than half their children and young people without any serious religious education. Evangelicals, fearful of "secular humanism" and racial inte-

---

7. These and many other goal statements are discussed in Randolph Crump Miller, "The Objective of Christian Education," in Taylor, *An Introduction,* pp. 95, 97, 101.

8. Shinn, "The Educational Ministry of the Church," in Taylor, *An Introduction,* p. 12.

gration, turned more and more to private weekday schools to protect their younger members.

These demographic and cultural ground shifts also brought new pressure on the "mainline" denominations. For more than a century they could take for granted an identity between their religious traditions and the "Christian" culture. Thus they had been able, through the "culturally Protestant" public schools and through their own part-time educational efforts (Sunday school, summer programs, etc.), to educate Christians to become contributing members of the society. But as the "liberal" culture in which they had wielded dominant religious power began to erode, their identification with it resulted in strategic disarray in their educational work. Sensing the need to become more critical of the emerging and newly dominant ideology, they found it difficult to become countercultural in their educational efforts. The shift from the "Christ of culture" to the "Christ against culture" and the "Christ transforming culture" patterns called for a radical reorientation in their understanding and strategy of religious education.[9] As Stephen A. Schmidt stated in his history of the Religious Education Association: "Visions of a public paideia were domesticated into styles of church renewal."[10]

The ethos of comfortable culture-dependent religion, which had shaped the educational strategies of the major religious communities, was eroding. Because the ground shifts were glacial, as Marty suggests, the resulting dislocations in religious education were not easy to figure out or overcome. The varieties of curriculum experimentation and development, the somewhat frantic search for ways of recovering "the good old days," and the uncertainty that increasingly permeated the discussions in religious education all indicated the depth and scope of the changes taking place.

II. The Questions of Basic Strategy: When, Where, and How to Pursue Religious Education?

a. When?

Since the early development of public schools in the United States, the separation of church and state forced religious education to use "spare time" outside the regular school schedule. That meant weekends, after-

9. The patterns are delineated in H. Richard Niebuhr, *Christ and Culture* (New York: Harper and Row, 1951).

10. Stephen A. Schmidt, *A History of the Religious Education Association* (Birmingham: Religious Education Press, 1983), p. 159.

school hours, and summer. In some, but not all, provinces in Canada religion could be taught in the public schools. The Sunday school strategy therefore developed alongside of and in partnership with the public schools. Such a strategy had to depend upon a strong religious culture that "taught" religion indirectly.[11]

When education is thus more broadly defined, religious education occurs when there are crisis events in the society or in the church. Photos of the Rev. Martin Luther King, Jr., leading civil rights marches and of Eugene Carson Blake, the dignified stated clerk of the Presbyterian Church, being arrested while trying to integrate an amusement park, dramatically "taught" people how the church could act for justice. The recent Catholic and Methodist statements on nuclear war and the Catholic statement on the economy challenged accepted views and are teaching people about justice and peace. Just as educators perceive how public life influences peoples' worldviews, so they also see how religious bodies educate by reinforcing or opposing particular ideologies and actions of the powerful forces in society.

b. Where?

In addition to carrying out basic religious education in parish schooling and in gatherings for worship and work, the church also established institutions of higher education to train clergy and lay religious leaders. North American higher education developed under Christian auspices, but after 1950 church-related colleges became more and more a minority in the total picture as regards both numbers and influence. Campus ministries supported by the churches worked effectively on many large university campuses during the middle years of the period, but then they declined, except for evangelical programs that seemed to capture more student attention during the recent period of social uncertainty.[12]

---

11. For historical studies of this development, see William B. Kennedy, *The Shaping of Protestant Education* (New York: Association, 1966); Robert W. Lynn and Elliott Wright, *The Big Little School*, 2nd ed. rev. (Birmingham: Religious Education Press, and Nashville: Abingdon, 1980); Jack L. Seymour, *From Sunday School to Church School* (Washington: University Press of America, 1982); and Jack L. Seymour, Robert T. O'Gorman and Charles R. Foster, *The Church in the Education of the Public* (Nashville: Abingdon, 1984). For helpful chapters on Roman Catholic and evangelical developments, see D. Campbell Wyckoff, ed., *Renewing the Sunday School and the CCD* (Birmingham: Religious Education Press, 1986).

12. See J. Edward Dirks, "Religious Education in Church-Related Colleges and Universities," pp. 294-305, and Robert Michaelsen, "Religious Education in Public Higher Education Institutions," pp. 306-15, in Taylor, *A Comprehensive Survey;* also John E. Cantelon, "The Campus Ministries," in Taylor, *An Introduction,* pp. 340-49.

Despite the separation of church and state, many state institutions have had outstanding departments of religious studies. In fact, the growing predominance of these university departments in religious studies led to some concern in the seminaries that their future professors, holding advanced degrees from such departments, would lack the firsthand experience of the church that education in theological seminaries had traditionally provided. The positioning of Christian and Jewish studies within a much broader spectrum of world religions and ideologies dramatized what many saw as the increasing marginalization of the church in the modern world.[13]

In the 1930s religious educators spoke of common laws of learning in both general and religious education and in character education in the public schools.[14] By the time of the 1950 survey volume, they were reporting dissatisfaction with and disapproval of the partnership because of "secularism in the schools," "the weakening influence of the traditional religions," "widespread moral laxity," "disagreement on basic social values," and "the threat of radical social action."[15] Following Supreme Court decisions in the 1960s forbidding prayer and Bible-reading in public schools, many religious people and groups felt a sense of loss, and some participated in conservative political efforts to legislate religious exercises in classrooms and to provide public support for religious schools. Earlier hopes for effective cooperation in released time or after-school programs had not worked out. Many religious bodies were perturbed by the absence of any serious teaching about religion in the schools, and they were increasingly driven to find time outside of school for religious activities with their children and adolescents. With the increasing pressure for extended student and family involvement in school activities, that option did not prove easy.

In their educational work Protestant churches used a wide variety of agencies, including city and state councils of churches, the National Council of Churches, the World Council of Christian Education, the World Council of Churches, and the Religious Education Association. Roman Catholic and Jewish educational efforts employed similar agencies, including the REA. Specific programs were developed for family, children, youth, adults, Sunday church school, vacation church

13. Charles S. McCoy provided a useful summary of the situation and its history in "The Churches and Higher Education," in Taylor, *Foundations*, pp. 259-70.

14. Hugh Hartshorne, "The Relation of Religious Education to General Education," p. 434, and Edward R. Bartlett, "The Character Education Movement in the Public Schools," pp. 450-71, in Lotz and Crawford, *Studies*.

15. J. Paul Williams, "The Relation of Religion and Public Education," pp. 491-500, and Arlo Ayres Brown, "Protestantism's Strategy for Religious Education," pp. 553-54, in Lotz, *Orientation*.

school, weekday religious education, camps and summer conferences, and colleges and theological seminaries. The size of some of these programs is evident from a report that in the fifties "some one hundred to one hundred and fifty million dollars" were spent on church camp development.[16]

c. How?

The questions of "when?" and "where?" merge with the broader question of "how?" in regard to educational strategy.

A significant change in conceptualizing education came in 1960 with Bernard Bailyn's revisionist history of U.S. education. He redefined education as involving more than public schools by including libraries, lecture series for adults, and other such shapers of public understanding that compose what Lawrence Cremin would later call a "configuration" of educative agencies.[17] At about the same time a broadening of the concept of education was also occurring in religious education. In 1967 C. Ellis Nelson's *Where Faith Begins* used a sociological interpretation to emphasize the primary influence of the religious community on the development of faith.[18] Likewise, John Westerhoff blended "enculturation" and a cultural anthropological interpretation with the tradition of catechesis.[19]

Major new denominational programs after World War II put the "school of the church" in a broader context. The Episcopal Seabury Series built its nurture program on a renewal of parish life. Both the Presbyterian Faith and Life Curriculum and the Covenant Life Curriculum of the Presbyterian Church U.S. tried to reestablish the family as a basic part of Christian nurture, but the modern family was no longer stable enough for the attempt to succeed. The latter program also emphasized the importance of congregational worship and work in nurturing the faith of members young and old, but that effort at integration failed, in part because leaders of organized worship and mission activities saw such integration as an attempt to "take over" all corporate religious life for education.[20]

16. Maurice C. Bone, "Camps and Conferences," in Taylor, *Comprehensive Survey,* p. 222.

17. Bernard Bailyn, *Education in the Forming of American Society* (New York: Vintage Books, 1960). See also Lawrence A. Cremin, *Public Education* (New York: Basic Books, 1976), pp. 27ff.

18. Richmond: John Knox.

19. See John Westerhoff, "A Socialization Model," in his *A Colloquy on Christian Education* (Philadelphia: Pilgrim, 1972), pp. 80-90.

20. See David R. Hunter, *Christian Education as Engagement* (New York: Seabury,

The socialization approach related well to a new emphasis on worship and "liturgical renewal" in many religious bodies. This emphasis challenged the preoccupation with cognitive learning in religious education, and theorists and practitioners began serious efforts to engage persons in many aesthetic and "holistic" learning experiences.[21] Others concentrated on the church as an organization with nurturing potential and trained people in "organizational development," for which the new D.Min. programs provided network support.[22]

Others criticized religious education for failing to educate religious people for justice and peace in the world. In 1976 Grant Shockley charged that the white church was apostate in its racism: "It had acquiesced in segregation—failed to identify, define, or articulate critically or challenge effectively a single aspect of the problem of racism faced by 10 percent of its national population, 80 percent of whom were fellow Christians." What, he asked, is the responsibility of education in that situation? Also in 1976, Emily Hewitt examined the ways in which church and social structures inhibited the educational development of women. In the 1984 volume, Gloria Durka made a strong ideological critique of the way power was used covertly to repress and oppress women in religious institutions. From their minority experience Jewish, Catholic, and evangelical educators also called attention to the pervasive power of the white Anglo-Saxon Protestant ideology dominant in the United States.[23]

This approach focused attention on the educative power of the culture itself. In 1960 C. Ellis Nelson observed that "Floyd Hunter's *Community Power Structure* [showed] how powerful are the informal lines of control that regulate a community," and Howard E. Tower noted that "mass communications are often used as a means of manipulation of persons to the end that they buy or do what the program wants." In analyzing group theory in a 1966 article, Ross Snyder wrote that "society-as-it-functions is the fundamental educator." Robert W. Lynn

---

1963); William B. Kennedy, "Neo-Orthodoxy Goes to Sunday School: The Christian Faith and Life Curriculum," *Journal of Presbyterian History* 58/4 (Winter 1980) 326-70; and Byron H. Jackson, "The Covenant Life Curriculum Within Its Historical Setting" (Ed.D. diss., Teachers College, Columbia University, 1980).

21. See Ross Snyder, "Worship as Celebration and Nurture," in Taylor, *Foundations*, pp. 171-85.

22. Robert C. Worley, "Church Education as an Organizational Phenomenon," in Taylor, *Foundations*, pp. 117-26.

23. Shockley, "Liberation Theology, Black Theology, and Religious Education," p. 84, and Hewitt, "Women, Ministry and Education," pp. 96-106, in Taylor, *Foundations*. Durka, "Women, Power, and the Work of Religious Education," in Taylor, *Changing Patterns*, pp. 169-80.

asked whether religious education could work in a media-oriented society when "network moguls are, in effect, the value-brokers of contemporary America."[24]

This cultural perspective ran counter to a deep change taking place in the field, as the emphasis shifted from the community to the individual. Stephen Schmidt connected Lewis J. Sherrill to this change: "Because of his psychoanalytic orientation, [his] accent was on the individual rather than the community or the larger cultural context." Sherrill and others thus contributed to future developments as "depth psychology replaced social theory as the paradigmatic location for future strategies of religious education."[25]

Educators concerned about community and society criticized the individualistic and privatistic bent of western psychology, which seemed to accept the social situation as a given, to which religion helped persons adjust. That bent ran counter to the sociological concern for justice in the social structures. The tension between saving individual souls and social action also characterized religious education. Questions were raised by those with firsthand experience of oppression: blacks, women, and Latin Americans, who from their religious experience gained clarity and courage to challenge the cultural captivity of religious education. Their protests against the injustices embedded in the larger structures of society, combined with the socialization approach to church education, led to efforts to improve the quality of religious community life in order to engage and challenge the power of society. Roger Shinn argued that the familiar patterns of religious education had "too often been introverted, concerned to develop Christian character and Christian institutions by protecting persons and church from the world. . . . They have organized the educational process itself so as to draw persons from life in the world instead of driving them into the world, where Christian witness and service are most meaningful." Christian education takes place "before action, during action, and after action," and is education by engagement in mission in the world.[26]

These pressures from oppressed groups and sociologically oriented educational theorists pointed toward a more radical orientation: particular Jewish and Christian traditions called upon religious ed-

---

24. Nelson, "Group Dynamics and Religious Education," p. 180, and Tower, "The Use of Audio-Visuals in the Church," p. 202, in Taylor, *A Comprehensive Survey.* Snyder, "Group Theory and Christian Education," in Taylor, *An Introduction,* p. 279. Lynn, "A Historical Perspective on the Futures of American Religious Education," in Taylor, *Foundations,* p. 17.

25. Schmidt, *A History of the Religious Education Association,* p. 139.

26. Shinn, "The Educational Ministry of the Church," in Taylor, *An Introduction,* p. 18.

ucation to bring a sharp counterideological challenge to the dominant views in U.S. society and to the policies and practices of the powerful private and governmental forces that maintained and profited from the hegemonic ideology. As organized religion recognized its increasing marginality, it also became ever more conscious of the cultural captivity of its traditional educational activities. But how to change this society? The search for answers to that question has increasingly animated recent writings in religious education.

Evangelicals took two main approaches: opposing "secular humanism" by mobilizing religious-political activity to change the social order so that it would more directly support religion; and developing private day schools where socialization resistant to the larger and dangerous societal conditioning processes could be intentionally fostered. The commitment of the Roman Catholic church to its own system of schools for more than a century involved the same rationale and strategy.

In her 1984 article "Women, Power, and the Work of Religious Education," Gloria Durka urged women to direct their energies away from the personal-interpersonal to the structural, from influencing attitudes to changing organizations, from naming evil as personal sin to seeing it as social sin, and to move away from the humanities and psychological disciplines for interpreting reality to the social sciences, economics, sociology, political science, and anthropology.[27]

In this context, the rise of "civil religion" can be understood as an ideological instrument of education to marshal people's religious beliefs and feelings in support of national security or other values labeled "good" by the dominant ideology. Some religious educators and theologians from the oppressed sectors of society joined in challenging the inherited patterns of religious education and demanded clearer counterideological education for critical Christian consciousness of what God has willed for human beings in the world.

As communities of faith, the various religious bodies were "swimming in a common ideological sea," largely unaware of the water itself but manifesting in their practices and rationales many signs of that shared location. The dominant ideology of U.S. and Canadian culture exercises heavy influence in and through religious thought and practice on this continent. The educational activities of the church reflect that influence. But in the church and its educational activities also appear prophetic challenges, counterideological and countercultural affirmations and actions that keep the society changing. Understanding re-

---

27. Durka, in Taylor, *Changing Patterns,* p. 177.

ligious education in a web of socioeconomic and ideological connections, as a part of that larger struggle, helps to open up helpful ways of interpreting its course during these fifty years.

A growing awareness of the church as a whole facing the society made the separated churches aware that their impact could be much greater if they presented a united front. Moves toward ecumenical cooperation in the denominations and in religious education gained from this sociological and political analysis. The establishment of the Division of Education and Ministry in the new National Council of Churches in 1950 provided a central forum for Protestant mainline Christian education, and the Religious Education Association has continued to bring together Catholic, Protestant, and Jewish educators through conferences and in the pages of its journal, *Religious Education*.

III. The Question of Content: What to Teach?

Church education was deeply affected by the theological trends and controversies of the period 1935-1985. In the 1930s the religious education movement was strongly tied to so-called liberal theology. The "realistic" theologies of Barth and the Niebuhrs and others challenged that theology. A famous confrontation between two leaders of the movement, Harrison S. Elliott and H. Shelton Smith, who published major books in 1940 and 1941, sharpened the debate. Elliott defended liberal theology, while Smith attacked it owing to his alignment with the new theologies.[28] In 1947 Paul Vieth summarized the ongoing debate in his report on the work of a study committee of the International Council of Religious Education.[29] Three years later Randolph Crump Miller, theologically trained at Yale under D. C. Macintosh and soon to teach Christian education there, affirmed that *The Clue to Christian Education* is "the rediscovery of a relevant theology," which he described as "the truth-about-God-in-relation-to-man."[30]

The 1931 survey volume had hardly noted the theological problems then emerging. In the 1950 book, John Bennett described the "basic Christian convictions" that religious education had to deal with, including not only the "classical" doctrines but also social ethics, the Christian social imperative, and the kingdom of God. By that time the

28. Elliott, *Can Religious Education Be Christian?* (New York: Macmillan, 1940); and Smith, *Faith and Nurture* (New York: Scribner's, 1941)

29. Vieth, *The Church and Christian Education* (St. Louis: Bethany, 1947).

30. New York: Scribner's, 1950. A very helpful account and analysis of this theological struggle can be found in Schmidt, *A History of the Religious Education Association*.

Presbyterian Faith and Life Curriculum had been launched, with its strong neo-orthodox approach and its modern study of the Bible. In 1960 Daniel Day Williams delineated some of the newer approaches: Barth's emphasis on the absoluteness and exclusiveness of the biblical witness to God's grace, Buber's and Brunner's emphasis on faith as personal encounter, and Bultmann's and Tillich's theology in correlation with ultimate questions. Williams saw Christian education as theological inquiry:

> Since theology in the church is an interpretation of the Christian way of believing and living, all those who reflect critically upon Christian experience become theologians. Christian educators therefore not only draw upon theological insight provided by the tradition and thought of the church; but they help to create the body of materials and the reflective criticism which make a living theology possible.[31]

In the 1960 volume Gerard S. Sloyan referred to an "objective element, sacred truth" and a "subjective one, the states of heart and mind necessary to come into possession of that truth," which he considered integral to Roman Catholic religious education.[32] In 1966 Sara Little emphasized the "'rediscovery' of the doctrine of revelation and of the centrality of the Bible to the life of faith," and pointed to growing Roman Catholic interest in Bible study in the development known as "kerygmatic catechetics." That development, she noted, paralleled the theological renewal in Protestantism.[33] In the 1976 book, Little reaffirmed the relevance of theology as the "clue" to Christian education. And, in this same volume, H. Edward Everding discussed "A Hermeneutical Approach to Educational Theory" in light of new developments in interpretation theory, with special emphasis on the student as interpreter and the need to reshape educational goals and teaching styles.[34]

During the post–World War II period the curricula of some denominations brought church history, systematic theology, and ethics directly into their recommended study programs, especially for adults. This broadened curriculum began to resemble the curricular pattern in theological seminaries and represented an effort to put biblical studies

---

31. Williams, "Current Theological Developments and Religious Education," in Taylor, *A Comprehensive Survey*, p. 52.

32. Sloyan, "Roman Catholic Religious Education," in Taylor, *A Comprehensive Survey*, p. 396.

33. Little, "Revelation, the Bible, and Christian Education," in Taylor, *An Introduction*, pp. 42, 45.

34. Little, "Theology and Religious Education," pp. 30-40, and Everding, pp. 41-53, in Taylor, *Foundations*.

into a more historical and contemporary context. Evangelical curricula continued to resist modern critical study of the Bible and the more recent theological trends. Although the theological struggles were acute in the seminaries and church educational agencies, the older patterns of Bible study tended to remain basic for local Sunday school classes. Sales of conservative and independent publishers' materials, which generally avoided historical and ecclesiological emphases in what could be called "sola Scriptura" curricula, continued strong throughout the period.

IV. The Question of Participation: Who?

The modern religious education movement proceeded on the basis of a corollary to the Reformation doctrine of the priesthood of all believers: the notion of a "scholarhood of all believers," with the goal of educating all Christians to know the meaning of their faith. The goal was never satisfactorily reached, but during this half-century Protestants, Catholics, and Jews alike realized that the future of their faith communities depended on rooting their younger members and new converts in their specific religious traditions. Such mass education of all members required the special education of leaders and teachers.

Early in the century a new profession emerged. The director of religious education became popular in Protestant churches. Drastic layoffs of these newest staff persons came during the Depression, but the office rebounded with larger numbers after World War II. After Vatican II, various forces led to a dramatic rise in that professional function within Catholic circles, as competent lay educators took up this specialized work. Central to this development was the so-called catechetical movement connected with Josef Jungmann and Johannes Hofinger and the work of the Confraternity of Christian Doctrine, which, through a series of congresses, stimulated interest in religious education that was attuned to Catholic parish life as well as to Catholic schools.[35] By 1965 one author called the profession a "flourishing, important church vocation," numbering some 11,000 persons exercising ministerial, educational, and supervisory roles in religious education.[36]

35. Mary Charles Bryce, "The Confraternity of Christian Doctrine in the United States," in D. C. Wyckoff, ed., *Renewing the Sunday School and the CCD*, pp. 27-44.

36. Gentry A. Shelton, "The Director of Christian Education," in Taylor, *An Introduction*, pp. 117-29. For helpful historical analysis, see also Dorothy Jean Furnish, "The Profession of Director or Minister of Christian Education in Protestant Churches," pp. 193-204, and Maria Harris, "U.S. Directors of Religious Education in Roman Catholic Parishes," pp. 205-19, in Taylor, *Changing Patterns.*

The new profession, however, faced many problems having to do with status, title, instability of office, and even with the expectation that the educator would perform other jobs such as church visitor, secretary, and janitor. Moreover, the relationship of the professional educator with the pastor or priest was problematic. Clergy holding power in traditional church organizations did not easily share it or relate cooperatively with the new specialized educational activity and its leadership.

Advanced degree programs in religious education grew in numbers and quality during the period. Major graduate centers such as Union Seminary and Teachers College (Columbia University), Yale University, and New York University, as well as the larger denominational seminaries, developed strong doctoral programs. Their graduates moved into leadership positions in seminaries and colleges and in church agencies.

Well-organized ecumenical Protestant training for lay leaders also occurred during this period. In 1936 the International Council of Religious Education launched the Standard Leadership Curriculum with "more than 150 courses, covering the whole range of church work, both in content and method." In that year alone more than 150,000 credits were given.[37] In more recent years large Catholic gatherings provided training opportunities for both professional and lay educational leaders. Throughout the period workers' conferences, workshops, and lesson previews provided training for volunteer teachers and leaders in local congregations.

V. The Question of Past, Present, and Future Identity and Function

As the problems attaching to religious education became increasingly severe, many leaders began to search for a better historical understanding of the church's teaching and of the religious education movement. Lewis Sherrill wrote *The Rise of Christian Education* in 1944, tracing its development from biblical times to the Reformation.[38] Others published subsequent studies that attempted to locate the field in its historical framework. Sherrill's own summary chapter appeared in the 1950 survey, and the chapters in the 1960 and 1966 volumes generally

37. Herman J. Sweet, "The Education of Lay and Professional Religious Education Leaders," in Lotz, *Orientation,* pp. 396-97.
38. New York: Macmillan, 1944.

followed his interpretation.[39] The search then turned toward investigation of the continuing influence of nineteenth-century beliefs and ideologies in the new, more secular situation of the mid-twentieth century, as Robert T. Handy has suggested.[40] In the same vein Robert Lynn referred in the 1976 book to two dominant nineteenth-century images: "Paideia in a Protestant Zion" for those who belonged, and "Aliens in Zion" for the marginalized minorities. He noted that mainline Protestants were experiencing system-wide distress in a context of "increasing systemic disarray in the ecology of educational institutions," and he raised critical questions about the future of religious education.[41]

During this half-century the field also expanded its focus to include religious education developments outside the U.S. and Canada. A 1950 essay by James Luther Adams on "Basic Causes of Progress and Decay in Civilization" analyzed the relationship of religion to western civilization and, in particular, of Protestantism to root causes of its progress and decay.[42] The 1976 volume reported on the integration of the older World Council of Christian Education and the World Council of Churches in 1971 and included chapters on religious education in the world ecumenical movement, in Europe, and in the Third World.[43] The 1984 volume filled a lacuna in historical and global understanding of the field with two informative chapters on Protestant and Catholic religious education in Canada.[44]

During this period religious education has moved from its early and tentative "glory days" of development through decades of major effort, only to find itself in the swirl of historical changes that have decreased the effectiveness of its traditional forms and that are calling for newer and larger structural rearrangements than it knows how to make. The implication of this interpretation is clear: if the church is to

39. Lewis J. Sherrill, "A Historical Study of the Religious Education Movement," in Lotz, *Orientation*, pp. 13-26; Marvin J. Taylor, "A Historical Introduction to Religious Education," in Taylor, *A Comprehensive Survey*, pp. 11-23; William B. Kennedy, "Christian Education Through History," in Taylor, *An Introduction*, pp. 21-31.

40. Handy, "The Long Spell of Christendom," *Soundings* 60/2 (Summer 1977) 123-34.

41. Lynn, "A Historical Perspective on the Futures of American Religious Education," in Taylor, *Foundations*, pp. 7-19.

42. Adams, in Lotz, *Orientation*, pp. 61-74.

43. William B. Kennedy, "Education in the World Ecumenical Movement," pp. 208-18; Krister A. Ottosson, "Religious Education in Western Europe," pp. 219-30; and Gerson A. Meyer, "Patterns of Church Education in the Third World," pp. 231-41, in Taylor, *Foundations*.

44. Doris Jean Dyke, "Protestant Religious Education in Canada," pp. 144-54, and Martin Jeffery, "Roman Catholic Religious Education in Canadian Churches," pp. 155-68, in Taylor, *Changing Patterns*.

act effectively as educator in the future, it must address very seriously the fundamental strategic questions facing religious education today.

Encouraging movement toward that end has begun, as indicated, in revisionist historical studies, analysis of the social context and its ideological influences, and interest in aesthetics and more holistic learning. The very turbulence of this period leads to fresh excitement, curiosity, and expectation about the church as educator in the years ahead.

17. Christian Ethics as Responses to Social Conditions

Edward LeRoy Long, Jr.

Theological formulations about ethics often arise in response to social events and cultural trends that challenge existing ways of thinking. This is the case regardless of whether these historical phenomena belong to the category that Martin Marty, in his introductory essay, calls "hurricane events" or to what he calls "glacial movements."

The first part of this essay will examine changes in Christian social attitudes and teaching with respect to five areas of public concern between 1935 and 1985, showing how Christian understandings of social and moral issues have been responses to historical events during this period. While primary attention will be given to the distinguishing features of such Christian social witness, some attention will also be given to the foundational theological positions that have informed that witness.

A second, quite brief part of the essay will comment on some current changes in these foundational outlooks—developments that are not necessarily tied to the social experiences of the present.

I. Christian Social Concerns as Responses to Social Changes

a. War, peace, and international affairs

Late in 1933, Harry Emerson Fosdick preached a sermon at the Riverside Church entitled "My Account with the Unknown Soldier," in which he expressed disillusionment with the First World War and pledged that he would never again support the use of arms for purposes of seeking peace. The following year he addressed a gathering in New York City that rallied support for a pledge to refuse to sanction war and to participate in armed conflict. Kirby Page persuaded nearly 13,000 clergy to sign this pledge. Fosdick's oratorical skill dramatized a widespread attitude, chiefly among the clergy of the mainline Protestant denominations, that Christians should rely upon the way of love in the public sphere rather than the way of Mars. This high idealism of Christian leaders was accompanied by an isolationism then prevalent in the culture, which, while not constituting a moral repudiation of international violence, showed no taste for participation in the world's power struggles.

Almost simultaneously with the crystallization of these strong pacificist convictions in many of the mainline clergy, ominous threats to the vision of the world united by good will began to appear in both Europe and Asia. Hitler was confirmed as Fuehrer in Germany by a plebiscite in 1934, and Japan renounced its long operative naval treaties with western nations. Mussolini began a series of aggressions that prompted sanctions from a limping League of Nations at the very time that the United States (which never joined the League) was dissociating itself from the World Court.

All of these trends provoked intense debate within American Christianity about the proper way to deal with the rising threat of totalitarianism. While many prominent Christians—Fosdick among them—remained steadfastly opposed to participating in war, others changed their minds when faced with the specter of European and Asian totalitarianism. Reinhold Niebuhr was the spiritual father of a large group of Christians who responded to this threat by acknowledging the need to take power seriously as the price of being politically responsible and who draw upon a refurbished Augustinianism to give their position theological depth. Though Niebuhr early shared the pacifism of many liberal Christians, he slowly came to see its inadequacies. His *Moral Man and Immoral Society* (1932) drew a sharp contrast between the morality that applies between individuals and that which obtains between groups. His *An Interpretation of Christian Ethics* (1935) cast even more explicit doubts on the possibility of using love as a programmatic model for dealing with the political world. Eventually, Niebuhr's thought was to inspire a Christian realism steadfastly at odds with the pacificism of Fosdick, Page, and others.

During the Second World War this pacifist/nonpacifist split had several consequences unique in church history. It forced persons of sharply differing views on a momentous issue to live together in the same ecclesial groupings even while they were debating their respective convictions; it opened the way for the extension—widely supported by all concerned—of the right of conscientious objection to members of every branch of Protestantism, not merely to members of historic peace churches; it tempered the spirit in which the conflict was fought and helped to keep jingoistic fervor at bay; and it prompted the churches to speak with conviction about the need to build a just and durable peace after the cessation of armed conflict. Thus, though the ethical issue as to the legitimacy of Christian participation in war was never settled in theory, an enormous contribution to cultural maturity resulted.

The insistence of Christian leaders on the importance of seeking a just and durable peace rather than vindictive settlements after the hostilities; the contribution of church groups to fostering public support for the founding of the United Nations; and the witness of the religious community to the importance of caring for human well-being on a global scale were all crucial factors in creating one of the most positive thrusts in international public policy in America's history. But the Cold War would shortly take its toll of such gains.

Soon after the armistice, deep suspicions developed between the U.S. and the U.S.S.R. These suspicions steadily intensified, so much so that by the mid-1980s both nations found it difficult to coexist in the same world. The tension between these two superpowers dominated the international "politiscape." Each claimed for itself a vast sphere of influence, which it sustained largely by flexing military and economic muscle. Each brought social, economic, and political pressures to bear against those nations that did not align themselves with one in opposition to the other. Both sometimes overrode the sovereignties of smaller nations and acted unilaterally in opposition to international laws and conventions in order to maintain a balance of power or to achieve strategic advantage.

Among the nations of Western Europe the policy of collective security, as implemented in NATO, was generally supported, as it largely succeeded in holding Communist expansion at bay. The story in Asia unfolded differently. The military action taken in Korea was understood by many at the time as applying the same realism that informed European policy, and the limited nature of the engagement allowed it to be interpreted as more a policing effort than a full-scale conflict. President Truman's recall of General MacArthur was taken as proof that civilians could keep the military in check and hostilities well controlled. However, the American experience in Vietnam produced an entirely different scenario. The political situation was less promising, the military enterprise floundered, and the electronic media brought the horrors of the conflict into most living rooms. The public slowly became disillusioned, and many Christian ethicists turned to just war teaching as a means of mounting a critique of the nation's policy. While it was generally realized that resort to atomic/nuclear warfare was too dangerous to contemplate, massive bombing with conventional explosives was carried out against largely defenseless populations. While this war of attrition gnawed at the nation's resources, opposition to it grew increasingly vocal, although not necessarily more explicit in articulating its theoretical foundations. The most vocal opponents, curiously enough, were those who had been nonpacifist in conviction, rather than pacifist, during the Second World War.

The Vietnam War resulted in an enormous public turmoil rather than a mature consensus about the proper public policy. Efforts to obtain the right of selective conscientious objection to a particular conflict, based on just war criteria rather than on unswerving pacifist convictions, were given practically no hearing in domestic policy, though Christian ethicists discussed this issue at length. America's withdrawal from the conflict was sensed less as a victory for policy than as a concession to internal dissent. This had the latent potential to produce a national sense of defeat, for which there was no theological preparation or spiritual amelioration. Subsequent nippings at America's presence in the world, such as the hostage crisis in Iran and the rise of terrorism, had to be faced without any compelling theological rationale for patience and reserve. In understandable reaction, a trend toward national truculence slowly came to dominate the making of administrative policy. Under Ronald Reagan, the concept of peacekeeping took on an essentially military cast, and the quest for nuclear superiority seemed unremitting.

In 1985, instead of a League of Nations, there was a United Nations to which the U.S. often refused to listen — most obviously whenever that body adversely interpreted the role of America in the world. A third world had grown in both self-awareness and power. Peoples who previously could be ignored had become forces to be reckoned with as they aspired to enter the mainstream of global commerce and community. Oceans no longer provided immunity from external threats and even the heavens themselves were liable to become an arena for conflict. A human error with a switching sequence in a little black box or a computer failure in some automated chain of response might unleash a destructiveness that could abolish viable human life from the planet, perhaps forever.

Many saw nuclear weapons and warfare as the overarching problem of the eighties. Extensive efforts were made to address the issue, even by such unexpected bodies as the National Conference of American Roman Catholic Bishops—not heretofore noted for opposition to public policy matters of defense and national security. The bishops drew upon just war theory as a basis for questioning the wisdom of nuclear policy. This was probably one of a very few times when this theory had been used to qualify and criticize rather than legitimize the policy of a nation state. There was also a large public outcry against the nuclear arms race, symbolized by the nuclear-freeze movement and by nuclear pacifism. These latter responses categorically repudiated the policy of nuclear deterrence, but their theological foundations were not articulated as clearly as those of the Catholic bishops. A third response to these developments focused on the importance of Christian fidelity and witness. Cogent statements by John Howard Yoder and Stanley Hauerwas showed that this approach (like that of radical Christianity in other eras) placed a greater stress on the church's faithfulness as an alternative community of witness than on the church's successful exercise of public influence.

A number of persons whose Christian vocations brought them to serve America's poor and disinherited, like the late William Stringfellow, came to speak of America as a new Babylon—the antithesis of all that is Christian.[1] Nuclear pacifism, tax resistance, the sanctuary movement, and related trends were, in effect, the antiwar sentiments of the thirties writ even larger, and were potentially even more resistant to the policies of a military colossus than was the pacifism of an earlier time. Meanwhile, theological conservatives who once eschewed public advocacy of policy positions became far more active in supporting the policies of a government increasingly prone to rely upon military solutions to Cold War problems. A patriotism rooted in civic religion, rather than a carefully articulated theological position, was often evident in these responses. Unlike the tensions in the late thirties between pacifists and nonpacifists, which had the constructive results noted above, the tensions in the middle and late eighties between the resisters and the bellicose seemed to generate little but polarizing division in both church and culture.

b. Economics and social welfare

In 1935 President Franklin Roosevelt, then approaching the height of popular support, signed the Social Security Act into law. This symbol-

---

1. William Stringfellow, *An Ethic for Christians and Other Aliens in a Strange Land* (Waco, TX: Word Books, 1973).

ized an emerging concern to protect the welfare of the individual within the framework of an entrepreneurial society. John L. Lewis, no doubt encouraged by the legality accorded collective bargaining by the just-enacted Wagner Labor Relations Act, was organizing the Committee of Industrial Organizations (later to become the Congress of Industrial Organizations). This movement helped propel a goodly number of semi-skilled American workers toward the economic mainstream, although it did so at first by using sit-in strikes and other unprecedented and quasi-violent forms of labor struggle that aroused much public anger. The memory of bread lines was still sufficiently vivid in 1935 to create a political majority that looked to government to alleviate human misery. Moreover, both the Social Gospel and the ecumenical movement were identified with a concern for economic justice. Both had long been sympathetic to the efforts of labor to secure the right to bargain collectively.

The degree to which the country as a whole embraced the vision of a welfare state varied considerably in the half-century under review. In the 1930s, after the Great Depression, moves to extend the welfare state had a large base of political support. The political successes of the New Deal, while remaining anathema to conservatives, convinced many of those who once favored socialism to put a greater degree of confidence in a mixed economy.

There has always been disagreement among Christians about economic matters, and the period 1935-1985 was no exception. In the 1930s many were committed to free-market capitalism. Almost three-quarters of a sample of more than 21,000 clergymen were opposed to the New Deal as late as 1936.[2] But some small groups of very articulate Christian leaders expressed considerable doubt about the capacity of the entrepreneurial system to establish and maintain a fair society. At the beginning of the thirties, leaders like Sherwood Eddy, Kirby Page, Reinhold Niebuhr, John Bennett, Roswell Barnes, and Buell Gallagher formed the Fellowship of Socialist Christians, whose members accepted a voluntary tax on their salaries to provide relief funds for the poor. The group advocated democratic socialism as an alternative to capitalistic individualism. Subsequently the group's name was changed first to Frontier Fellowship and then to Christian Action. Each change signaled a move to a position a bit closer to the political middle.

Gathering toward the other end of the spectrum were leaders like the Los Angeles pastor James Fifield, organizer of a conservative group called Spiritual Mobilization, one of whose aims was a defense

2. Sydney E. Ahlstrom, *A Religious History of the American People* (New Haven: Yale University Press, 1972), p. 924.

of entrepreneurial capitalism. More extreme groups on the far right attacked the Federal Council of Churches (and its successor, the National Council of Churches) for having Communist tendencies. The outlook of Norman Vincent Peale, whose career spanned the entire period 1935-1985, was typical of the majority of church leaders, who had little to say about issues of social justice and thus seemed to uphold the economic status quo.

Ecumenical thinking came to focus more and more on the idea of the responsible society—one in which all persons could develop their potential and might expect to share in society's rewards with some semblance of distributive justice. While the idea of the responsible society strongly emphasized social welfare and approved governmental action to redress economic injustices, it did not envision the destruction of capitalism as a precondition of those results.

The moral issues related to economics and welfare may not have the life and death implications of the nuclear problem, but they are nevertheless momentous and are closely bound up with the prevailing tensions between the two great world powers. Through most of the period under review it was difficult to consider economic matters apart from this Cold War context. On one side of this precarious international divide, attempts to overcome the terrible ravages and economic inadequacies of the past were wedded to an ideology that suspends freedom in order to foster planned economic change. On the other side, a long experiment to combine political freedom with a welfare vision was severely truncated by the recent resurgence of a laissez-faire ideology that engenders callousness toward a large but not politically decisive group of indigent citizens shunted aside by the forces of economic growth. A new Social Darwinism replaced public compassion as the prevalent philosophy.

On one side of this ideological divide, the practice of psychiatry was subverted by political purposes; on the other, the practice of medicine came to be dominated by economic considerations that subordinate therapeutic concerns to monetary ones. Social planning did not bring great economic well-being to the Communist world, and in the "free world" enormous debts cast the future viability of essential human services into considerable doubt. While the quasipublic sectors that provided escape (whether at the stadium or the casino) were thriving, the philanthropic enterprises that free societies depend upon for the cultivation of learning, high culture, and charity were increasingly threatened. Under the one system people could be victimized by political terror; under the other, by economic vicissitudes, like inflation, that they cannot foresee or control.

The right to collective bargaining, achieved at great cost in the thirties, once enjoyed decisive support from ecumenical agencies inspired by the teachings of Walter Rauschenbusch and others associated with the Social Gospel. The labor movement in America did much to bring the working class and the middle class closer to each other in economic status, but in the eighties it no longer enjoyed widespread support from socially concerned Christians.

The rise of liberation theologies, particularly in the third and fourth worlds, helped revive attention to the plight of the poor, but the insights of these theologies were often deemed inapplicable to the first world. Moreover, liberation theology (which has not called itself a social ethic) did not always address the difficult strategic and moral issues involved in shaping public policy in complex democratic societies. It was often influenced by a Marxist outlook that made its approach to economic issues more ideological and less pragmatic than that of much liberal social Christianity.

Late in 1985, the Roman Catholic bishops surprised many by issuing a pastoral letter that scrutinized American economic achievements with the same critical thoroughness that they had applied to nuclear issues and the making of peace a few years before. While not rejecting capitalism, the bishops did repudiate the exemption from moral scrutiny often claimed by a market system. They also reiterated the importance of testing economic life by canons of distributive justice, not merely by measures of logistical success.

In the period 1935-1985 biomedical issues and business practices became new fields of inquiry. While these fields are not unrelated to how people earn their livelihood, neither field showed much interest in questions of social justice. Only as a market approach came to be used to bring health care costs down did those doing bioethics begin to address the problems of equity surrounding the delivery and allocation of health care services.

It may well be that current disenchantment with the welfare idea, and the dismantling of governmental services that were long considered staple components of a mixed economy, will result in a reappearance of the kind of unrelieved poverty that produces hunger pains in the stomachs of the needy and gnawing doubts in the consciences of the sensitive. Such poverty could, at the price of horrible suffering, once again put economic justice at the center of public attention. It may be possible for the private sector to find ways to alleviate the crying need of the poor without making charity an instrument of dehumanization; but, should that happen, it will be a new American achievement.

c. Race relations, civil rights, and black power

If the story of ethical concern about economic matters chronicles the gradual loss of an initial radicalism and even the eclipse of urgency about such matters, the story of changing attitudes about the plight of racial and ethnic minorities is one of an initial indifference giving way to significant changes in outlooks and policies.

In the 1930s Jim Crow reigned legally in the South and unofficially in the North, although some unease with this situation was beginning to appear in morally sensitive circles. It was quite unpopular, even outside the South, to suggest that whites and Negroes (as they were then called) should live in a pattern of social interaction providing equal access to the American dream. Paul Carter, in *The Decline and Revival of the American Social Gospel 1920-1940,* maintained that the churches of America were unusually slow in responding to the dawning realization that the cause of justice between blacks and whites could not be served within a system overtly or covertly premised on white supremacy.[3] Reinhold Niebuhr found his Detroit parish unsympathetic to the advocacy of open housing. While supported in the abstract by liberal Christians, the call for integration was not the focus of widespread popular concern. Sydney Ahlstrom, in his single reference to these matters in his account of the sixties, tersely observed: "racial inequities had a minor place in the protest literature of the period."[4]

As the Second World War came to an end, President Truman proposed a "Fair Deal" for American society, including an end to discrimination in employment. In 1950 he abolished segregation as an official policy of the armed forces. Four years later the Supreme Court ruled that segregation in public schools was a violation of the equal protection clause of the Fourteenth Amendment. These changes provoked much grumbling, but support for racial equality that had been voiced by an ever growing minority in the churches during the previous twenty years limited the degree to which such grumbling could claim moral credibility. Although the churches continued to be among the most segregated of American institutions, by the 1960s opposition to desegregation was openly expressed only in the theologically and culturally most conservative religions.

The relationship of blacks to American society began to undergo important changes in the 1960s—owing not least to an adventurous

3. Paul A. Carter, *The Decline and Revival of the Social Gospel: Social and Political Liberalism in American Protestant Churches, 1920-1940* (Ithaca: Cornell University Press, 1954; rev. ed., Hamden, CN: Archon Books, 1971).

4. Ahlstrom, op. cit., p. 923.

heroism born of the religious fervor of the black church. The struggle for civil rights showed that legal protections and official policies could not effect dramatic change until the victims of oppression and exclusion were motivated to claim their just due. When, in 1955, Rosa Parks refused to sit in the rear of a Montgomery bus, she did as much to catalyze social change as the nine venerable judges of the Supreme Court had done in declaring segregation in public schools unconstitutional. The freedom rides, in which both blacks and whites participated, transformed theory and ideal into practice and process. Martin Luther King, Jr., combining a Christian liberal theology with a Niebuhrian tough-mindedness about the need to exercise power (albeit a nonviolent form of power), became one of America's finest exemplars of the use of theological proclamation in the service of action.

Some important theological work explored the phenomenon of racism as a form of idolatry, thereby pushing the analysis of segregation beyond the categories of prejudice and injustice to fundamental questions about the underlying faith commitments that divide a society.[5] Such analysis promotes a salutary awareness that, despite social changes that may have reduced the degree of segregation and helped achieve some justice, there is still a long way to go before full justice and full community are attained. Subsequent accounts of the black experience appealed more and more to black identity as the *fons et origo* of both freedom and justice. Black liberation theology insisted that equality must be personally experienced as a source of identity and dignity, which cannot happen if equality is merely "bestowed" by someone holding a higher status.

d. The protest against oppression broadens

In recent years other oppressed groups—women, American Indians, and homosexuals—made known their grievances against a social system that denied them full status and equality of opportunity. These protests ranged widely and pushed deeply into the fabric of the social consciousness. Churches and theological seminaries provided, with varying degrees of effectiveness, intellectual and community support for these agendas.

Women were notably successful in developing a theological movement with feminist perspectives at its center. Not only did they press for inclusion in ecclesiastical roles, chiefly the ordained ministry; they also provided a new kind of theological/ethical reflection replete

---

5. George D. Kelsey, *Racism and the Christian Understanding of Man* (New York: Scribner's, 1965).

with historical and systematic contributions consciously derived from women's experience of oppression. They likewise pressed for modifications of language, both of an ordinary discourse dominated by male generic terms and of a traditional theological vocabulary in which terms like Father, Son, King, Lord, and Master connoted patriarchy and male hierarchical rule. They thereby asserted that something even more basic than a change of ethical outlook is needed if cultural conditions are to shift. Writers like Mary Daly, Beverly Harrison, Nelle Morton, and Letty Russell called for a theological reorientation of the very conceptual world out of which ethical reflection comes. Some of them took this to require the repudiation of the entire Hebraic-Christian heritage, while others believed that its radical reconception would suffice. The literature of the women's movement has made plain that theological ethics cannot be done without taking into account what is being said in *all* the other theological disciplines.

While the cause of gay liberation was promoted with considerable fervor, it produced no extensive theological reconceptualization comparable to that produced by both blacks and feminists. Much the same can be said about the cause of native Americans. The claim of these groups—that they have been miserably treated and excluded from the protections of the moral covenant that governs the mainstream of American life—was substantiated by many writers, but it did not lead to new ways of thinking theologically about moral issues.

e. The debate about private behavior in the American ethos

Americans entered the mid-30s with a vivid memory of an unsuccessful effort to control individual morality by public law, namely, Prohibition, which was a complex and cumbersome attempt to legislate against what was considered unacceptable private behavior. In 1935, the repeal of the Eighteenth Amendment was still only thirteen months old. The failure of the "noble experiment" to deal with the prevalent and problematic use of liquor created doubts in many minds about all efforts to control individual behavior by governmental proscription. There will always be types of behavior that are thought to be more appropriately determined by private discretion than by public policy. Throughout the fifty years following the repeal of Prohibition—possibly in reaction to its failure—there was a tendency to relegate more and more behavior to the discretionary realm of private determination rather than to the realm of criminal activity. Arguments still occur, for instance, as to whether motorcycle helmet laws and seat belt requirements should carry criminal sanctions.

In the mid-80s the private use of both legal and illegal drugs for pleasure and escape consumed enormous resources and undercut the resolve, alertness, readiness for service, and productivity of many affluent as well as marginalized members of American society. This behavior may be part of a larger pattern of social irresponsibility that threatens the viability of western society. Several astute social observers, writing from very different perspectives, have described the present condition of American society with phrases like *The Broken Covenant*,[6] *The Culture of Narcissism*,[7] and *The Naked Public Square*.[8] These studies criticized aspects of the American scene that involve far more than the misuse of chemical substances. They differed sharply in what they would do about the problems that they identified as manifestations of cultural disintegration. However, they all agreed that something is seriously amiss in our culture that warrants grave concern and will require a spiritual refurbishing to overcome.

The mores of the eighties are less restrictive than were those of the thirties. The intervening half-century witnessed strong impulses to "de-Puritanize" society. Violation of drug laws became widespread possibly because many people felt that drug use, like alcohol use, is a private matter. The outlook may now be shifting. Smoking has been prohibited in more and more places in order to guard against harm from mere proximity to the fumes. Public support has been rallied for strict enforcement of the laws against drunk driving. As of this writing, one house of Congress has been considering a bill to launch a massive public campaign against the use of drugs.

The reluctance to use public sanctions against unacceptable private behavior has also been evident in responses to the sexual revolution of the last two or three decades, from the standpoint of both legislative policy and moral reflection. Stanley Hauerwas correctly pointed out that mainstream Christian ethics has been confusedly silent before the "sheer sexual anarchy characteristic of much of our culture."[9] The reticence of mainline Christian thinkers to treat sexual behavior as a social matter may stem from an understandable desire to avoid the prudery of conservative religiosity—lest one do with sex what Prohibition did

6. Robert N. Bellah, *The Broken Covenant: American Civil Religion in Time of Trial* (New York: Seabury, 1957).

7. Christopher Lasch, *The Culture of Narcissism: American Life in an Age of Diminishing Expectations* (New York: Norton, 1978).

8. Richard John Neuhaus, *The Naked Public Square: Religion and Democracy in America* (Grand Rapids: Eerdmans, 1984).

9. Stanley Hauerwas, *A Community of Character: Toward a Constructive Christian Social Ethic* (Notre Dame: University of Notre Dame Press, 1981), p. 176.

with the use of alcohol, i.e, make it cruder and less responsible by driving it underground. In any event, the rise of publicly exploited sex (from sensate advertising and pornography to the proliferation of plush as well as sordid brothels) has served to remove sexual activity still further from the frameworks of covenant and commitment that enhance its human value. The sexual exploitation of children is especially disturbing. The overall result is a social condition against which there has been an understandable and growing revulsion. Situation ethics, which sought to emphasize the importance of context for sexual activity, came on the scene in the sixties, when broad cultural trends legitimated behavior that gave little heed to traditional morality. "Freedom" was then the byword and situation ethics was unfairly identified with a cultural climate that did little to keep sexual behavior from becoming crass and merely sensual.

These developments evoked a moral response that was no less theologically oriented and impelled by social malady than were the aforementioned liberal responses to other issues. This particular response, however, came from conservative religious forces historically aligned with prudish moralities and with views that assign a repressive role to public order. This reaction may well have tipped the scales in recent American elections toward candidates who condemned these developments most vocally, and it has even brought theologically conservative Christians, who once repudiated social action, to take up the cause with crusading ardor. Crusades against personal misconduct are to conservative Christians in the eighties what crusades against war were to liberal Christians in the thirties.

Opposition to abortion is not unrelated to these changes in ethos. The scale on which abortions are being performed in America today should sober even those who feel that a moralistic prohibition is an unsatisfactory response. Not only are fetuses often treated casually, but the bodies of women are assaulted without sufficient sensitivity to physical and psychic consequences. It has become hard for one even to point this out without being identified with persons whose opposition to abortion shows remarkable similarities in stance and tactics to the anti-drink crusades that resulted in Prohibition. Just as the one group attacked saloons, so the other bombs abortion clinics. Just as did the one, so the other would amend the Constitution if appeals to legislative action prove fruitless. This issue has engendered some of the most intransigent moralizing of our time, making it impossible to break through the bitter divisions to a more sensitive and constructive way of dealing with the problem.

II. Some Comments about Theological Perspectives

Ethical engagement with the specific issues and problems arising from the cultural context has significantly influenced American ecclesiastical life. The appearance of a conservative social activism has altered the meaning that can be ascribed to "private party" and "public party" religion.[10] For most of the past fifty years these terms denoted predictable stances about social issues. The "public party" was liberal, whereas the "private party" was conservative. (Many conservatives argued that religious bodies should not even seek to influence public policy.) This simple correlation has now been upset. The religious right has mounted a public party behavior on the conservative side. This may make for a repositioning of American religious life; it could also make for better theological discussion—one that has to consider the substance of moral debates rather than merely contend that the church should or should not be active in public controversies.

These changes in social outlooks and in church life have also influenced the foundational theological methodologies employed in Christian ethics. Liberal social Christianity, Protestant political realism, liberation theology, and—in its own way—right-wing political conservatism all belong to a particular type of Christianity: one that seeks the transformation of society in conformity to God's will. This type responds to felt social needs by thinking theologically about how Christians ought to address such needs. The fundamental methodology used in such approaches often starts with problems in the world at large and then prescribes a Christian response on the basis of a conceptually defined set of Christian ideals.

A variation on this method appeared in the idea of a *koinonia* ethic, which Paul Lehmann advanced in his writing. It approaches Christian decision making as an effort to deal with what God is understood to be doing in a particular historical context.[11] This ethic turns directly to God's self-revealing activity in the world and stresses the significance of the church (or Christian community) for guidance as to what the Christian believer is to do. Likewise, divine-command morality is often quite contextual in determining its response, rather than de-

10. See Martin E. Marty, *Righteous Empire: The Protestant Experience in America* (New York: Dial, 1970), p. 179.

11. See Paul L. Lehmann, "The Foundation and Pattern of Christian Behavior," in John A. Hutchison, ed., *Christian Faith and Social Action* (New York: Scribner's, 1953), pp. 93-116.

pending upon a set of norms or principles that are thought to embody the Christian ideal.[12]

The work of some recent Christian ethicists, such as Stanley Hauerwas and John Howard Yoder, has a still different emphasis. While by no means oblivious to the perceived social needs of the time, this approach concentrates on the paradigmatic qualities of Christian discipleship as known from the Bible and history. It eschews the use of cultural trends as guides to Christian discipleship. This way of thinking about Christian ethics is often presented under the rubric of an ethic of character and virtue.

Moral development theory introduces yet another perspective. While some of its ablest originators, like Robert Coles, have been interested in the impact of social change on individual lives, moral development theory as such tends to be more concerned with what constitutes viable and mature decision making than with what problems in society must be faced.

Some Christian ethicists have also been intent upon using their discipline "apologetically," i.e., to speak to particular groups that might be interested in a morally based religion but not in a dogmatic Christianity. James Gustafson's *Ethics in a Theocentric Context* was probably intended more to address such groups than to respond to widely felt social imperatives.[13] Its most interesting feature is the way it uses terminology of a Reformation provenance to make a case for a religion that is largely oriented to the perspectives of a scientifically dominated modernity.

It may well be that, as we move from the mid-80s into the 1990s, a sharp debate will again arise as to how important it is for Christian ethics to be an autonomous discipline. The theological liberals of half a century ago, working from Kantian assumptions, stressed the independence of morality from dogmatic versions of faith, but they did not seek to break entirely with the Christian heritage. Writers like Karl Barth, Paul Lehmann, Joseph Sittler, and Nels Ferré rejected the rationalistic version of autonomy associated with such liberalism. They tried to work out an ethic that was derived more directly from theological premises, without being slavishly dependent on dogma.

Today there is an increasing polarization among ethicists over the degree to which normative authority is to be accorded to the Christian tradition and heritage. The Roman Catholic church is anxious to re-

---

12. The reference here is to the positions of Karl Barth, Emil Brunner, and Rudolph Bultmann.

13. James M. Gustafson, *Ethics in a Theocentric Context* (Chicago: University of Chicago Press, 1981).

assert strict hierarchical control over specific moral teachings in the name of fidelity to its tradition. Similarly, the Protestant right-wing seems to look upon conformity to particular biblical teachings as the test of moral legitimacy. On the other side, claims for the value of an autonomous morality are advanced ideological constructs that do not take pains to preserve a connection with the Christian heritage. Less by polemic than by neglect, this approach undercuts the decisive significance of the dynamic factor that classical and Reformation theology designated as the "in-breaking Word."

The separation of Christian ethics from a dogmatic/kerygmatic framework manifests itself in many ways. One way appears in the work of those ethicists who simply declare the experience of certain oppressed groups to be exclusively decisive, without consideration of a more inclusive set of concerns. Another appears in an explicitly psychological examination of moral decision making and moral development, which uses biblical categories as nothing more than illustrations of its insights. Yet a third appears in ethical deliberations based upon the phenomenological analysis of moral experience, which examines the moral life as a human enterprise (including attention to the contributions of comparative religious ethics), but which also regards observable human experience as itself a sufficient guide to moral maturity.

When the Christian tradition is utilized in ways that undercut and destroy the free and authentic response of individual believers, an autonomous approach to morality that discounts or disclaims that tradition will appeal to many. The most challenging task facing Christian ethics is to keep attuned to the particularities of concrete and changing historical movements, while remaining loyal to the perspectives and normative implications of biblical and historic Christian faith. The best in American Christian social ethics during the past fifty years has shown that it is possible to be at once evangelically committed and socially relevant. Both liberal and neo-orthodox theologians did that, the former with a strong stress on discipleship as a form of *imitatio Christi,* the latter with an equally strong stress on justification by faith as the soteriological context of Christian obedience. It remains to be seen how well some of the trends and movements that now vie for our allegiance will do this in the future.

18. A Changing Historiography: From Church History to Religious History

David W. Lotz

Church historians in the United States have never been a notably contentious lot, perhaps owing to their relatively small numbers and an attendant esprit de corps. If not given to intramural warfare, however, they have certainly been at pains to "explain" their enterprise to a wider public, including the parish clergy and interested laypersons as well as their professional peers in the academy and the general guild of historians.

Ever since the mid-nineteenth century, when church history became a regular part of the seminary curriculum and full-time instructors were first appointed, America's church historians have displayed a heightened self-consciousness about their craft, particularly in comparison to their colleagues in other areas of theological study. George H. Williams has justly said that "probably no theological discipline has been more self-conscious, at least in America, than Church history. Again and again, Church historians have felt called upon to defend or define their field."[1]

In support of Williams's observation, one can point to the hundreds of essays and books relative to the nature, function, and worth of their discipline that American church historians have produced since the appearance, in 1846, of Philip Schaff's memorable *What Is Church History?*[2] This extensive "apologetic" literature constitutes a large part

---

1. George Huntston Williams, "Church History: From historical theology to the theology of history," in *Protestant Thought in the Twentieth Century: Whence and Whither?*, ed. Arnold S. Nash (New York: Macmillan, 1951), pp. 147-78; citing p. 167.

2. Cf. David W. Lotz, "Philip Schaff and the Idea of Church History," in *A Century of Church History: The Legacy of Philip Schaff*, ed. Henry W. Bowden (Carbondale: South-

of the record for that comprehensive history of church historiography in the United States that still remains to be written.

The word "historiography" denotes both the actual *writing* of history and the *study* of such writing. My intent in this essay is to identify the most important changes in the writing of church history during the years 1935-1985 and also to account for these changes. To this end I will employ the aforementioned literature in which church historians have periodically defined and defended the points of view that both inform and mirror the history that they actually write. I thus propose to consider church historiography in the first sense by examining church historiography in the second sense.

The history of church historiography in the United States during the past half-century can be periodized as follows:

(1) *1935-1965:* the period of *church* history, characterized by a renewed emphasis on the discipline as a specifically theological enterprise whose proper object of study is the church catholic, namely, the unique community called into being by God's redemption of sinful humanity through the person and work of Jesus Christ, and called to be the witness to and the bearer of divine revelation in history.

(2) *1965-1985:* the period of *religious* history, characterized by a renewed secularizing of the discipline on the ground that theological constructs such as the church catholic, redemption through Christ, and God's self-revelation in history are metahistorical constructs (thus transcending the historian's purview) and that, in any case, the traditional focus of leading church historians in the United States on so-called mainline Protestantism failed to do justice to the manifest pluralism of American Christianity and religion (thus necessitating a comprehensive "religious" history in place of a constrictive "church" history).

The nature and significance of historiographical developments during the past fifty years, however, can be properly gauged only against the backdrop of earlier developments from the 1880s to the 1930s—a period when church historians "emphasized *history,* rejoiced in it as a method, . . . [and] were conspicuously eager to assimilate their field and methodology to that of their secular or academic colleagues. . . ."[3] Accordingly, one must also identify the leading features of this formative period from about *1888 to 1935.*

Before proceeding to an exposition and analysis of each of these

---

ern Illinois University Press, 1988), pp. 1-35. This entire volume, commemorating the centenary of the American Society of Church History (1888-1988), is relevant to the present essay. See especially H. W. Bowden, "The First Century: Institutional Development and Ideas about the Profession," pp. 294-322.

3. G. H. Williams, op. cit., p. 148.

three periods, I want to consider some of the factors that make for change in the writing of history, including the dramatic changes in church historiography since the 1880s.

I. Some Causes of Historiographical Change

Nothing is more evident than the fact that history is always being written anew. But how to explain this ever-changing historiography? The answer stands ready to hand: because history itself is ever changing! This reply will surprise only those who wrongly equate history with the past (which is presumed to be unchanging, forever fixed).

It is necessary, therefore, to identify four operative meanings of the word "history," namely, (1) history-as-*actuality:* all that has happened in the human past and that is knowable from its surviving traces; (2) history-as-*record:* the extant evidence for past events, in the form of documents, artifacts, monuments, etc.; (3) history-as-*inquiry:* the disciplined endeavor to give a true account of past events on the basis of methodical (critical) research into the record; and (4) history-as-*written:* the account itself, the story of some part of the human past so far as that past can be reconstructed through inquiry.

Thus, while historians do indeed study and write about the past (history-as-actuality), the immediate, proper object of their research and writing is always history-as-record (for if past events have left no vestiges or record of themselves, they have literally vanished without a trace). The term "history," therefore, as indicated by the Greek and Latin noun *historia* ("investigation"), refers first and foremost to history-as-inquiry, whose goal or chief purpose is history-as-written on the basis of history-as-record. From this it should be plain that changes in historiography—in the actual writing of history—are mainly attributable to two factors: (1) historians' changing understandings of history-as-inquiry; and (2) changes in history-as-record and in historians' approaches to this record. Each of these factors calls for elucidation.

1. History-as-inquiry is rooted in historical thought or theory. Changes periodically occur in this philosophy of history, in the discipline's epistemological foundations, as succeeding generations of historians entertain new (different) views of historical objectivity, of history as art vis-à-vis history as science, and of the relationship of history to literature, philosophy, theology, and the natural and social sciences. Church historians in the United States, whatever the distinctiveness of their subject matter, have always thought of themselves as bona fide

historians; as such, they have not been immune to changes in the conceptual underpinnings of the discipline.

Given the widespread tendency to conceive of "the modern historical consciousness" as *one* thing—as a basically homogeneous phenomenon, it is necessary to stress that history-as-inquiry has undergone significant transformations since the eighteenth-century Enlightenment. To be sure, most modern historians have shared fundamental agreements about the nature and value of their enterprise. Nonetheless, over the centuries and not least in the United States since the last quarter of the nineteenth century, they have manifested striking differences in their understanding of historical cognition, of the canons or rules of historical method, of the proper objects of historical study, of the role of interpretation and hypothesis in historical research, of the place (legitimacy) of moral judgments in historical exposition, and of many other such central issues.[4] These changing views of history-as-inquiry have, perforce, wrought changes in the writing of history, including church history.

2. Change also characterizes history-as-record. The record of the past is constantly subject to expansion and contraction as evidence is newly created by the course of events, is newly discovered (cf. the Dead Sea Scrolls), and is forever lost to sight (cf. the destruction of irreplaceable archives by fire and war). Historiography thus changes because the record itself is ever changing. Historians, moreover, both by virtue of their training and in response to the pressure of events, learn how to question the record anew and thereby to elicit from it answers (data) that they had not previously observed. In this instance, what changes is not the record itself but the informed *use* of the record. Historiography thus changes because historians' approaches to the record are ever changing. Such new readings of the record underlie the recent development of minority history, women's history, and so-called popular history (or "history from below").

But *why* do historical theory (history-as-inquiry) and historians' uses of the record change? In partial answer, one can point to three further factors that make for a changing historiography: (3) significant developments within the *multiple societies* to which the historian simultaneously belongs; (4) the articulation of *new perspectives* on past events in the light of more recent events; and (5) the emergence in historical theory and practice of *exigent problems* whose resolution seems to re-

---

4. See John Higham, *History: Professional Scholarship in America*, rev. ed. (Baltimore: Johns Hopkins University Press, 1983; originally published by Prentice-Hall in 1965). [Hereafter referred to as *History*.]

quire new strategies in both history-as-inquiry and history-as-written. In addition, as regards church historiography proper, another key factor has come into play: (6) the presence of a *fundamental tension* (if not contradiction) between "church" and "history." Each of these factors also requires explication.

3. It is clear that important changes in historiography have attended important changes in American culture, western civilization, and the global society; in the historian's professional society or guild; in the historian's immediate milieu, namely, the academy (university and seminary); and, in the case of most church historians, changes in the churches (denominations) of which they are members or, at least, interested observers. Historiography, in short, has a social locus and is invariably socially conditioned.

For example, the patterns of historical research and writing have changed in response to societal crises (such as two world wars, the Great Depression, the nuclear age, the civil rights movement, the student revolution and counterculture of the late sixties and early seventies). They have also changed in response to developments in higher education, most notably, perhaps, the professionalization of historical study in the United States during the later nineteenth century owing to the rise of the modern university, with its provision for the training and employment of Ph.D.s in history. With professionalization, especially with the burgeoning number of new Ph.D.s following World War II, came specialization—the rapid proliferation within the guild of new areas of intensive historical study (including the history of religion). Likewise, the changing patterns of church historiography have reflected changes in the churches (e.g., the ecumenical movement, Vatican II, the resurgence of evangelicalism), as well as changes in the curricula of seminaries and divinity schools (where church history has repeatedly had to establish its relevance, even its right of existence, vis-à-vis the fields of Bible, systematic theology and ethics, and "practical" theology).

4. Historians constantly turn (return) to the record of past events with eyes newly sensitized by more recent events. Accounts of history-as-actuality are always open to revision—and so new(er) accounts are produced—because history-as-record is always open to re-examination in light of ongoing historical experience. In short, the history of earlier events is reappraised and revised on the basis of new angles of vision supplied by later events.

For example, the history of peacemaking in the the decades prior to World War I was refashioned, after 1914, by the experience of that terrible war. The civil rights movement of the sixties occasioned a fundamental reappraisal of the history of slavery in the United States (and the western world) and has also had a profound revisionary effect on historical study of such topics as racism, race-relations, and minorities in American society. This reading of the record of past events in response to present historical experience can fall prey to anachronism, but, properly controlled, it often results in a more complex, more subtly nuanced historiography.

5. Sweeping historiographical change normally transpires over the long-term and occurs in reaction to the appearance of anomalies in the prevailing paradigm of inquiry, i.e., in the discipline's theoretical basis. Stirred into reflection on their craft by the presence of such anomalies, some historians—usually, at first, a small and highly self-conscious group—call for a reconceptualization of the discipline and proceed to define and defend their new strategies.

Thus, by way of illustration, American historiography underwent a basic shift toward relativism (or pragmatism) in the 1930s and 40s, in line with the influential views of Carl L. Becker and Charles A. Beard.[5] Duly awakened from their dogmatic slumbers, Becker and Beard discovered that the prevailing "scientific" notion of history-as-inquiry, in which both had been schooled, could not adequately account for the manifest interests and values that historians bring to their research (and, indeed, *must* bring if they are to fulfill their vocational obligations to society). Hence, far from being an entirely dispassionate process of arriving at historical actuality (the truth) by minute inspection of, and simple inference from, the historical record (the facts), history-as-inquiry was seen to be value-laden from the outset, ever guided in its selection (!) of past facts by present-day interests.

Basic theoretical changes in history-as-inquiry bring with them, of course, comparable changes in the use of history-as-record and, consequently, in history-as-written. Relativism, for example, opposed scientific determinism by emphasizing the role of subjective and unpredictable elements in history, especially individuals and their ideas, and thereby engendered a heightened interest in biography and intellectual history. As will be seen, church historiography in the years after 1935 was directly affected by relativism and, in addition, generated its *own* paradigm shift owing to the presence of certain anomalies in the traditional understanding of church history as a theological discipline.

6. The theory and practice of church history in America have undergone striking changes since the mid-nineteenth century due to the ever-present tension—perhaps even contradiction—between "church"

---

5. Cf. *History*, pp. 117-31; also Cushing Strout, *The Pragmatic Revolt in American History: Carl Becker and Charles Beard* (New Haven: Yale University Press, 1958).

and "history." The problem, at root, is this: if the church be understood *theologically* as the Body of Christ—the community of those redeemed by God through the life, death, and resurrection of Jesus Christ—how can such an understanding be reconciled with a *strictly empirical* understanding of history that rules out all appeals to acts of God for interpretive and explanatory purposes? Thus church history, as traditionally understood and pursued, appears to land its practitioners in the proscribed territory of metahistory.

One radical solution, which has been favored since the mid-1960s (as it also was from about 1900 to the mid-1930s), is to abandon any and all theological definitions of "church" (e.g., the elect people of God), turning instead to phenomenological definitions (e.g., the institutional churches), on the supposition that theology *necessarily* entails metahistory. In effect, then, "the church" disappears as a working construct and, in its place, one finds "the churches/denominations" or "Christianity/the Christian religion" or, most broadly, "religion" (in North America, Europe, etc.).

It now remains to trace this changing historiography from 1935 to 1985, seen in light of developments from the 1880s to the 1930s. One may observe that all the factors discussed above, making for changes in history-as-inquiry and history-as-written, have been operative in the craft of church history during the past century.

II. 1888-1935: The Period of Church *History*

The professionalization of church historical scholarship in the United States can be dated from the founding of the American Society of Church History in 1888. The society's guiding spirit and first president, until his death in 1893, was Philip Schaff of New York's Union Seminary. Swiss-born, German-trained, and resident in the United States from 1844, Schaff was the best known and most highly regarded American church historian of the nineteenth century. He was also the foremost representative of the theological conception of church history as "salvation history." For Schaff, that is, the church is rightly understood as the Body of Christ: "the dwelling place of Christ, in which he exerts all the powers of his theanthropic [divine-human] life, and also the organ, through which he acts upon the world as Redeemer. . . ." Church history, therefore, "is simply the progressive execution of the divine kingdom in the actual life of humanity; the outward and inward development of Christianity; the extension of the church over the whole earth, and the infusion of the spirit of Christ into all the spheres of human existence. . . ."[6] This idea of the church and its history received consummate expression in Schaff's magnum opus, *History of the Christian Church* (7 vols., 1882-92).

Already by 1888, however, Schaff's perspective was becoming passé, being steadily replaced by the new orthodoxy gaining ground among America's professional historians, namely, the idea of history as an empirical science.[7] Presumably modeled on the natural sciences, history-as-inquiry was now declared to be presuppositionless, purely inductive, objective, and antispeculative. In view of its commitment to a "realistic reproduction" of the record of the past, it also scorned the preoccupation with dramatic effect and rhetorical elegance of the traditional literary or romantic historians. It was this multifaceted idea of history-as-science that animated the newly established American Historical Association (founded in 1884). Among church historians its stoutest advocate was Ephraim Emerton of Harvard, himself a founding member of both the AHA and the ASCH (and instrumental in the merger of the ASCH with the AHA from 1896 to 1906).

In his 1882 inaugural address as the first Winn Professor of Ecclesiastical History at Harvard, Emerton observed that "even the history of the Church was coming to be considered as only a part of the great story of humanity, that its study was to be undertaken with the same methods and the same materials that were employed in other branches of historical inquiry. . . ." Hence it was entirely fitting that church history "should be viewed as a department of historical rather than of theological science." Even so, Emerton invited his "fellow-students" to join him in studying "the history of the Christian Church as a great human institution," for if history is "the record of human life, then whatever has to do with the life of humanity is part of history; whatever goes beyond the life of humanity passes the boundary line of history. . . ."[8]

Emerton's idea of the church as "a great human institution"—his decisive break with Schaff's idea of the church as the divine-human Body of Christ, the agent of the world's redemption—was, in his own judgment, the result of a strict adherence to "the science of modern Historical Criticism." He took it to be axiomatic that "the method of natural science is the method of history; namely, the observation of facts and inductions from them." As an inductive science, history-as-inquiry works from observable facts to warranted generalizations, not from

6. *History of the Apostolic Church, with a General Introduction to Church History*, trans. Edward D. Yeomans (New York: Scribner's, 1853), pp. 8, 16.

7. Cf. *History*, pp. 92-103.

8. "The Study of Church History," *Unitarian Review and Religious Magazine* 19 (January 1883) 1-18; citing pp. 11, 16.

a priori constructs (theories, hypotheses, speculative schemes) to the investigation of particular phenomena. But theology *must* have its preconceptions since it deals with the supernatural (the unobservable). Hence, for Emerton, it was no less axiomatic that theology (and any "Christian philosophy of history") is synonymous with metahistory.[9] Theology and history, therefore, are two radically different enterprises, and so the traditional subsumption of church history under historical theology (or salvation history) is untenable since it robs history-as-inquiry of its independence, its critical autonomy, by allowing the presuppositions of faith (belief in God) to condition, and therewith to corrupt, the impartial observation of facts (history-as-record).

To be sure, there is no essential antagonism between history and theology: the former, while it must be independent of the latter, is not indifferent to it in principle. The *results* of historical inquiry may subsequently enter into theological and philosophical speculation: history may then serve theology as an "auxiliary science." And, ultimately, in the actual life-situation of the student of church history, the findings of history and the concerns of faith may "weave themselves together" into a *conviction* (value judgment) about the church as a "divine creation."[10] Moreover, while the *reality* of the superhuman is beyond the reach of historical evidence, *"belief* in the superhuman is a profound fact of human experience" and so can be studied in a fully historical manner.[11] The critical church historian, therefore, does not recount the actual history (or "progressive execution") of the world's redemption by God through Christ and his Body the Church, but traces the genesis and the consequences of the faith of Christians that "God was in Christ reconciling the world unto himself."

This putatively scientific view of church history thus entailed

(1) A rigid distinction and division of labor between history and theology, between the empirical and the speculative;

(2) A rejection of traditional supernaturalism in favor of a new naturalism that interpreted and explained historical phenomena, including the church's existence and its faith, without any recourse to "acts of God" or "miracles" (a necessary methodological atheism);

(3) A rejection of the dualism of salvation history, which wrongly separated sacred (church) history from secular (world) history and subordinated the latter to the former, thereby treating the church as the one true key to the meaning of humanity's total story rather than as

9. Ibid., pp. 3, 6, 7, 9.
10. Ibid., pp. 8, 9, 17.
11. "A Definition of Church History," *Papers of the American Society of Church History,* 2nd series, 7 (1923) 55-68; citing p. 62 (italics added).

"only a part of the great story of humanity" (a correct historiographical monism);

(4) A rejection of salvation history's rhetoric of commitment (the language *of* faith) in favor of a neutral, impartial, objective rhetoric of description (the language *about* faith);

(5) A vindication of the parity of church history with all other branches of history and of the legitimacy of church historical study in the modern university, on the ground that church historians use "the same methods and the same materials" as their professional peers; and

(6) A confidence that church history, though not itself a theological discipline, is of material importance for the work of theological construction and, above all, is of indispensable service to vital religion (e.g., by its critical dismantling of a "dogmatic [metaphysical] Christianity" and its attendant recovery of Jesus Christ in his fully human lineaments).

Church history in this "scientistic" guise was regnant from about 1900 until the early 1930s. While much history of a Schaffian sort continued to be written, the luminaries of the profession had, on the whole, opted for the Emertonian perspective (which Emerton himself was still vigorously promoting in the 1920s). The latter viewpoint, with various modifications, was also represented by Williston Walker (at Yale), Arthur Cushman McGiffert (Schaff's successor at Union), Frank Hugh Foster (at Oberlin), and Shirley Jackson Case and William Warren Sweet (both at the University of Chicago), as well as by Walter Rauschenbusch (a professor of church history at Rochester Theological Seminary from 1902 until his death in 1918, albeit better remembered as a leader of the Social Gospel).[12] Case and Sweet, it should be noted, were much influenced by James Harvey Robinson's *The New History* (1912): a manifesto enjoining scientific historians to move beyond their usual focus on institutions ("past politics") to a penetrating investigation of "social forces" (e.g., industrialization) and the "environment" (e.g., the American frontier), to the end that history might intentionally ally itself with the social sciences in searching for laws and regularities of predictive value and thereby demonstrate its relevance to present problems and needs.[13]

Yet another leading representative in the 1920s of the social-

12. The views of Schaff, Emerton, Walker, McGiffert, Foster, and Rauschenbusch—as well as the idea of "scientific history"—are examined by H. W. Bowden, *Church History in the Age of Science: Historiographical Patterns in the United States 1876-1918* (Chapel Hill: University of North Carolina Press, 1971).

13. Cf. *History*, pp. 104-16; also S. J. Case, "The Historical Study of Religion," *The Journal of Religion* 1 (January 1921) 1-17.

scientific approach to church history was the ethicist and historical theologian, H. Richard Niebuhr (at Yale from 1931). In the preface to his
widely influential book, *The Social Sources of Denominationalism* (1929),
Niebuhr declared that "The effort . . . to approach the problem of church
unity from a purely theological point of view appeared to [the author]
to be a procedure so artificial and fruitless that he found himself compelled to turn from theology to history, sociology, and ethics for a more
satisfactory account of denominational differences and a more significant approach to the question of union."[14]

Eight years later, however, in the preface to an even more influential book, *The Kingdom of God in America* (1937), Niebuhr expressed
dissatisfaction with his earlier work for the following reasons:

> Though the sociological approach helped to explain why the religious
> stream flowed in these particular channels [of race, class, and sectional
> interests] it did not account for the force of the stream itself; while it
> seemed relevant enough to the institutionalized churches it did not ex-
> plain the Christian movement which produced these churches; while it
> accounted for the diversity in American religion it did not explain the
> unity which our faith possesses despite its variety; while it could deal
> with the religion which was dependent on culture it left unexplained
> the faith which is independent, which is aggressive rather than passive,
> and which molds culture instead of being molded by it. . . .[15]

Niebuhr's remarkable change of mind (and method) between
1929 and 1937 bespoke a profound transformation occurring in the
church historian's craft during these very years: by the later 1930s (and
for at least two decades thereafter) a majority of church historians were
intent on reforming their discipline by again making it theological and
churchly in something like the old Schaffian sense.

III. 1935-1965: The Period of *Church* History

In 1935 (the year of Emerton's death) H. R. Niebuhr and church historians Wilhelm Pauck and Francis P. Miller published *The Church
Against the World.* Their book was intended as a declaration of the
church's independence "from its bondage to a corrupt civilization,"
specifically from its entangling alliances with modern capitalism, nationalism, and, above all, anthropocentrism: each being a form of idolatry,

14. *The Social Sources of Denominationalism* (New York: Holt, 1929), p. vii.
15. *The Kingdom of God in America* (New York: Harper & Row, 1937), pp. ix-x.
[Hereafter referred to as *Kingdom of God.*]

of perverted religious faith.[16] Concluded Niebuhr: "There is no flight out of the captivity of the church save into the captivity of God"—where *God* stands not as a symbol of human aspirations but designates that ultimate reality "whose ways are again evident in historic processes, . . . a redeeming and saving reality" who effects such salvation "only through the event called Jesus Christ." Even so, for Niebuhr, Pauck, and Miller, a truly independent, dynamic, culture-shaping church was best spoken of as "a revolutionary community in a pre-revolutionary society"—a community whose "main task always remains that of understanding, proclaiming, and preparing for the divine revolution in human life."[17] In this light Emerton's idea of the church as "a great human institution" appeared woefully inadequate—itself a sign of the church's radical dependence on culture and of its captivity to anthropocentrism.

The new perspectives that informed *The Church Against the World* and *The Kingdom of God in America* were largely to shape the theory of church history for the next quarter-century and more. The reconceptualization of the discipline that was gradually carried out during these years was, in fact, a "re-theologization." Church historians, that is, while remaining insistent on their status as scientific historians, were again fully prepared to operate with a theological concept of the church, specifically that of the redeemed community called into being not simply by human *faith* in God but, decisively, by God's own saving *act* in the life, death, and resurrection of Jesus Christ. (Church history would then have to be written in such a way as to make plain the ontological priority of the divine action to the human response.) The particular theology (in a formal sense) that entered into any given interpretation of "church" was not the same for all church historians. Most of them, however, employed some recognizable version of what is variously called neo-orthodox, neo-Reformation, neo-Augustinian, dialectical, or crisis theology, as it came to expression in seminal writings by Karl Barth, Emil Brunner, Rudolf Bultmann, Anders Nygren, Paul Tillich, the brothers Richard and Reinhold Niebuhr, and many others (including St. Augustine and, especially, Luther and Calvin).

Forming the background to this renewed theological approach to church history—and to the development of the "new" theologies themselves—was the experience of a profound and prolonged cultural crisis in the West: a catastrophic "Thirty Years' War" from 1914 to 1945, punctuated by the Wall Street Crash, the Great Depression, the rise and threatened global spread of political totalitarianisms, the advent of the

---

16. *The Church Against the World* (Chicago: Willett, Clark, 1935), p. 124.
17. Ibid., pp. 150-51, 153-54.

nuclear era, and followed by an intractable Cold War between the victorious superpowers. From the 1930s into the 1960s church historians felt obliged to work and write in response to this "age of anxiety" (W. H. Auden). Dozens of books devoted to "The Meaning of History" and "The Christian Understanding of History" were published during these years by leading historians and theologians—among them Nicholas Berdyaev, Paul Tillich, Reinhold Niebuhr, Karl Löwith, Herbert Butterfield, Christopher Dawson, Jean Daniélou, Martin D'Arcy, Oscar Cullmann, and Rudolf Bultmann.[18]

An examination of representative church historical literature from the mid-30s to the mid-60s shows that the discipline during this period was in theory, if not always in practice, (1) *church-centered* in its content, i.e., focused on a unique Holy Community; (2) *ecumenical* or catholic in its scope; (3) *antipositivist* in its method; and (4) *committed* in its rhetoric.

1. Writing in 1952, Wilhelm Pauck hailed "the re-discovery of the 'church' in our time" and approvingly observed: "Thus the whole life of contemporary Protestantism is loosened up and everywhere people search for a fresh understanding of the distinctive functions and mission of the Christian church."[19] Among the notable rediscoverers of the church and its distinctiveness was Cyril C. Richardson, author of *The Church Through the Centuries* (1938). In 1949, on the occasion of his entrance into a professorship once held by Philip Schaff, Richardson declared that "Church history is the tale of redemption; and . . . its central thread is the story of the Holy Community (known under various guises and found in manifold and surprising places), which is the bearer of revelation and through which God acts in human history."[20] Likewise, in a series of essays published in the forties and early fifties, James Hastings Nichols insisted—in opposition to a secularized historiography—that church history is "the story of God's redemption of mankind" and that the chief task of church historians, accordingly, is "to trace the actualization of the Gospel in human history, to discern and describe the signs of the Kingdom, to reveal the subtle indications of the presence of the Risen Christ to his adopted brethren."[21]

18. Much of this literature was surveyed by E. Harris Harbison, "The 'Meaning of History' and the Writing of History," *Church History* 21 (June 1952) 97-107. Representative selections may be found in *God, History, and Historians: Modern Christian Views of History,* ed. C. T. McIntire (New York: Oxford University Press, 1977).

19. "The Idea of the Church in Church History," *Church History* 21 (September 1952) 191-214; citing p. 192.

20. "Church History Past and Present," *Union Seminary Quarterly Review* 5 (November 1949) 1-11; citing p. 9.

21. "The Art of Church History," *Church History* 20 (March 1951) 3-9; citing p. 9

Central to this rediscovery of the church as God's work of redemption in human life was the intent to underscore the church's uniqueness vis-à-vis the "world," i.e., its independence from the immediate environment, its culture-transforming power, and its prophetic, reformist-revolutionary mission. Nichols, for example, attacked "the positivist blight" that had led historians "to concentrate on 'environmental factors' in religious history, to put second things first," thereby neglecting "the specifically religious, the creatively religious."[22] One recalls H. R. Niebuhr's discontent with the sociological approach to church history that had failed to do justice to the creative power of religion by focusing almost exclusively on the social conditions of religion—an egregious example of missing the forest for the trees. Preeminent among mid-century historians in his emphasis on Christianity's intrinsic power of world redemption and transformation was Kenneth Scott Latourette, whose two monumental works—*A History of the Expansion of Christianity* (7 vols., 1937-45) and *Christianity in a Revolutionary Age* (5 vols., 1958-69)—were designed to show that universal history is at root the history of salvation.

2. Central to the new historiography was also the determination not to lose the Church in the churches by simply becoming "the [specialized] study of those institutions called churches."[23] The Christian church, that is, must not be identified with its institutional or denominational embodiments, which are only the relative, time-bound carriers of the Christian faith, of the dynamic movement of prophetic Christianity throughout the ages. "The true church," said Niebuhr, "is not an organization but the organic movement of those who have been 'called out' and 'sent.'"[24] The true church, in sum, is the church catholic: the invisible or spiritual church of the truly redeemed, transcending space and time yet also finding its embodiment, with relative degrees of adequacy, in the visible or institutional churches.

This ecclesiology provided the impetus for a self-consciously ecumenical historiography that sought to discern the *universal* church within the particular churches and thus to disclose the hidden *unity* of the church in the midst of its manifest diversity (especially on the American scene). Confronted by the weighty problem of theological and ecclesiastical pluralism, church historians and church leaders alike were

---

(= 1950 presidential address to the ASCH). See also J. H. Nichols, "Church History and Secular History," *Church History* 13 (June 1944) 87-99.

22. "History in the Theological Curriculum," *The Journal of Religion* 26 (1946) 183-89; citing p. 183.

23. J. H. Nichols, "The Art of Church History," p. 6.

24. *Kingdom of God*, p. xiv.

enjoined "to explore more deeply . . . that common history which we have as Christians and which we have discovered to be longer, larger and richer than any of our separate histories in our divided churches."[25] Spurred on by the gathering force and conspicuous mid-century successes of the ecumenical movement, church historians—notably Albert C. Outler and Georges Florovsky—devoted much of their best effort to exploring and articulating "the [same] Tradition within the [different] traditions."[26]

3. In the 1920s Ephraim Emerton still entertained no doubt that a truly scientific history is altogether objective and value-neutral, eschewing all interpretive schemes in deference to a pure induction from critically established facts. In the course of the 1930s and 40s, however, this conception of scientific history was equated with positivism or "fact-mongering' and came under concerted attack by professional historians in the United States, led by Carl Becker and Charles Beard, who, in turn, were profoundly influenced by such antipositivist European philosophers of history as Benedetto Croce, Karl Heussi, and R. G. Collingwood.[27] The result was the hegemony in the historians' guild of a new relativism: the view, namely, that history-as-inquiry, while guided by the ideal of objectivity and impartiality, is always relative to the standpoint of the inquirer and so is invariably informed by the historian's own presuppositions, value judgments, and working hypotheses. History-as-inquiry, in short, is an art no less than a science, based on the imaginative patterning of the record of the past no less than on the scrupulous effort to read that record in a fair-minded, nonpartisan fashion. This relativist idea of history was enshrined in the famous "Bulletin 54" of the Social Science Research Council: *Theory and Practice in Historical Study,* published in 1946.

Church historians during this period were quick to avail themselves of relativism's conceptual (and polemical) resources. Here, for example, J. H. Nichols found the weapons for his running battle with a positivist church historiography that, by a "misconceived scientific method," had abandoned "the Christian vision of history," thus showing itself naively oblivious to the fact that *all* history is at once art and

25. *Report of the Third World Conference on Faith and Order,* Lund, 1952, Faith and Order Commission Papers No. 15 (London: SCM, 1953), p. 15.

26. Cf. Albert C. Outler, *The Christian Tradition and the Unity We Seek* (New York: Oxford University Press, 1957); and "Our Common History as Christians," in *The Nature of the Unity We Seek,* ed. Paul S. Minear (St. Louis: Bethany, 1958), pp. 78-89. Cf. Georges Florovsky, *Bible, Church, Tradition: An Eastern Orthodox View* (Belmont, MA: Nordland, 1972; vol. 1 of his collected works).

27. See above, note 5.

science and that church history, in particular, is "at the same time a product of religious imagination and thought and a scientific discipline."[28] Likewise Sidney E. Mead, whose writings in these years were replete with references to Becker, Beard, Collingwood, and "Bulletin 54," maintained that "every written history is at least implicitly an explanation and defense of the allegiance—the faith—of the historian. . . . In this respect the Christian historian does not differ from the non-Christian historians. His conflict with them, if any, is a conflict of allegiances—of faiths—and should be recognized as such."[29]

The method of church historical study, then, is antipositivist but not anticritical, for the historical-critical method itself is based on a subtle reciprocity between "facts" and "interpretation." The truth about "what really happened" in the past cannot be established apart from the historian's own imaginative "reconstruction" of that past, which, in turn, is inseparable from the historian's own system of values or "faiths." Hence church historians may legitimately elect to tell the church's story by embedding the facts of the matter in the particular interpretive framework supplied by the Bible and the catholic faith (the common history, the Tradition), namely, the interpretation that the church is God's own creation in Christ, the Holy Community that is the witness to and bearer of God's work of redemption in human life.

Opposition to positivism also showed itself in a new interest in the history of ideas, to which was attributed a causative power. Ideas, that is, possess their own autonomy and creativity; they cannot be simply or fully explained by reference to social and economic conditions; they are not mere rationalizations of more basic environmental factors. It is not surprising, then, that during this period intellectual history in the United States entered its golden age, as attested by the writings of Samuel Eliot Morison, Perry Miller, Ralph Gabriel, Merle Curti, F. O. Matthiessen, and Arthur O. Lovejoy. Church historians not only drew upon these writings, especially those of Miller on the Puritans, but found in them an important impulse and warrant for their own "recovery of interest in doctrines as successive transcripts of divine realities traced for the community of faith out of faith and as such charged with a potency of their own in shaping events."[30] A theological understanding of the church correspondingly required a sophisticated understanding of theology, of the distinctive preaching and teaching—the normative message—of a distinctive community.

28. "The Art of Church History," pp. 3, 6.
29. "Church History Explained," *Church History* 32 (March 1963) 17-31; citing pp. 22-23.
30. G. H. Williams, op. cit., p. 163.

4. Since church history is "the tale of redemption" and since this story is told from the perspective of "the Christian vision of history," it is a matter of principle that church historians should occupy a standpoint within the church and should encode their story in an appropriate rhetoric, namely, the language of faith. "If we are to understand American Christianity," asserted Niebuhr, "we must take our stand within the movement so that its objects may come into view."[31] So also Mead counseled that "every historian of 'the church' ought ideally to be a practicing, responsible member of a denomination."[32] History, moreover, is to a people what memory is to an individual: the ground of self-knowledge and continuing self-identity. In the words of William A. Clebsch: "The historian tells [his] story for the sake of his people, that they may know, and now act in the light of, the kind of people they have come to be. . . . The church historian, working by the same methods and under the same limitations, tells us who we are as church, as God's people."[33] In thus telling "our" story, the church historian perforce speaks "*from* faith *for* faith" and so speaks in the recognizable accents *of* faith. In these ways, then, a methodological, epistemological, and rhetorical significance came to be attached to Christian commitment.

So much for the general idea of church history during the period 1935-1965. It was admirably clear and coherent, yet it was beset by serious internal difficulties that rendered it suspect in theory and ineffective in practice. The paradigm of *church* history, in short, generated its own anomalies.

First, it proved impossible to write the actual history of the church catholic. For how can the earthbound historian recount the story of the *invisible* church, of God's hidden work of redemption in human life? This neuralgic issue exercised Leonard J. Trinterud in his 1955 presidential address to the ASCH. "The Church Catholic," he concluded, "regards itself as coming into being, and continuing in existence, through the activity of God himself. To be the Church, therefore, is always a confession of faith and not a matter of historical investigation and proof. How, then, can you write the history of the work of God, unless you are a Prophet or an Apostle? . . . The answer, of course, is that you cannot." Lacking empirical criteria for identifying those elect people who have truly experienced redemption through Christ and for determining which of the many competing denominations, if any, is the

---

31. *Kingdom of God,* p. 12.
32. "Church History Explained," p. 27.
33. "Church History," in *Viewpoints: Some Aspects of Anglican Thinking,* ed. John B. Coburn and W. Norman Pittenger (Greenwich, CN: Seabury, 1959), pp. 58-70; citing p. 60.

genuine church catholic, historians can only investigate all those diverse groups—the visible institutional churches—that have claimed to participate in redemption, showing how they have understood and acted out this claim. "Here then," confessed Trinterud, "is laid bare my bad conscience. I assume that I ought to present *church* history, but I end up with only the history of Christianity."[34]

Second, the idea of church history as "the tale of redemption" was seen to involve certain presuppositions that either transgress or transcend the established canons of critical historiography: a predicament that engaged Albert Outler in his 1964 presidential address to the ASCH. "The peculiar problem of interpreting *church* history," said Outler, "comes from the historian's obligation to rehearse the Christian past in the light of the Christian world view," which attributes the Christian community's self-identity and continuity through time to "the action of God in history," namely, to divine providence. Outler frankly acknowledged that this providential interpretation of history amounted to a "Christian metahistory" and he was thus constrained to ask: "Can some such vision of God's *pronoia* be conveyed in a critical narrative of the Christian past without debasing the canons of honest historiography?"[35] Many of his professional colleagues, from the later sixties onward, were increasingly inclined to answer no.

Third, the pivotal argument that history-as-inquiry always involves value judgments or "allegiances" or "faiths," and that church historians, therefore, need have no qualms about employing "the Christian vision of history" for interpreting their facts, proved to be less than compelling. This contention seemed to entail that all interpretations are equally valid and that the choice among them is entirely preferential. Yet historians themselves adjudicate among competing interpretations on the ground that some are *better attested* than others; i.e., that their empirical and logical warrants are more persuasive. But how can church historians adequately back up their claim that God acts (in Christ, in the church), since such divine agency is not a matter of ordinary historical experience but requires appeal to privileged sources of information (revelation)? In the epistemology of critical historiography, faiths are one thing, warrants quite another, and the two must not be facilely equated: a point that was underscored by Van A. Harvey in his influential *The Historian and the Believer* (1966).

By the mid-60s, then, the stage was set for another dramatic par-

---

34. "The Task of the American Church Historian," *Church History* 25 (March 1956) 3-15; citing pp. 11-12.
35. "Theodosius' Horse: Reflections on the Predicament of the Church Historian," *Church History* 34 (September 1965) 251-61; citing pp. 258, 261.

adigm shift as church historians began anew to rethink and refashion their discipline.

IV. 1965-1985: The Period of *Religious* History

Significant changes taking place in the church historian's craft during the sixties were signaled by the publication in 1968 of *Reinterpretation in American Church History,* a volume of essays edited by Jerald C. Brauer. In his own introductory essay Brauer observed:

> The assumptions on which the church historian used to function are no longer valid. His discipline developed at a time when it was a commonly held assumption that the church was a unique institution grounded in the supernatural and fulfilling a transcendent will in history. . . . There was sacred history and secular history, which, though intertwined and closely related, were clearly distinguishable. No such distinction is any longer possible. This raises serious questions about the function of the church historian.

Taking special note of L. J. Trinterud's painful realization, in 1955, that one cannot actually *write* church history on the assumption that "the church exists as a community of people redeemed by God in history through Jesus Christ," Brauer concluded: "Perhaps the day of the church historian, as he was long known, is now past, and we can speak only of historians of Christian religion. At this point the church historian becomes a particular kind of historian—a historian of religion, of the Christian religion in Europe or in America."[36]

Writing in the same volume, Martin E. Marty observed that church history was now being pushed "in a 'secular' direction," namely, toward the unreserved acceptance of its cognitive status as a strictly historical-critical discipline, not as a specifically theological discipline operating with its own faith assumptions. Concluded Marty:

> We picture church history in a crisis, then. In its bearing toward "church" it "barely maintains its existence as a discipline." In its stance toward "history" it carries the burden of some sort of theological or ecclesiastical concern in a secular environment and shares with all the humanities a crisis of status and role. Therefore, this is a promising time to study religious history, to examine its roots and its goals. . . .[37]

36. "Changing Perspectives on Religion in America," in *Reinterpretation in American Church History,* ed. J. C. Brauer (Chicago: University of Chicago Press, 1968), pp. 1-28; citing pp. 20, 21.

37. "Reinterpreting American Religious History in Context," in ibid., pp. 195-218; citing pp. 197, 198.

For Marty, then, the crisis besetting the discipline, marked chiefly by a loss of "church," could be offset by a promising new venture: the study of religious history (though this shift, it seems, also confirmed and even compounded the crisis!).

Similar observations and conclusions were advanced, in 1970, by Sydney E. Ahlstrom, who likewise spoke of a secularizing of the discipline. He underscored "two methodological corollaries" of this transformation: "First of all, religious history has become a field of study within the larger frame of world history. It no longer enjoys any rights of sanctuary. . . . Providence cannot be invoked as an explanatory principle. Supernatural sources of insight or knowledge cannot be claimed. . . ." Second, "the concept of 'religious history' becomes a far more comprehensive term than formerly. It is no longer a synonym for 'church history.'"[38]

By 1970, therefore, old-style church history, grounded on Christian theology and its faith claims, had given place to new-style religious history, grounded on the methodology of secular history and its demand for empirical warrants. Just as Philip Schaff's idea of the church as the transcendent Body of Christ had come to new expression in the period 1935-1965, so also Ephraim Emerton's idea of the church as an integral part of human history has been given a new lease on life in the period since 1965 (though these revivals of earlier standpoints have often gone unremarked). This secularizing of the discipline, or "de-theologizing" as it may also be termed (so reminiscent of Emerton's break with Schaff), has continued in force from the mid-60s to the present day, notwithstanding some occasional opposition and some continuation of more traditional patterns of interpreting and writing church history.

By way of clarification, it must be emphasized that secularization does not logically entail "irreligion" or the inevitable "decline and disappearance" of religion. (Indeed, empirically considered, religion may flourish in a secular age.) As used here, rather, in respect of church historiography, the term refers to the gradual loss in the modern world of the *self-evident validity* of all that is metaphysical and metahistorical—including, not least, the *supernatural* grounding of religious belief. A secularized historiography, therefore, is not as such indifferent or inimical to religion but is committed to investigating it "from below" as a matter of ordinary human experience rather than "from above" as a matter of divine revelation. To be sure, as Emerton long ago observed, belief

---

38. "The Problem of the History of Religion in America," *Church History* 39 (June 1970) 224-35; citing pp. 233, 234. [Hereafter referred to as "The Problem."]

in such revelation, and the consequences of this belief for the lives of individuals and groups, are themselves historical phenomena and so demand historical study.

How can one explain this remarkable development since 1965— this intentional break with the venerable and previously prevailing idea of the Christian church as the unique Holy Community whose history is "the tale of redemption"? As already noted, the break occurred in large part because the older paradigm generated its own anomalies: it proved to be *historiographically barren* inasmuch as none but a seer could know and narrate the story of the invisible church catholic (cf. Trinterud's "bad conscience"); and it proved to be *methodologically illicit* inasmuch as a "Christian metahistory" could not justify itself before the bar of critical-historical thinking (cf. Outler's "predicament").

The practical necessity of conforming church history to the canons of secular historiography can be explained, in turn, by developments in the sociology of the discipline. As J. H. Nichols already acknowledged in 1965: "In the United States between 1930 and 1960 the historians of culture and thought [e.g., Miller, Gabriel, Lovejoy] contributed more to the literature of church history than did the occupants of chairs assigned to the discipline."[39] These historians of ideas did not, of course, work and write from a distinctively Christian or theological perspective. Since 1965 this secularizing trend has become ever more pronounced owing to the rapid growth of departments of religion in state-supported universities (and the further expansion of such departments in private universities). During the last generation the great bulk of the writing in church history—and most of the *best* such writing— has been done by scholars situated in university departments of religion, history, and literature, as well as in seminaries and divinity schools related to universities. In such contexts one can legitimately investigate all religious phenomena, including the history of the Christian religion in its intellectual and institutional manifestations; but the study, teaching, and writing of church history as the story of the unique community of those redeemed by God in Christ is regarded as at once sectarian and unscientific.

Concurrent with these developments in the church historian's professional society and academic milieu was an even more foundational and far-reaching change in American society as a whole: what Robert T. Handy has called "the decline of Christendom." By the later sixties growing numbers of people in the United States and Canada

39. "The History of Christianity," in *Religion,* ed. Paul Ramsey (Englewood Cliffs, NJ: Prentice-Hall, 1965), pp. 157-74; citing p. 166.

were forced "to admit that these countries could no longer be considered to be Christian nations in the old sense."[40] What amounted to a further disestablishment of religion was made plain by two landmark decisions of the U.S. Supreme Court in 1962 and 1963 that declared unconstitutional, respectively, the use of prayer and the devotional reading of the Bible in public schools. Moreover, the election in 1960 of the first Roman Catholic president in U.S. history made it no less plain that the old, lingering idea of a *Protestant* Christian America was a myth (one that soon came under critical scrutiny in important books by William Clebsch, Martin Marty, and Robert Handy).[41] Meanwhile, Christian theology itself—far from declaring "the church against the world"—was becoming increasingly "worldly" in its basic orientation, holding itself answerable to "a world come of age" (Dietrich Bonhoeffer) and so questing for "the secular meaning of the Gospel" (Paul van Buren); celebrating the liberties and disciplines of "the secular city" (Harvey Cox); and even announcing "the death of God" (Gabriel Vahanian, Thomas Altizer, William Hamilton). The secularization of church history in America was thus attended, and abetted, by the secularization of both American culture and American theology.

Perhaps the main social factor in secularizing church history, however, in turning the profession away from theological study of the church catholic to phenomenological study of the Christian religion (and religion in general) has been the growth of a radical religious pluralism in the United States since the 1960s. During the past quarter-century, religion on the American scene has presented an increasingly bewildering aspect as the varieties of religious experience proliferate apace. One now encounters a veritable supermarket of faiths, ranging from the traditional denominations through newly emergent or resurgent sects and cults to groups and individuals preoccupied with "spiritual 'self-cultivation,'" with diverse techniques of prayer and meditation, and with the occult.

Denominational lines, moreover, have been blurred by transdenominational charismatic, neo-fundamentalist, neo-evangelical, and other renewal movements, as well as by the impact of media evangelism. The Roman Catholic church, long the country's largest Christian

---

40. *A History of the Churches in the United States and Canada* (New York: Oxford University Press, 1977), p. 419 and the title of Chapter XII (pp. 377-427): "North American Churches and the Decline of Christendom."

41. Cf. W. A. Clebsch, *From Sacred to Profane America: The Role of Religion in American History* (New York: Harper & Row, 1968); M. E. Marty, *Righteous Empire: The Protestant Experience in America* (New York: Dial, 1970); R. T. Handy, *A Christian America: Protestant Hopes and Historical Realities* (New York: Oxford University Press, 1971).

body, has become its single most influential denomination in the wake of the reforms and restructuring mandated by Vatican II. The civil rights movement and the subsequent black power movement have brought the black churches into national prominence. Other heretofore marginalized churches and religious communities—Eastern Orthodox, Pentecostal, Mormon, Jewish, Muslim—have prospered and are impinging on public awareness to an unprecedented degree. The rise in women's consciousness has found expression in feminist theologies and is transforming much of Protestantism through the ordination of women to the ministry, even as Catholicism is being transformed by its Hispanicization. Theologies of liberation have drawn widespread attention to the concerns of Third World churches and peoples. Meanwhile, a public or civil religion has manifested itself at the same time that a privatized religion is flourishing outside the organized religion of church, synagogue, and temple.

This religious pluralism has been attended by a new tribalism, by a celebration of group autonomy and social distinctiveness—racial, ethnic, and gender-based. Little wonder, then, that the idea of the church catholic—with its bias toward unity (consensus), homogeneity (sameness), continuity (self-identity through time)—has lost much of its historical relevance, its interpretive scope and explanatory power, in a religious context marked by dissensus, diversity, discontinuity, and, in sum, differentiation.

Religion in America, to be sure, has been notable, indeed notorious, for its "sheer multifariousness" since at least 1700; but church historians were long able to master—and mask—this diversity by various stratagems, chiefly by annexing the complex story of American religion to the relatively simple story of American evangelical-revivalistic Protestantism (the religion of the "WASPs"), which was thus assumed to be both mainline American religion and normative Christianity.[42] This "Protestant synthesis" dominated the historiography of American religion from the works of Robert Baird (1788-1863) to those of William Warren Sweet (1881-1958) and his successors in the "Chicago School." Its arbitrary, anachronistic character has been made painfully plain by developments since the 1960s. In its stead one now finds a pluralist paradigm, i.e., an interpretive framework congruent with the religiously pluralistic ethos of late twentieth-century America.

In sum: *church* history since the sixties has been secularized and rendered pluralistic, and therewith has been transmuted into *religious*

---

42. The phrase "sheer multifariousness" is S. E. Ahlstrom's in "The Problem," p. 224. Ahlstrom here surveys the traditional "Protestant synthesis," as does J. C. Brauer (see above, note 36).

history. Among the more important consequences of this development are the following:

(1) The discipline continues to bear its traditional name, but this title is now largely honorific since the historian's actual object of study is no longer "the church" in a theological sense. The erstwhile church historian has become a historian of religion—primarily of the Christian religion or Christianity as embodied in the empirical churches (denominations, associations) and their doctrines, creeds, polities, liturgies, missions, etc., as well as in parachurch organizations and transdenominational movements. The discipline also properly includes study of religious communities and groups outside the Christian orbit (history of religions) and, indeed, of all phenomena that may plausibly be designated religious (many of which lack institutional embodiment and ideological articulation). Thus, as Sydney Ahlstrom emphasized, religious history is a "far more comprehensive enterprise" than church history in the old sense.

(2) Normed as it is by the canons of secular historiography, religious history has no way of breaking "the confining circle of immanence" on strictly historical-critical grounds.[43] A historian's belief in God's existence and providence cannot directly enter into the explanation of events, which must be comprehended from within history itself (the natural nexus of cause and effect), though the observable belief of some historical agents that God is acting in their history (and all of history) may properly be invested with explanatory import. The historian's own beliefs may, and no doubt do, influence his or her choice of subject matter, degree of empathy with it, and overarching perspective on it; but one does not rightly expect to be able to tell from the history-as-written whether it has been composed by a believing or an unbelieving historian. The difference that faith makes relates primarily to the historian's understanding of his or her *vocation:* one's calling to speak responsibly and meaningfully to both church and academy, to Jerusalem and Athens, and to bring them into fruitful dialogue. The new religious historiography, in brief, has largely reinstated the old Emertonian position, save that it remains an heir of relativism and so rejects Emerton's naive notion of scientific history, while also rejecting a no less naive relativism that makes all interpretation a matter of competing faiths. The role of subjectivity (presuppositions, hypotheses, points of view) in his-

43. The quoted phrase is from M. E. Marty, "The Difference in Being a Christian and the Difference it Makes—for History," in *History and Historical Understanding,* ed. C. T. McIntire and Ronald A. Wells (Grand Rapids: Eerdmans, 1984), pp. 41-54; citing p. 48. In this same volume, see also R. T. Handy, "Christian Faith and Historical Method: Contradiction, Compromise, or Tension?," pp. 83-91.

tory-as-inquiry is readily granted, but the ideal is that of a *controlled* subjectivity—one regulated by a verifiable appeal to the record of the past, by empirical warrants, and by the rules of simple formal logic.

(3) Church history concerned itself with the Christian community's self-understanding as "people of God." It issued in Christian autobiography (our story), couched in a rhetoric of commitment. Religious history, by contrast, displays a quite different concern, narrative form, and rhetorical style. Thus, in identifying some consequences of the discipline's secularization and speaking as a historian of American religion, Ahlstrom concluded that "the religious historian assumes a new burden—a responsibility for interpreting the moral and spiritual history of the American people."[44] Here the focal concern—while still oriented to communal self-understanding—shifts from church to nation, from people of God to American people, from sacred to profane America, from Christ to culture. The resultant history-as-written is biography (a religious history of the American people), couched in a rhetoric of description. Likewise, the new historiography's shift from the *church* to the *churches* involves a parallel shift from autobiography to biography and from the language of faith to the language about faith. Yet if catholic Christian self-identity and self-knowledge are to be preserved and promoted in a religiously pluralistic culture, there remains a pressing need, it seems, for church histories expressly written for ecumenical Christians by ecumenical Christians out of ecumenical Christian commitments, and unabashedly written in a confessing style. Ironically, the rise and rule of religious history has made a revival of old-style church history a genuine, even urgent desideratum.

(4) Religious history, working out of a pluralist paradigm and focusing on religion and society, is more naturally allied with the social sciences than (as was old-style church history) with intellectual history and the history of theology. Thus the new historiography is often informed, even guided, by the writings of such noted anthropologists and sociologists as Anthony F. C. Wallace, Clifford Geertz, Victor Turner, Peter Berger, Thomas Luckmann, and Robert Bellah. The history of ideas, by contrast, has fallen upon hard times, partly in justifiable reaction to the treatment of ideas, in some older histories, as free-floating, timeless, quasimetaphysical entities. In this connection one should note that Reformation historiography, in particular, has been revolutionized since the 1960s by its disavowal of an earlier "theological captivity" of Reformation research (i.e., a preoccupation with the reformers' doc-

---

44. "The Problem," p. 234. Cf. S. E. Ahlstrom, *A Religious History of the American People* (New Haven: Yale University Press, 1972), p. xiii.

trines), in favor of a social-historical approach that studies the complex links between the reformers' religious message and contemporary social groups in the towns, cities, and territories of the German Empire and Swiss Confederation: all with a view to accounting for the popular reception and spread of Protestantism in its time-specific sociopolitical, economic, and intellectual milieu.[45] This programmatic turn from theological history to social history—so characteristic of religious history *in toto*—is partly attributable to the change in the discipline's primary institutional locus from seminaries to university departments of religion and history. Most of the more recent Ph.D.s in religious studies lack formal, seminary-based theological education. In consequence, as Jaroslav Pelikan has remarked, "young scholars have been entering the field of the history of Christianity without adequate preparation in the biblical, ecclesiastical, liturgical, and theological issues with which, after all, much of that history has been preoccupied, and have therefore been compelled to acquire, only after the doctorate (if then), what seminary graduates used to bring as a prerequisite to graduate study and research."[46]

(5) A pluralist religious history has helped to accord previously marginalized groups their historical due, has thus counteracted elitism, racism, ethnocentrism, sexism in historiography (although the no-longer-marginalized, in turn, may be inclined to their own historiographical triumphalism!). At the same time, the pluralist emphasis on differentiation has served to obscure the presence of pervasive *continuities* in the religious experience of different ecclesial communities (e.g., of northern black Methodists and southern white Baptists, of midwestern Lutherans of German descent and southwestern Mexican-American Catholics). These communities, notwithstanding their rightful claims to distinctiveness, in fact share religious symbols and rites that encode common religious values and viewpoints—a common worldview. To a certain degree, moreover, political communities—not least the American nation itself—share these same symbols (e.g., a monotheistic concept of God). One expects that the new religious historiography will give increasing attention in coming years to this significant phenomenon of unity-in-diversity. (The new historiography ap-

45. Cf. Bernd Moeller, *Imperial Cities and the Reformation: Three Essays*, ed. and trans. H. C. Erik Midelfort and Mark U. Edwards, Jr. (Philadelphia: Fortress, 1972), p. 7: "In the last decades [i.e., prior to 1965] our research has been concentrated almost exclusively on Reformation theology. . . . Consequently, we have frequently lost sight of the Reformation as an event in the distant past and as a complex network of historical relationships."
46. J. Pelikan, "Foreword" to *A Century of Church History*, pp. vii-xi; citing p. x.

pears to require a notion of religious universality akin to that of church catholic in the old historiography.)

(6) So far as theory is concerned, the transformation of church history into religious history has proceeded on the assumption (already operative in Emerton's critique of Schaff) that *any* theological concept of the church is *necessarily* metahistorical, and, hence, methodologically untenable.[47] Yet, strange to say, this key assumption has largely gone *unexamined* by American church and religious historians.[48] Granted, "church" understood in a Schaffian sense as "the divine-human Body of Christ" or "the community of those redeemed by God in Christ" or "the invisible church catholic" is metahistorical. But Christian theology surely knows of other, nonmetahistorical ways of speaking of church: for example, following the Augsburg Confession (1530), as the community of believers called into being and preserved throughout time by the Word (the Gospel or oral proclamation of Jesus Christ as Savior and Lord) and the sacraments (the "visible words" of baptism and the eucharist). Word and sacraments are themselves fully empirical phenomena; yet they are also constitutive of "the church." Church history, accordingly, can properly (on critical-historical grounds) be construed as *the history of the communal handing on and down—the traditioning—of the Christian Gospel,* of the Jesus story, as this continuously occurs in preaching and sacramental observance, in worship and witness (mission), in catechesis and biblical interpretation, etc.

"The church," therefore, does not hover *over* or exist *beyond* "the churches" (as must always be the case when "church" is theologically understood according to the long-favored "visible/invisible" dichotomy); but it is ever present precisely *in* and *with* their distinctive activity of traditioning the Gospel. ("Church," in brief, is not a Platonic construct!) Likewise, "redemption" (God's saving activity) does not occur from *above* as a miraculous divine action interrupting the natural causal nexus; but it transpires from *below* through ordinary, observable "means of grace" (human speech, common water, bread, wine), whenever this traditioned Gospel elicits a response of faith ("I/we believe"). Only faith, to be sure, can "see" and confess that *God* is savingly at work here; but the historian (even an unbelieving one) can observe and describe the *work* itself, i.e., the actual, indispensable traditioning of the Jesus story

47. This assumption is operative throughout W. A. Clebsch's important "History and Salvation: An Essay in Distinctions," in *The Study of Religion in Colleges and Universities,* ed. Paul Ramsey and John F. Wilson (Princeton: Princeton University Press, 1970), pp. 40-72.

48. Cf. D. W. Lotz, "The Crisis in American Church Historiography," *Union Seminary Quarterly Review* 33 (Winter 1978) 67-77.

in a communal setting. Even so, the *church* historian is one whose distinctive vocation it is to know and to narrate just what it is that is always going on *inside* Christian gatherings that both *makes* and *keeps* them what they are, namely, the church catholic. As such, the church historian does not rest content with a description of the churches as social institutions of a religious character; rather, proceeding theologically as well as sociologically, he or she is especially intent upon identifying and describing the church *within* the churches, so far as the former reality manifests itself in the latter's church-creating-and-sustaining activity of traditioning the Gospel through Word and sacraments (and, indeed, through the many evangelical ways of handing on the Christian message).

This model or paradigm of a new-style church history is, I judge, *at once* theological and critical-historical. It thereby serves to obviate any necessary contradiction between "church" and "history." It also promises to overcome the crisis in the discipline occasioned by religious history's loss of "church."

Looking to the future, one reasonably expects that some such reinterpretation of church history will commend itself as the anomalies in the paradigm of religious history become more apparent, above all its seeming incapacity to account for the *sine qua non* nature of the biblical Gospel in making "Christianity" *Christian* and "the churches" *the church*.

Historians, of course, are not prophets. One does not have to be a prophet, however, but only an observant student of history, to predict with confidence that the years ahead will witness, in any case, an ever-changing historiography.

PART THREE

Reflections on Religion in a Changing America

19. The Biblical Life in America: Which Past Fits Us for the Future?

Donald W. Shriver, Jr.

As historians, the majority of authors in this collection share a common anxiety: they have been asked to write about an era that roughly corresponds to their own lifetimes. As a rule of thumb, historians hold that no era is ripe for investigation unless it is at least twenty-five years in the past. They require that long to achieve proper intellectual distance from journalism and autobiography.

The people who compose my own discipline—Christian social ethics—tend to entertain quite the opposite anxiety about the work of historians. While historians want to understand the past, ethicists want to influence the future. Ethics always stands on a line that divides the future from the past; it assumes that human beings will tilt themselves in one direction or another according to perceptions, standards, goals, and meanings that obtain in the present. Ethics, basically, concerns the turns we *should* prefer to take, or to avoid, as we move into the future.

Here there emerges one of the great classic issues of historiography: Should one always seek to disengage his or her account of the past from the biases of the present? One recent historian, George F. Kennan, responds with an unmistakable no.[1] The particular past of which Kennan writes coincides not only with his own lifetime but also with his active participation in its affairs, namely, United States–Soviet relations since 1917. His books on this history ride a tide of great political fear and hope about the future relations of these two countries, which, as Tocqueville discerned a century and a half ago, hold much of the

---

1. George F. Kennan, "History, Literature and the Road to Peterhof," *The New York Times Book Review*, June 29, 1986, p. 42.

world's immediate future in their shaky institutional hands.[2] Kennan offers a passionate moral justification for the project of understanding this history, including its most recent twenty-five years:

> . . . In this bewildering and dangerous age, when the very preservation of civilization has been placed, as though by some angry and impatient deity, in the weak and trembling human hands that have so long ago abused it, what greater cause, what nobler commitment, could there be than *to help people to see themselves as they really are?* And what generation could ever have been more in need of that self-scrutiny, that self-awareness and that self-judgment than the one to which we, poor denizens of the twentieth century, have the fortune, and the misfortune, to belong?[3]

This vision of the historian's vocation allies itself with ethicists' vision of their vocation. The present essay consists of a few suggestions for how historians, especially church historians, and ethicists, especially church-related ethicists, might help each other to help American Christians "see themselves as they really are."

I.

Historical knowledge and perspective do not belong constitutionally to all versions of ethical discourse, but it seems impossible to dub an ethic "Christian" without implying its historical roots. An unavoidable methodological question for Christian ethicists, however, will always be: *Which* history is normative for Christian ethics? What strains of church and world history compose the core by which the other strains are to be understood and evaluated?

No theological ethicist of the mid-twentieth century focused this question more astutely than did H. Richard Niebuhr. In his writing and teaching, Niebuhr regularly sought to alert his students to the historical tendency of all Christian theologians to live, work, and have their intellectual being in more than one communal history. Characteristically, he observed, biblicist Protestants—scorning the dual authority of "Scripture and Tradition" in Roman Catholicism—have proceeded to rely on their own community's tradition, which functions powerfully in their interpretation of the Bible. In American history, that community has often shifted from a Reformation church to an allegedly reformed nation—the American people.

---

2. Cf. Alexis de Tocqueville, *Democracy in America,* ed. J. P. Mayer, trans. George Lawrence (Garden City: Doubleday, 1969), pp. 412-13.

3. Kennan, p. 42 (emphasis added).

American church history is replete with illustrations of this tendency, as documented at length by Robert T. Handy in his classic *A Christian America,* which shows that nineteenth-century Protestants embarked on a crusade to bring the people and the institutions of the United States under the suzerainty of *the* Christian ethic. Ever and again this mighty project stumbled over two obstacles: the gathering religious pluralism of this nation, whose resemblance to a Protestant preserve was steadily eroding, and the doubt that Protestant prescriptions for American life assuredly accorded with ancient Christian standards. Many late-nineteenth-century church programs for "cleaning up" the politics of the new cities, for example, looked like an attempt to keep old-line Anglo-Saxon elites in control over and against newly arriving south Europeans. Anglo-Saxon racism often hovered in the background of these programs. Towering over all, however, was a supremely confident nationalism, a belief that the United States of America was a modern version of ancient Israel, a people chosen to bring enlightenment, civilization, and democracy to the rest of the world.[4]

The upshot of analyses such as those of Niebuhr and Handy is that every particular proposal for a Christian ethical stance in American society has been born of at least double parentage: a particular recollection of the Bible and a particular interpretation of the American nation itself. "New Israel" has been a persistent theme in Protestant Christian-European reflection on their settlement of these shores since at least 1620. Down to Ronald Reagan, American presidents have rung changes on the powerful, religiously tinged notion of Lincoln that the United States is "the last best hope" of the nations. Nothing less than binocular vision accounts for what Protestant Americans have thought about the meaning of the American segment of world history.

Often enough they have retained a third lens: that of a specific denominational or theological tradition drawn from portions of church history that appear esoteric to those who do not share them. For example, notorious among historians is the persistent (and sectarian) Protestant tendency to skip lightly over the thousand years of church history between Constantine and the Protestant Reformation. Here, "real" church history, after biblical times, concerns the increasing corruption of early church devotion to the Gospel, a corruption not decisively cured in principle until the time of the sixteenth-century reformers. Normative church history arrives with the Reformation, and this view leads easily to the notion that the "New World" is the new base of

---

4. Robert T. Handy, *A Christian America: Protestant Hopes and Historical Realities* (New York: Oxford University Press, 1971).

Gospel advance in the world at large. As late as 1981, Jerry Falwell was sure that the United States is God's chosen instrument for keeping the church free to preach the Gospel to the whole world and for protecting the state of Israel until the Last Times. In these opinions Falwell was not out of step with many a "mainline" nineteenth-century perspective recorded in *A Christian America.*[5]

If, in their ethical reflection, Christians appropriate not only a history, but multiple histories, whether doing so wittingly or not, the question of how these histories *should* relate to each other is unavoidable for the academic ethicist. Some historians may try to bypass this question in the name of scholarly objectivity. Others, like Kennan, may explicitly ally themselves with ethicists in making this question a focus of their methodological reflections. In any event, identification of the multiple histories of any contemporary Christian ethical claim may be an indispensable service of the church historian to the church ethicist. In turn, a service of the ethicist to the churches has to be a relentless inquiry, preliminary to every specific ethical deliberation, for answers to the question: "What have we learned from our past that fits us for ethical deliberation as that past becomes a part of a different future?"

These observations suggest that all Christian ethical reflection involves three "timely" components, namely, (1) some continuity with what Christians believed and did in the past, (2) some discontinuity with the same on the basis of contemporary judgment about the inadequacy of "ancient good" when measured by the unrealized ancient norms themselves, and (3) an interpretation, including new norms, that takes account of something unprecedented in the present moment, heavy with portent for the future. The first two components commit the ethicist to intrachurchly debate over the nature of the "real" norms associated with the faith of Christians. Typically, this means raising old normative questions that are never out of date: "Did the ancient standards take full account of the whole Bible? The teachings of Jesus? The beliefs of the early church, whether or not recorded in the Bible?" It also may mean pitting one period of church history normatively against another: "Did the reformers of the sixteenth century understand the meaning of human work better than did the medieval monastics?" And implicitly this may involve the acknowledgment that (as John Robinson told the Pilgrims in 1620) "God has yet more light to break forth from His Holy Word." That is, the Holy Spirit illumines some generations of believers in ways different from the illumination accorded other generations.

---

5. Cf. "An Interview with the Lone Ranger of American Fundamentalism," *Christianity Today* 25/15 (September 4, 1981) 22-31.

All such questions involve a mixture of claims, normative and empirical, drawn from certain readings of church and general history. Christians are not unique in their dependence upon such a mixture. Jews rely on a formally similar mixture when they tie their current ethical reflections to the Hebrew Bible, the Talmudic and Mishnaic writings, and their reading of the millennia-long experience of the Jewish people. But a uniquely difficult, not to say upsetting question in all such reasoning, inside a historically oriented religious community, arises in connection with the third component. *What do we have to learn from this present moment in history for which no precedent suffices to illumine us? What does our present experience teach us about the traditional norms that still bind us?*

These questions suggest a formal way to describe a historically conscious and conscientious Christian ethical method. For those who cherish regularity and order in ethical method, the most disturbing element in this proposed method is its expectation, paralleled in much historiography, that knowledge in the present can upset previous "knowledge" of the past, or can at least invest that previous knowledge with a new and heretofore unappreciated significance. In this context it is not so much that "new occasions teach new duties" as that they equip people in the present to understand what was happening in the past better than the people of the past could have understood it. Not superiority, but a new point for viewing, attends human experience here.

II.

What might such an analysis of Christian ethical method have to do with ethical thinking in American church history during the period 1935-1985? My thesis is that the past fifty years have seen significant— not to say portentous—changes in "mainline" church thinking on three crucial themes in American society, and that these changes consist, in part, of new church viewpoints prompted by the new historical occasions of this era. As Edward Long's essay above demonstrates abundantly, more than three themes have dominated American Christian ethical reflection during these years. My purpose here is not to deal comprehensively but illustratively with the phenomenon that, on some issues central to the life of Americans, the churches have undergone something of a collective change of mind. In a historical as well as a moral sense, human beings never quite "know what they do." It remains for their descendants to understand something of what they did that they themselves could not have understood. One could speak here of the similarity of theology and history to science: scientists ask their successors to improve on, even refute, their discoveries.

Ingrained conservatives, inside and outside the Christian movement, may blame the mainline "liberal" churches for too much mind-changing on ethical issues; but vital religious commitment in these churches will always remind their critics that "change of mind" and "repentance" translate the same word in New Testament Greek. "Think that you may be wrong" is as good a rule for contemporary Protestants as it was for Cromwell's contentious Scots. For illustration, I will trace briefly what these churches have tended to say publicly, and in their own deliberations, on three major themes in American society in the past half-century: (a) war, (b) poverty, and (c) pluralism. In all three illustrations my principal interest will be to discern the catalytic impact of major events on the way official church bodies conducted their ethical reflection, especially on the way they used old standards, via this new experience, to come to new conclusions.

a. War

The American republic was born in war, and the majority of church people in this country have not been pacifist. Among some of the churches pacifism has survived as one of three ethical critiques of warfare, but the other two theories—the Just War and the Crusade—have tended to dominate. In the period 1935-1985, few advocates of the crusading spirit could be found among the major historic "public" churches, with the possible exception of some "new evangelicals" who in the 1980s saw the United States, with its nuclear weapons, as the protector of the churches' freedom to evangelize. To find the theory and enthusiasm of the crusade, one has to return to the America of 1917-18.

Disillusion with the results of American participation in the "Great War" had set in for large segments of the public by the 1930s, and pacifism, along with resurgent isolationism, gained new favor among liberal church leaders during this decade. Harry Emerson Fosdick and (early on) even Reinhold Niebuhr took this stance. As the Second World War was beginning, a politic Franklin Roosevelt sought a third term as president by assuring the country that he would not lead it into war. Against the tide of pacifism and isolationism the voice of a mind-changed Reinhold Niebuhr spoke often and loudly in these latter years; but his advocacy of violent defense of justice against violent injustice did not prevail among mainline church leaders until the climactic event that turned the entire American public toward that view: Pearl Harbor.

Few if any official church bodies in the early forties criticized the unanimous American resolve to rid the world of the menace of totalitarianism in its German, Italian, and Japanese versions. Fueled by a sense that the institutions of democracy and the very existence of the nation were at stake, the churches supported the war effort almost without exception. But they did so with a sobriety that distinguished them and the country at large from the outburst of patriotism that greeted U.S. entry into the war of 1917. This time, "preachers" were not so ready to "present arms." Instead they supported the war in terms well represented in the so-called Calhoun Report of 1943-44, authored by a committee of some two dozen seminary theologians, chaired by Robert Calhoun of Yale Divinity School, and including a mixture of pacifist and just war advocates such as Roland Bainton, Douglas Steere, Reinhold Niebuhr, and H. Richard Niebuhr.

This long report contained memorable moral distinctions between degrees of justification and guilt for the prosecution of international war. Memorable also were the overtones and explicit themes of neo-orthodox theology:

> [One] can still be a devoted patriot if the well-being of [one's] nation is clearly seen to be inseparable from the well-being of the wider society and its members. But this is different from the patriotism of the unawakened nationalist.
>
> Without minimizing the fateful consequences of the policies and decisions of the Axis governments, we can say that war comes not because the people on both sides deliberately will it, but because enough people on each side willed, half-gropingly, half-wittingly, their own apparent advantage without due regard to the obligations of human community and divine order.
>
> What thus came to horrid fruitage in the war had its roots, once again, in the behavior of [people] and nations before the war broke out. Hideous brutalities, cold-blooded treacheries, cowardly evasions, callous stupidities—all these and more we must charge against our present enemies, our allies, and ourselves in varying proportions during the years of miscalled peace. . . . Though all were involved in sin, their ways of sinning were not identical in the sight of God, we believe, nor in their portent for the common life. . . . In the actual course of events, dominance by the Axis powers would have fastened upon their own peoples and upon conquered lands a reign of tyranny and terror full of danger to human living everywhere. Resistance to such rule, whether by armed force or by more peaceful means, became imperative.

The report ended with an imperative hope: "World society must become world community."[6]

So, though preachers flocked during World War II to military chaplaincy, though theological schools trained chaplains, and though local churches adorned sanctuaries with "Christian" and American flags, support of war this time was grim rather than bombastic. Most church people understood Reinhold Niebuhr's point about the ambiguity of ethical violence: "Christians may sometimes have to carry guns, but they will do so with a heavy heart."[7] If World War II was the last "good" war in twentieth-century American experience, it was mostly so as a necessary evil rather than as a crusade.

Seldom in the war years did any church body take upon itself the task of criticizing the methods by which the war was prosecuted — an important element of just war theory. A few Christian individuals and an occasional church body raised questions about the internment of Japanese civilians, the obliteration bombings of 1945, and the dropping of the atomic bomb; but, on the whole, the churches rallied unambiguously to the national cause. When on June 6, 1944, the president, announcing the allied invasion of Europe, invited Americans to join with him in an extended prayer to the God of Righteousness for victory, few ministers across the land failed to join their congregations in that prayer. Indeed, the rhetoric of religion, like the rhetoric of the politicians, escalated in its righteous fervor as the war proceeded.[8]

During the next forty years, what happened to religious feeling and religious argument in relation to war? For the first fifteen years after 1945, one might say that Reinhold Niebuhr's view came into its own. His careful balancing of power against power, social justice against personal love, seemed to be an ethic whose time had come, reflecting as it did the lessons of World War II for pacifist and isolationist America, now faced with another competitor in the shape of the Soviet Union. Enunciated by solid Presbyterians in government like John Foster Dulles and by the vigorous new mass evangelism of Billy Graham, re-

6. Cf. Ray H. Abrams, *Preachers Present Arms: The Role of American Churches and Clergy in World Wars I and II with some Observations on the War in Vietnam* (Scottsdale, PA: Herald Press, 1969). For the quotations from the Calhoun Report, see "The Relation of the Church to the War in the Light of the Christian Faith," in *Creeds of the Churches*, ed. John H. Leith (Garden City: Doubleday, 1963), pp. 546, 548, 550-51, 554.

7. Like many of Niebuhr's aphorisms, this entered my memory long ago, and I cannot locate its printed source.

8. For a local illustration of this escalation in the rhetoric of churches and community news media, see John D. Earle, Dean D. Knudsen, and Donald W. Shriver, Jr., *Spindles and Spires: A Restudy of Religion and Social Change in Gastonia* (Atlanta: John Knox, 1976), pp. 60-61.

ligious reasons for opposing communism were never lacking in religious gatherings of the fifties. With the coming of the "Korean Conflict" in the early fifties, however, most Americans began to experience war in a new mode. For the first time in its history the United States had determined to become a worldwide military power, in reluctant response to the threats of communism. But confronting that threat in Korea was quite unlike confronting Germans on the beaches of Normandy. As the "police action" of the United Nations dragged on, debate about the necessity of this undoubted war seethed in the country at large; and, almost for the first time in their history, Americans stood baffled before the complexities of their unprecedented military strength, the limits on that strength that could be imposed by a large undeveloped Asian country, the further limits imposed by the new reality of nuclear weaponry, and the difference between the "new civilization" of communism and the "corrupt civilization" of Nazism. Meantime, in deference to some of these new realities, Reinhold Niebuhr himself was changing his opinion about the tenability of the new sort of war America had pioneered: nuclear war.[9] Against much in their national tradition, Americans now found themselves engaged in global power struggles but unable to promote their interests and values unambiguously anywhere.

An age of limit, compromise, frustration, and even defeat in war was about to dawn ironically in (what Henry Luce had called) the "American century." Most Americans were not ready for the change, as would be painfully documented in the struggle inside churches to come to grips with the ambiguities of the Vietnam War of the sixties. By the end of this decade, most mainline church bodies had joined in opposing this war, but their path to doing so was as beset by ethical and political agony as that of the politicians. Theological ethicists in the sixties tested this war by the standards of just war theory. Some found it met the standards;[10] others found it wanting by the same tests.[11] Often, in less disciplined ways, debates within church bodies touched on the same implicit ques-

---

9. Cf. *Christianity and Crisis*, Nov. 13, 1961, p. 202; March 19, 1962, p. 38; April 2, 1962, p. 48; and *Union Seminary Quarterly Review* 17 (March 1962) 239-42, as quoted in Richard Fox, *Reinhold Niebuhr: A Biography* (New York: Pantheon, 1985), p. 278.

10. Most notable exponent of the Just War theory was Paul Ramsey. Cf. his *War and the Christian Conscience: How Shall Modern War be Conducted Justly?* (Durham: Duke University Press, 1961) and *The Just War: Force and Political Responsibility* (New York: Scribner's, 1968).

11. John C. Bennett became the leading critic of the Vietnam War among Christian ethicists of the era. Cf. his *Foreign Policy in Christian Perspective* (New York: Scribner's, 1966) and his earlier edited work, *Nuclear Weapons and the Conflict of Conscience* (New York: Scribner's, 1962).

tions: Was the government of South Vietnam an object of unjust invasion by the North, or was this a civil war irrelevant to territorial imperatives? Is the expenditure of American and Vietnamese life and treasure proportional to the human gains to be expected from victory in the war? In such a war is it possible to discriminate between civilian and military targets? Is it possible for the United States to win such a war at all? Does it have any major national interest in doing so?

Debate on these questions, all appropriate to just war theory, simmered in church assemblies of this period, producing perplexity, troubled patriotism, and equally troubled consciences. Notably lacking in these debates, and in the documents that came from them, were the naive enthusiasms of World War I or the sober confidences of World War II. Large numbers of Americans inside and outside the churches began to suspect that it was wrong, unpatriotic, and against the national interest to support this war. Add length of years and looming defeat to the political-moral calculus, and American Christians had an unprecedented theological surmise to ponder: Was God warring against the Americans in this war? Many a voice from the churches of the world joined in fortifying this contention.[12]

Although no radically new ethical critique of warfare emerged among the churches in any of these debates, new prominence was accorded one old and one new variation on the just war theory: (1) conscientious objection to a particular war and (2) nuclear pacifism. The former emerged as an agonizing issue of debate among those local pastors and families who had to cope with the determination of some of their young parishioners to avoid participating in the Vietnam War. The pacifist tradition and the law that sustains the military exemptions of pacifists have never sanctioned selective nonparticipation in war. Public protest and intrachurch debate on U.S. military policy left a new residue of sympathy for the particular-war viewpoint, however, just as reflection on nuclear weaponry brought some individuals and church bodies to the "nuclear pacifist" positions. This position is perhaps misnamed, for many of its advocates brought nuclear war to the bar of just war theory and found it wanting by that very measure.[13]

12. Two meetings of the World Council of Churches in this period amplified these voices: the one, the 1966 World Conference on Church and Society in Geneva, and the other, the Fourth Assembly of the W.C.C. in Uppsala in 1968, overwhelmingly rejected U.S. involvement in the war.

13. The best summation of the 1960s debate in the churches and among Christian ethicists is Ralph B. Potter, *War and Moral Discourse* (Richmond: John Knox, 1969). See the biographical essay at the end of this book, pp. 87-123, as well as the clear analysis of the major positions in Edward LeRoy Long, Jr., *War and Conscience in America* (Philadelphia: Westminster, 1968).

In 1985, American defeat in Vietnam remained an undigested irritant in the body politic. While major church groups and assemblies did their part in pushing for the national consensus that finally pulled Americans out of the war, church reflection on "the lessons of Vietnam" seems rare. The one exception, in 1985, was widespread criticism by the churches of U.S. government policy in Nicaragua, where they found, along with many Congressional critics, the shadow of "another Vietnam" looming large. Some evangelical church bodies found the anti-communist rhetoric of the early fifties still useful here, but other churches exhibited caution, high regard for empirical investigation, and fear of old-style North American imperialism in Central America.[14] The Vietnamese experience, if it did nothing else, taught many church members to look beneath the surface of the government's claims about its military policies.

The great new political circumstance, looming over all post-1945 wars of the republic, has been the world's burgeoning nuclear weapon systems. But some thirty-five years of the nuclear age would pass before major church bodies collected their thoughts about nuclear weapons into major public statements, which, in turn, helped launch major new programs for "peacemaking" in the churches. Three statements in the early 1980s—Presbyterian, Roman Catholic, and Methodist—all agonized over the unprecedented threat of nuclear weapon systems to human existence itself, and all weighed facts of those systems in the balance of the just war theory. Though the Catholic bishops, in the final draft of their "Pastoral Letter," allowed nuclear deterrence a tentative place on the basis of this theory, the Methodist bishops declared the very existence of nuclear weapons a sin against God and a crime against humanity.[15]

The contrast with 1945 was stark. Then, few church leaders protested the dropping of the first atomic bombs.[16] Now, with 50,000 bombs in place, many, even Billy Graham, concluded that the invention

14. One exemplification is supplied by the papers and debates on U.S. policy in Central America of the 1983 General Assembly of the Presbyterian Church, U.S.A. Cf. *Minutes* (New York: Office of the General Assembly, 475 Riverside Drive, New York, NY 10115).

15. See the three statements: *Peacemaking: The Believer's Calling* (New York: United Presbyterian Church, 1980); *The Challenge of Peace: God's Promise and Our Response,* in *Origins* 13/1 (Washington, D.C.: National Catholic Documentary Service, May 1983); and *In Defense of Creation* (Washington, D.C.: United Methodist Church, 1986).

16. In 1946 the Federal Council of Churches reconvened the "Calhoun" commission, a majority of whose twenty-two members deemed the Hiroshima and Nagasaki bombings "morally indefensible." Cf. Federal Council of Churches, "Atomic Warfare and the Christian Faith" (New York, 1946), and Reinhold Niebuhr, "The Atom Bomb," *Church and Society* 10 (Fall 1945) 4.

of this weapon had been a great human mistake.[17] Equally mistaken, said all these statements, is the view of apocalyptically inclined evangelicals who see nuclear weapons as instruments of God's own ending of human history: Why should the creator God revealed in Jesus need nuclear bombs for ending or preserving the world? To suppose *that* is to make an idol of the human capacity for destruction and to sanctify the demonic. With striking clarity, this debate demonstrated how very old theology and very new human history have mingled, clashed, and issued in unprecedented questions in the modern ethical deliberation of American churches.

b. Poverty and affluence

Few people on earth have told their national story so consistently as one of progress from poverty to wealth as have Americans. With their Protestant ethic of work, their this-worldly sense of divine calling, and their access to exploitable land and other resources, many European settlers of North America came here with an abiding hatred of poverty and an abiding ambition for wealth. These feelings were often couched in religious terms. It has always been difficult for Americans to believe that a person could display the dignity of a child of God apart from economically productive work and its reward, wealth. When joblessness and intransigent poverty struck large numbers of Americans in the 1930s, therefore, the shock had religious dimensions. For the most part the churches had minimal public wisdom to offer for saving the dignity of lives caught in the grip of the Great Depression. Again, the voice that many began reluctantly to hear on the subject of the new poverty was that of Reinhold Niebuhr, who, against the tradition of individualistic economic achievement, analyzed individual suffering as derivative from webs of social-institutional injustice. In this he drew extensively from Marxist perspectives.

In the thirties white Protestant church bodies were filled with constituents ambivalent about or hostile to the Roosevelt New Deal. In their occasional public expressions on the subject, however, the churches were likely to concede that central government now had some responsibility for keeping Americans out of poverty—whether by jobs, minimum wage law, retirement income, and public works, or by protecting the right to join unions.[18] All these measures conflicted with

17. Said Graham: "I honestly wish we had never developed nuclear weapons." As quoted in *Pastoral Care Network for Social Responsibility Newsletter* 3/4 (April 1986).
18. For a sample of writings from this period by theologians sympathetic to the New Deal, many of them influenced by Reinhold Niebuhr, see William Scarlett, ed., *Chris-*

Protestant traditions of work and individual initiative. And the real "solution" to the Depression—World War II—conflicted with the same traditions. Hardly equipped by heritage to mount serious economic analysis and ethical critique of economic systems, the Protestant churches carried with them into the post-war era the old set of individualistic economic ethics.[19] The post-war economy would soon seem newly hospitable to that old individualism.

For the next twenty-five years the nation seemed invulnerable to another major depression. Korea, even Vietnam, seemed to fuel, not diminish, rising prosperity. The true middle-classing of America was at hand, sweeping all but a decreasing percentage of the population into home ownership, salaries with fringe benefits, and a growing share in American economic dominance of the world marketplace. Liberal church support gathered for the Lyndon Johnson "War on Poverty" but was largely silent on the dangers of inflation arising from the real war in Vietnam. Church participation in this era of unprecedented affluence consisted of enormous outlays for new church construction in the new suburbs; expansion of staffs and programs on all organizational levels for ministries to diverse age groups, locales, and social crisis areas such as inner cities; a rise in the sense of professionalism among clergy, with accompanying salary expectations; and a new concern, among the most internationally sensitive leaders of the churches, for the ethical question: What is the obligation of Christians, in a situation of rising affluence, to the majority of their world neighbors situated in poverty? An affluent era put this question on the ethical agenda of the churches. Liberation theologies, in the seventies, helped keep it there.

Debate on the world poverty issue frequently focused on church contribution to economic development in the poorer countries of the world. Many liberal church leaders urged the U.S. government to

---

tianity Takes a Stand (New York: Penguin, 1946). On the tendency of many unemployed and destitute people of the Depression era to blame themselves for their misfortunes, see Studs Terkel, *Hard Times: An Oral History of the Great Depression* (New York: Pantheon, 1970). On the ambivalence of church bodies toward the New Deal, see Kenneth K. Bailey, *Southern White Protestantism in the Twentieth Century* (New York: Harper and Row, 1964), pp. 114-15.

19. For all its putative contributions to the "Protestant ethic" in capitalist America, Protestantism has never developed a systemative economic ethic in relation to the working of large modern economic systems, a point made repeatedly in Reinhold Niebuhr's *Moral Man and Immoral Society* (New York: Scribner's, 1932). Cf. R. H. Tawney, *Religion and the Rise of Capitalism* (New York: Harcourt, Brace and World, 1926); Max Weber, *The Protestant Ethic and the Spirit of Capitalism* (New York: Scribner's, 1958); (especially) Liston Pope, *Millhands and Preachers: A Study of Gastonia* (New Haven: Yale University Press, 1942); and Earle, Knudsen, Shriver (above, note 8).

strengthen its economic rather than its military aid to these countries. Meantime, a new philosophy of missionary work in these churches had encouraged partnership for economic development with indigenous churches. Only slowly did the politically and economically astute among these leaders begin to question the effect of both government and church economic programs upon fundamental causes of poverty in Asia, Africa, and Latin America. Precisely the same causes, some began to suspect, were at work inside the United States: obsolescence of industries in a changing international marketplace; resulting loss of jobs; educational requirements for work in sophisticated industries that poor people, by definition, could not meet; and economic decisions affecting millions made by multinational corporations loyal to the needs of no nation in particular.

Like students who led the protest against the Vietnam War in the late sixties, most church people and leaders of this 1950-1970 era assumed the continuation of relative affluence in America. Protest they might against the uses of this unprecedented prosperity by corporations, governments, individuals, and churches themselves. Assume it they did, little suspecting that a war-related inflation rate, quadruple OPEC oil prices, and hugely successful foreign industrial competition lay immediately ahead. Hardly settled in their new affluence, middle-class Americans were unsettled by the economy of the seventies. From the viewing point of the eighties, a return to that affluence was not in sight. In 1985 only unshakable devotees of the American dream were sure that such prosperity would ever return.

When they write the church history of the 1970s, historians will locate the rise of the so-called new evangelicals in a context that includes these economic anxieties along with the assaults on American political prestige during these years. Evangelicals made their militant entry into American politics in the seventies. Many saw the "mainline liberal" churches as intimidated into passivity before the economic and political traumas of the era. One manifest reason for the rise of evangelical patriotism was the ongoing multiple assault upon the collective American ego: Vietnam, OPEC, inflation, foreign competition, unemployment, slipping middle-class security, the Iranian hostage crisis, and declining certainty that the U.S.A. can dominate the world in any sense whatsoever, in spite of its continuing wealth and military might. Only in the post-1945 era had the majority of U.S. citizens begun to rest comfortably with the idea that their country was by might and right a world power. Only in the post-1970 era have they had to cope with an array of severe world challenges to this idea. One response to these challenges has been the reassertion, by evangelicals, of old American claims to moral superiority, economic ambition, and political will sufficient to overcome the nation's "enemies."

Though the "public" churches may not yet have found a consistent voice for addressing this range of public anxiety, it was evident, in 1985, that their ethically reflective leaders were at work on quite a different response—one crafted in part from some careful listening to the critics of America in churches around the world. This openness accounts for some of the opprobrium that critics of the public churches heap upon them: "Who can trust members of the World Council of Churches to say what is just and good for the people of the United States in their relations with other peoples of the world?" In fact, leaders associated with the National Council of Churches often felt biblically obligated, in the new "global village," to listen to their Christian colleagues across the world as diligently as to their patriotic evangelical neighbors at home.

The ethical counsel of extra-American churches tends to be painful for Americans of all ecclesiastical stripes, for the gist of the world church message seems to be: The time of your dominance of the world was brief; let it be over! Your share of the world's resources has been disproportionate; let it decline! Your national affluence was bought in some measure by your ability to buy cheap and sell dear in world markets; let others buy cheap and sell dear for a change! Christians among you experience guilt because they live in an island of affluence amid a sea of poverty; let Asian competition be a sign that even through markets God can bring justice to nations other than your own! For long you have been proud to be a generous nation; now be content that economic justice, however painful, is better than charity, however great![20]

In 1985 an ethic of national self-denial, deference to the needs and powers of international competitors, and consent to declining affluence had not yet taken definitive shape in the documents or other public utterances of denominational and ecumenical agencies. But such an ethical stance is in the making. It draws on ancient themes of social justice in the Hebrew prophets and in the teachings of Jesus. It criticizes the accumulation of wealth in anyone's hands alongside anyone's poverty. This ancient biblical norm of justice, fitfully asserted in American church history by such theologians as Walter Rauschenbusch and

20. These themes were frequently sounded in many a gathering of the World Council of Churches, especially in the years 1966, 1968, 1975, and 1983. For example, see the papers preparatory to the Geneva Conference on Church and Society (1966), *Economic Growth in World Perspective*, ed. Denys Munby (New York: Association, 1966). American theologians of "liberation" were deeply influenced by these meetings.

Reinhold Niebuhr, found new expression in the early seventies in black theology and various forms of liberation theology. Large differences loomed between those open to such perspectives and the "new evangelicals." Evangelicals espoused an "America first" position; black and liberation theologies insisted that the United States had to see itself as but one nation among others. The difference was very large, and by 1985 the dividing line between the two positions was theologically, politically, and economically momentous. Crucial to the entire discussion was the moral and theological meaning of the American economic experience during the two hundred years since the nation's founding. Are we justly or unjustly rich? Debate on this question is far from over in any of the churches of the land.

c. Pluralism and the American national identity

The paradox of religion in the United States, noted at least as long ago as Tocqueville, is that religion flourishes here under an institutional structure that makes it legally separate from government and barred from special privilege.[21] Nonetheless, ever and again, including the period 1935-1985, organized religion has risen to public influence. The recent upsurge of evangelical participation in American politics is only the latest example of this phenomenon. In the early eighties some evangelical leaders claimed that they represented a new majority of American Protestants—60 million—a figure that George Gallup reduced to 30 million. (In 1985 the thirty-one member churches of the National Council of Churches had a total membership of 40 million, and Roman Catholic Americans numbered some 52 million.[22])

Multiple possible interpretations of such statistics lay in the background of Sydney Ahlstrom's statement, in his landmark history published in 1972, that the year 1968 marked the end of the Protestant "establishment" in the religious life of the United States.[23] In that year, not only was there new interest in nonwestern religions among adherents of the campus "counter culture," but by then it was apparent that with the exception of Martin Luther King, Jr., no religious leader or institution in America could speak confidently about public policy in ways that drew together classic religious concepts and classic American political philosophy. In the early eighties, Martin Marty described "mainline" denomina-

21. Cf. Tocqueville, p. 47.
22. Cf. *1985 Yearbook of American Churches,* Office of Research, National Council of Churches (New York, 1986), pp. 247, 90.
23. Sydney E. Ahlstrom, *A Religious History of the American People,* 2 vols. (Garden City: Doubleday, 1975), 2:612ff.

tions and congregations as representing a "public church" that brought together people of diverse theological, ideological, and social opinion. In contrast to the alleged sectarian uniformity of the "evangelicals," the public church affirmed a profound unity in face of profound diversity. Such a church, implied Marty, is analogous to and supportive of the democratic concept of a public open to many opinions and cultures.[24]

From the Puritans on, accommodation by American Protestants to growing public diversity has seldom been enthusiastic. From the nineteenth century into the twentieth, leaders of major Protestant groups could still hope for a "Christian America" in face of historical realities already contradicting this hope. In the late seventies their view was republished by many vocal evangelical leaders who seemed unaware of the evidence for Ahlstrom's thesis that the day of their hegemony in America was over, too.

Perhaps no trend in the period 1935-1985 among American churches has been more pervasive than the growing diversity of religious bodies, religious claims urged as public policy, and religions as such. In no other period have the churches had to think of "freedom," "democracy," and "justice" in reference to so startling a diversity of groups clamoring for the right and the power to define these values in the nation of the future: blacks, Hispanics, Asians, women, the handicapped, Buddhists, Muslims, Hindus, agnostics, and varieties galore of Christians.

In another of his striking proposals for understanding the role of religion in America, Ahlstrom says that church historians may eventually come to appreciate that the religious group which came closest to being "a paradigm of restoration" of authentic Christianity in America has been black Protestantism.[25] These churches, Ahlstrom suggests, have brought an integration to American religious life more profound than the integration sought by the civil rights movement. They have combined personal religion and social relevancy, church integrity and public witness.

Recently, Robert Bellah and his colleagues have echoed Ahlstrom's view of the exceptional combination of church and public leadership in the career of Martin Luther King, Jr. Under his leadership, they say, the civil rights movement "explicitly aimed at broadening and strengthening effective membership in the national community, involving biblical and republican themes on an international as well as

24. Martin E. Marty, *The Public Church: Mainline-Evangelical-Catholic* (New York: Crossroad, 1981).

25. Cf. Ahlstrom, 1:40-41.

national level." The movement "called upon Americans to transform their social and economic institutions with the goal of building a just national community that would respect both the differences and the interdependence of its members. It did this by combining biblical and republican themes in a way that included, but transformed, the culture of individualism."[26]

This combination was abundantly evident in King's now famous "I Have a Dream" oration at the March on Washington in August 1963. Americans find that speech memorable precisely because it fitted together themes that so often fall apart in the rhetoric of religious leaders seeking to address public issues in the United States: belief in God, the Gospel of God's love for all persons, the freedoms of the democratic tradition, the freedom to be different from one's neighbors, and the freedom to love one's neighbor in his or her differences from oneself. Who else in the period 1935-1985 had integrated these themes as eloquently and as convincingly as had this black Baptist minister? And who else, in the church history of this period, had proven themselves more qualified as teachers of what pluralism really means—in terms at once Christian and democratic—than the leaders of the American black churches? If the variety of human experience, including religious experience, is to combine with a common social loyalty in pluralistic America, some such synthesis of religious and democratic thought is required. By their experience of being shoved to the sidelines of this national society, black Americans may be the minority best equipped to help the majority know what a democratic society really looks like.

At their democratic best, Americans have defined their country as a home for people of all nations. In their service to democracy, Christian Americans have proclaimed the biblical promise of a universal, loving, just human community without national boundary. Early and late in our history, the tension between universal humanism and national community has seldom been honestly and clearly identified, even inside American churches. At their nationalistic worst, patriots of every stripe have regularly reverted to some form of "chosen people" analogy. Often this chauvinism has been fueled by churches that identified themselves so fully with an ethnic, racial, or ideological past that their public role came down to protecting the integrity of the past from dilution by "foreign" immigrants. But the most nearly biblical side of the American dream has always been that "with God there is no respect

---

26. Robert N. Bellah, Richard Madsen, William N. Sullivan, Ann Swidler, and Steven M. Tipton, *Habits of the Heart: Individualism and Commitment in American Life* (Berkeley: University of California Press, 1985), pp. 213, 249.

of persons," and that with democracy there should be none also. Tocqueville, with his usual ironic wisdom, saw religion as the one force in the equalitarian democratic ethos that countered its natural tendency to "isolate men from each other so that each thinks only of himself." Democracy encourages individualism; religion promotes a world community that draws its adherents away from merely "thinking about themselves."

> Thus religious peoples are naturally strong just at the point where democratic peoples are weak. And that shows how important it is for people to keep their religion when they become equal.[27]

Protecting Americans from each other and from the world was a poor vocation for the churches in isolationist 1935; it was increasingly impossible in 1985. In that year, Presbyterians in New York acknowledged that the fast-growing congregations in their local presbytery were Korean; Lutherans in New York, that their two largest congregations were black and Chinese, respectively; Methodists in Los Angeles, that their church services, on any given Sunday in the metropolitan area, used a total of twenty-four languages; Roman Catholics in Chicago, that in some neighborhoods no priest could function without a knowledge of Spanish; and Missouri Synod Lutherans in Peoria, that the Gospel and recent American history required then to open doors to refugee families from Vietnam.

Perhaps no general issue of social meaning demands more courageous, careful reflection among American Christians in the late eighties than does this: What does it mean to be Christian and American? In the past fifty years, the question itself may not have changed radically, but the conditions and the urgencies for asking it have multiplied. The answers may not be more difficult than they were in 1935, but they are now more urgent because the American Christian today is inescapably a part of a much larger world.

27. Tocqueville, pp. 444-45.

20. Religion at the Core of American Culture

John F. Wilson

In the last half-century there have been immense changes in American Christianity as well as more generally in religion in America. The history of this period is complex, consisting of partly realized dreams and failed expectations, of morally sensitive leaders and frustrated crusades, of individual idealism and weakness as well as collective power. No less has the writing about religion in American history, the historiography, been complex and diversified, for it has both registered the changes and searched for new and more adequate ways to interpret them.

Robert T. Handy has been both churchman and historian, at once involved with the sweep of events and one of their notable interpreters, placing especially American Christianity in the larger perspectives of national and finally world history. This volume, which pays tribute to him, inevitably addresses both the history and the historiography of these years. In responding to both, this essay will explore the relationship between the last half-century of religion and culture in America and the much larger question of cultural identity in America, especially as it may be presented in a religious idiom.

How may we adequately frame this discussion? Any exploration of a tumultuous period must address the reality of social change. Major events—world depression and world war, a successful internal struggle for civil rights, an external military defeat, and a conservative sea change in politics—frame and punctuate this era. But we need to reach more deeply in our quest, recognizing that the period is characterized by continuity as well as change. However it is finally interpreted, the long-standing religiousness of the American people, both in how they see themselves and in their behavior, is a fundamental given.

The Gallup Report recently summarized a range of data related to religion in America from 1935 through 1985.[1] Of course, strictly comparable statistics do not exist for the whole period, since the art of opinion sampling was perfected only during these years. But even if one allows for development of method and difficulties in constructing instruments, and takes due account of shifting values and cultural climates, what nonetheless leaps from Gallup's page is the sustained high degree of commitment to religion that characterized Americans throughout this period. Space does not permit (and our purposes would not be served by) exploring all the relevant aspects of the Gallup data. Selective attention to them will, however, help to focus this discussion.

With respect to the percentage of the population that claims membership in churches or synagogues, for example, annual rates have ranged between 76 percent (1947) and 67 percent (1982).[2] This relatively constant rate, at approximately 70 percent of the population, is remarkable. Rates of average attendance at religious services per week have also held stable. For more than a dozen years this rate has remained at just about 40 percent, after ranging as high as 49 percent in the middle years of the 1950s.[3] Equally noteworthy are the statistics about the percentage of Americans believing in God (no lower than 94 percent across four decades)[4] and in life after death (a constant 70 percent or so of the population over the same period).[5] So however much emphasis is given to changes in religious institutions and in overt behaviors during this epoch, or to dramatic events, both this remarkable degree of religious practice and its relative constancy throughout the half-century must be taken into account.

Balancing the continuity, however, there are the changes, and these are as striking as the relative constancy of the religious practices. Composite figures on religious preference in the four decades since World War II show a roughly 15 percent decline in the sector of the population identifying itself as Protestant, while the percentage identifying itself as Roman Catholic increased by approximately 40 percent. Concurrently, the percentage identifying itself as Jewish has been reduced by at least 50 percent, and the number of those more comfort-

1. Gallup Report. *Religion in America: Fifty Years, 1935-1985.* Report No. 236, May 1985.

2. Ibid., p. 41.
3. Ibid., p. 43.
4. Ibid., p. 50.
5. Ibid., p. 53.

ably identified as "others," while small in absolute terms, has multiplied by approximately four times, now totaling some 4 percent of the population. Finally, the category "none" has increased by 50 percent so that it approximates 10 percent of the population.[6] While these gross figures on religious preference show very marked changes, they mask yet greater shifts that have occurred in the last half-century. These shifts involve a redistribution of membership within broad families of denominations; accordingly, they may not show up in the data.

First let us look at the striking changes that have taken place at the simple level of institutions. These are most obvious within Protestant ranks, owing to the differentiation of Protestantism into denominational bodies with distinctive profiles. It seems clear that denominations that were deeply influenced by theological liberalism, simultaneously concerned and involved with social issues, and dedicated to fostering respect for individuals and sensitivity to moral actions have suffered a marked loss of members and significant erosion of influence. Many of these denominations are rooted in the older Anglo-American heritage—among them the United Church of Christ (successor to the Congregationalists), the Presbyterians, the Methodists, and the Northern Baptists. These bodies, which formed the core of the old religious mainline or establishment, have certainly declined in their percentage of membership and perhaps in absolute numbers. At the same time, cognate denominations like the Southern Baptists and the more rigorous Lutheran bodies have flourished. So there has been a redistribution of population, wealth, and influence away from relatively liberal bodies with early roots in colonial life and ties to the economic and political power of the Northeast toward more conservative denominations with bases of power located elsewhere. Of course, movements like the resurgence of evangelicalism and the extension of Pentecostalism must be seen as flowing across the nominal lines of denominational affiliation. Indeed the proliferation of vigorous free-standing congregations, often unaffiliated with others, represents a related development.[7]

Such shifts are even less easy to chart within the institutional life of the Roman Catholic church. The last half-century has seen this church's emergence into full maturity within both American society and the international Roman Catholic community as well. It is indisputably

6. Ibid., p. 27.

7. These broad trends are widely recognized and frequently commented upon. Among many relevant studies, see especially Wade Clark Roof and William McKinney, *American Mainline Religion* (New Brunswick, NJ: Rutgers University Press, 1987). See also James Davison Hunter, *American Evangelicalism* (New Brunswick, NJ: Rutgers University Press, 1983).

the largest single—and most influential—American denomination. But this shift in status, which may be amply documented by data ranging from hard statistics to evocative literature, is not unambiguous. For in this same half-century, American Catholicism has disclosed the variety of its inner life and has acknowledged the tensions that make it something of a microcosm of American society more generally. Furthermore, its leadership, which once was predominantly Irish, is now more broadly representative of the church. Within Catholicism the crosscurrents have been as strong as those within Protestantism, but they have served chiefly to highlight its internal pluralism.[8]

For the much smaller Jewish community, the shifts of the last generations have been no less dramatic. External events, such as the systematic destruction of European Jewry in World War II and the at least partial fulfillment of Zionist dreams in the creation of a state of Israel (albeit surviving in a hostile environment), continue to have deep effects on the domestic community. Linked to these developments has been a pronounced conservative shift, or a renewed appreciation for traditions, that has served to undercut the more extreme Reformed end of the spectrum of Jewish congregations. While the Jewish community has become manifestly a part of the American mainstream, its more sensitive members have agonized about whether it is the destiny of the ancient Jewish traditions to become but one more religion within an American nation. Here too, as in the Protestant ranks, the emergence of conservative impulses has been very clear.[9]

Some interpreters have observed that beneath these reconfigurations of religious bodies and traditions there is the common thread of a deeper shift toward more demanding kinds of religion. What we have seen, the argument goes, is a revolt against easy forms of religion in favor of a more disciplined and intense religious commitment.[10] This revolt may be one element in the larger picture, but it must be balanced against others. Surely as important is the vastly extended, and almost completely Protestant-inspired, utilization of the media by religious en-

8. The most recent comprehensive history of Roman Catholicism in the U.S. is Jay P. Dolan, *The American Catholic Experience* (Garden City, NY: Doubleday, 1985). It delineates the church's marked adaptation over the modern centuries, which has been continued in the changes of the last fifty years.

9. A brief, poignant discussion of the fate of Judaism in America is the "Epilogue" to Nathan Glazer's *American Judaism*, rev. ed. (Chicago: University of Chicago Press, 1972), pp. 151-86. Glazer subtitles it "The Year 1967 and Its Meaning, 1972." For a recent comprehensive analysis of the Jewish community in America, see Charles E. Silberman, *A Certain People: American Jews and Their Lives Today* (New York: Summit Books, 1985).

10. Dean M. Kelley's *Why Conservative Churches Are Growing* (New York: Harper and Row, 1972, 1977) stood at the center of this discussion.

trepreneurs.[11] Television, especially the availability of networks through cable or satellite systems, has enabled the evangelist, healer, and aspiring politician alike to create and shape a clientele. The anxious bench and the sawdust trail have been succeeded by chargecard piety and checkbook sanctification.

These few paragraphs are a cursory attempt to suggest some salient characteristics of Christianity, and indeed of religion, in America for the last half-century, namely, that the general culture of religious attitudes, behaviors, and actions manifests deep-seated continuities, while the institutional and social aspects of American religious life simultaneously reveal dramatic changes. One theme of this essay is that historians, not least among them Robert T. Handy, have recognized the sweep and the significance of the changes and have interpreted them for the culture at large more effectively than they have dealt with the continuities. The historiography of the last half-century has registered many of these changes—indeed, in the process of analyzing religion in our culture, it has become a distinctive field of historical scholarship—but it has nevertheless failed to do equal justice to the substantial cultural continuities that have been noted above.[12]

Systematic attention to the religious aspects of American history began in the nineteenth century. Early and noteworthy examples of the genre, such as Robert Baird's comprehensive survey and Philip Schaff's pointed essays, were primarily intended to explain this strange new world of America to Europeans.[13] At the end of the century, through the work of the American Society of Church History, and in the early decades of the next century, through the efforts of pioneering figures like Peter G. Mode and William Warren Sweet, a field of historiography began to coalesce that was specifically concerned with the interpretation of religion in American society.[14] By the 1930s, when the half-century of particular concern to us began, the work of intellectual

---

11. See Jeffrey Hadden and Charles E. Swann, *Primetime Preachers: The Rising Power of Televangelism* (Reading, MA: Addison-Wesley, 1981).

12. Henry May, who himself contributed much to this development, discussed "The Recovery of American Religious History" in *American Historical Review* 70 (1964) 79-92.

13. Baird's *Religion in America* was first published in 1844; a critical abridgement by Henry Warner Bowden was published in 1970 (New York: Harper and Row). Schaff's *America* (New York: Scribner, 1855) grew from two addresses he gave in Prussia in 1854. They are most accessible in an edition by Perry Miller (Cambridge, MA: Harvard University Press, 1961).

14. See the thirteen-volume set of denominational histories sponsored by the American Society of Church History as the American Church History Series, edited by Schaff and others (New York: Christian Literature Company, 1893-97). Mode was influential through his *Sourcebook and Bibliographical Guide for American Church History* (Menasha,

historians, especially Perry Miller, gave additional stimulus to the field.[15] Through the intervening decades that historiography has developed into a mature field. Many scholars have contributed, including Sydney Ahlstrom, Winthrop Hudson, Sidney Mead, H. Shelton Smith, and Martin E. Marty, to name only some of the better known.[16]

Among authors in this field none has had more influence through his publications and training of graduate students than Robert T. Handy. Indeed the work of Handy and his professional colleagues, while often moving back to earlier periods or out to other cultures, has been fundamentally responsive to and shaped by the period we have described in terms of simultaneous change and continuity. Thus the historical field that Handy represents itself exemplifies the leading religious characteristics of this era.

It is important to note briefly how Handy's work typifies the broader field. His contribution has been noteworthy for many reasons, not least the variety of historical genres through which he has exerted influence. Carefully crafted essays, such as "The American Religious Depression" and "Fundamentalism and Modernism in Perspective," have helped orient, or reorient, later scholarship.[17] Judicious monographs—the best example is probably *A Christian America*—have chronicled significant cultural epochs with a skill that has established his stature.[18] His edition of *The Social Gospel in America* can be held up as a model for comparable endeavors.[19] His collaborative efforts, such as the two-volume sourcebook edited with Lefferts Loetscher and H. Shelton Smith, have had long-term use as basic instructional tools.[20] Finally, his magisterial survey in the Oxford series, *A History of the Churches in the United States and Canada*, at once provides a standard

WI: Banta Pub. Co., 1921). Sweet's many publicatons were widely utilized, especially *The Story of Religions in America* (New York: Harper and Brothers, 1930).

15. Miller was best known for *The New England Mind*, a two-volume reinterpretation of Puritanism in seventeenth-century America and its transformation (Cambridge, MA: Harvard University Press, 1939, 1953). The full range of his interests—and influence—is evident in the essays collected as *Errand Into the Wilderness* (Cambridge, MA: Harvard University Press, 1956).

16. Representative publications are: Sydney Ahlstrom, *A Religious History of the American People* (New Haven: Yale University Press, 1972); Winthrop S. Hudson, *Religion in America* (New York: Scribner's, 1965); Sidney Mead, *The Lively Experiment* (New York: Harper and Row, 1963); H. Shelton Smith, *Changing Conceptions of Original Sin* (New York: Scribner, 1955); Martin E. Marty, *Righteous Empire* (New York: Dial Press, 1970), reissued as *Protestantism in the United States*, 2d ed. (New York: Scribner's, 1986).

17. *Church History* 29 (1960) 3-16; *Religion in Life* 24 (Summer 1955) 381-94.

18. New York: Oxford University Press, 1971; 2d rev. ed., 1984.

19. New York: Oxford University Press, 1966.

20. *American Christianity: An Historical Interpretation with Representative Documents*, 2 vols. (New York: Scribner, 1960, 1963).

narrative account of institutions and introduces important comparative data.[21] The virtuosity of Handy's work insures it a central place in the scholarship on Christianity and religion in America in the last decades. It also shows how well established and substantial the field as a whole has become.

As already suggested, one dominant feature of the historiography of this period has been attention to the increasing differentiation of religion, thus leading to the rapid development of specialized studies. Even summary volumes, including those produced by Handy himself, show that historians of religion have been obliged to recognize the ever greater inclusiveness of American society and to take its essential pluralism as a fundamental premise.[22] The serious study of the manifold religious life of black Americans, of which Handy was an early advocate, and the heightened appreciation for Spanish influence in the New World pre-1600, as well as post-1950, are examples of inevitable and important developments.[23] Certainly this new, wide-ranging historiography more faithfully reconstructs the past, even as it effectively responds to the present social and religious reality of American life. The necessary correlate to this emphasis on differentiation and change, however, has been decreased attention to the continuities in the religious components of the culture. This observation leads to the question: Is there a core or focal point at the center of our culture? Are there fundamental premises that give meaning to the whole? Are these expressed through religious commitments? Such an attempt to "define America," however, has been notably lacking in the extensive historical literature called forth by the rich and diverse religious culture of our time.

Thus, in the flowering of history writing about Christianity and religion in America during the last half-century, so fully exemplified in Handy's work, what has remained largely unexplored is the conjunction between the obvious and remarkable differentiation of the subject and the undergirding continuity of the culture. We must say "largely unexplored," because one member of the guild of church historians, Catherine Albanese, has effectively played upon the contrast between the manyness and the oneness of American religion as the theme of a recent textbook.[24] We might also point to the discussion of civil religion

21. New York: Oxford University Press, 1977.
22. See Handy's edited volume, *Religion in the American Experience: The Pluralistic Style* (New York: Harper and Row, 1972).
23. See Handy's early article, "Negro Christianity and American Church Historiography," in *Reinterpretation in American Church History*, ed. Jerald C. Brauer (Chicago: University of Chicago Press, 1968), pp. 91-112.
24. Respectively the subjects of Parts One and Two of *America, Religions and Religion* (Belmont, CA: Wadsworth Publishing Co., 1981).

during the last decade as, in part, an attempt to deal with this subject.[25] But that discussion has proved equivocal as it bears on this point, for it has given rise to the commonplace that civil religion in America is but one religious ingredient within the broader cultural matrix.

So the burden of this essay centers in the observation that while there have been occasional approaches to the study of continuity in American culture and religion, the subject has not been systematically explored. This inattention to continuity is boldly displayed in Sydney Ahlstrom's arresting suggestion that "a distinct quadricentennium" ended circa 1960, namely, an Anglo-American epoch beginning with the accession of Elizabeth I to the throne of England and ending with the election of John F. Kennedy as American president, whose close simultaneously marked the end of a Protestant axis to American culture.[26] From the vantage point of the late 1980s that judgment appears to have been premature, but that it was offered as the summary conclusion to Ahlstrom's massive volume—and was taken so seriously in discussions surrounding it—indicates something about the conflicting positions in contemporary historiography. Against this background let us ask how we might do justice to the relatively neglected continuities.

We can possibly profit from an approach that proved effective in probing the relationship of cultural continuity to manifest change in another social context. In his "Quicunque Vult," R. G. Collingwood posited that through metaphysical inquiry one can discover first principles that serve as the presuppositions of social life.[27] He thought it possible, by analyzing these presuppositions, to explore deeper cultural patterns beneath relatively superficial appearances. These first principles are taken for granted, that is, they do not have the status of logical propositions nor do they serve as explicit norms of behavior and belief. They are, rather, cultural givens, hidden under, and only expressed through, symbols and rituals, in short, in a religious idiom. In this perspective, religion may be seen as the social location where the presuppositions of the common life are worked through, codified, and transmitted.

The power of presuppositions lies in their capacity to make the world intelligible within a given culture, that is, to make ideas and ac-

25. Discussions most usefully represented in Russell E. Richey and Donald G. Jones, eds., *American Civil Religion* (New York: Harper and Row, 1974).

26. See Chapter 63, "The Turbulent Sixties," in *A Religious History of the American People,* pp. 1079-96.

27. *An Essay on Metaphysics,* vol. 2 of *Philosophical Essays* (Oxford: Clarendon Press, 1940), Chapter 21, pp. 213-27.

tions within it effective and coherent. According to Collingwood, classical culture had a metaphysical flaw that fatally limited it. It failed to understand and conceptualize the relationship between realm and movement, form and flux, structure and change. The church fathers identified this flaw and corrected it with the Trinitarian formulations of the Creed. For Collingwood the magnitude of their achievement was demonstrated by the progressive advance of science in subsequent western culture, which was itself decisively recast on the basis of Christian assumptions.

Collingwood's interest in metaphysics centered on the link between religious doctrine and scientific inquiry with respect to nature. His argument was carried a step further by Charles N. Cochrane in his *Christianity and Classical Culture,* suggestively subtitled "A Study of Thought and Action from Augustus to Augustine."[28] Cochrane held that metaphysical assumptions also determine the operative views of human nature and political society, in short, that whole range of valuing actions we identify as culture. Does Cochrane's adaptation of Collingwood's approach help in our exploration of the sources, significance, and continuity of American religious culture in the last half-century?

To properly identify and understand the first principles embedded in religious ritual and symbol may be very difficult. It may even be that, as Collingwood attests, such principles can be analyzed in a fully rational way only retrospectively, that is, as a historical subject matter. In this light the study of metaphysics becomes a historical analysis of culture, for while first principles lie behind or under culture, so to speak, they can only be approached through it. Taking inspiration from Cochrane's analysis of classical culture, therefore, let us ask: Is it possible to identify distinctive metaphysical presuppositions that have defined the form of American culture and shaped the content of its social order in distinctive ways, even through these five decades of the twentieth century? (This way of putting the question, while possibly pretentious, is certainly a more exact way of framing it than simply by asking: Is America a civilization in its own right because it manifests a unique culture?) If such presuppositions can be identified, might these explain the pronounced continuity of American religious life in the last half-century, and its sources in earlier periods, notwithstanding all the specific changes to which we have called attention? And can that continuity be explored as the means for us to understand, through the religious idiom, the core of American culture?

28. Oxford: Clarendon Press, 1939; London: Oxford University Press, 1944.

It is surely plausible to argue that American society and its culture have, in general, embodied the basic metaphysical postulates of the western Christian tradition rather than first principles antithetical to it such as might have been derived initially from indigenous cultures in the New World or, subsequently, from eastern sources. If we accept Collingwood's formulation, this tradition entails, first, the assumption that the world is one and coherent. He argued that this assumption is expressed in religious terms by the presupposition that there is only one God. (By contrast, polytheism, or any position short of theism, implies that the world is at root plural.) Most certainly the course of modern science, including the drive toward universal explanatory theories, is predicated upon this assumption. At least as clear is that our political approaches to other societies, including a drive to establish hegemony over them and our idealized perceptions of America's role in world history, reflect a comparable metaphysical assumption. So the theistic postulate, which Collingwood saw as the symbolic means of asserting the oneness of the world, continues to operate as a basic presupposition of American culture.

Second, American society and culture retain from Christian Europe the assumption that the world is ordered. Collingwood, and Cochrane following him, identified this postulate with the central position Christianity gives to the symbol of the logos or Christ figure. For Collingwood, emphasis upon Christ as the "Word made flesh" is—at the cultural level—a claim that the world and the realms of experience within it are comprehensible, albeit only in light of correct principles. In this respect also, therefore, traditional assumptions of European Christian societies have been continued in America and still inform its culture.

Beyond these principles, American culture also embodies what Collingwood saw as a broadly Christian understanding of events or movement. In particular, its emphasis upon the Holy Spirit is a means of symbolizing the significance of change in relationship to structure, or of spirit in relationship to logos. In this broad generic sense the historic American presuppositions or accepted cultural principles are Trinitarian, compatible with—because continuing—Christian rather than pagan formulations. We must, however, recognize that the American metaphysic has represented a specific version of western Christian first principles. It is to this point of difference and its implications that we must turn our attention.

A half-century ago, in an immensely influential book, H. Richard Niebuhr proposed that the religious symbol of the kingdom of God has played a critical role in American religion and, by implication, also in our social and cultural history.[29] His discussion not only called attention to this symbol's continuing prominence but also analyzed the transformations it had undergone during three centuries of American history. He suggested that for the Puritans the kingdom signified God's sovereignty, while in the Great Awakening, and for the evangelicals of the nineteenth century, it signified the rule of Christ. Finally, in the late nineteenth and the twentieth centuries, he saw the Social Gospel emphasis upon a kingdom on earth as an expression of the social implications of Christianity. This latter development completed or filled out the American interpretation of the kingdom of God symbol and made it uniquely an American cultural possession.

Following Niebuhr's lead, a considerable literature has explored millenarianism, the conviction that divine rule over America—however that rule might be construed—is critical to understanding America's development as a society.[30] But no one, so far as I know, has turned the question around in order to ask whether the manifest American preoccupation with the kingdom of God represents a working out of a set of metaphysical assumptions distinctive to American culture, though by no means exclusively expressed through the symbol of the kingdom. While the metaphysical first principles of American culture are surely within the generic set of assumptions derived from Christian Europe, the question remains: Have those first principles undergone significant adaptation or transformation in the New World?

To explore this question, it is useful to hypothesize that the first principles of American society and culture represent a projection, by an emerging people, of a particular relationship between order and movement, form and flux, or continuity and change. As regards the Trinitarian symbols to which Collingwood directed attention, this projection has been signaled by two developments: first, increased emphasis within American Christianity upon the third person of the Trinity, the Holy Spirit; and, second, a marked reduction of the scope of religious action identified exclusively with Christ or the second person of the Trinity. This redistribution of the dynamic relationships within the economy of the Trinitarian Godhead explains why, virtually without exception, American versions of Christianity are essentially directed to building up this-worldly communities, whether viewed exclusively or inclusively. Under this set of assumptions, the reality of the new life available to members of the American republic of the spirit is more sa-

---

29. *The Kingdom of God in America* (Chicago: Willett, Clark and Co., 1937).
30. Among the more influential studies has been Ernest L. Tuveson's *Redeemer Nation* (Chicago: University of Chicago Press, 1968).

lient than the status and significance of Christ, whatever role he is thought to play in bringing it about.

It is frequently argued that the millennial premise of American life derives from seventeenth-century English roots and was expressed as such from the outset of New World colonization.[31] But this premise was decisively reformulated in colonial experience, and that legacy was worked through in more detail during the nineteenth century.[32] Thus the American collectivity (meaning republic, nation, church, or whatever) was from the beginning thought to be infused with and inspired by the Spirit. While the kingdom of God symbol has never been as prominent in the European Roman Catholic or Lutheran traditions as in the Reformed, these traditions, like the Reformed, have become transformed in the course of American residence. As in no other society, the Holy Spirit, or its cultural equivalent, has become the animating principle of American corporate activity. The cultural outcome is that change (movement) is accorded primacy over form (order) as the foundation of life in this world.

One means of charting the evolution of these distinctive presuppositions is to note how the American Augustine, Jonathan Edwards, shaped his discussion of the relationship between religious and political ends. For the bishop of Hippo in antiquity, human beings lived simultaneously in the City of God and in the cities of this world, and separate and distinctive claims appropriate to each locus defined human life. For the sage of Stockbridge, by contrast, redeemed humanity was moving toward a kingdom of heaven on earth, one which he believed was dawning in the spiritual troubles of the Awakening in his time. While Edwards insisted, in orthodox terms, that there would be a final loosing of the devil before the Last Judgment (which is to say historical life would not cease), for him the redeemed were already experiencing the rule of Christ through the Holy Spirit within history. In this step, then, from Augustine to Edwards, I am suggesting we may see a critical reorientation of the Christian legacy. Following Collingwood, we could describe this reorientation as a transformation of those metaphysical presuppositions that lie behind the culture of the New World and that have become its common possession.

Edwards's discussion of the coming of Christ in the dispensation

---

31. Among the many books on millenarianism in sixteenth- and seventeenth-century England, see Bryan W. Ball, *A Great Expectation* (Leiden: Brill, 1975), Paul Christiansen, *Reformers and Babylon* (Toronto: University of Toronto Press, 1978), and Christopher Hill, *The World Turned Upside Down* (New York: Viking Press, 1972).

32. C. C. Goen's "Jonathan Edwards: A New Departure in Eschatology," *Church History* 28 (1959) 25-40, was an early and important discussion of this question.

he thought then under way clearly identified it as one of a series of effusions of the Holy Spirit.[33] The coming age, prior to the Last Judgment, would be dominated by the Spirit, in both individual and social senses. It would be wrong, however, to interpret this emphasis upon the Spirit as a technical Sabellianism, that is, as one construed in modalistic terms. Nor should it be seen as standing in the tradition of Joachim of Fiore. For Edwards, and in the American set of first principles generally, there is no separation of these outpourings of the Holy Spirit from Christ as their true form. Rather, the American reformulation displays a pattern of peculiarly intensive linkage between form and spirit.

We should emphasize two aspects of this comparison and contrast between the presuppositions of classical Roman antiquity and of American culture. First, classical antiquity was oriented to an idealized past. The ideal of pagan or pre-Christian classicism was to conform the Roman *imperium* to the golden age of the *respublica*. Thus the normative age was retrojected, and the goal was to return the present to that ideal past, so far as possible. In its critique of this classical ideal, orthodox Christianity removed the golden age from this world to another and future one. Likewise, the American first principles are unrelievedly forward-facing. The ideal lies not in the past but in the future (albeit, *pace* Christian orthodoxy, a future construed wholly in "this-worldly" fashion). Viewed in this context, the Western European Christian tradition appears as something of a middle term: it accepted both a past golden age and a future fulfillment, but held that history is cut off from the one by the Fall and from the other by the Last Judgment. American culture, however, has resolutely maintained that history is *not* cut off from a golden age and from its consummation. By diminishing its attention to an Eden before history began, by minimizing the consequences (or even denying the reality) of a Fall from original perfection, and by locating the "heavenly city" in time rather than in eternity, this culture has constructed its own distinctive ideal of a golden age as a fully historical reality—one existing even now in vision and hope, one that will assuredly come to fruition in the future. American culture, in short, takes for granted that this ideal is historically available *in toto*.

Second, classical Roman antiquity emphasized order or form as basic to society rather than movement or change. Change was seen as an erosion of form; movement threatened the order which was reality. By contrast, we can almost say that for American culture change or

---

33. I have suggested the importance of this interpretation in "Jonathan Edwards as Historian," *Church History* 46 (1977) 5-18. It will be further developed in the introduction to my critical edition of Edwards's *A History of the Work of Redemption*, forthcoming in the Yale edition of his works.

movement is reality, and that form or order (while often viewed with nostalgia) is seen as an impediment to it. Put in religious terms: the Holy Spirit is present and continuously available and is the manifestation of fundamental reality. Christ as the logos is experienced in the movement of Spirit rather than as an independent principle that transcends the apparent reality of change.

Theologically considered, this new American emphasis upon the Spirit helps to explain the oft-repeated lament that American theology has so little attended to Christology in comparison with its European counterpart. But if the Christ figure has been underemphasized in American religious thought, then from the outset the Spirit—and experience of it and in it—has been correspondingly emphasized and repeatedly prominent in thought and action. This theological anomaly of American Christianity lies behind the growth of the "Third Force" of Christendom that H. P. Van Dusen remarked upon several decades ago.[34] The rise of Pentecostalism to such extensive influence in the twentieth century, and the subsequent emergence of charismatic emphases especially within the Roman Catholic tradition, are indications that the last half-century has but consolidated innovations that have deep roots in our history.[35] From its beginnings, Christianity in America has had a very particular texture or tonality that has set it apart from the great churchly European versions of Christianity, Roman Catholic, Lutheran, and Reformed. It may not be too much to say that American Christianity, indeed religion in America, has been preoccupied with possession by the Spirit. In its relentless affirmation of change, American culture embodies the principles that are religiously expressed through emphasis upon this symbol.

The recognition that emphasis upon the Spirit has been uniquely strong in American theology and that it is linked to preoccupation with change in American culture, especially in the twentieth century, returns us to our starting point. There we remarked upon the striking juxtaposition of change and continuity during the last half-century of American religion. The point may finally be, however, not that continuity has contrasted with change but that the continuity of the last half-century has manifested itself precisely in the cultural embrace of relentless movement. Thus, far from arguing that modern American society has lost its moorings, this essay proposes that modern American culture, so preoc-

34. In an article titled "The Third Force" appearing in *Life*, June 9, 1958, pp. 122-24.

35. Among the many discussions of the Pentecostal and charismatic movements, see especially D. E. Harrell, Jr., *All Things Are Possible* (Bloomington: Indiana University Press, 1975), and Meredith B. McGuire, *Pentecostal Catholics* (Philadelphia: Temple University Press, 1982).

cupied with or directed to change, has fulfilled very amply the specifically American rendering of the presuppositions that have undergirded western Christian culture more generally. By deemphasizing the place of order or structure and by increasingly emphasizing the centrality of change or movement, this society has pushed beyond specific formulations that underlie European cultures in their characteristic theological forms. Indeed, this is but another way to say that American culture has ushered in a consistent commitment to modernity.

Those seeking to understand the religious history (and also the historiography) of the last half-century need to relate the manifest differentiation of the subject to the basic presuppositions of American culture. The approach suggested here is to analyze the religious symbols, rituals, and actions of the society in order to identify its first principles— a task for which students of religion are especially well equipped. In carrying out this task, these students will inevitably need to focus upon the metaphysical assumptions (in Collingwood's sense) that are fundamental to American society. The importance of this goal is self-evident in any attempt, such as this volume represents, to assess religion in the last half-century and, in particular, the significance of the recent history of Christianity in the United States.

Index